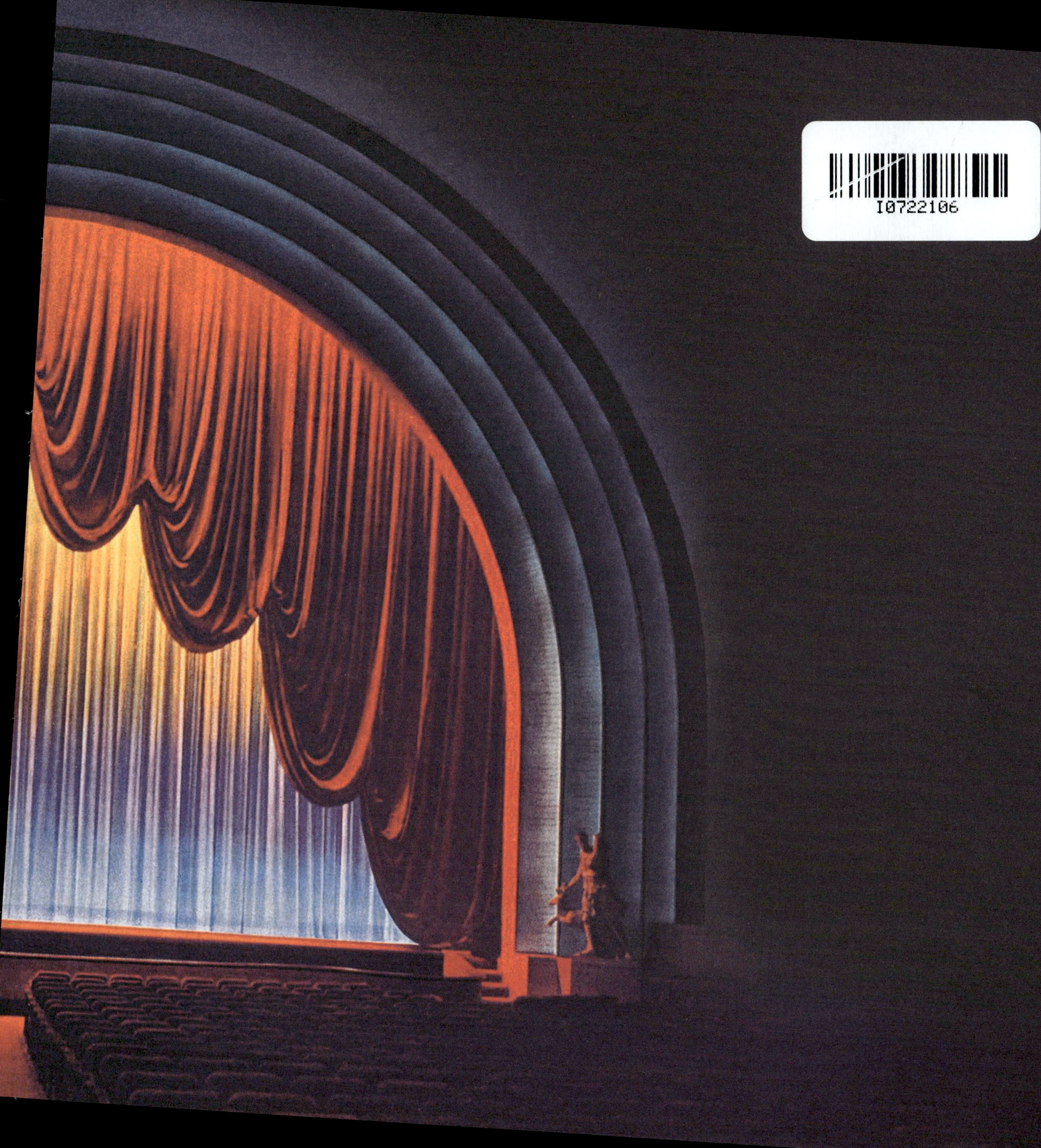
I0722106

RED

First published in the French language by Éditions du Seuil, Paris,
under the title: *Rouge: Histoire d'une couleur* by Michel Pastoureau
Copyright © 2016 Éditions du Seuil, Paris

Translated from the French by Jody Gladding

English translation copyright © 2017 by Princeton University Press
Requests for permission to reproduce material from this work
should be sent to permissions@press.princeton.edu

Published by Princeton University Press,
41 William Street, Princeton, New Jersey 08540
99 Banbury Road, Oxford OX2 6JX

press.princeton.edu

Jacket illustration: Raphael and Giulio Romano, *Portrait of Isabel
de Requesens, Vicereine of Naples* (detail), formerly *Portrait of
Giovanna of Aragon*, 1518. Lens, France, Musée du Lourvre-Lens

ISBN 978-0-691-17277-4
Library of Congress Control Number: 2016949541

British Library Cataloging-in-Publication Data is available

This book has been composed in Lyon Text and Brandon Grotesque

Printed on acid- free paper. ∞

Printed in Portugal

3 5 7 9 10 8 6 4 2

MICHEL PASTOUREAU

RED

The History of a Color

Translated by Jody Gladding

Princeton University Press

Princeton and Oxford

A bull becomes furious
only if he is presented
with a red cloth;
a philosopher, on the other hand,
goes into a rage as soon as the color
is mentioned.

—GOETHE

n the human sciences, to speak of the "color red" is almost a redundancy. Red is the archetypal color, the first color humans mastered, fabricated, reproduced, and broke down into different shades, first in painting, later in dyeing. This has given it primacy over all other colors through the millennia. This also explains why in many languages the same word can mean "red," "beautiful," and "colorful" all at once. Even though blue is by far the favorite color today in the West, and even though red's place in our daily lives has diminished—at least in comparison to the place it held in Greco-Roman antiquity and the Middle Ages—it still remains the strongest, most remarkable color, and the one richest in poetic, oneiric, and symbolic possibilities.

In the following chapters, I have attempted to trace the color's long history in European societies, from the Paleolithic age to the present. That was no easy task, given the many areas in which red plays a role and the many questions its study raises. The historian, like the linguist, sociologist, and anthropologist, always has much more to say about red than any other color. Red is an ocean! In order not to drown in it, in order for this work to remain a reasonable size, in order for it to be comparable to the ones preceding it, I had to—regretfully—omit or condense some material, skim over certain eras, avoid certain questions, and give priority to a few leading threads (the lexicon, clothing, art, fields of learning, symbols). These choices allowed me to find my way in a particularly rich chromatic labyrinth.

*

The present book is the fourth in an ongoing series, beginning with *Blue: The History of a Color* (2001), followed by *Black: The History of a Color* (2009) and then *Green: The History of a Color* (2014), all produced by the same publisher. A fifth, devoted to yellow, should come next. As with the books that have appeared before it, this one follows a chronological plan; it is very much a history of the color red, not an encyclopedia of red, and even less a study of the color in the contemporary world alone. It is very much a history book that examines red over the long term and in all its aspects, from the lexical to the symbolic, and including everyday life, social customs, scientific knowledge, technical applications, religious moral codes, and artistic creations. Too often histories of color—the few that exist at all—are limited to the most recent time periods or to pictorial matters alone, which is very reductive. The history of painting is one thing; the history of colors is another, and much more vast.

As with the three preceding works, this one only appears to be a monograph. A color never stands alone; it only derives its meaning, it only fully "functions" from the social, artistic, or symbolic perspective, insofar as it is combined or contrasted with one or many other colors. Hence, it is impossible to consider it in isolation. To discuss red, we must also discuss blue, yellow, green, and especially white and black.

These first four books (and the one to follow) constitute the stones of an edifice whose construction has occupied me for almost half a century: the history of colors in European societies, from Roman antiquity to the eighteenth century. Even if, as you will read in the following pages, I often look back to before that first period and ahead to beyond the last one, it is within this already quite broad chronological slice of time that my research essentially lies. Similarly, my research is limited to European societies, because for me the issues of color are first of all social issues. As a historian I am not competent to speak about the whole planet, and not inclined to compile, second- or third-hand, works done by other historians on non-European cultures. In order to avoid making foolish claims or plagiarizing or recopying the books of others, I will limit myself to what I know and what was the subject of my seminars at the École Pratique des Hautes Études and the École des Hautes Études en Sciences Sociales for more than thirty years.

*

Constructing a history of colors, even one limited to Europe, is not easy. In fact it is a particularly arduous task that historians, archaeologists, and art historians (including those who study painting) have refused to tackle until recently. There are multiple difficulties; that is true. Reviewing them in the introduction to this book is worthwhile, because they are fully part of its subject and can aid us in understanding the gaps in our knowledge. With regard to color, there is no real boundary between history and historiography.

These difficulties can be grouped into three categories. The first are documentary. We see the objects, images, artworks, and monuments that past centuries have bequeathed us not in their original colors but as time has made them. Sometimes the disparity between the original state and the present state is immense. What to do? Must those supposedly original colors be restored, rediscovered at any cost, or must we acknowledge that the work of time is a historical document that the historian must accept as such? Moreover we are seeing those colors in lighting conditions very different from those of the societies preceding ours. The torch, oil lamp, candle, and gaslight produce different illumination than electricity provides. That much is clear. But who among us remembers this when visiting a museum or exhibition? And what historians take it into account in their work? Furthermore, for decades, researchers were in the habit of studying objects, artworks, and monuments by means of black-and-white reproductions—first engravings, then photographs—so much so that over the course of time their ways of thinking and perceiving seemed to have become black and white as well. Accustomed to working from documents, from books and collections of images largely dominated by black and white, historians and archaeologists considered and studied the past as a world from which color was absent.

The difficulties in the second group are methodological. Historians are often stymied when they try to understand the status or the function of a color in an image or artwork. All the problems—material, technical, chemical, iconographical, ideological, symbolic—present themselves at the same time. How to organize them? How to conduct an analysis? What questions should be asked and in what order? To this day, no researcher and no research team has yet proposed relevant methods for helping the entire scholarly community better study the issues of color. That is why, facing the proliferation of inquiries and the multitude of vested interests, all researchers—and me first among them, no doubt—tend to retain only what suits them in relation to whatever they are in the process of demonstrating and, inversely, to overlook whatever does not suit them. That is clearly a faulty way of working.

The difficulties in the third group are epistemological: we cannot thoughtlessly project our present-day definitions, classifications, and conceptions of color, just as they are, onto the past. They are not those of the societies preceding ours (and will not be those of the societies following ours). This is all the more so because what is true of knowledge is also true of perception: the antique or medieval eye, for example, did not perceive colors or contrasts as the twenty-first-century eye does. Whatever the historical period, perception is always cultural. Therefore, for the historian, the danger of anachronism seems to lurk behind the corner of every document, especially when it is a matter of the spectrum (unknown before the late seventeenth century), the theory of primary and complementary colors (of no concern in the human sciences), the distinction between warm and cool colors (pure convention), the principal of simultaneous contrast, or the alleged physiological or psychological effects of colors. Our knowledge, our sensibility, our present-day "truths" are not those of yesterday and will not be those of tomorrow.

*

All these difficulties together underscore the strictly cultural nature of the questions that color poses. For the historian, color is defined first as a social phenomenon, not as a material or a component of light, still less as a sensation. It is the society that makes the color, that gives it its vocabulary and its definitions, that constructs its codes and values, that organizes its uses and determines its stakes. That is why any history of color must first be a social history. Unless we acknowledge that, we could lapse into reductive pseudo-neurobiology or fruitless scientism.

To construct this history, the researcher's work is twofold. The first task is defining what the universe of colors could have been for the societies of the past, taking into account all the components of that universe: the lexica and phenomena of language, the chemistry of pigments, dyeing techniques, systems of dress and the codes that accompanied them, the place of color in everyday life, rules handed down by authorities, church moral codes, scientific speculation, and artistic creation. The areas of inquiry and reflection are endless and present the historian with complex questions. After defining a given cultural area, the second task in a diachronic study is to examine the changes, losses, innovations, and mergers that affect all historically observable aspects of the color in question.

In that dual process all available documents must be examined. Color is essentially an interdocumentary and interdisciplinary area. But certain areas prove to be more fruitful than others, vocabulary first of all: the history of words always provides our knowledge of the past with much original and relevant information. With regard to color, that history underscores how much color's primary function in any society is taxonomic: to classify, associate, oppose, hierarchize. Second of all is the area of fabric, dyes, clothing, and appearances. This is probably where chemical and technical issues merge most closely with economic, social, and symbolic ones. Dress constitutes the first color code established by social life.

Lexica, fabrics, clothing: in matters of color, the poets and dyers have at least as much to teach us as the painters, chemists, and physicists. The long history of the color red in Western societies is exemplary in this regard.

Red Is Not Alone

A color never appears in isolation. It takes on its whole meaning only when it is combined or contrasted with one or several other colors. Red is no exception to this rule, despite its preeminence among the colors. An anonymous author from the late fifteenth century, proposing styles for livery and assigning them symbolic meaning, maintained that "red with gray is a sign of high expectations."

Serge Poliakoff, *Composition in Gray and Red*, 1964. Montpellier, France, Musée Fabre.

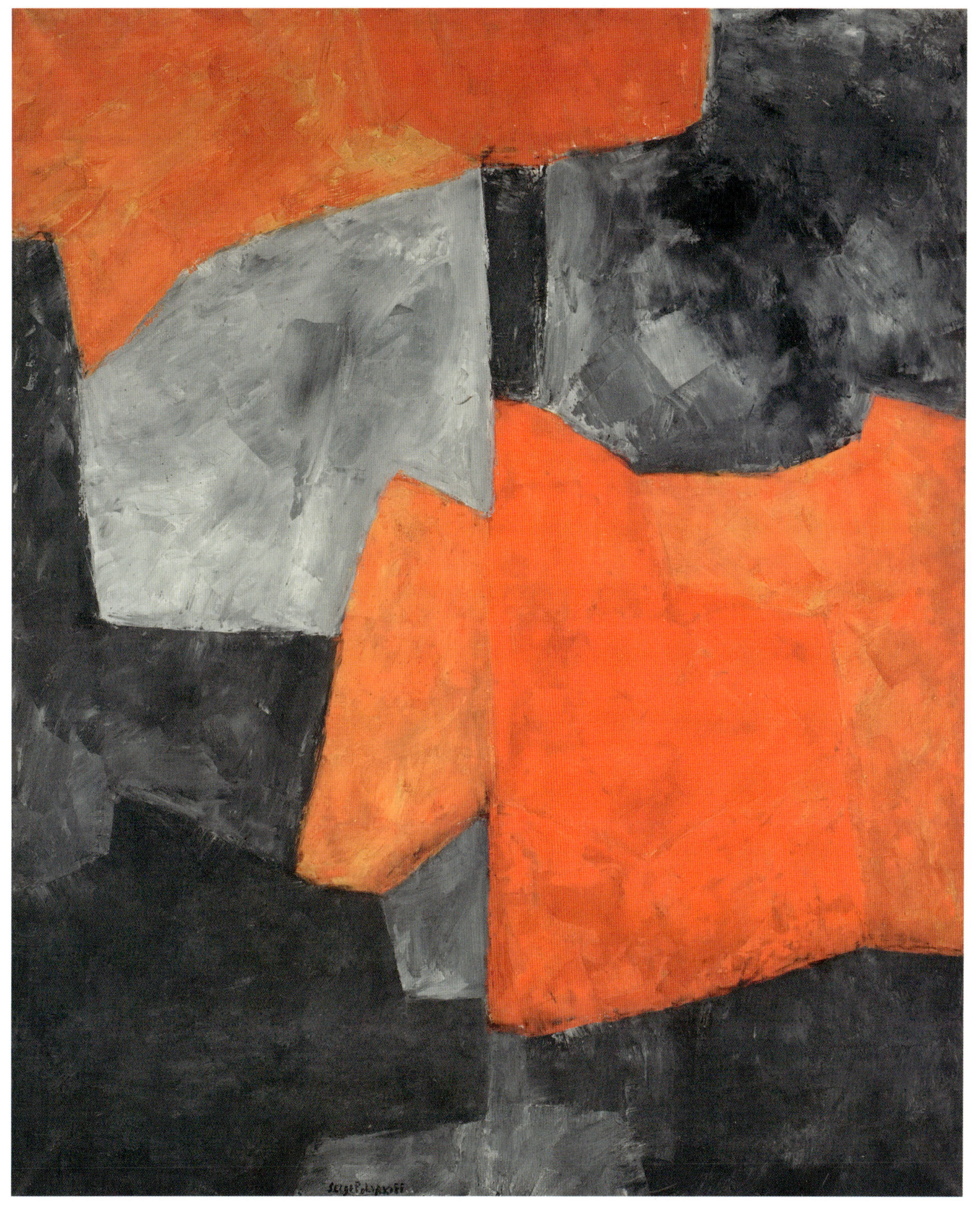
Serge Poliakoff

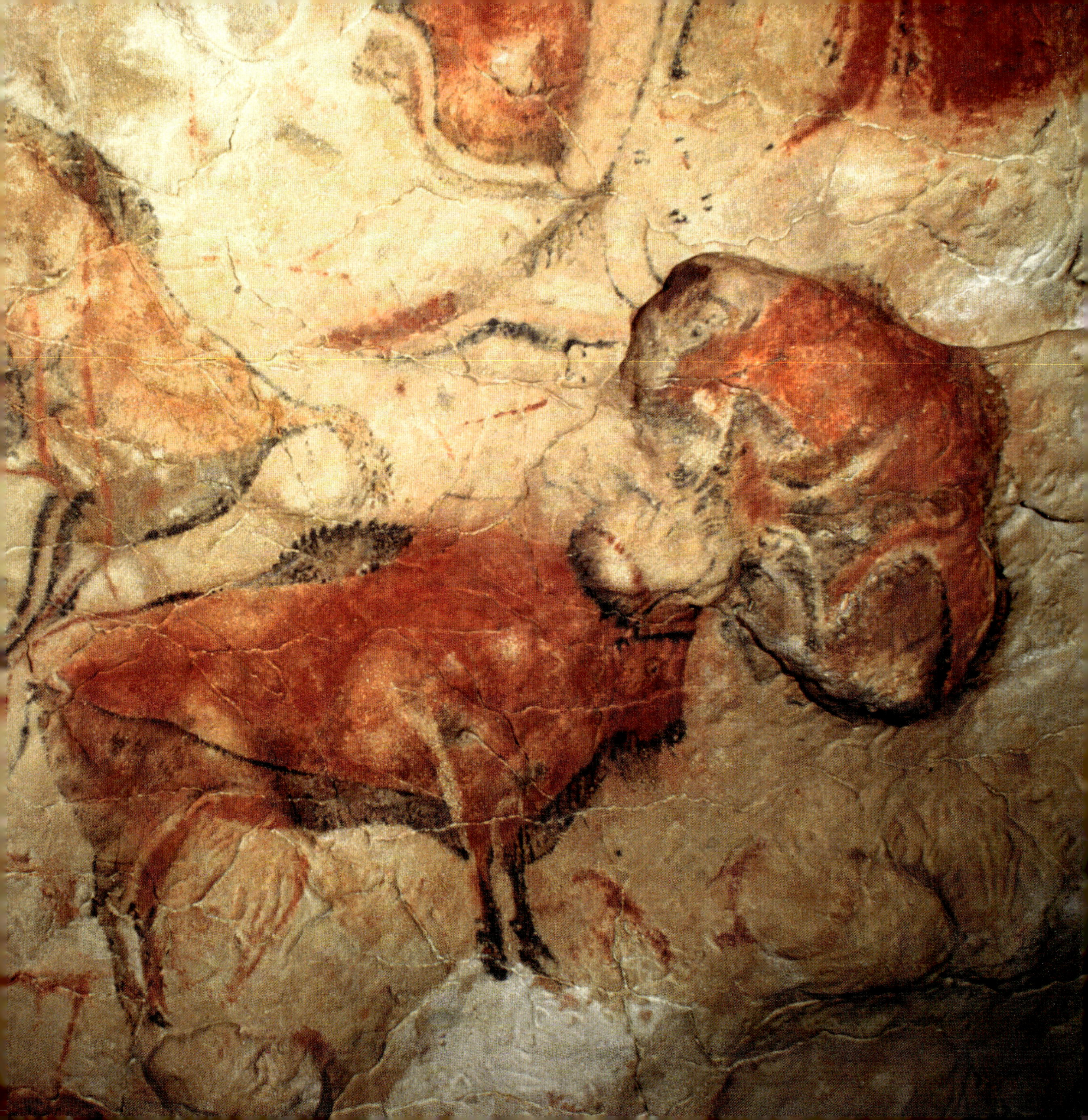

THE FIRST
COLOR

FROM EARLIEST TIMES
TO THE END OF ANTIQUITY

For thousands of years in the West, red was the only color worthy of that name, the only true color. As much on the chronological as hierarchical level, it outstripped all others. Not that they did not exist, but they had to wait a long time before they were considered colors and then played a comparable role in material culture, social codes, and systems of thought.

It was with red that humans did their first color experiments, achieved their first successes, and then constructed a chromatic universe. It was also within the range of reds that they learned early on to diversify the palette and to produce varied tones and shades, as the oldest known color terms demonstrate. Here the lexicon seems in keeping with pictorial practices and tinctorial techniques. In certain languages, the same word can mean "red" or simply "colored," depending on the context, such as *coloratus* in classical Latin or *colorado* in modern Castilian.[1] In other languages, the adjectives meaning "red" and "beautiful" share a common root; for example, that is the case in Russian, in which the terms *krasnyy* (red) and *krasivy* (beautiful) belong to the same lexical family.[2] And in still other languages, only three color terms seem to exist: white, black, and red. But the first two are not always recognized as true chromatic adjectives; essentially, they describe darkness and light. Only the third is an authentic term for color.[3]

Red's preeminence is found again in everyday life and in material civilization. Around the Mediterranean it occupied an early place in the building of houses and towns (bricks, tiles), on movable objects (various ceramics and pottery), on fabrics and clothing (red tones had prestige), as well as on finery, jewels, and personal accessories, where it served as protection, embellishment, or a source of good luck. Similarly, in representations and rituals it was often associated with power and with the sacred. A very rich symbolism accompanied it, and it sometimes seemed endowed with supernatural powers. In many respects, in ancient societies, red appeared not only as the first color, but also as the color par excellence.

PAGE 12

Great Red Bison of Altamira

When they were discovered in 1879, the paintings in the Cave of Altamira in northern Spain prompted skepticism from specialists. Their authenticity was long in doubt for some, until comparable groupings were gradually discovered. The ceiling in Altamira's great hall displays sixteen bison, accompanied by horses, deer, and wild boar, to which the painters gave the illusion of volume by using the natural relief of the cave walls.

15,500–13,500 BCE. Santillana del Mar, Spain, Cave of Altamira, hall of the bison.

Ships of Tanum

The various protohistoric sites of Tanum, on the southwestern coast of Sweden, present a total of about two hundred drawings engraved or hammered into the rock, then painted red. Numerous ships can be seen there, and in some of them the rowers' gestures can be clearly distinguished. Are they heading toward the realm of the dead?

c. 800–750 BCE. Tanumshede, Sweden, Vitlycke site.

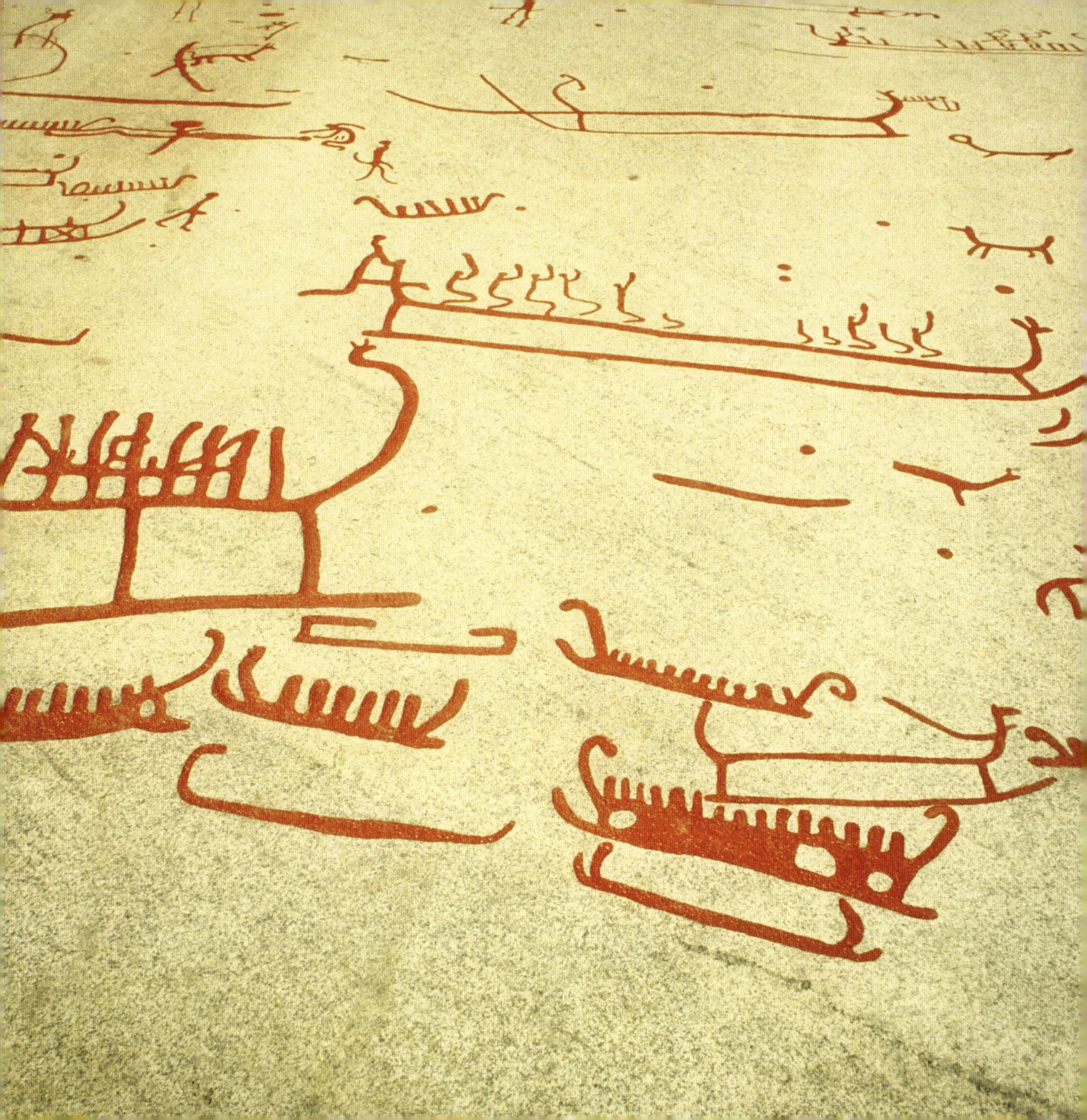

The First Palettes

Humans painted long before they used dyes. On the walls of caves, the widest array of paintings now known dates back about thirty-two or thirty-three thousand years—that is, more than twenty-five thousand years before the appearance of dyeing. And new discoveries may well predate that first bestiary in the Chauvet Cave in Ardèche. But is this truly the beginning of painting? Did Paleolithic man paint on the walls of caves before painting on stones or rocks? Prehistorians debate this question. Furthermore, what is painting? Some pebbles, bones, statuettes, and even tools bear various traces of color: lines, points, smears, spots. Can they be called paintings? It is an open question, especially since it is difficult to date them. Nonetheless, what matters for our purposes is that traces of red prevail, as if red had been the color of the sign or mark even before being the color of art. Later, in the Lower Paleolithic or Magdalenian period (15,000–11,000 BCE), such objects exhibiting the remains of color became more numerous; the materials varied (stone, bone, ivory, antler), the palette was more diversified, but red remained the dominant color.

Moreover, even before they put colors on walls, stones, or bones, it is likely that human beings applied them to their own bodies, and that body painting is older than painting on walls or objects. But does this represent the first artistic expression? It is impossible to say. At most, we can assume that there as well red was the principal shade because it remains so even today; women continue to adorn their cheeks and lips with this color, and the world of cosmetics remains one that offers the most diverse and subtle hues of red.

Thus early on, red played an important role in the practices of adornment. Bearing witness to this fact are all the red stones and pierced shells, and all the painted red pieces of bones and teeth, which in the Paleolithic period were used to make amulets, necklaces, bracelets, and pendants. Found abundantly in burial places, these objects are also hard to date, but they were probably related to body paintings and fall into the range of reds because that color was thought to have protective or magical properties. For example, there are pieces—"beds" or pallets—of red ocher found among funeral materials in some tombs. Were these beds meant to protect the dead on their last journey? To restore them to life in the beyond? We do not know. But it is clear that the reds used on bodies in prehistoric times served three functions, deictic, prophylactic, and aesthetic. In those remote times, men and women were already drawing attention to themselves, protecting themselves, and adorning themselves with red. They would continue to do so for a long time—a very long time.

Let us leave the grave sites and linger in the halls and corridors of the caves where the most famous European wall paintings are found: Chauvet, Cosquer, Lascaux, Pech-Merle, Altamira, and a few others. Let us observe the palettes of the painters. In relation to our modern practices, it is limited: blacks, reds, browns, sometimes (less frequently) yellows, more rarely whites (undoubtedly more recent); never green or blue. The black pigments have a manganese oxide or plant carbon base; the yellows come from clay soils rich in ocher; the reds are most often extracted from hematite, one of the most widespread iron ores in Europe. Thus the question is not so much one of supply as one of transformation: how did Paleolithic humans learn to transform a natural earth element, an ore, into a product that could be used for painting—a pigment? Can we call this chemistry already?

In fact, recent analyses have shown that certain yellow ochers were heated in stone crucibles to rid them of water and thus transform them into red ochers; a few of those crucibles that survive today still show traces of red. Similarly, some pigments were enriched with products meant to alter their covering power, to change their relationship to light, or even to make them easier to apply to the wall: talc, feldspar, mica, or quartz. Surely, chemistry is

Bear in the Chauvet Cave

More than all others, the Chauvet Cave "smells of bear" (Jean Clottes). The walls display many drawings in which cave bears appear side by side with brown bears, while in the back of the cave, in the center of one chamber, there is a bear skull mounted on a rock and surrounded by twelve other skulls arranged in a semicircle on the ground. This presumed sanctuary, as well as many others scattered throughout Europe and Siberia, suggests that Paleolithic people worshipped this animal. But that hypothesis is far from generally accepted by prehistorians.

33,000–29,000 BCE. Vallon-Pont-d'Arc, Ardèche, France, Chauvet Cave, "negative hands" wall.

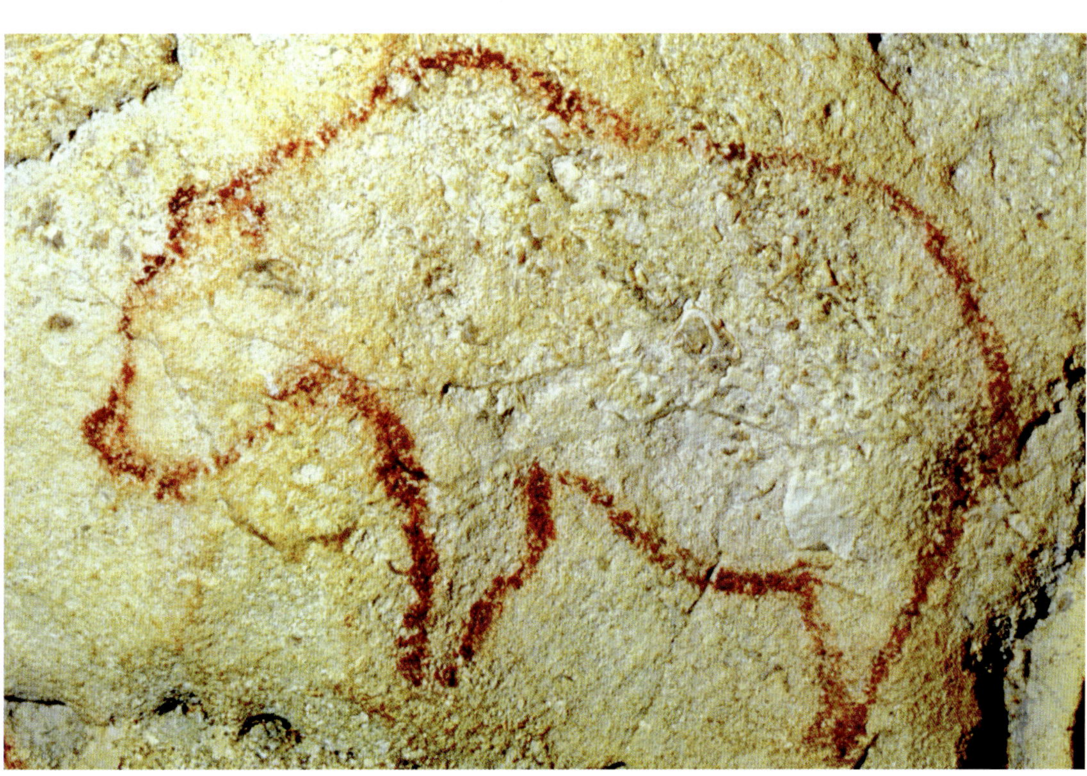

very much present here. Burning wood to make charcoal to use for drawing is a relatively simple technique. But extracting plates of hematite from earth, washing, filtering, and grinding it with a mortar and pestle to obtain a fine reddish powder, and then mixing that powder with feldspar, vegetable oils, or animal fats to give it different shades or make it adhere better to a rock surface is another, much more complex one. And the painters of Niaux, Altamira, Lascaux, and other caves were already familiar with it, as perhaps were the painters of the even more ancient Cosquer and Chauvet Caves.

With regard to pictorial practices, it may be too early to speak of true color formulas, but we can observe a great diversity of red tones on the wall paintings that have come down to us. Is this diversity deliberate, determined in advance, implemented using learned procedures (mixing, diluting, adding charges, choosing specific binders)? Does it correspond to specific intentions or meanings? Or is it the result of the work of time? It is difficult to know, because we are not seeing the colorings produced by these pigments in their original state but as time has transformed them. In any case, even in caves that remained sealed until the twentieth century, the gap between the original state and the present state is always a significant one. Moreover, we are looking at these paintings in light conditions that bear no relationship to those experienced by the prehistoric painters. Electric lighting is not the same as torch light (it goes without saying). But how many specialists bear that in mind when studying the cave paintings? And simply among visitors, who is really aware that between these paintings and the present,

millions—billions?—of color images from all eras have intervened, images that neither our gaze nor our memory has been spared? These images have the effect of a distorting filter; we have consumed, digested, and recorded them in a kind of collective unconscious. Time has done its work, millennia have passed, art has continually been transformed. That is why we cannot see and will never be able to see as our distant ancestors did. This applies to forms and is even more true of colors.

Let us now leave prehistory. Between the most recent paintings of the Paleolithic period and the most ancient paintings of Near Eastern and Egyptian antiquity, many millennia passed, during which pictorial techniques evolved and were enriched with new pigments, notably in the range of reds. In pharaonic Egypt for example, although hematite was still widely used, painters used other materials as well: cinnabar, a natural mercuric sulfide, and more rarely, realgar, a natural arsenic sulfide. Both of them were very expensive, imported from far away, and used only in small quantities; moreover, they were very toxic.[4] Dyeing lacquers that required elaborate technical knowledge were also used. It is often said that the Egyptians invented the oldest known artificial pigment—almost three thousand years before our era—the famous Egyptian blue, obtained from copper filings that were heated and combined with sand and potash.[5] This process provided those splendid blue and blue-green tones that were then considered beneficial and that win our admiration even today. But the Egyptians could hardly be outdone in the range of reds as well, since they knew how to transform animal or vegetable matter—madder, kermes,

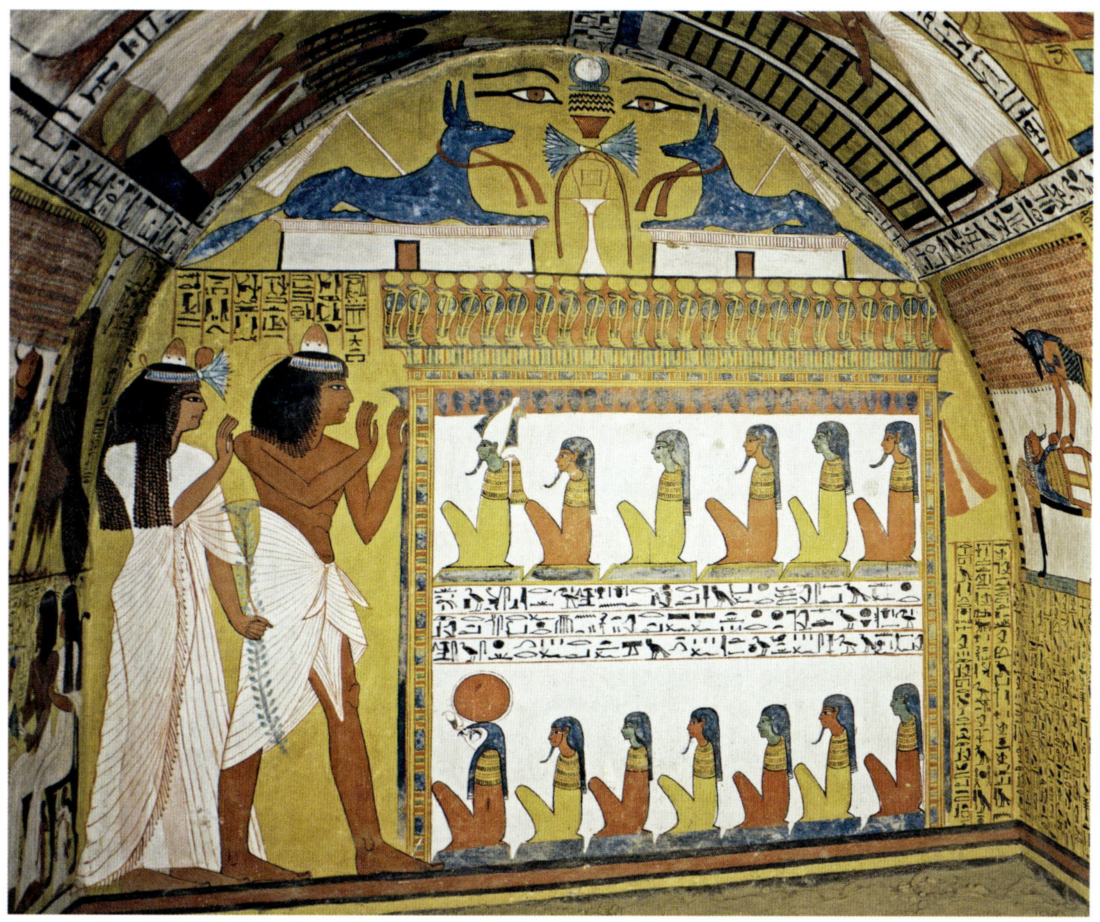

murex—into pigment. To do this, they reprocessed pieces of fabric dyed in red, extracted from them the remaining dyestuffs, and chemically precipitated them onto a mineral powder. The material thus obtained became a pigment. And, without even considering such delicate operations, what about the transformation of yellow ochers into red ochers through simple cooking?[6] Doesn't this transform a natural pigment into an artificial pigment? As we have seen, the Paleolithic painters already knew how to do this.

The Egyptians loved colors and made a business of them. In Egyptian culture, as later in Phoenician culture, the same artisans made pigments, dyes, makeup, glass, soap, and certain remedies. Moreover, many materials served a variety of uses; hematite, for example, was simultaneously a red pigment meant for paintings, a light dye that easily colored water, and a medicine that supposedly cured diseases of the blood and stopped bleeding. Throughout the first millennium BCE, Egyptian merchants supplied a large part of the Mediterranean basin with these various products; in return they received raw materials that Egyptian artisans were expert in transforming. Hence, for making red pigments, cinnabar came from Spain and red ochers from Bithynia and the Pontus region, on the shores of the Black Sea.

In Egyptian funerary painting, the colors, still so bright and clean that they sometimes seem almost new, reflect conventions. For

Isis Welcoming Thutmose IV

Discovered in 1903 in the Valley of the Kings, the tomb of Pharaoh Thutmose IV (r. 1397–1387 BCE) did not use yellow and red to distinguish the bodies of the gods from those of humans, but instead resorted to differences in shades; humans have dark skin and gods have light skin. That is the case here with the goddess Isis, who is holding the famous ankh, an object-ideogram in the form of a cross with a handle, symbolizing life.

c. 1380 BCE. Luxor, Egypt, Tomb of Thutmose IV, vestibule wall.

example, male figures display red or reddish-brown complexions, thus distinguishing them from women, whose bodies are lighter in color, beige or yellowish. Those of divinities are a more vivid yellow, often drawn from orpiment, a natural arsenic sulfide reserved for this purpose. Similarly, the arid red of the desert is generally contrasted with the fertile black of the Nile's alluvial valley. Added to this strictly iconographic function is a symbolic dimension; red is more often negative than positive. Not only was it the color of the desert burned by the sun, but it was also the color of the people who lived there or who came from there, all enemies of the Egyptians. It signaled violence, war, and destruction. It was also the color of the god Seth, brother of Isis and Osiris, who often embodied the forces of evil. He was sometimes given red hair or was dressed in red. The murderer of Osiris and the rival of Horus, he symbolized cruelty, ruin, and chaos. His name was generally written in red.

Indeed, language and writing cannot be outdone for underscoring the evil nature of red. The same word can, according to the context, mean "to redden" or "to die," and sometimes "to inspire terror." Expressions like "having the red heart" (being angry) or "committing red acts" (doing evil) are negative as well. Similarly, scribes sometimes drew in red the hieroglyphs that evoked danger, misfortune, or death.

Nevertheless, all Egyptian reds were not evil. Some signified victory, others power, and still others, the most numerous, blood and vital powers. There were even reds that protected against evil: red jasper amulets, for instance, which were thought to be dyed with the blood or tears of Isis, goddess of fertility, often represented in the form of a heifer with a red coat. All the same, the symbolic world of pharaonic Egypt was neither constant nor univocal; between the ancient empire and the Hellenic epoch, between Upper and Lower Egypt, the meanings of colors were not the same. Moreover, all their mysteries have still not been revealed to archaeologists.

The same is true for the ancient Near East; colors occupied an important place in the decoration of walls and furnishings, but their interpretation remains difficult. Here red seems positive, linked to creation, prosperity, power, and the worship of certain divinities, especially representing fertility. The Sumerians and Assyrians, for example, painted the statues of their gods in vivid colors; whether the statues were in stone or clay, their dominant color was almost always red. It was at once the color of the sacred and the color of the living world.

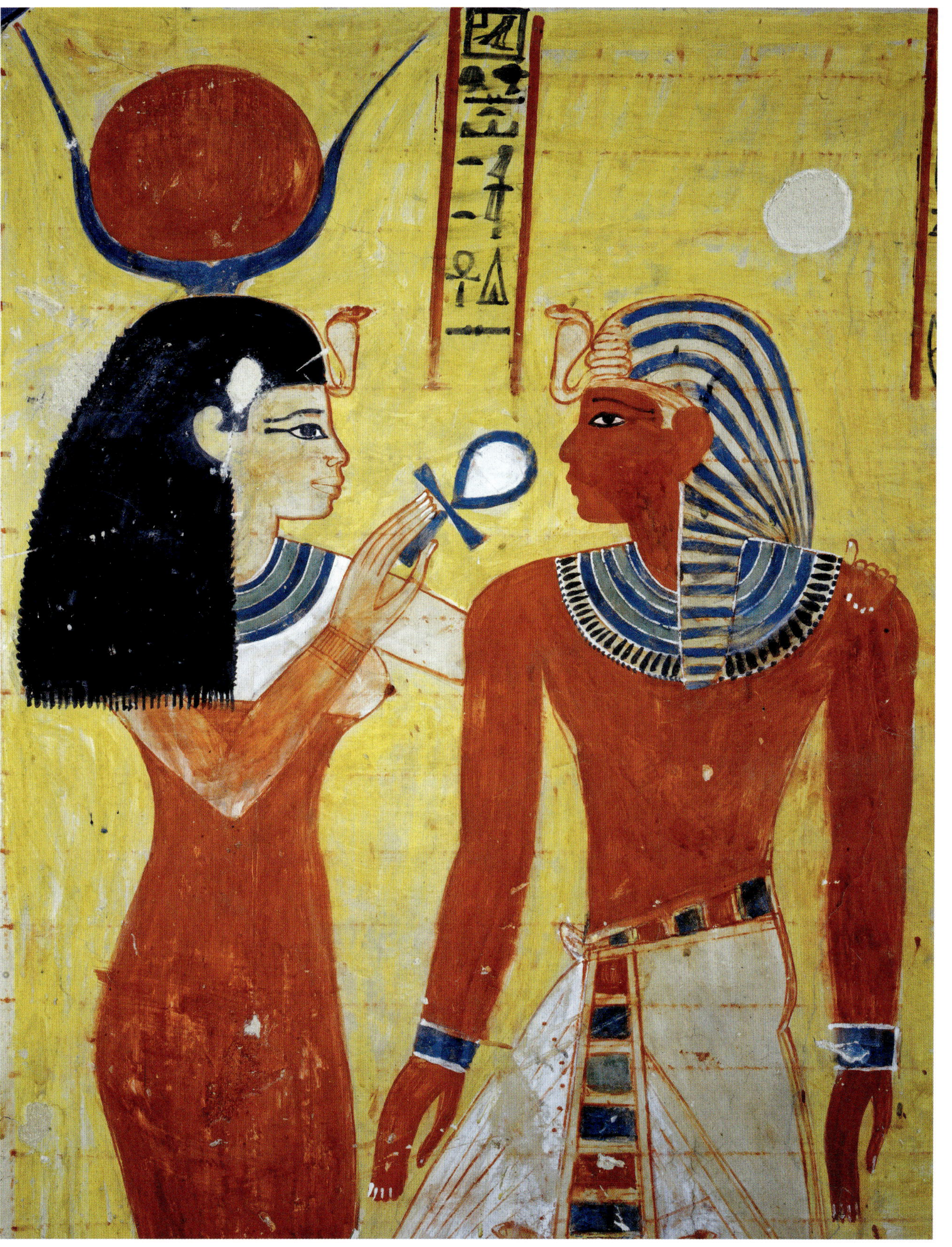

Fire and Blood

The symbolic primacy of red in ancient societies is thus a firmly established fact, which was in place for a very long time, from the Upper Paleolithic period, or even earlier, until the first millennium BCE. Establishing why, on the other hand, is not easy. The theory that color vision in humans may have evolved over millennia, and that humans may have perceived red before all other colors, appealed for a time to some scholars and scientists. In the second half of the nineteenth century, fierce debates thus divided philologists, neurologists, archaeologists, and ophthalmologists over whether a given ancient people were blind or not to a given color. Were the Germans more advanced than the Greeks and Romans in the perception of blues and greens? Did the peoples of the Bible and the ancient Near East see red better than all other hues? To answer these questions, scientists assembled texts and explored lexica, thereby transforming language itself into a kind of code whose study would allow the mechanisms of perception to be discerned.[7]

Today those evolutionist theories—linguistic and biological—have been abandoned.[8] Language is not a code, and vision mechanisms for ancient populations differ not in the least from our own. But the perception of colors is not just a biological or neurobiological phenomenon; it is also a cultural phenomenon that calls upon knowledge, memory, imagination, feelings, relations with others, and more generally, life in society. It is not because a color is not named that it is not seen; it is because there is little or no opportunity to name it. Which place does which society grant to which color, not only in its material life, institutions, and social codes, but also and especially in its rituals, beliefs, and symbols? That is where the real issues lie. In these areas, it is undeniable that red has played the primary role for a long time, a very long time, as if it were granted more or less magical powers that other colors did not possess. Why?

One answer can probably be found in the two principal referents for this color: fire and blood, two natural elements that are almost immediately associated with red and encountered in almost all societies in every period of their history. Even today, nearly all language dictionaries define the adjective "red" with a phrase like "having the color of fire or blood." Of course other colors have one or many powerful referents in nature, but they seem less universal and immutable.[9] Red, on the other hand, refers always and everywhere to fire and blood. Now if the bond between red and blood goes without saying—all living vertebrates have red blood—the association between red and fire is less obvious. In reality, a flame is rarely red, but rather orange, yellow,

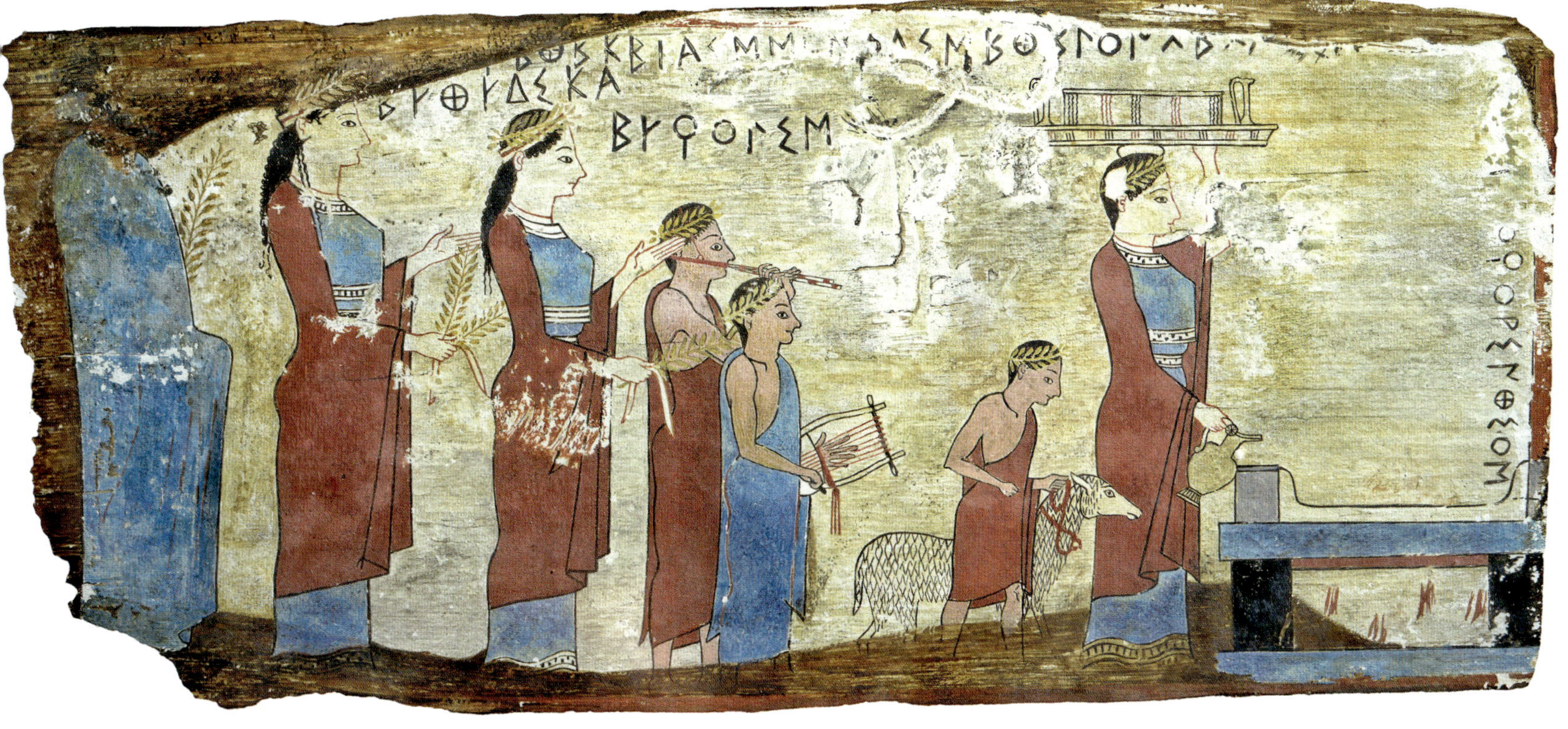

Sacrificial Procession

On this exceptional painted wooden tablet, a sheep is being led to the sacrificial altar. Around its neck is a red cord, a symbol of its consecration to the gods.

c. 530 BCE. Athens, National Archaeological Museum.

blue, sometimes white, colorless, or polychromatic. Even live coals tend more toward orange than red. Why is it that in the world of symbols and representations fire is always red?

Perhaps it is because fire was perceived as a living being, at least by ancient societies in which red was the color of life. As a source of light and heat, like the sun, to which it is related, fire does indeed seem endowed with an autonomous life force. Its domestication by humans, at a much debated date—between five hundred thousand and three hundred fifty thousand years ago, or even earlier

still—undoubtedly constitutes the most important event in the history of humanity, an event that completely changed the conditions of existence and formed the basis for what can be called "civilization."[10] Numerous stories arise in all mythologies recounting how humans took possession of fire, usually stealing it from the gods, as Prometheus does, for example, in Greek mythology.[11]

As a living, supernatural being, fire was an early object of worship, and was still so in documented historical times, in India and Persia, for example, where fire had its temples and

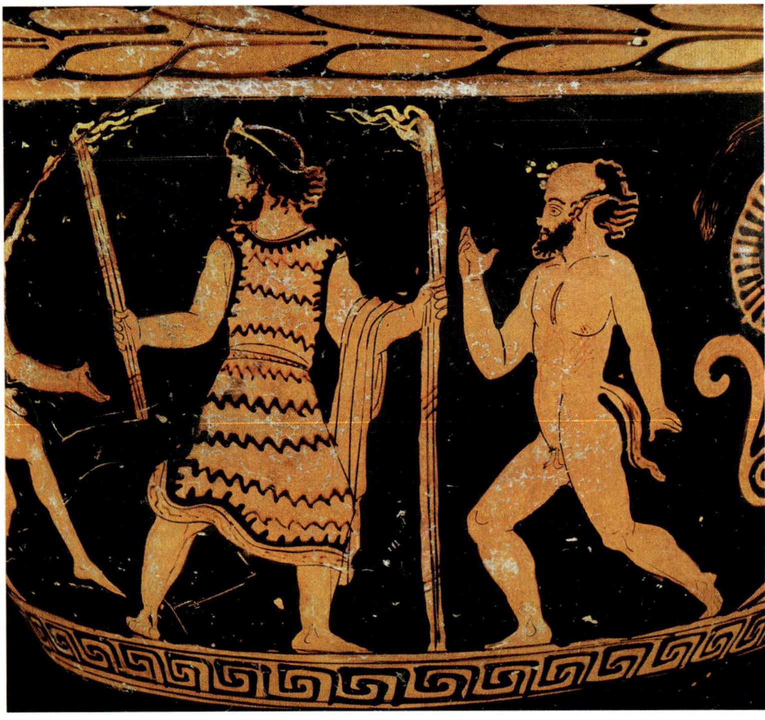

Prometheus Bringing Fire to Mortals

This detail from a red-figure krater, in an excellent state of preservation, may represent a comic scene, especially because the satyr on the right is imitating Prometheus's gestures.

c. 450 BCE. Lipari, Italy, Museo Archeologico Regionale Eoliano.

its high priests, dressed in red, not surprisingly. Fire allowed humans to communicate with the gods and sometimes to identify with them. Moreover, fire divinities, which maintained strict relationships with the color red, existed everywhere and, like the color and like fire itself, were a matter of ambivalent symbolism. That is the case with the Greek Hephaestus (who later became the Roman Vulcan), the god of fire and metal, by turn either a beneficent, ingenious creator or a vindictive, harmful magician. The oldest texts call him lame, ugly, and red—that is, red like the fire and the iron over which he is master.[12] In his image, all the blacksmiths in Western traditions are ambiguous figures, both industrious and magic. Sometimes fire is favorable, fertile, purifying, regenerative; sometimes, on the contrary, it is treacherous, violent, and

destructive, the enemy of humans and all living beings. Sometimes it must be tended, watched, not allowed to go out because it is the source of good things; sometimes it must be protected against, fled, extinguished, or tamed. Red follows in its image, often beneficent, sometimes malefic, but always stronger symbolically than any other color.

That symbolic ambivalence also characterizes the other referent for the color red, blood. Blood, too, is both the source of life and death, according to whether it circulates in the bodies of animate beings or it escapes from them. Blood also allows humans to communicate with the gods, generally in the form of bloody sacrifices that form the subject of very ancient and carefully controlled rituals. Blood gave rise to a whole set of beliefs and superstitions, stories and myths, magic and preventive practices against which early Christianity would wage war. These included offering a certain divinity the blood of a certain animal; bathing in the blood of another animal; drinking the blood of yet another animal; exchanging one's blood with that of a comrade in arms or the hunt. Sometimes pure, sometimes impure, sometimes sacred, sometimes taboo, blood can bring salvation or fertility, just as it can bring peril or death.[13]

The idea that blood belonged to the gods and constituted their food dominated for a long time. Thus arose the sacrifice of animals, whose blood served to sprinkle temples, altars, and even the faithful in order to purify them or to satisfy the divinities or obtain pardon from them. Already evident in the Neolithic period, these sacrifices are still abundantly present in the Old Testament (it was only in the first

The God Mithras Slaying a Bull

On this white marble bas-relief, which retains a few traces of red paint, the central scene of the cult of Mithras is represented: the bloody sacrifice of a bull.

c. 260–80. Rome, Museo Nazionale Romano.

century CE, after the destruction of the Second Temple, that they disappeared among the Jews).[14] Sometimes the sacrificed animals had to have a red coat or fur, as though that color was favored by the gods or perhaps conveyed the presence of richer, stronger, more fertile, or more nourishing blood in the animals in question, most often bovines. For example, that was still the case in the first centuries CE for the cult of Mithra, a religion of Eastern origin that spread widely throughout the Roman Empire; its central ritual revolved around a

bull with a red hide or cloaked in red. Prudentius, a Christian author from the fifth century who was violently opposed to Mithraism, left us a striking description of it:

The high priest, you know, goes down into a trench dug deep in the ground to be made holy. . . . Above him they lay planks to make a stage, leaving the timber-structure open, with spaces between; and then they cut and bore through the floor, perforating the wood in many places with a sharp-pointed tool so that it has a great number

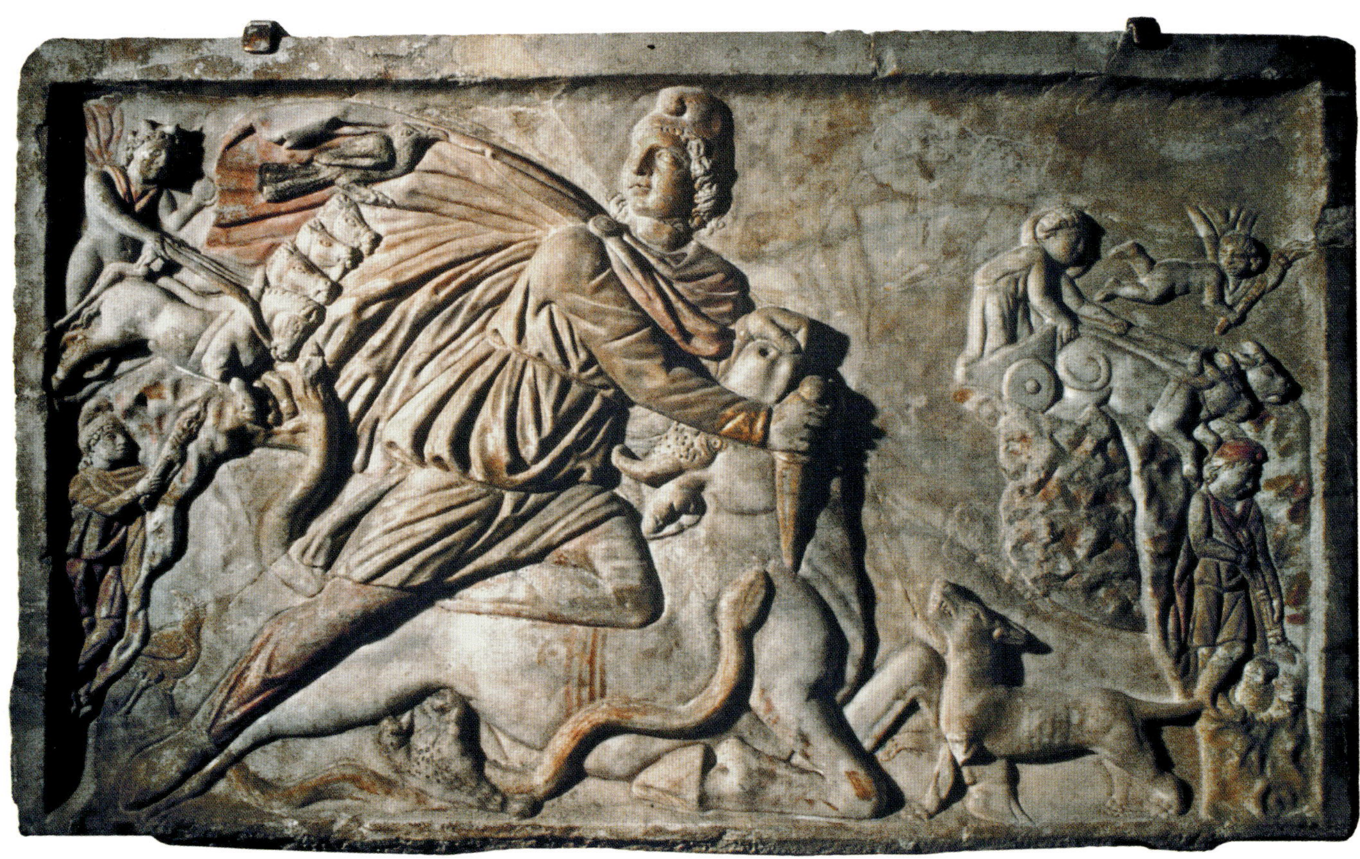

Dionysus Riding a Panther

God of the vineyard, wine, and all related excesses, Dionysus is often represented with the color red, as is the case for this mosaic from Delos. Yet the god is not wearing his usual red cloak but rather a long tricolor robe that gives him an effeminate appearance, all the more so because he is beardless. Nevertheless, his attributes allow us to identify him without hesitation. First is the panther (or leopard), which he is often seen riding; second are the objects he holds in his hands, a tambourine and a thyrsus, which are associated with him.

c. 180–170 BCE. Delos, Greece, House of Masks.

of little openings. Hither is led a great bull with a grim, shaggy brow, wreathed with garlands of flowers about his shoulders and encircling his horns, while the victim's brow glitters with gold, the sheen of the plates tinging his rough hair. When the beast for sacrifice has been stationed here, they cut his breast open with a consecrated hunting-spear and the great wound disgorges a stream of hot blood, pouring on the plank-bridge below a steaming river which spreads billowing out. Then through the many ways afforded by the thousand chinks it passes in a shower, dripping a foul rain, and the priest in the pit below catches it, holding his filthy head to meet every drop and getting his robe and his whole body covered with corruption. Laying his head back he even puts his cheeks in the way, placing his ears under it, exposing lips and nostrils, bathing his very eyes in the stream, not even keeping his mouth from it but wetting his tongue, until the whole of him drinks in the dark gore. After the blood is all spent and the officiating priests have drawn the stiff carcase away from the planking, the pontiff comes forth from his place, a grisly sight, and displays his wet head, his matted beard, his dank fillets and soaking garments. Defiled as he is with such pollution, all unclean with the foul blood of the victim just slain, they all stand apart and give him salutation and do him reverence because the paltry blood of a dead ox has washed him while he was ensconced in a loathsome hole in the ground.[15]

Prudentius wrote in a time when the worship of Mithras was in decline, and few followers of that religion continued to believe in the purifying virtues of bull's blood. Alternatively, some Christian authors enjoyed recalling how the Greeks and Romans had once considered it a deadly poison, citing many famous figures who committed suicide by drinking bull's blood: King Midas, Aeson (father of Jason), Themistocles, Hannibal, and a few others.

Moreover, in some religions, as in the cult of Dionysus in Greece, wine had replaced blood early on, thus actually contributing to the slow decline of animal sacrifice. Henceforth, it was spilled on the altar, on the ground, on fire, on priests and followers, as blood had been in the past. Wine is indeed an equivalent of blood, but blood of a specific kind, that of the vineyard. It is also the drink of life and immortality; source of energy, health, and joy; symbol of knowledge or initiation. It consoles men, inspires poets, brings pleasure to all. The vineyard itself was a gift from the gods, and wine sometimes constituted their own blood, sometimes an offering made to them. Whatever its actual color, it was associated symbolically with red and has remained so to the present. In this sense, white wine is not really wine. Dionysus himself, god of the vineyard and of wine, was frequently represented dressed in a red cloak, or given a ruddy face and sometimes red hair. Like all the gods, he did not experience drunkenness, a transgressive state reserved for mortals. Hence, for a human, not to get drunk is to show oneself worthy of the gods. Weak and corrupt beings, tyrants and barbarians are incapable of this.

This privileged bond that most ancient religions established between the color red and vital powers can even be observed in funeral practices. As in prehistoric times, a very widespread belief held that the dead lived or should live in their tombs. Thus, everywhere

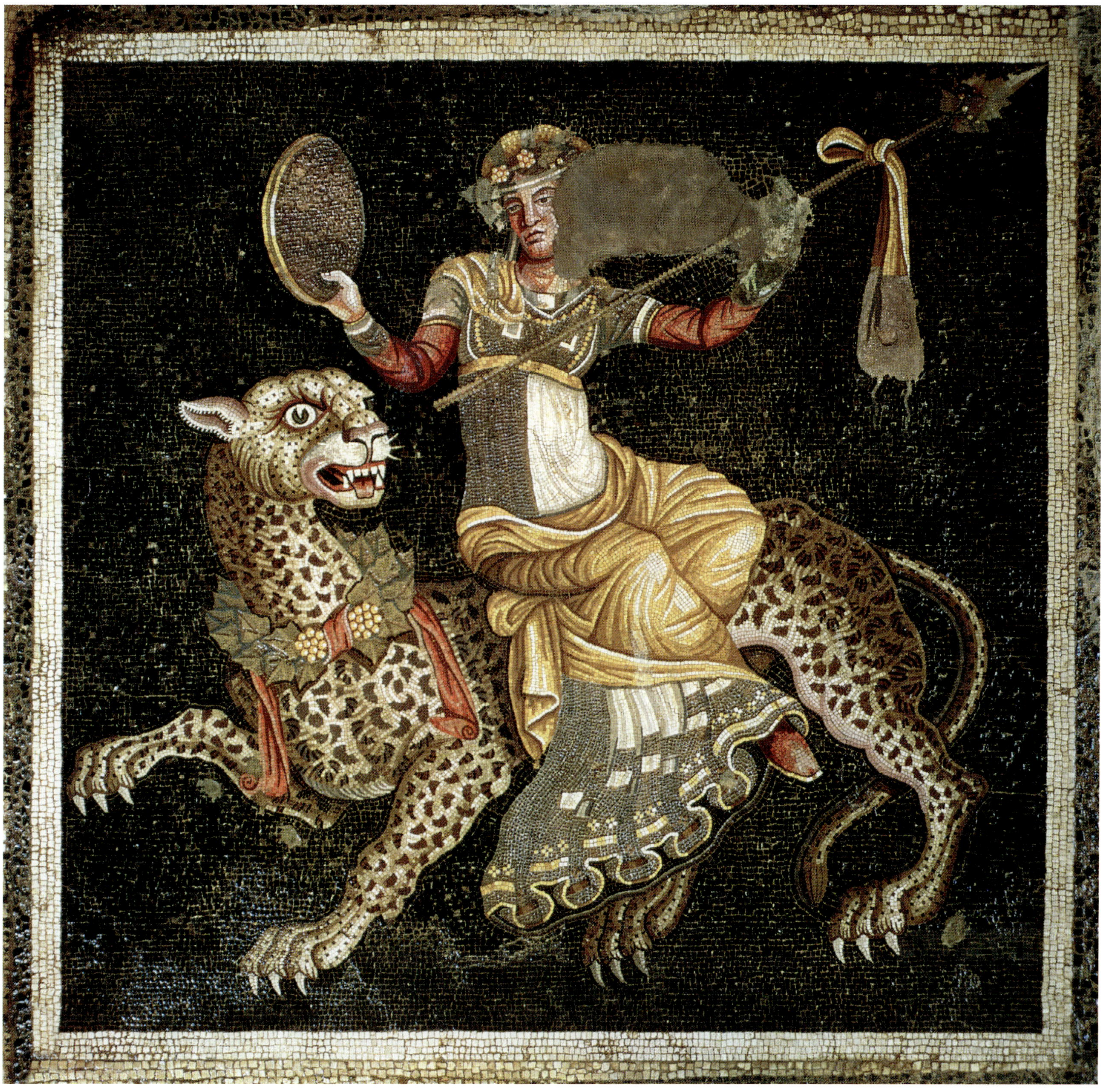

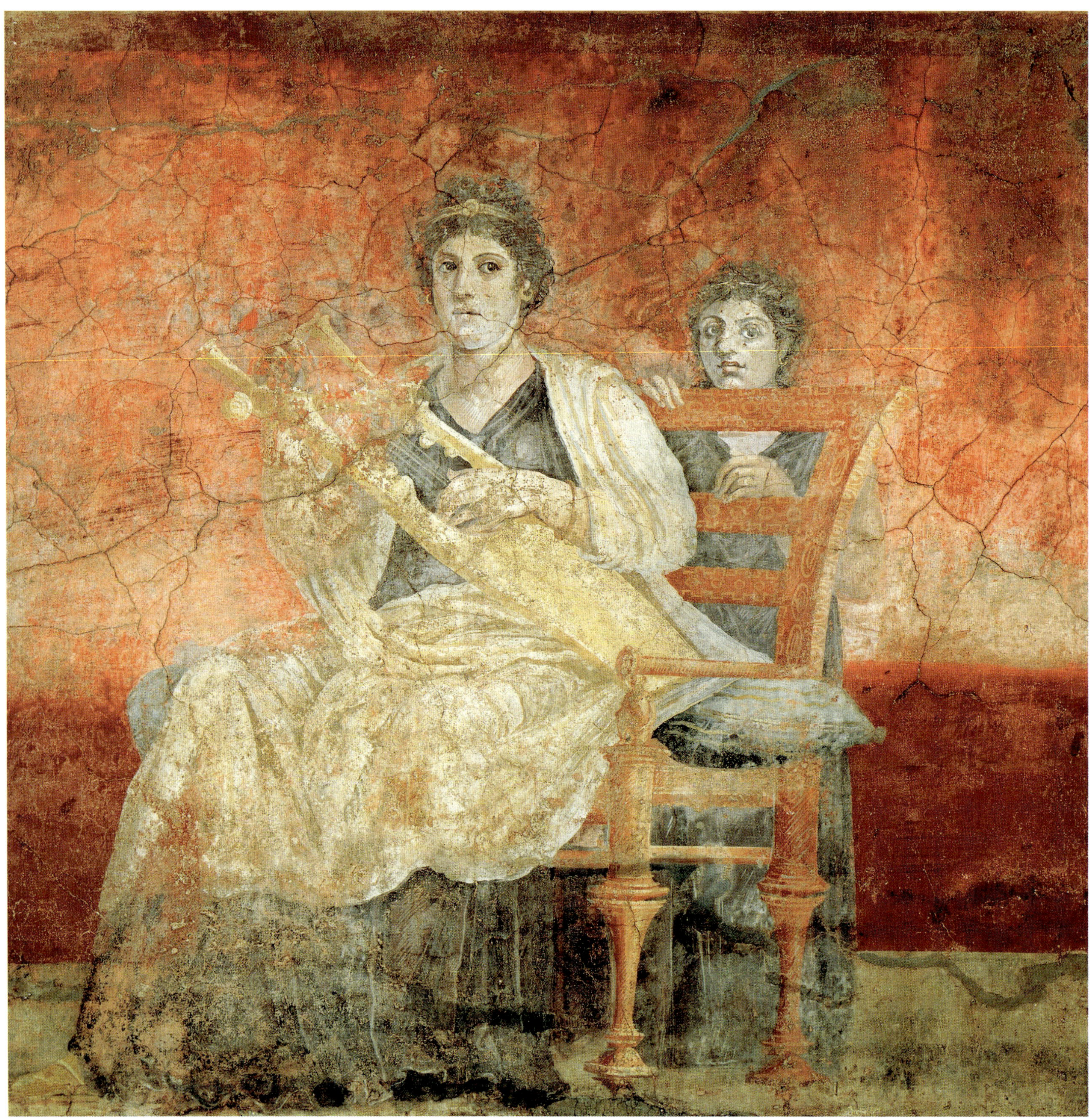

Cithara Player

The rural villa in Boscoreale in Campania was buried under ashes from the eruption of Vesuvius in 79 CE. Its owner must have been of high standing, if we are to believe the clues left in this surviving mural painting. First, cinnabar, a very expensive pigment, is used abundantly; second, it portrays a woman seated on a kind of throne, playing the cithara and wearing a luxurious tiara. A variant of the lyre, the cithara had a tone both soft and low, and was a prestigious instrument.

c. 40 BCE. New York, Metropolitan Museum of Art.

throughout the Near East, Egypt, Greece, Rome, and even among the barbarians of Brittany, or Germania, an abundance of materials is found in tombs. And just as some of the dead from the Paleolithic period rest on beds of red ocher, many of the deceased from the first centuries BCE are surrounded by red objects or elements in their tombs or sarcophagi, the red meant to protect them in the beyond and allow them to recover a share of their vital powers. There are blocks of hematite or cinnabar; red stones (carnelian, jasper, garnet) and red molten glass; vessels containing wine or blood; fabrics, jewels, and statuettes in the color red; and fruits and flower petals of this same color.[16] Virgil gives us a literary account of those enduring rites in Book 5 of the *Aeneid*, when he presents Aeneas returning to the tomb of his father Anchises and performing various libations:

> Leaving the council now with thousands in his wake, amid his immense cortege, Aeneas gains the tomb and here he pours libations, each in proper order. Two bowls of unmixed wine he tips on the ground and two of fresh milk, two more of hallowed blood, then scatters crimson flowers with this prayer: "Hail, my blessed father, hail again! I salute your ashes, your spirit and your shade—my father I rescued once, but all for nothing.[17]

In Rome, red and purplish flowers were often used for funerals, especially those that lost their petals quickly, like poppies and violets. They symbolized the briefness of life. The rose itself assumed funereal connotations during the Rosalia, a series of ceremonies to honor the spirits of the dead that took place from May to July. On the other hand, the amaranth, another red or crimson flower that does not wilt, represented immortality. Poets sometimes contrasted it to the rose, whose brilliance is fleeting. That is the case with this short anonymous piece, possibly inspired by one of Aesop's fables:

> "How beautiful you are!" said the amaranth. "Your scent and your splendor are the delight of gods and mortals." "Of course," replied the rose, "but I live only a few days, and even if no one picks me, I rapidly fade. But you, amaranth, you remain young forever and you keep your blossoms eternally."[18]

With Pliny among the Painters

Let us leave flowers and funeral customs behind and return to pictorial practices. Contrary to what one might think, Greek painting is less well known to us than Egyptian painting. In truth it is much more varied and complex, and most of the works and evidence of this have disappeared.[19] Let us begin with polychromatic architecture and sculpture, long unknown to historians and archaeologists and then denied, rejected, or reduced to a minor role. Only in recent times was the fact finally accepted that all statuary was painted, including the most modest examples, as well as most architecture and its decoration.[20] What place did red take in this? First place, probably, as least if we rely on the polychromatic traces that survive, as well as the lists made in the field by young architects in the eighteenth and nineteenth centuries.[21] The attempts at simulated reproduction, carried out in recent years on replicas with the aid of increasingly sophisticated techniques, offer proof.[22] But here again it is necessary to distinguish periods, as was the case with the Near East. Red for Greek statuary and architecture was undoubtedly more pervasive in the Archaic period than in the Classical and especially the Hellenic period; over the course of time, the palette diversified. In this regard, the image of a white, somber Greece, inherited from historians and theoreticians of neoclassicism, must be corrected once and for all. That is a false image. The Greeks loved vivid, contrasting colors; on stone, polychromatic painting was intense.[23]

Was the same true of the large wall paintings seen in public or sacred buildings? It is difficult to know, because they have almost completely disappeared. Despite recent major discoveries—such as the painted funeral chambers of the Macedonian kings—we know them primarily through a few texts, especially through Book 35 of Pliny's *Natural History*, compiled about 60–70 CE and entirely devoted to Greek and Roman painting. But while he teaches us the names of the great artists, cites a few famous works, and mentions the main subjects (mythology and history), Pliny says hardly anything about color, not from the perspective of iconography at least, only from the perspective of pigments. We must thus look to everyday production—that is, to the artisans who left more evidence (private dwellings, votive scenes, funerary paintings, various signs) and above all to ceramics. Vase painting constitutes the principal iconographic source available to historians of ancient Greece for studying not only mythology and religion but

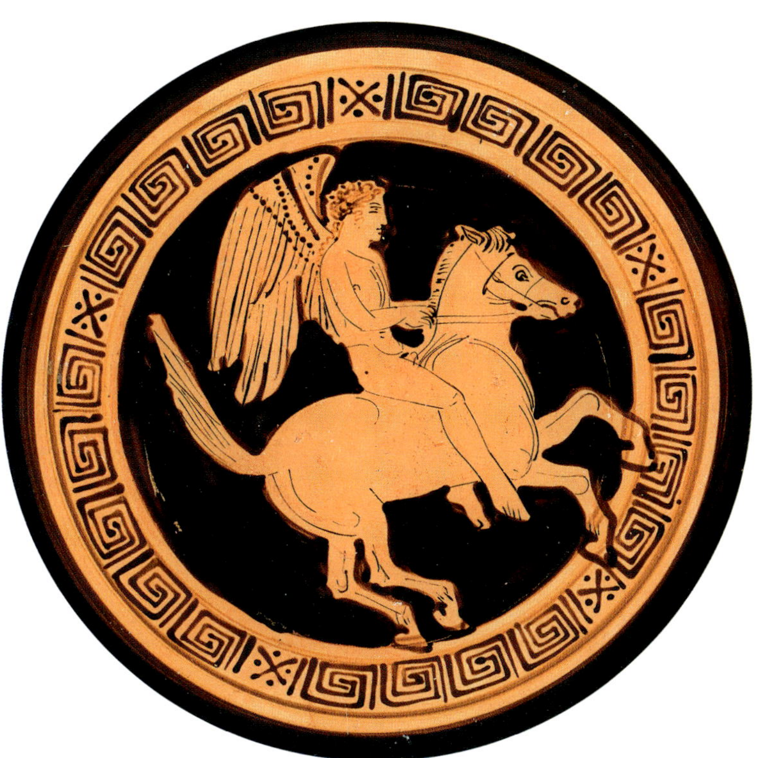

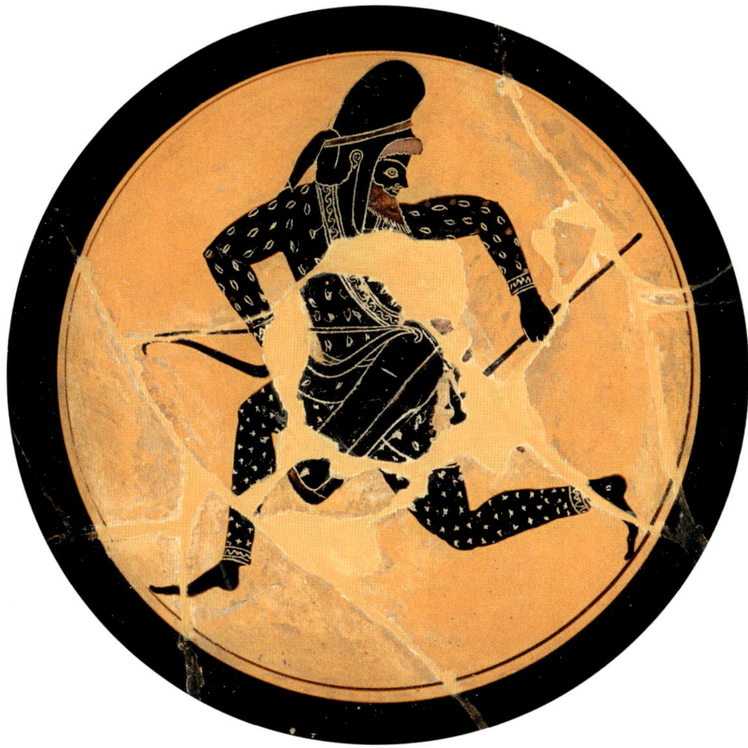

also the bestiary, war, clothing and weapons, material culture, and social relationships of the period. Colors hold the place of honor there. Decoration on the oldest vases is primarily geometric and polychromatic. Then came the widely distributed vases with black figures, originating in Corinth in the seventh century BCE. The figures were incised or painted on a clay background, generally left bare. Then came vases with red figures for which the technique was reversed. Appearing in Athens about 530–520 BCE, they present a background painted uniformly black, with figures worked in relief that, upon firing, take the red color of the clay. The drawing is more precise, the realism greater, the subjects more varied. All traces of white or polychromy henceforth disappeared, and the palette was constructed essentially around two colors: red and black.[24]

Roman painting is better known to us than Greek painting, not only because Roman works and decorations have been preserved in greater numbers but also because Roman texts are more long-winded, if less precise.[25] Pliny's *Natural History* remains our primary textual source here as well. But Pliny's meaning is not always clear. His vocabulary especially presents difficulties for interpretation. Like other Latin authors (and like some present-day art historians), Pliny constantly conflates the terms designating pigments and those that designate the colorings obtained from those pigments.[26] The word "color" itself

Greek Pottery: Red Figure and Black Figure

This black-figure (archer) dish belongs to a period of transition that produced "bilingual" vases, with black figures on the interior and, already, red figures on the exterior. That is the case with this one, the work of the Athenian painter Oltos.

4th and 6th centuries BCE. Paris, Musée du Louvre, Department of Greek, Etruscan, and Roman Antiquities.

is sometimes applied to the coloring matter, sometimes to the color effect produced. And because Pliny is often elliptical, it is also hard for the reader to tell exactly what level of the pictorial practice is under discussion. Among modern historians of ancient painting, a certain number of misunderstandings and debates have arisen from this imprecise vocabulary.[27]

What is more, that imprecision has not disappeared today. For example, is a "vermilion red" simply a red coloring that tends toward orange or rather, more accurately, is it a red pigment derived from the synthesis of sulfur and mercury? One may well wonder. But we moderns are more guilty than Pliny and the ancients, because we have known since the Middle Ages how to abstract the color from its medium or its material. We can speak in the absolute, in a conceptual way, of red, green, blue, and yellow. A Latin author from the first century had a hard time doing this; for him, a color was difficult to envision apart from its materiality and rarely constituted a thing in and of itself.

Art historians have sometimes compounded these lexical difficulties by adding anachronistic comments or questions.[28] This practice has transformed Pliny's remarks, which are sometimes technical and sometimes historical, into aesthetic judgments similar to those made by art critics today. That is to ask of Pliny's discourse on painting something that is foreign to it. Pliny (born in 23 and dead in 79) is of his time, not our own. If he judges, it is as an ideologue, glorifying Rome and its history, not as an aesthete. Moreover, he was an enemy of novelty and preferred earlier painting to the painting of his time, the time of Nero and the first Flavian emperors. In matters of color, he denounced the frivolous, garish tones (*colores floridi*) that pleased his contemporaries, and lamented the matte, somber tones (*colores austeri*) favored in the past.[29] Similarly, with regard to pigments, he could not find words strong enough to criticize and even ridicule those imported henceforth from the most distant Asian countries, those red pigments "drawn from the mud of the Indies . . . and from the blood of their dragons and elephants."[30] This was an allusion to a legend, still well attested in the Middle Ages, that attributed the presence of the blood of a dragon killed by an elephant to many red resins that painters used. Here as elsewhere, in each of the books in his *Natural History*, Pliny appears to be very conservative, if not reactionary.[31] The beautiful, the worthy, the virtuous was the old.

That said, Pliny's *Natural History* provides us much information on the pigments used in Greece and Rome, not only in the well-studied Book 35 but also in other books and chapters concerning minerals, dyes, makeup, and even cures. The bits of information he gives us complement those we can draw from other authors (notably Dioscorides and Vitruvius) as well as analyses done on the paintings themselves.[32] These analyses have proliferated in recent years and have advanced our knowledge considerably, especially with regard to painting in the first century BCE and in the two centuries that followed.[33]

Roman painters used more pigments in the range of reds than in any other range of colors—which is in itself major evidence of the primacy of red tones and the favor they enjoyed throughout the empire.[34] We have already mentioned red ocher, hematite, and cinnabar, well known among the Egyptians and the Greeks. Although hematite seems to have been slightly in decline in Rome, at least for the most refined painting, cinnabar was much in vogue despite its high price and dangerous nature (it is a powerful poison). For example, it was present throughout Pompeii in wall painting, where it was used ostentatiously for painting backgrounds. Hence, it was the dominant red displayed on the walls of many villas that today we would be quick to label as properties of the nouveaux riches. Pliny does in fact inform us that cinnabar cost "fifteen times more than red ocher from Africa" and that its price was equal to that of "blue from Alexandria" (that is, the Egyptian blue we discussed earlier), otherwise the most expensive pigment. In the first century BCE, the most expensive cinnabar was extracted from mines in Almadén, located in the heart of Spain. Shipped to Rome in its raw mineral form, it was processed in many workshops operating at the foot of the Quirinal. This was a true industrial neighborhood, bustling, noisy, foul-smelling, and dangerous. There was another, more ordinary kind of cinnabar that came from mines located below several volcanic mountains in the Apennines, but the painters of Pompeii seemed to disdain it. Their rich sponsors

House of the Griffins in Rome

Located on the Palatine Hill, this residence includes a great hall displaying a beautiful group of trompe-l'oeil paintings belonging to the Pompeian Second Style. The pigments used vary: cinnabar, hematite, *rubrica*.

c. 80 BCE. Rome, Casa dei Grifi.

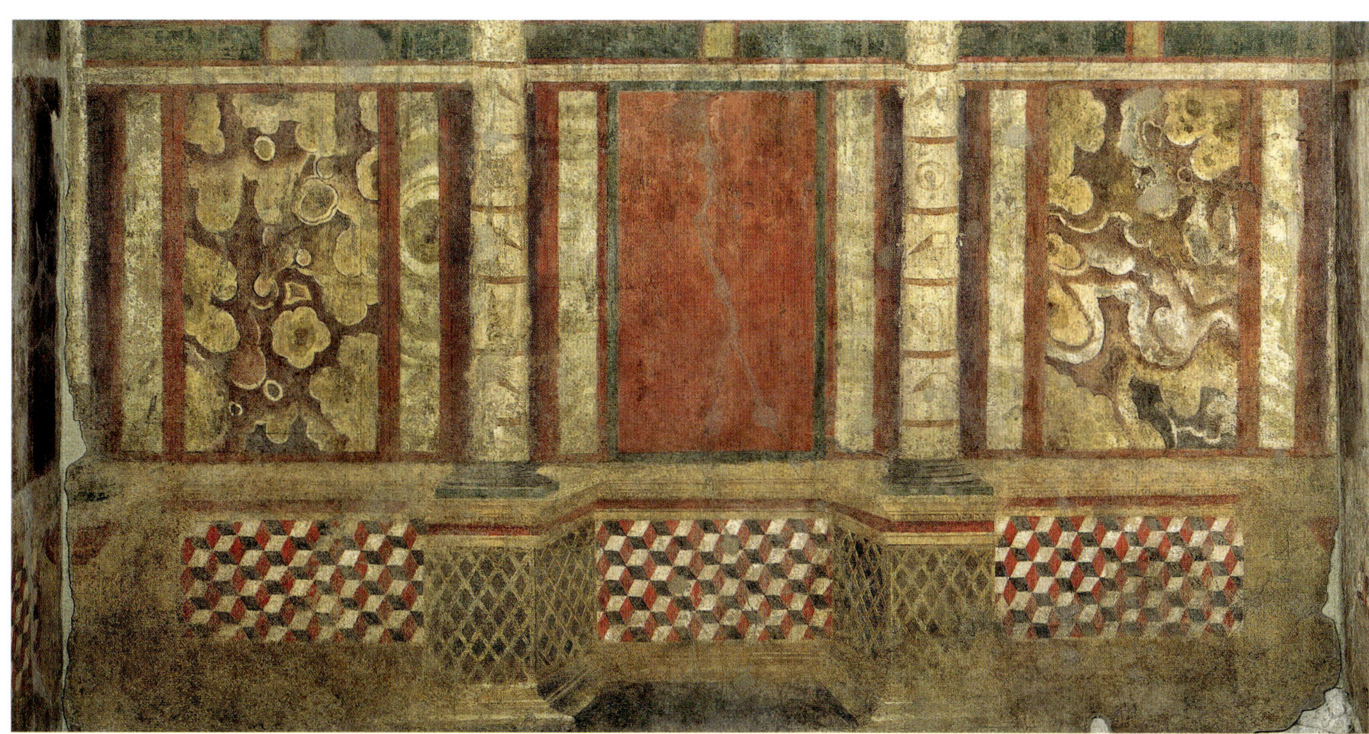

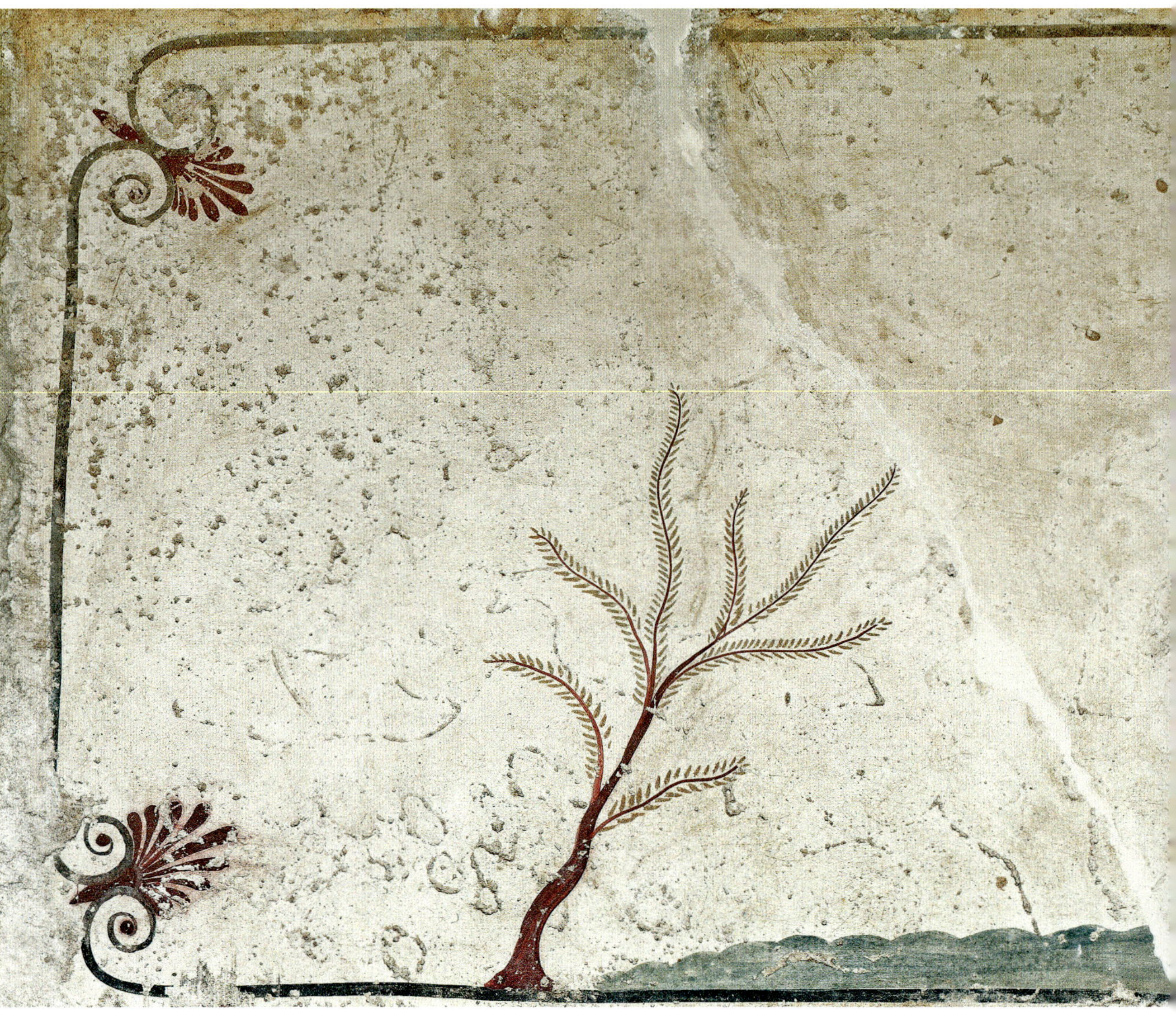

Diver of Paestum

What is he diving into, this unexpected figure in a funerary painting? Another life? The beyond? The world of Hades? Or just simply into his daily bath? The scene is painted in red on the interior face of a stone slab covering a tomb discovered in Paestum in 1968. The trees seem to be olives.

c. 480–470 BCE. Paestum, Italy, Museo Archeologico Nazionale di Paestum.

wanted whatever was most beautiful, expensive, and ostentatious.

Ancient cinnabar was a naturally occurring mercury sulfide. Methods for producing it artificially were not yet known. That would have to wait for the early Middle Ages and the appearance in the West of a new synthetic pigment: vermilion, which will be discussed further on. But Roman painters used many other red pigments, notably ochers of various qualities—to which Pliny gives the generic name *rubrica*. Red ochers were frequently used as an undercoat for cinnabar. Sometimes they were derived from yellow ocher, which was heated and, according to the temperature, transformed into orange, red, purple, or brown.[35] But red pigment could also have come from natural hematite or other types of

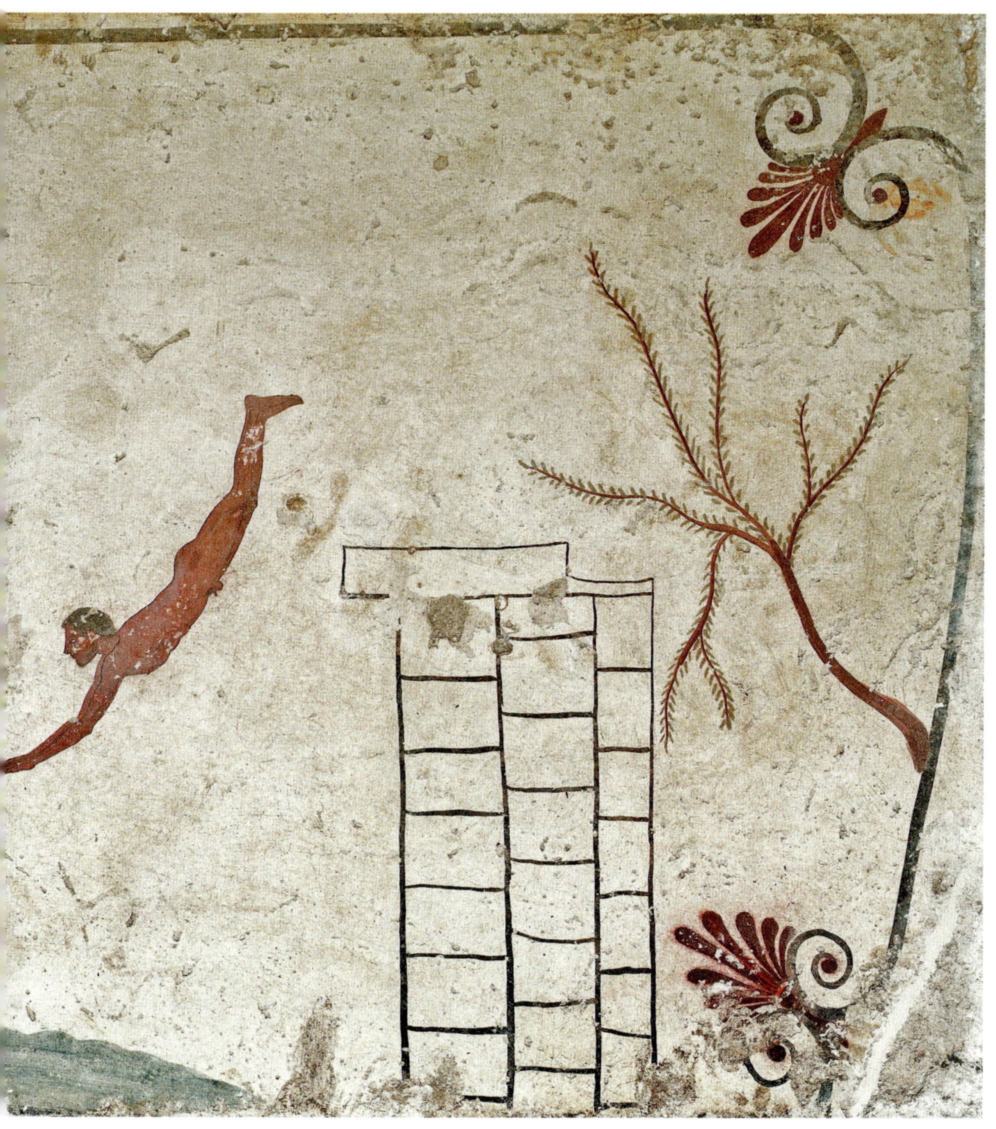

because from one end of it to the other, artists and artisans used the same, or nearly the same colorings—let us again mention realgar (natural arsenic sulfide), which we noted in connection with Egyptian painting.[37] Let us also mention minium, an artificial pigment produced by heating white lead to a high temperature.[38] The term *minium* is particularly ambiguous among Latin authors. Sometimes it refers to minium itself (that is, red lead), sometimes to cinnabar (as is the case with Pliny), sometimes to a mixture of various mineral pigments falling into the range of reds. As "chemists," Roman painters and artisans could resort to mixtures, which the Egyptians rarely did. To obtain beautiful tones of pink, for example, they burned together ceruse (white lead) and *rubrica*.[39] Similarly, they introduced a bit of cinnabar into hematite to give it a sheen. In Rome, painting practices were often learned skills.

To this list of mineral pigments can be added a few pigments of plant or animal origin. Among these are the reddish resins from certain native (thuja, cypress) and exotic (dragon) trees, and especially lacquers—dyestuffs (madder, kermes, murex) used to color a white mineral powder (kaolin, alumina) prepared in advance.[40] Like Egyptian and Greek lacquers, Roman ones primarily involved red tones (even if Vitruvius speaks of enigmatic yellow and green lacquers).[41] Painters valued them because they were particularly resistant to light.

red ores rich in iron oxide. The most prized of these was imported from the area of Sinop, an Asian mining town on the shores of the North Sea, and the town's name was given to the pigment, *sinopis* or *sinopia*.[36] Its cost was high because of the long sea voyage to the principal ports of the Roman west.

Among the red ore pigments used by Roman painters—and throughout the empire,

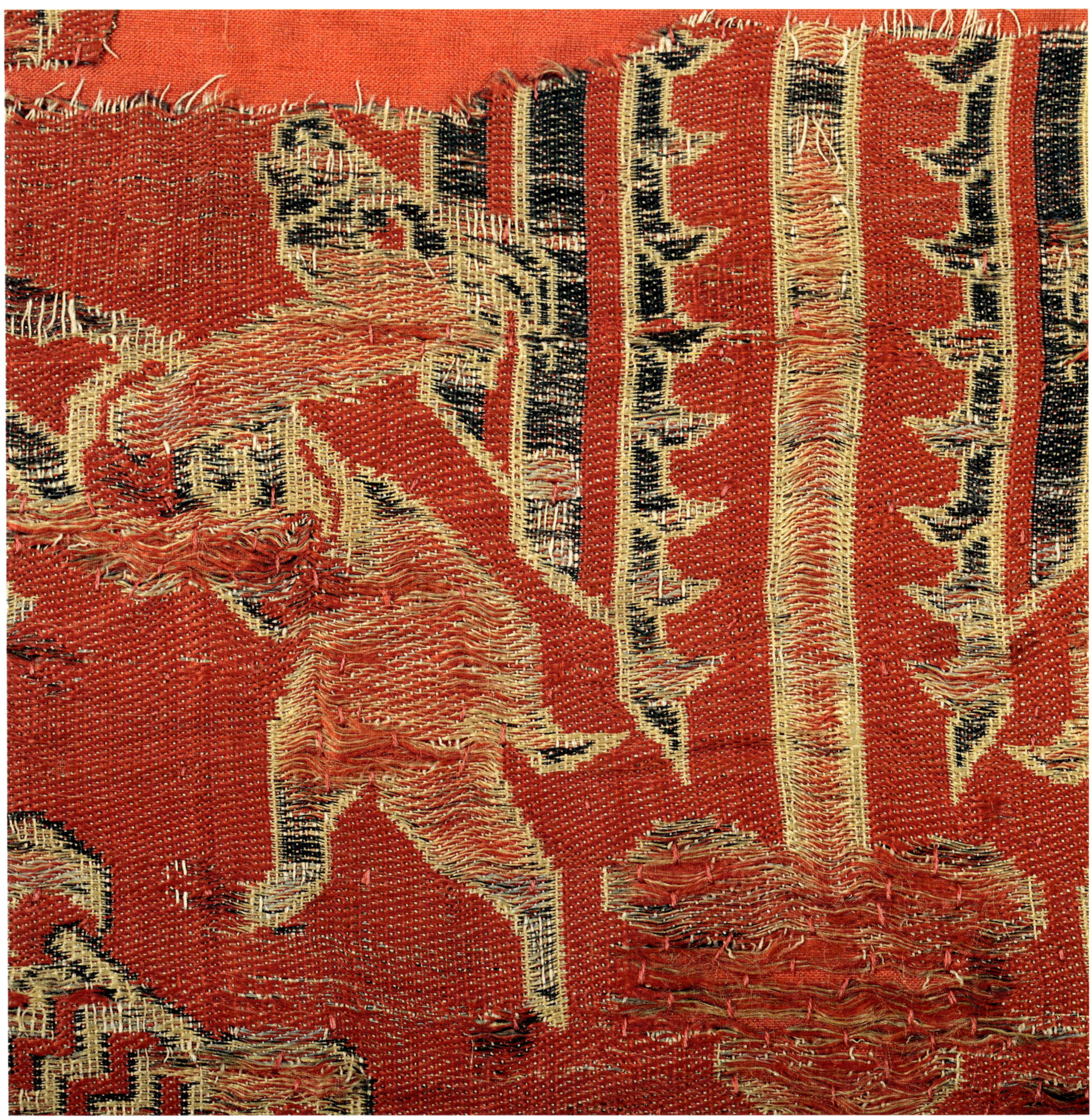

Dyeing in Red

Let us leave the painters and pay a visit to the dyers, those artisans who have so much to teach the historian of colors. Their early history is not well known. When did human beings begin to use dyes? Did they do so even before their populations became sedentary? Given the present state of our knowledge, it is impossible to answer these questions with certainty. However, we can speculate fairly safely that dyeing, like painting, was first achieved in the ranges of red. The oldest surviving fragments of cloth offer proof; they date back no further than the beginning of the third millennium BCE, but they all exhibit traces of red, and only red. Of course the iconography dating back further shows figures wearing clothes of different colors, but to what degree do these images convey reality with regard to color? Just because a figurative document shows a king or hero dressed in red, that does not mean he was really wearing that color. Nor does it mean that he was not. But documentary issues are not considered in this way, regardless of the document or era in question.

We have much written evidence that the Egyptians were skilled dyers. Pliny even attributes to them the invention of the mordant—that is, the use of an intermediary substance (alum, tartar, lime) that makes colors permeate the fibers of fabrics and firmly fixes them.[42] Moreover, funerary materials from tombs have offered various fragments of cloth and clothing, rarely from the early empire of course but more frequently from the Ptolemaic epoch. In the range of reds, the two principal colorants were madder and kermes, but traces can also be found of murex, carthamin, and henna. Those same dyestuffs were found in the Near East and through much of the Mediterranean basin in the first millennium BCE.

Henna is a bush that grows in warm regions whose leaves when dried and reduced to a powder provide a colorant for dyeing in red or in reddish brown, not only used for fabric but also for leather, wood, hair, fingernails, and skin on various parts of the body. Women used it for makeup on their faces (cheeks, lips, eyelids). From carthamus (safflower), a plant whose flowers have dyeing properties, a colorant was also drawn, sometimes yellow, sometimes red. Greek and Roman dyers used it for orange tones. For reds, they used madder, kermes, and murex abundantly. To these they added orcinol, a material provided by certain lichens growing on rocks (hence its Latin name *roccella*); according to Pliny, the most prized orcinol came from the Canary Islands. Orcein, the dyestuff, was a relatively expensive product, because orcinol was difficult to obtain and the processes for transforming it were complex. But orcein produces beautiful shades of more or less purplish red and requires a weak mordant.

Madder is a large, hardy herb that grows wild in various soils, especially wet or marshy ones, and whose roots have strong coloring properties. We do not know the date (fifth or sixth millennium BCE or even earlier?) or the place (India, Egypt, the West?) of the earliest dyeing practices, but we do know that they involved the range of reds. Therefore we may assume that madder was the first colorant used.[43] Madder produced solid, intense tones that dyers soon learned to vary by using different mordants (first, lime and fermented urine; later, vinegar, tartar, and alum). Over the course of time, techniques gradually improved, and by the first millennium CE, dyers in the Mediterranean basin had perfectly mastered madder dyes and the palette of red tones, which was not the case for other colors. The question remains: how did humans get the idea, as early as the Neolithic period, to dig underground for madder root, to remove its skin, harvest the red center, crush it, and use it as a dyestuff? How many aborted attempts, fruitless tries, errors and accidents of all kinds must they have made or suffered before they succeeded at dyeing? This remains a mystery.

In the Roman Empire, dyeing with madder (*rubia*) gradually became a true industry. Certain regions specialized in growing the plant: the Rhône valley, the Po plain, northern Spain, Syria, Armenia, and the Persian Gulf. Many authors give detailed descriptions: the soil had to be cool, calcareous, well watered; seeds were planted in March; after eighteen months the plant was tall enough to provide leaves and stems that served as fodder (which lightly dyed the milk of cows and sheep red), but it was three years before the roots could be dug; these were then dried, peeled, and crushed; the powder thus obtained would serve as dye.[44] Growing madder was easy but required rigorous protection against rats. The plants bore blackish berries that rats adored. The rats had to be driven away, for some of the berries were harvested because, according to Galen, they were the most powerful diuretic in existence. Ancient medicine made great use of them.

Madder demonstrated many tinctorial properties and offered a variety of deep, beautiful red tones. But they had the drawback of being dull. That was why Greek and Roman dyers sometimes preferred a different dyestuff—more expensive, of course, and much more difficult to obtain—that provided more striking reds: kermes (*coccum*). This was animal matter, extracted from the dried bodies of certain insects collected from the leaves of certain trees and bushes, most of which were varieties of oak, growing all around the Mediterranean. Only the female insect was used and had to be caught at the moment she was preparing to lay her eggs. Exposure to vinegar vapors and then drying in the sun transformed the insects into a sort of brownish seed (*granum*) that, when crushed, secreted a bit of intense red juice that was used as dye. The result was a uniform, intense, and luminous color, but it took considerable quantities of insects to obtain a small amount of dyestuff—hence the high price of kermes, the use of which was reserved for luxury fabrics.

Madder

With regard to these various dyes, Roman artisans had drawn upon the knowledge and expertise of the Egyptians, Phoenicians, Greeks, and Etruscans, and had improved upon them. Very early on these dyers seemed to specialize by color and by dyestuff. Thus, toward the end of the republic, the *collegium tinctorum*, a very ancient guild, distinguished six categories of artisans for red and its neighboring tones.[45] They were: the *sandicinii* (who produced all madder-based reds); the *coccinarii* (kermes-based reds); the *purpurarii* (vivid and purplish reds that were murex-based); the *spadicarii* (dark and brownish reds with various wood bases); the *flammarii* (carthamin-based reds and oranges); and the *crocatarii* (saffron-based yellows and oranges).[46]

In fact, throughout their history, Roman dyers seem to have been especially successful in the range of reds, purples, oranges, and yellows; a little less so in the range of blacks, browns, pinks, and grays; and mediocre in the range of blues and greens.[47] With regard to these last two colors, Celtic and German dyers seem to have been more skilled. But they transmitted their tinctorial expertise to the Romans quite late, when "barbarian" styles began to gain favor, first sporadically in the first century CE under Nero and the first Flavians, and then in the third century, a period when greens and blues became ubiquitous in women's clothing.

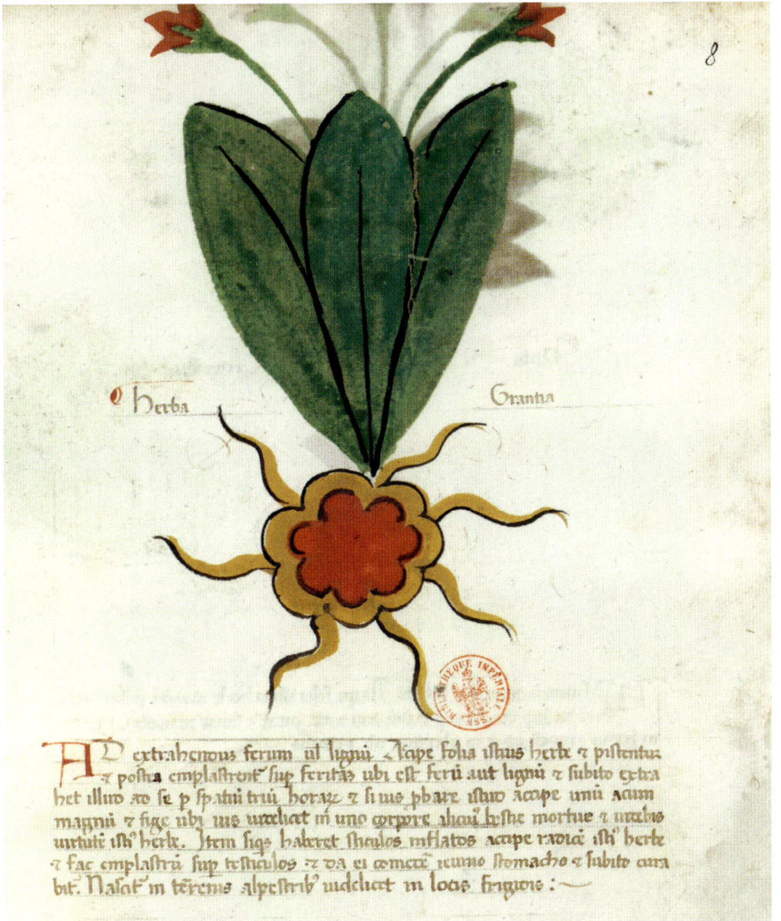

Roman Purple

Let us pause now to consider another colorant, even more prestigious than kermes, and which was the fame and glory of Roman dyeing: purple.

Actually, in this area, Roman knowledge was itself inherited, transmitted from the Greeks, Egyptians, and especially the Phoenicians. Well before Roman domination over the entire Mediterranean, fabrics dyed in purple were already the most prized and most expensive. As signs of wealth and power, they were considered treasures; leaders, priests, and kings dressed in them, and they were even used to adorn statues of gods.[48] There were two principal reasons for the prestige of purple fabrics: first, the incomparable brilliance of the dyes obtained from that somewhat mysterious colorant, murex; second, their solidity and resistance to light. Unlike the bases of other dyes, which faded, the coloring constituent of purple strengthened over time and was enhanced by the effects of light—sunlight, but also moonlight or a simple flame. Fabrics took on new shades and displayed changing, shimmering highlights they did not initially have. Hues varied from red to violet, from violet to black, sometimes passing through pink, mauve, or blue before returning to red. Purple appeared to be a living, magical material. Moreover, many legends circulated around its origins. In Greece, the most common one attributed the discovery of the dyestuff's properties to a dog—sometimes the dog belonged to Heracles, sometimes to Minos the king of Crete, sometimes to a simple shepherd—who, after nosing about in the sea sand and nibbling at the mollusks, was said to have dyed its muzzle red. In another less ancient and less poetic version, it was discovered by Phoenician sailors who, in trying to extract a few large murexes from their shells to make a meal of them, noticed their fingers becoming bright red as if they had been soaked in blood.[49]

Antique purple was indeed produced using the juice from many shellfish found on the eastern shores of the Mediterranean. The two main ones, which provided luxury purple, were *purpura*, which gave the dye its name, and *murex*, existing in two varieties: *Murex brandaris*, with an elongated shape, and *Murex trunculus*, more conical. The second one was the more coveted. It was collected abundantly on the Palestine coasts, especially in the areas of Tyre and Sidon, where today you can still see gigantic piles of shellfish debris at the sites of ancient workshops. But there are other species of mollusks whose juices possess dyeing properties and that were gathered on the coasts of Cyprus and Greece, the Aegean Islands, and Sicily, and even farther north on the shores of the Adriatic. Distinguishing them is difficult, because in Greek as well as

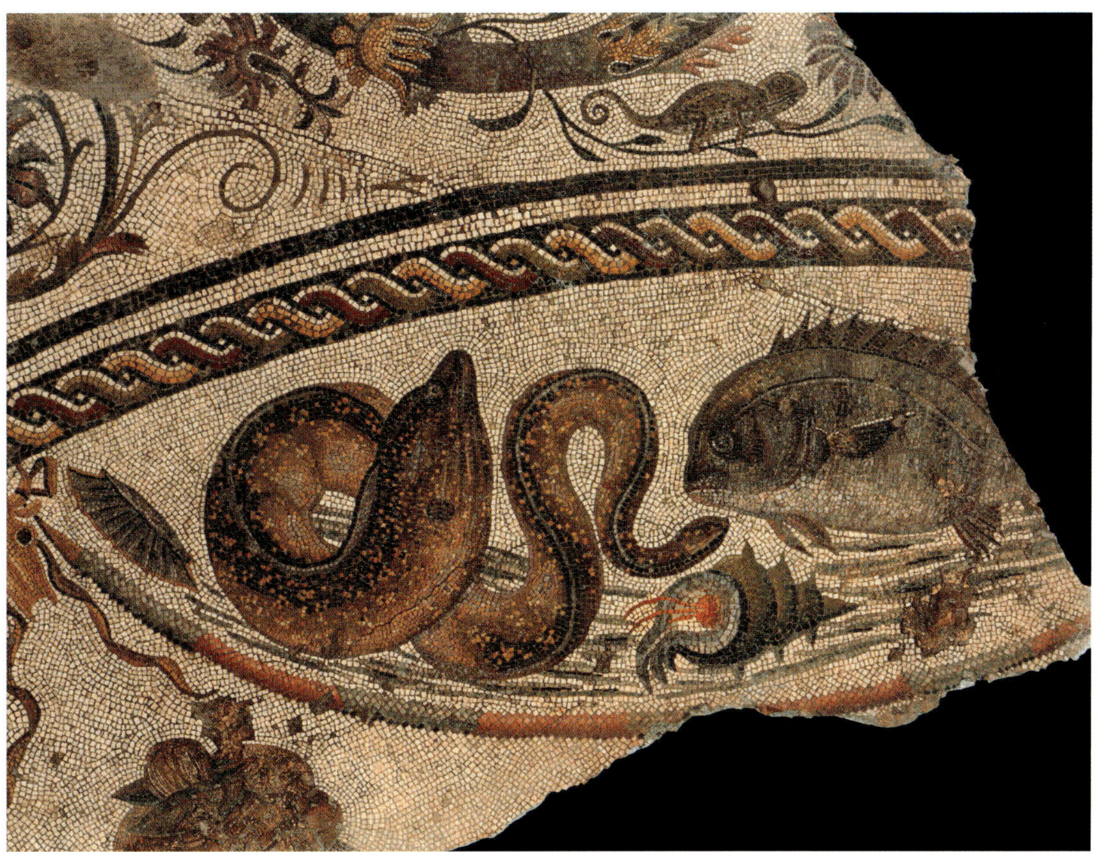

Murex trunculus

On this fragment of a circular border, between a moray eel and a big spiny fish, we can see a conical shellfish, *Murex trunculus*, from which the most expensive purple was extracted. This fragment of a lavish mosaic comes from a villa owned by a wealthy Roman, built in the area of Leptis Magna in Libya, one of the most prosperous provinces of the Roman Empire.

mid-3rd century. Tripoli, Archaeological Museum.

in Latin, the vocabulary that designates them is particularly unstable and the confusions numerous.[50]

For all these shellfish, especially for murex and purpura, harvesting conditions were difficult. Fishing could take place only in autumn or winter; in spring, the reproductive period, the juice lost its coloring power, and in summer the mollusks hid in deep water, sand, or under rocks to flee the heat. Thus they were harvested in the fall or early winter, at sea with bait and baskets for purpura, near shore from submerged rocks for murex. But most important, the shellfish had to be caught and kept alive, because when they died they released their juice. The juice was produced by a small gland—believed to be the animal's liver in antiquity—that had to be delicately extracted from the shell without damaging it. Once collected, the juice underwent various procedures (steeping in salt, boiling, reduction, filtering) before it was ready to be used as dye. This long process explains why the cost of purple was so high. It was all the more so because it took enormous quantities of shellfish to collect a small amount of juice, and during the transformation of the juice into dyestuff, 80 percent was lost. If we are to believe Pliny and other authors, it took fifteen or sixteen *libras* of juice to obtain one *libra*—about 325 grams—of dyestuff that the dyers could use.[51]

Despite scholarly analysis and a considerable bibliography, antique purple has still not revealed all its mysteries; workshop secrecy surrounds the chemical and technical processes by which shellfish turned into dye and dye into dyed fabric. Furthermore, procedures varied from one region to another, even from one workshop to another, and they evolved over time and according to fashions. The Romans no longer made purple as the Phoenicians had, the first inventors and traders in such a product. Tastes changed as well; as time advanced, dark reds that reflected gold in the light, in crimson, bluish, or purplish shades, became the most coveted. But the results obtained also differed widely according to the nature of the shellfish, the time of harvesting, the possible mixing of juices, their exposure to light, the expertise of the dyers, the nature of the textiles, and the nature of the mordants used.[52] Results also depended upon the shades and color effects desired. Between red, pink, mauve, purple, and black, anything seemed possible.[53]

We have better knowledge, on the other hand, of the organization of workshops and commerce, especially in the imperial period. Workshops required complex facilities, qualified workers, and capital outlay that only rich industrialists or merchants could provide. Purple was an export product and one of great luxury. Wholesalers supplied the major cities of the empire where specialized shops were located. For a small fortune, they sold the dye itself as well as dyed wool or silk, and sometimes even finished fabrics or clothing in the color purple.[54] In Rome in the second century CE, quality wools dyed in true purple from Tyre—the most expensive—sold for fifteen or twenty times the price of the undyed wool. Although severely punished, fraud occurred frequently. Its forms ranged from cheating on the quality or origin of the purple to resorting to a mixture of juices or employing preliminary dye baths secretly tinted with orcein or madder to lower production costs.

In the late empire, most of the large workshops became imperial industries with regional monopolies on shellfish gathering and manufacture, transport, and trade of the dye. Private enterprises became rarer and limited to local commerce and the sale of inferior quality purple. Roman emperors tried to curb extravagant expenditure among private individuals—this was considered to be unproductive investment—and reserved for themselves the right to wear purple fabrics of the highest quality. Moreover, throughout the time of the empire, the right to wear a purple garment or article of clothing was restricted and finally reserved for the functions of priests, magistrates, and military commanders. The expression "to take the purple" (*purpuram induere*) meant to rise to the highest military or civil offices. On the other hand, dressing entirely in purple cloth was an imperial privilege, symbolizing the absolute authority of the emperor and his divine essence. Infringing upon that privilege was a crime of high treason.[55] Suetonius recounts that during the reign of Caligula (37–41), the son of King Juba II of Macedonia, an elegant, insolent youth, was seen in Rome dressed in purple from head to toe, arrested, and put to death.[56]

Private individuals could however make use of purple on some part of their ceremonial attire, most often in the form of an added band or braid. On the white togas of patricians that band, long reserved for noble youths, was called a *clavus*. Its width and shade indicated the rank, age, quality, or degree of fortune of the one who wore it. Individuals could also own purple fabrics to be used for furnishings: covers, hangings, curtains, carpets, and cushions. The richest individuals indulged themselves. In one of Horace's *Satires*, written at the end of the first century CE, the poet mocks a certain Nasidenius, with his newly acquired but nonetheless fabulous wealth, who pushes ostentation and absurdity to the limit by having the table wiped with a purple towel (*gausape purpureo*) after a lavish feast.[57]

The Discovery of Purple

In ancient Greece there were many legends about the discovery of purple and its first inventor. Artistic and literary traditions of the modern period, on the other hand, have retained only one of them: after digging in the sand for shellfish to eat, Heracles's dog supposedly returned to his master with his muzzle dyed red. That is the scene represented here by Theodoor van Thulden, who collaborated with Rubens on a group of mythological paintings commissioned by King Philip IV of Spain.

Theodoor van Thulden, *The Discovery of Purple*, 1636. Madrid, Museo del Prado.

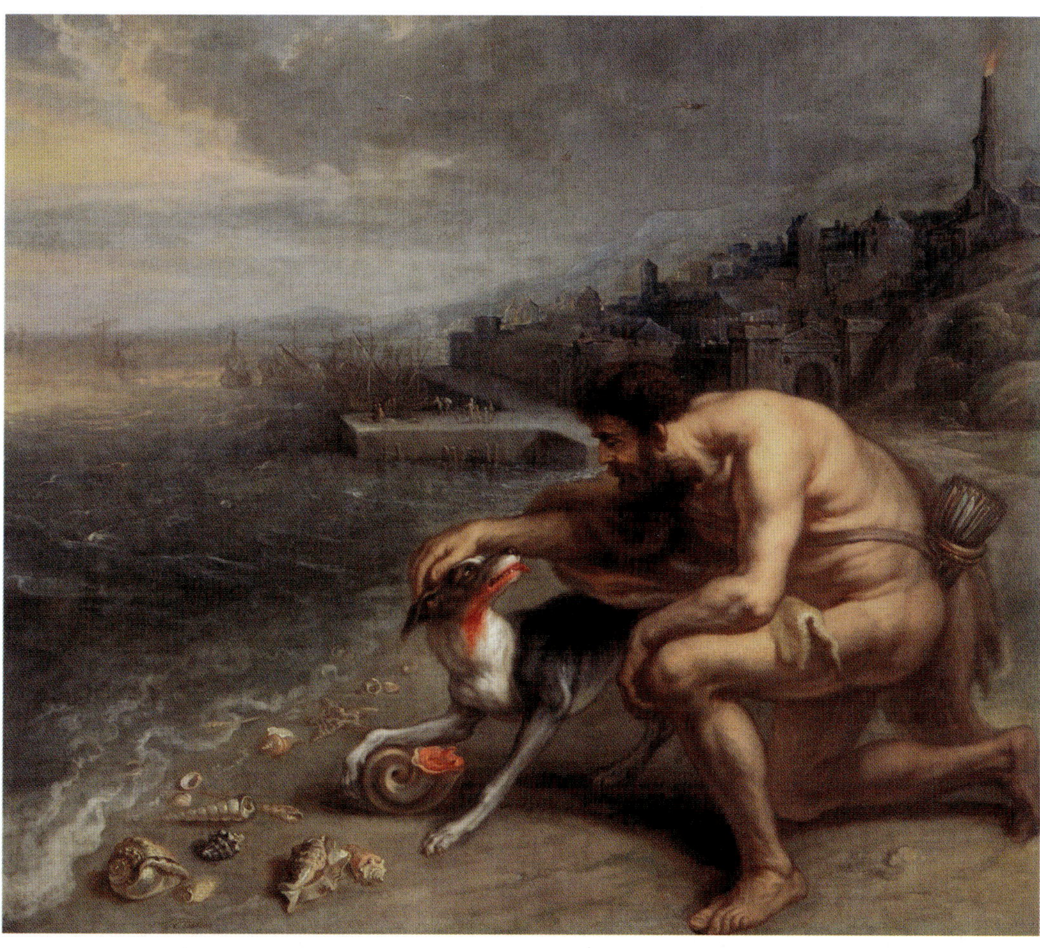

Red in Everyday Life

The many fabrics that the Romans used in their daily lives were not all dyed in purple, far from it, but they often displayed vivid colors. Like the Greeks before them, and like most of the peoples of antiquity, they loved eye-catching colors, strong contrasts, and polychromy. Polychromy, as we have said, adorned all statuary and a good part of the architecture. We must dispense with the image of a white Greece and Rome, inherited from the first neoclassical studies of the late eighteenth century, and passed down through academic scholarship and ideology, literature, and painting, and then through black-and-white photography, the cinema, and even comic strips. It is a false image.[58] In houses as well as in public spaces, colors were omnipresent. Most temples and public buildings were painted, both inside and out: polychromatic decors as well as vast surfaces of monochromatic colors, red dominating among them.

In large towns, what we now call house painting provided livelihood for a good number of contractors and workers. Only marble and expensive stone were left unpainted, but architects played with their coloration in pursuit of colorful effects. Emperor Augustus, the great prince of builders, boasted of inheriting a Rome of stone and leaving behind a Rome of marble. That was certainly true, but it was not in the least white, uniform marble, and furthermore, the claim was a bit exaggerated. For houses and ordinary buildings (*insulae*), the dominant material was neither stone nor marble but baked brick of all possible shades in the range of reds. It was that brick, along with tile (*tegula*), a material of the same color with multiple uses, that made Rome a city not of white but of red. Moreover, this was true of all the major cities in the empire.

We must not forget wood, another material widely used in Roman buildings, and the source of many fires. The fire of 64, which Nero attributed to larceny by the Christians—who had nothing to do with it—remains notorious,

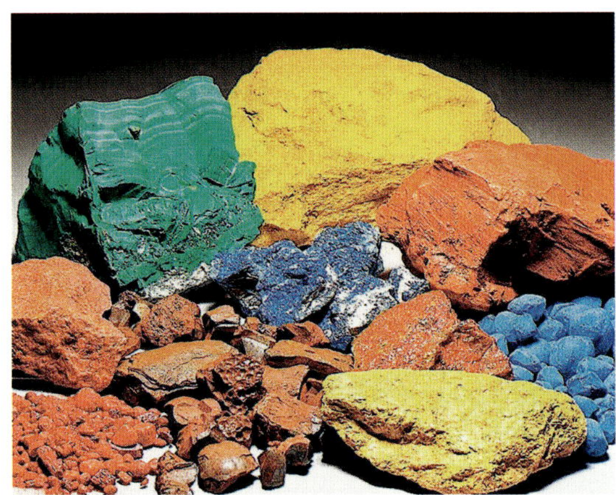

but it was one of many that destroyed various districts. In fact, fires were almost routine occurrences, as Juvenal emphasized at the end of the first century: "The ideal place to live is without fires and panics in the night."[59] Such lamentations are not just a literary cliché; they correspond to a certain reality that also made ancient cities into "red cities." Many authors stressed how quickly such fires spread in working-class neighborhoods, especially true because fire was present in most houses in the form of the domestic hearth, a veritable altar where fire burned throughout the day, presided over meals and ceremonies, and was used to communicate with ancestors, protect the family, and ensure its continuity. Letting it go out was a bad omen. On the other hand, observing the shapes and colors of its flames was a common divinatory practice. Very red flames, which were rare, heralded important events.[60]

Within patrician residences, things were not as somber as nineteenth-century archaeologists believed. Furniture hardly varied, of course, and decorative objects were relatively rare, but chairs were plentiful and served many different functions. There were chairs for sitting, lying down, or posing, for display, and for defining and organizing space. They were often covered with fabric, draped over them more or less carelessly; the colors varied and changed with the fashions, but red seems to have been dominant, as on walls and with decor, at least until the end of the second century.

Was red also commonly used for clothing? That is a difficult question. With regard to ancient Rome, as with all other historical periods, the study of clothing has ignored color.

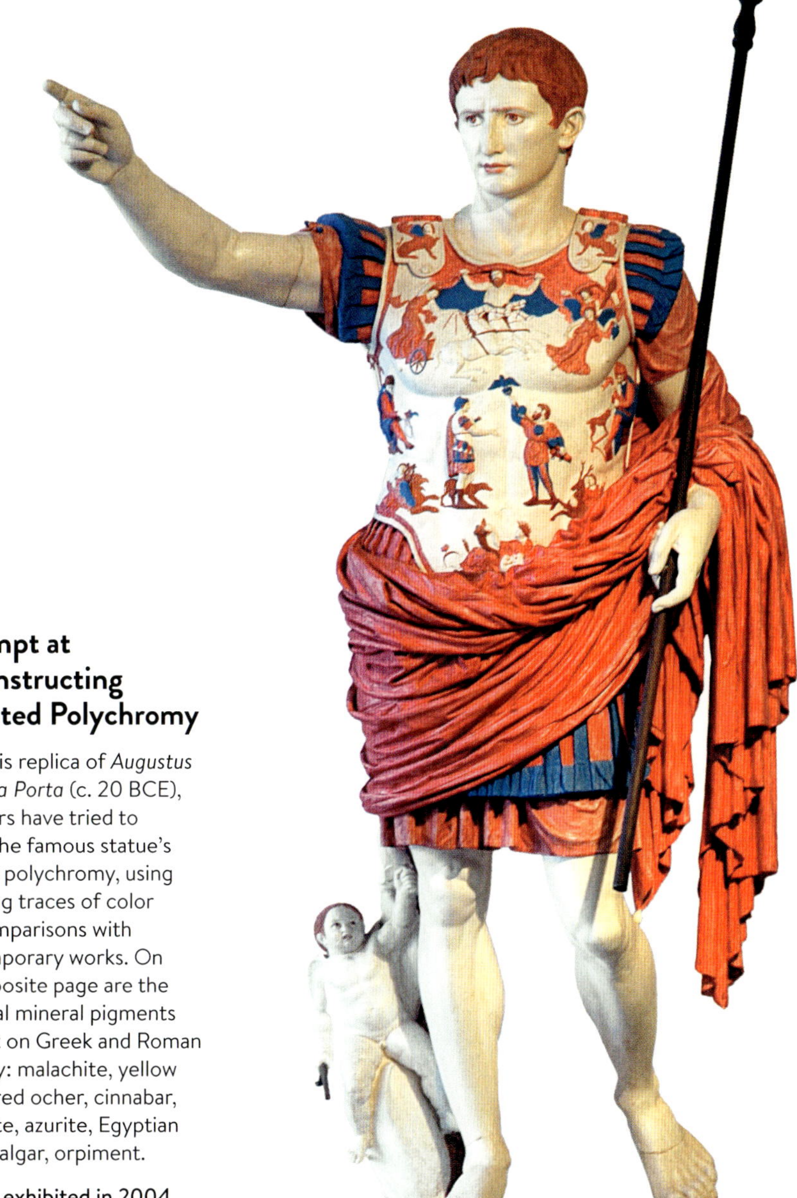

Attempt at Reconstructing Sculpted Polychromy

With this replica of *Augustus of Prima Porta* (c. 20 BCE), restorers have tried to evoke the famous statue's ancient polychromy, using surviving traces of color and comparisons with contemporary works. On the opposite page are the principal mineral pigments present on Greek and Roman statuary: malachite, yellow ocher, red ocher, cinnabar, hematite, azurite, Egyptian blue, realgar, orpiment.

Replica exhibited in 2004. Rome, Musei Vaticani.

LEFT PAGE

Copenhagen, Ny Carlsberg Glyptotek.

Priority has always been given to the archaeology of forms, lists of articles of dress, and the nature of fabrics and accessories, but colors have rarely captured the historian's attention. Moreover, texts from antiquity are taciturn and images deceiving. Authors report to us on the exception or the scandal but rarely on the colors worn in everyday life. Similarly, figurative documents more often present the special or the incidental rather than the ordinary. Nonetheless, four colors seem more common than others: white, red, yellow, and black, each in a range of various shades. Yellow and orange were reserved especially for women, and black for certain magistrates and those in mourning, although it was usually a matter of dark gray or brown rather than true black. During the empire, the nouveaux riches liked to be seen wearing red, whereas the "old Romans" remained faithful to white or undyed wool.[61] On many occasions and increasingly frequently over the course of time, the arrival of new fashions—Eastern or barbarian—diversified the clothing palette. Under Nero, some patricians and the emperor himself created a scandal by dressing in green. But it was the Roman matrons especially who broke with tradition and the required white-red-yellow triad. By the end of the first century they were dressing in blue, violet, and green, and like the Celts and Germans, they were wearing tunics (*tunicae*), robes (*stolae*), and cloaks (*pallae*) with stripes, checks, fretwork, and brightly colored patterns.

Better known than the color of clothing is the color of makeup those same matrons wore. From the beginning of the empire, the tendency was toward excess. They used white

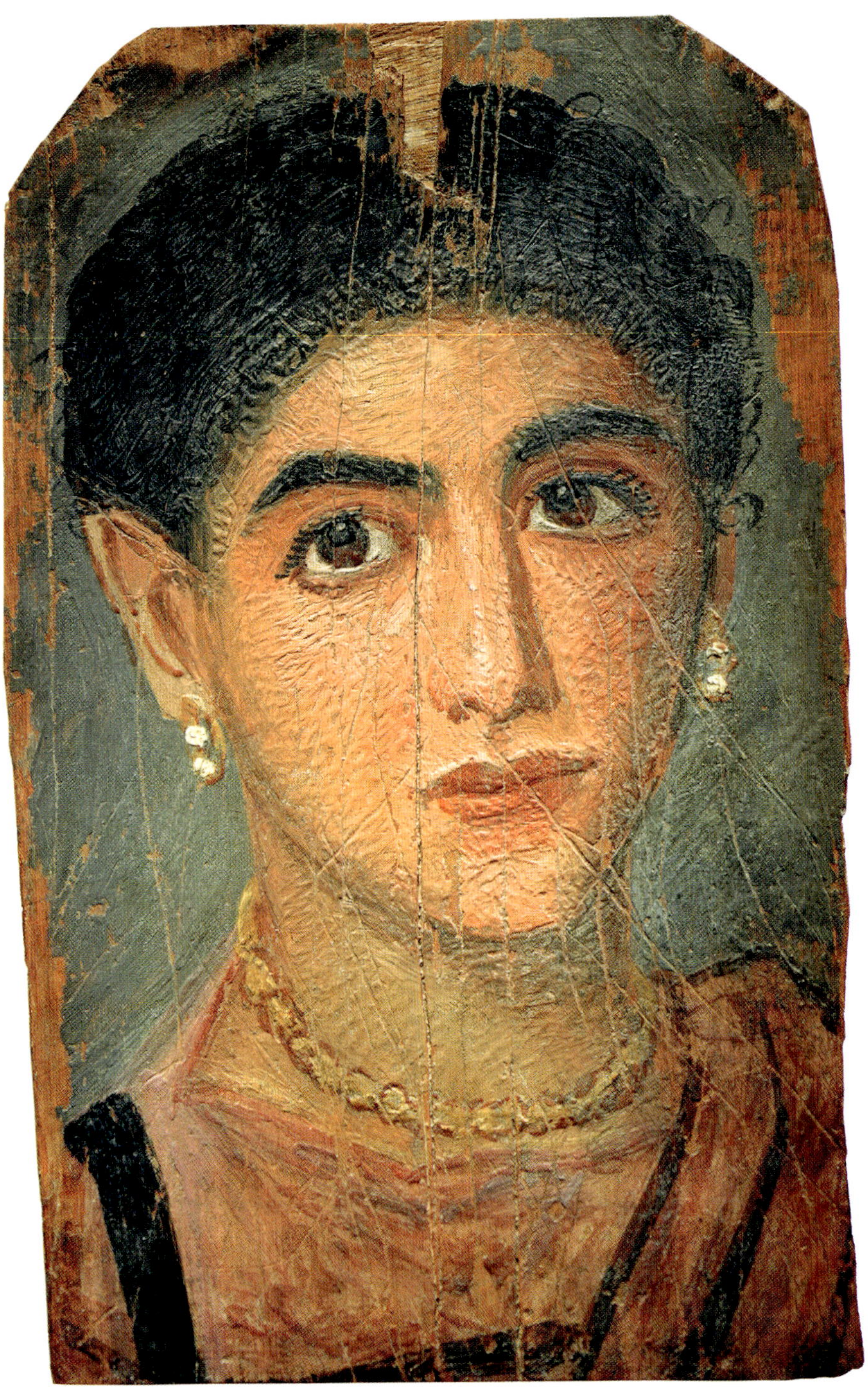

(chalk, ceruse) on forehead, cheeks, and arms; red (*rubrica, fucus*) on cheekbones and lips; black (ash, various charcoals, antimony powder) on eyelashes and around the eyes.[62] Many authors condemned those female faces "painted" by *ornatrices* (beauticians) and denounced the considerable arsenal of jars and bottles that each matron possessed to make herself beautiful. Moreover, by abusing makeup women made themselves ugly, as Ovid, an expert on feminine beauty, pointed out: "Your looks are aided by dissembled art."[63] He is echoed a few decades later in this criticism that Martial addresses to a certain Galla, who abuses cosmetics and does not present the same face by day as by night. "You are at home yourself, Galla, but you are made up in the middle of Subura. . . . Your face does not sleep with you."[64]

Jewels, amulets, and pendants of all kinds—precious stones (rubies, garnets, jasper, carnelian), cut and colored melted glass, pieces of cinnabar or coral set in precious metals—came to complete the feminine costume. Here again, red dominated, not only because it was considered beautiful and alluring but also because it was supposed to bring good luck. Some men, especially under the late empire, imitated the women and discreetly wore over or under their clothing red jewels or talismans to which they attributed protective powers—like beings of the Paleolithic age. The more pure and intense the red was, the more effective the stone or amulet. For this reason the ruby was particularly valued. It was the ultimate red stone, full of virtues and abilities thought to include warming the body, arousing sexual desire, strengthening the mind, and keeping away snakes and scorpions. It was often cut in the shape of a drop of blood. Coral was hardly to be outdone, as it was believed to provide

Funerary Portrait, Encaustic Painting

Inserted over the face of the mummy of the deceased, Egyptian funerary portraits from the Roman period can be very stereotypical or more or less realistic, as is the case here. For women, special attention was paid to makeup and jewelry.

c. 160. Paris, Musée du Louvre, Department of Egyptian Antiquities.

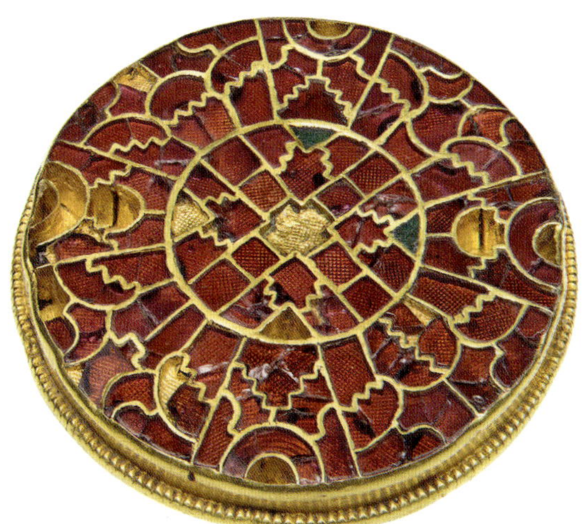

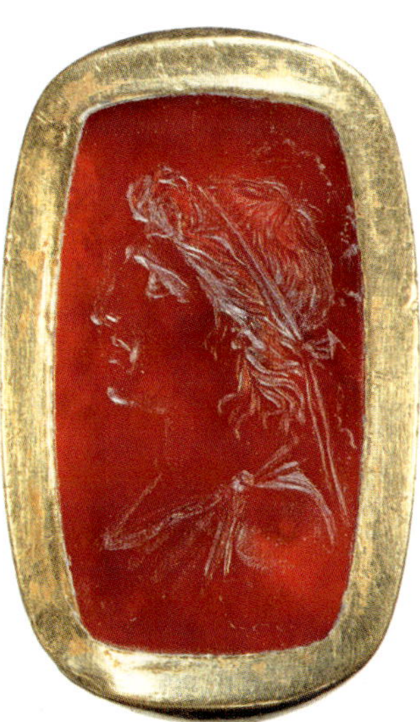

Gold, Garnet, and Ruby Jewelry

The circular clasp (gold and garnet) to the left was found at Saint-Denis, in the tomb of the Merovingian queen Aregund (deceased c. 570). The ring (ruby) to the right belonged to a Roman patrician from the first century BCE.

6th century. Brussels, Musees Royaux d'Art et d'Histoire.
50 BCE. Private collection.

protection from multiple dangers, especially lightning; many sailors set a coral "stone" (according to the Romans, coral was a mineral) at the top of their masts.

With regard to stones and fabric, a few authors compete in ingenuity and vocabulary in determining the most beautiful and brilliant shade of red.[65] Strangely, the winner of

this chromatic competition emerges as the red of a rooster's comb (*rubrum cristatum*), a choice that surprises us but would hardly have surprised the Romans, who had great admiration, even veneration, for this bird. Attribute of several divinities (Apollo, Mars, Ceres, Mercury), the rooster played a major role in divination. Its call and gait, how it

Mosaic Frieze with Rooster

Attribute of many divinities and a bird linked to divination, the rooster was revered by the Romans. The color of its crest, a red that signaled glory and victory, was considered the most beautiful shade of red to be found. Without quite the same admiration, Christianity continued to value the rooster and made it a symbol of courage and vigilance.

5th or 6th century. Madaba, Jordan, Archaeological Park, mosaic from Saint George's Church.

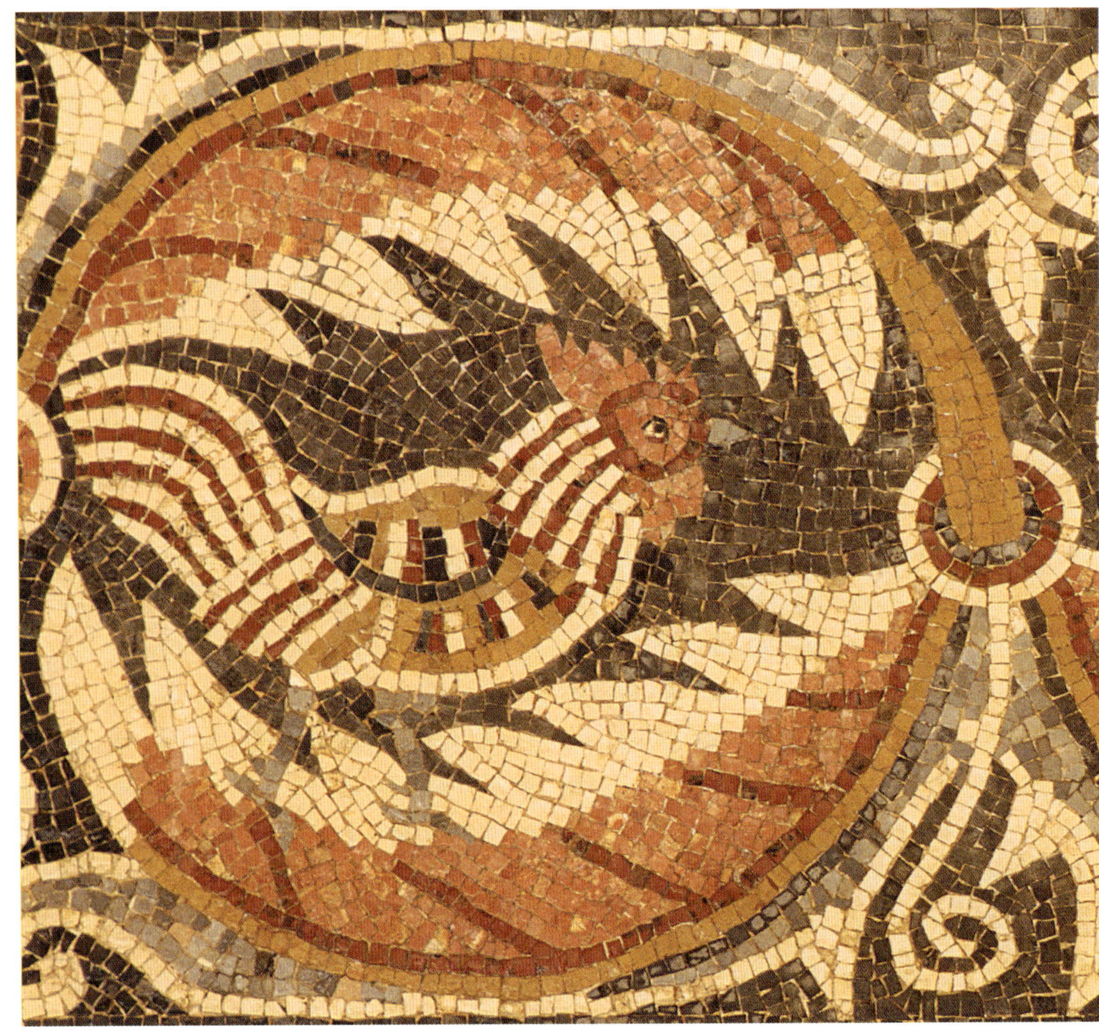

hopped, beat its wings, and behaved before food were all studied, and conclusions were drawn regarding the course of action to take or decisions to be made. In military circles, such practices were common for determining whether one should engage in combat or not. Many generals owed their most glorious victories to roosters. This led Pliny, a military man himself, to make this extraordinary pronouncement: "[Roosters] exercise royal sway in whatever household they live."[66]

The rooster owed that glory in large part to its brilliant red comb. A bird bearing such a crown on its head could only be loved by the gods and serve as their messenger. More generally, the Romans attributed greater symbolic power to red than to any other color and paid attention to all circumstances in which it came into play. Regarding the rooster, that symbolism was always positive, but elsewhere it could be negative or disturbing. Titus Livius (Livy) tells how in winter 217–216 BCE in Rome, in the midst of the Punic Wars, on the eve of Hannibal's attack against the Roman army, a red bull escaped from the cattle market (*forum boarium*), climbed the stairs of an *insula* as high as the third floor, and plunged to its death. This wonder was interpreted as an omen for the bloody defeats at the Battle of Lake Trasimene and the Battle of Cannae, two of the most horrific in all of Roman history.[67]

If animals with red crests, coats, or plumage prompted curiosity, worry, or admiration, the same was true with regard to humans. In Rome, red hair had a bad reputation. For a woman, it was a sign of a wicked lifestyle; for a man, it was ridiculous and a sign of Germanic ancestry. In fact, in Roman theater, the German barbarian is a caricature, gigantic (*procerus*), obese (*crassus*), curly-haired (*crispus*), red-faced (*rubicundus*), and redheaded (*rufus*). Moreover, in everyday life, calling a man a *rufus* was one of the most common insults and would remain so in clerical circles throughout a good part of the Middle Ages.[68]

Evidence from the Lexicon

Let us remain in this realm of vocabulary and examine the frequency, distribution, and declension of the different color terms in ancient languages. Even without conducting extensive surveys, we find that three colors appear to be named much more often than all the others: red, white, and black. And with regard to ancient lexica and all dictionaries, red tops the list; there is always the greatest number of terms for red, and that is as true in Hebrew as in Greek and Latin. Of course, we are speaking only of written language, but there is little reason to suppose it would be any different for oral language.

As a first example, let us consider the Bible and the scholarly studies done by François Jacquesson, beginning with the oldest version in Hebrew and Aramaic.[69] This entails lengthy reading for scant reward; the Bible is poor, very poor, in color notations. Entire books include not a single color term (Deuteronomy, for example); others limit their use to the domain of fabric alone; elsewhere, there is much confusion in the terminology between materials (shell, ivory, ebony, precious stones and metals) and the color. Moreover, in biblical Hebrew there is no generic term to designate color, and in Aramaic, the word *tseva'* refers more to the dye than to the color. Despite these difficulties and limits, one lexical and chromatic fact becomes very clear: the predominance of red. Three-quarters of the color notations fall into the range of red, an extensive range going from russet to purple and including all light, medium, and dark reds. Next follow—though far behind—whites and blacks, and even further behind are browns. Yellow and green are very rare; blue is totally absent. Let us turn to the words of the great linguist Jacquesson as he presents the results of his inquiries:

Colors are not common in biblical texts, and their appearance is very localized. Sometimes they describe livestock (in the same way as qualifiers like "spotted" or "striped"), sometimes diseased skin (here white dominates), sometimes the brilliance of fabrics used for holy ceremonies (red and purple dominate), and less frequently for royal pomp; in a few circumstances, they serve as part of symbolic systems still in their infancy. Being concerned with religious matters, the Bible highlights the sacred splendor of the nomadic temple, and with it, the purple-red range, statistically the most significant. Thus, red dominates and is highly valued; white follows far behind and is not good; black is hardly mentioned, but is not bad. Thus we are in quite a varied world of color, but in any case very far from the wicked red of hell, the black of terrifying darkness, and the innocent, angelic white that we sometimes very mistakenly associate with biblical representations.[70]

For a long time the primacy of red—and more generally the red-white-black triad—was emphasized by linguists and ethnologists. This was not so for all languages, as two American researchers, Brent Berlin and Paul Kay, maintain in their famous work *Basic Color Terms*, which appeared in 1969, but surely was for a great number of languages.[71] From studying the lexica of about one hundred languages, Berlin and Kay traced an order for the gradual appearance of color terms. According to them, all languages possess a word for white and another for black; if there is a third term, it always designates red; a fourth is sometimes green and sometimes yellow; a fifth is sometimes yellow and sometimes green, a sixth is blue, and so on. Such a sequence is supposedly universal and linked to the stages of technical evolution for the societies in question. The more technologically advanced a society is, the richer and more diversified its chromatic vocabulary. This last claim has legitimately given rise to numerous criticisms.[72] First, nothing is universal with regard to lexica. Some languages do not include a single color term, not even a word for "color." Others have no black or white or do not consider the words that designate them to be color terms. Second, and more important, the link between the richness of a vocabulary and technical development is far from proven. The modern languages of Europe, for example, use an everyday chromatic vocabulary that is much more limited than many indigenous languages of sub-Saharan Africa, central Asia, or Oceania spoken by very small populations.

Still it is true that in most ancient languages (and in the ancient forms of a great number of modern languages), *red*, *white*, and *black* are colors more often named than *green*, *yellow*, and *blue*. Moreover, these three colors have a more abundant vocabulary attached to them. That is the case with classical Latin, for example. In standard usage, black and white are expressed by two words each: *albus* (matte or neutral white) and *candidus* (brilliant or pure white); *ater* (ordinary or disturbing black) and *niger* (brilliant or prestigious black). By contrast, green is expressed by only one word (*viridis*), yellow by several ill-defined terms (*croceus*, *flavus*, *galbinus*), and blue by a few semantically uncertain terms (*caeruleus*, *caesius*, *lividus*). Saying "blue" in Latin is never an easy exercise. Red, on the other hand, benefits from a solid basic term (*ruber*), accompanied by a frequently used doublet (*rubeus*), and supplementing these is a rich, diversified lexicon that conveys a very extensive palette of red tones. Good Latin authors knew how to use the lexicon and did not substitute one adjective for another. Thus, with regard to the face, they knew to choose the term that was suitable for describing the vermilion cheeks of a pretty woman (*roseus*),[73] the bronzed skin of a sailor (*coloratus*), the ruddy complexion of a peasant (*rubidus*), and the hideous

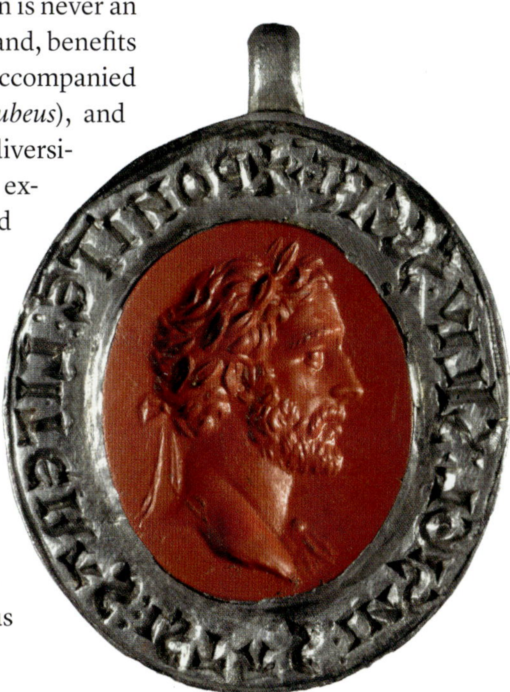

Intaglio with the Effigy of Antoninus Pius

This intaglio in red jasper, with the effigy of the most respected emperor in all Roman antiquity, was embedded in a silver matrix at the beginning of the thirteenth century, probably to be used as a seal by the English baron Robert Fitzwalter, famous opponent of King John Lackland.

2nd and 13th centuries. London, British Museum.

Caesar Preparing to Cross the Rubicon

A small coastal river, the Rubicon owes its name to the reddish color of its waters. It was not only a geographical boundary between Cisalpine Gaul and Italy; it was also a symbolic limit that a Roman general was not to cross with his army without authorization from the Senate. Caesar, in pursuit of Pompey, paid no heed and deliberately crossed this "red line," clearly highlighted in the foreground of this famous miniature by the painter Jean Fouquet.

Detached page from a lost, damaged manuscript of *Faits des Romains*, c. 1475. Paris, Musée du Louvre, Department of Graphic Arts.

rubicund face of a German barbarian (*rubicundus*).[74] Roman historians, poets, and orators carefully distinguished all the shades of red; they paid less attention to yellow, little to green, and almost none to blue.

They were also attentive to the history of words and knew that there was an etymological link between the adjective *ruber* (red) and the noun *robur* (the word for the king of trees, the oak, but also for solidity, vigor, force). Red was the color of strength, energy, victory, and power. On the symbolic level, it was sometimes paired with yellow—the color that evoked Greece for the Romans—and rarely with green or black, but never with blue (a barbarian color). In Rome, red was often combined with white. The two colors were both rivals and opposites and would remain so for many long centuries. In the West, from Roman antiquity until the turn of the year 1000, the true opposite of white was not so much black as red.

The primacy of the red-white-black triad did not involve only adjectives in everyday language. It can also be observed in proper names, in nicknames for individuals (*Rufus*: "the Red" or "the Redhead"; *Niger*: "the Black") and compound words or derivative phrases for place names. An individual nicknamed "the Red" often owed that name to his red hair or facial features, but he could also be described in that way because of his quick-tempered, cruel, or bloodthirsty nature. Similarly, for place names, the mention of a color could sometimes refer to the natural shade of water, land, or a mountain, but it could also underline a threatening, dangerous, or forbidden aspect of the place in question.

That was the case in January 49 BCE when Julius Caesar crossed the Rubicon (*Rubico* in Latin, a proper name formed from the adjective *ruber*) in pursuit of Pompey. He not only crossed a small coastal river in northern Italy, whose waters, because of the nature of the soils, exhibit a reddish hue. More important, he also crossed a dangerous "red line," a forbidden boundary. The Rubicon did indeed mark the separation between Italy itself and Cisalpine Gaul. No general could take his army across it without authorization from the Senate; that would be considered a sacrilegious act. Caesar paid no heed and entered Italy, provoking a long civil war that dragged on for years and had considerable consequences for the future of Rome.

In many respects, this red line, more symbolic than geographic, decided the fate of the empire, and the color of the river waters took on a dimension both political and proverbial. "To cross the Rubicon" is to violate a prohibition, to stake everything and leave the outcome to the will of destiny. *Alea jacta est*, "the die is cast," Caesar supposedly said, crossing the river.[75] The red waters of the Rubicon evoke those of the Red Sea in an earlier and different context, another symbolic barrier, this one crossed by the Hebrews leaving Egypt to gain the Promised Land.[76] Here again, red appears as a dangerous and foundational color that leaves an especially powerful mark on events and plays the role of a veritable driving force in history.

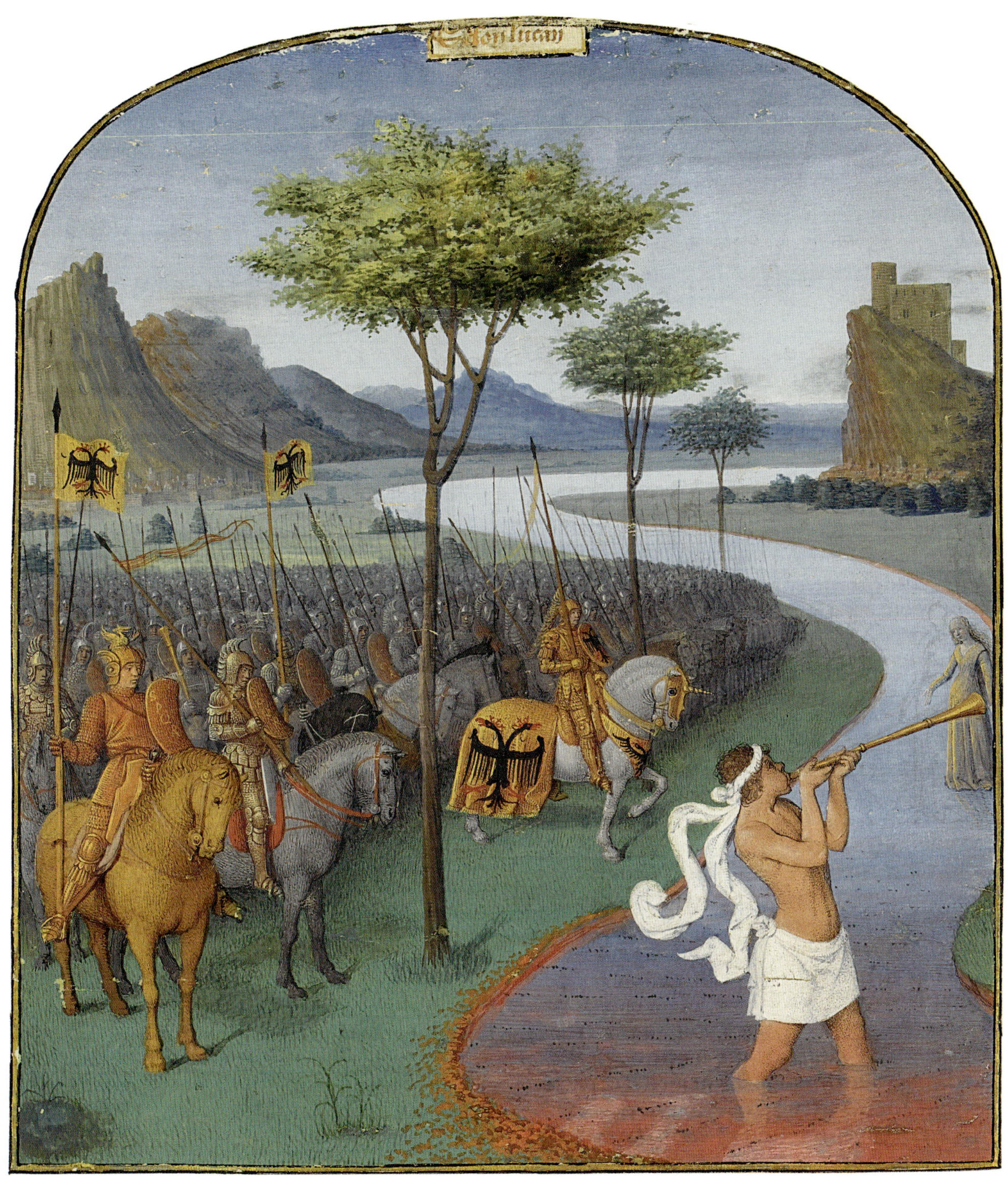
Confluent

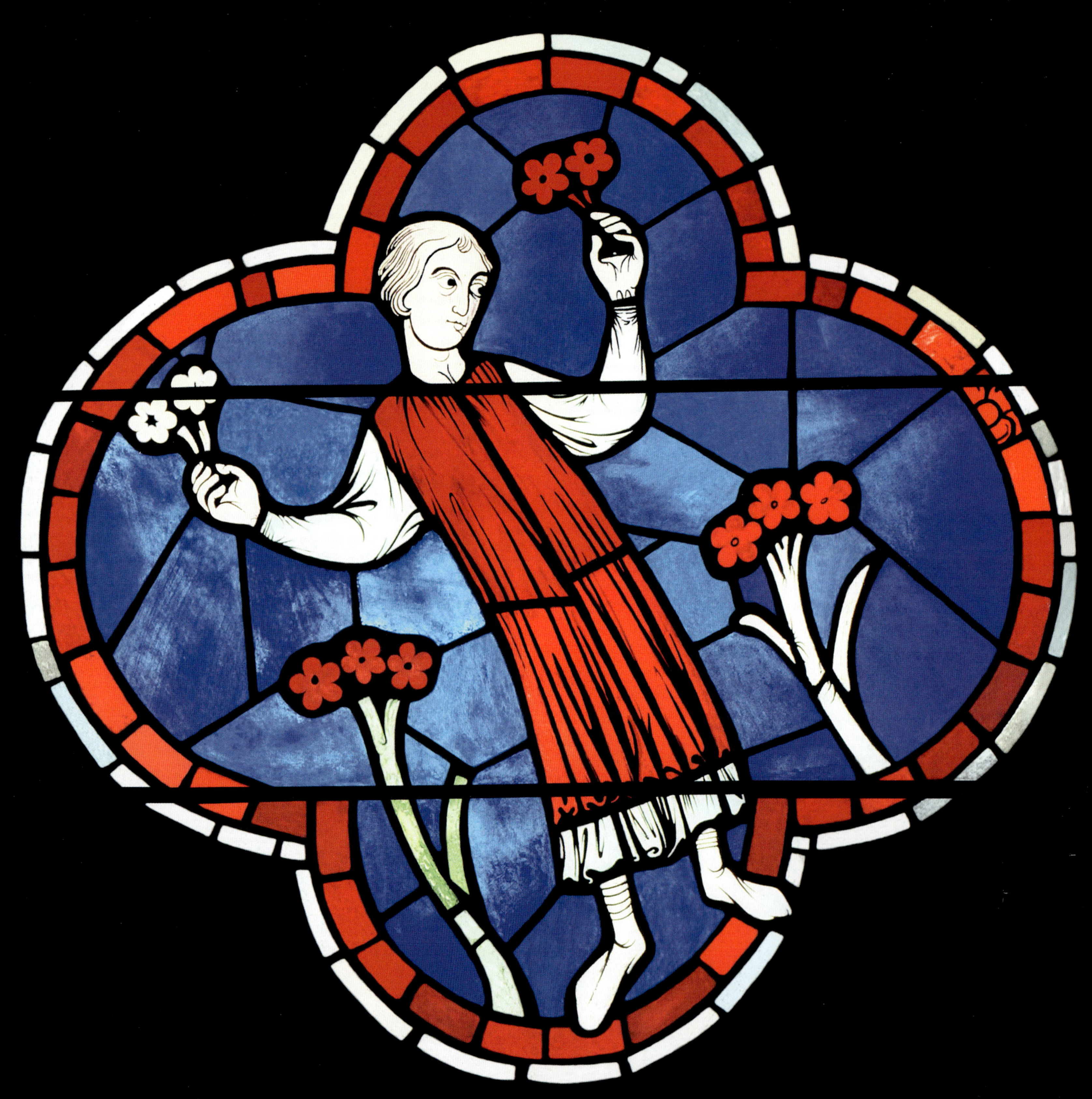

THE FAVORITE COLOR

SIXTH TO FOURTEENTH CENTURIES

For the Greeks and Romans, red was the first color, the color par excellence. And yet, can we say it was the favorite color? Probably not. It is not that red was not admired, sought-after, and celebrated, but the very notion of preference implies an abstraction, a conceptualization of color that antiquity hardly experienced. To say "I like red; I don't like blue" presents no difficulty today, in English or in French or any other European language. Color terms are not only adjectives; they are also nouns that designate categories of color in the absolute, as if it were a matter of ideas or concepts. In antiquity, that was not the case. Color was not a thing in and of itself, an autonomous abstraction. It was always linked to an object, a natural element, or a living being that it described, characterized, or individualized. A Roman could perfectly well say, "I like red togas; I hate blue flowers," but it was hard for him to declare, "I like red; I hate blue," without specifying something in particular. And for a Greek, Egyptian, or Israelite, it was even more difficult.

In what period does the change occur—that is, the shift from color matter to color concept? It is a difficult question to answer, because the evolution took place so slowly and according to different rhythms for different areas. But it does seem as though the early Middle Ages played a decisive role here, especially with regard to language and lexicon. Among the Church Fathers, for example, color terms were not only adjectives but also nouns. Of course we already encounter colors as nouns in classical Latin, but not frequently and more in connection to the figurative meaning than the actual chromatic meaning of a color. For certain Church Fathers, that was no longer the case; nouns spoke directly of the color. They might be actual common nouns, like *rubor* or *viriditas*, or adjectives in the neuter form and nominalized (*rubrum*, *viride*, *nigrum*): proof that color had lost its materiality and had begun to be considered a thing in and of itself.[1]

In the twelfth century, when first the system of liturgical colors and then the earliest coats of arms and the language of heraldry spread throughout the West, the matter seemed settled. Henceforth colors could be considered as abstract, general categories. Freed from all materiality, red, green, blue, and yellow were conceived in the absolute somehow, independent from their supports, their brightness, shade, pigments, or colorants. Among those colors now appreciated for themselves, red was the favorite.

The Rose, Flower of Love And Beauty

Like ancient roses, medieval roses were not pink but red or white, two colors that together constituted a particularly admired chromatic pairing. Here they are associated with spring, the favorite season.

c. 1260. Paris, Cathédral Notre-Dame, western rosace, calendar.

The Great Whore of Babylon

The text of Revelation dresses "in purple and scarlet" the great prostitute of Babylon with whom "all the kings of the earth fornicated." The illuminator here merely gives her a sumptuous red mantle, diamond-patterned and lined with vair. However, the feet and seven heads of the beast she is riding are very red, because it is "drunk on the blood of the martyrs."

Apocalypse en Français, detail (copy produced in 1313), c. 1310. Paris, Bibliothèque Nationale de France, French manuscript 13096, folio 56.

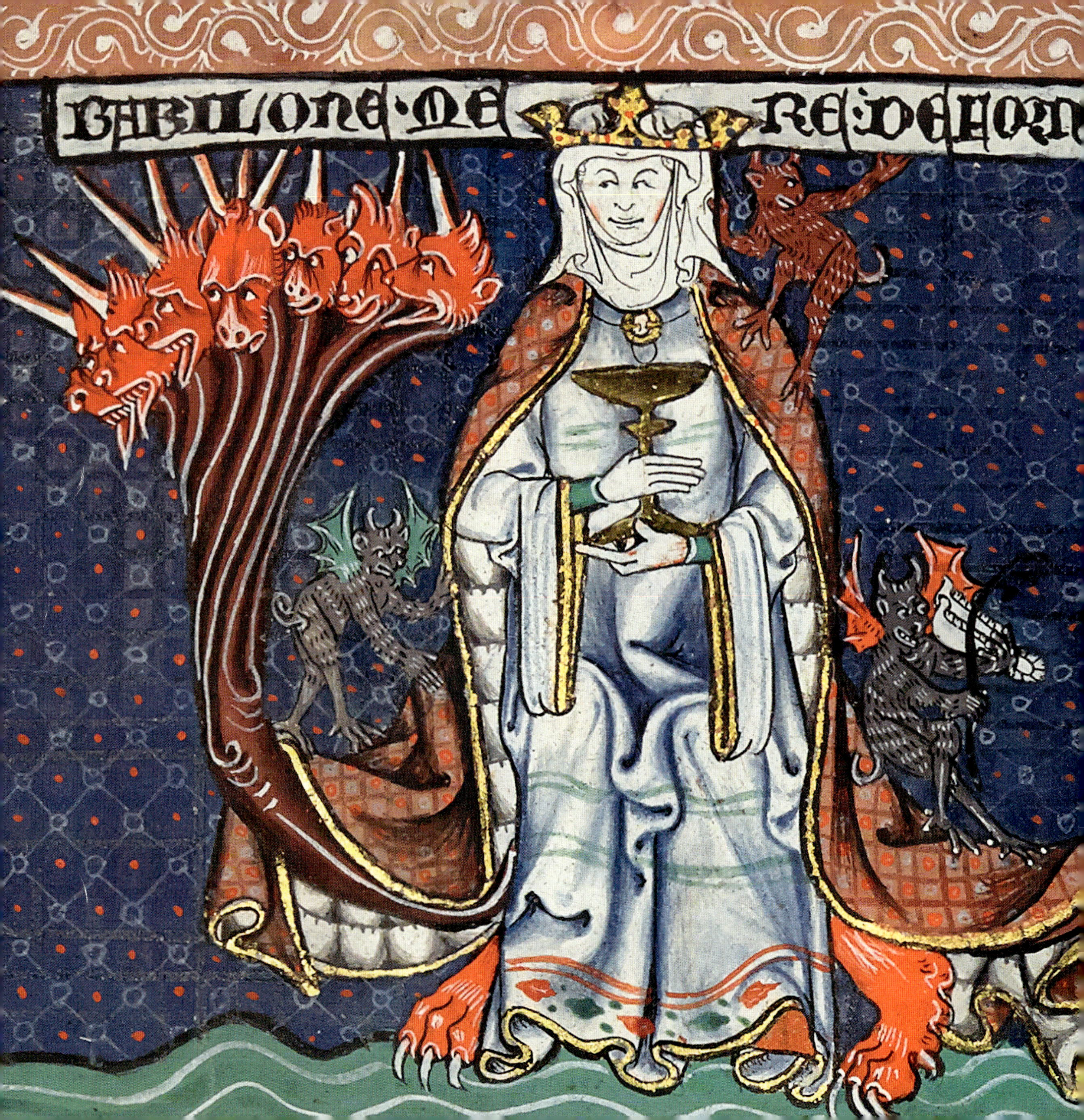

BABILONE·ME
RE·DE·HO

The Four Reds of the Church Fathers

The Pentecost

On the day of Pentecost, the apostles who gathered around the Virgin received the gift of the Holy Spirit, which descended from the heavens upon them in the form of tongues of fire. That is why the Pentecostal liturgy is celebrated in red, as are the festivals of the martyrs and the Cross. In the first instance, the color's referent is fire, in the second two, it is blood.

Hunterian Psalter, c. 1165–70. Glasgow, University Library, Hunter Manuscript 229, folio 12v.

As we have said, the Bible does not abound in color terms, at least not the Hebrew Bible and its Greek translation, the Septuagint, begun in Alexandria about 270 BCE. That was not the case with Latin. The first Latin translators had the tendency to introduce a certain number of chromatic adjectives where they had not been, and Saint Jerome, who followed them at the turn of the fourth century to the fifth, added still others when he revised the Latin text of the New Testament and retranslated the Old Testament directly from the Hebrew and Greek. A fluid text, the Bible thus tended to become increasingly colorful over the course of centuries and translations, and all the more so as vernacular languages accentuated this phenomenon in the modern era. Let us consider two examples in the range of reds. Where the Hebrew says "a magnificent cloth," the Latin translates as *pannus rubeus* (a red cloth) and

seventeenth-century French translates as *un tissu écarlate* (a scarlet cloth); where the Greek says "royal clothing," the Latin translates as *vestis purpurea* (a suit of crimson) and modern French as *un manteau cramoisi* (a crimson cloak).[2] Moreover, red tones have no monopoly on this addition of color at the whim of the translators. Adjectives in Hebrew or in Greek that mean "pure," "clean," "new," and "bright" were translated as *candidus* (white); and others like "dark," "disturbing," "obscure," "wicked," and "sinister" were translated as *ater* or *niger* (black). That was why, beginning from the fifth century and continuing until the turn of the first millennium, the Church Fathers and their successors became increasingly verbose with regard to colors when writing commentary on Latin biblical texts that had become ever richer in color notations. In so doing, they gradually constructed an ambitious symbolic system around these texts that exerted its influence for almost a millennium in many areas of religious life (liturgy, dress), social practices (clothing, coats of arms, insignia, ceremonies), and artistic and literary creation.[3]

Regarding red, the Christian symbolism inherited from the Church Fathers was organized around four poles, with each of the two principal referents for the color—fire and blood—being considered according to its good and bad aspects.[4]

Taken as evil, the red of fire was thus associated with the flames of hell and the dragon of the Apocalypse whose body is red as fire (Rev. 12:3–4).[5] This was a red that cheated and deceived, that ravaged and destroyed, emitting a light more disturbing than darkness, on

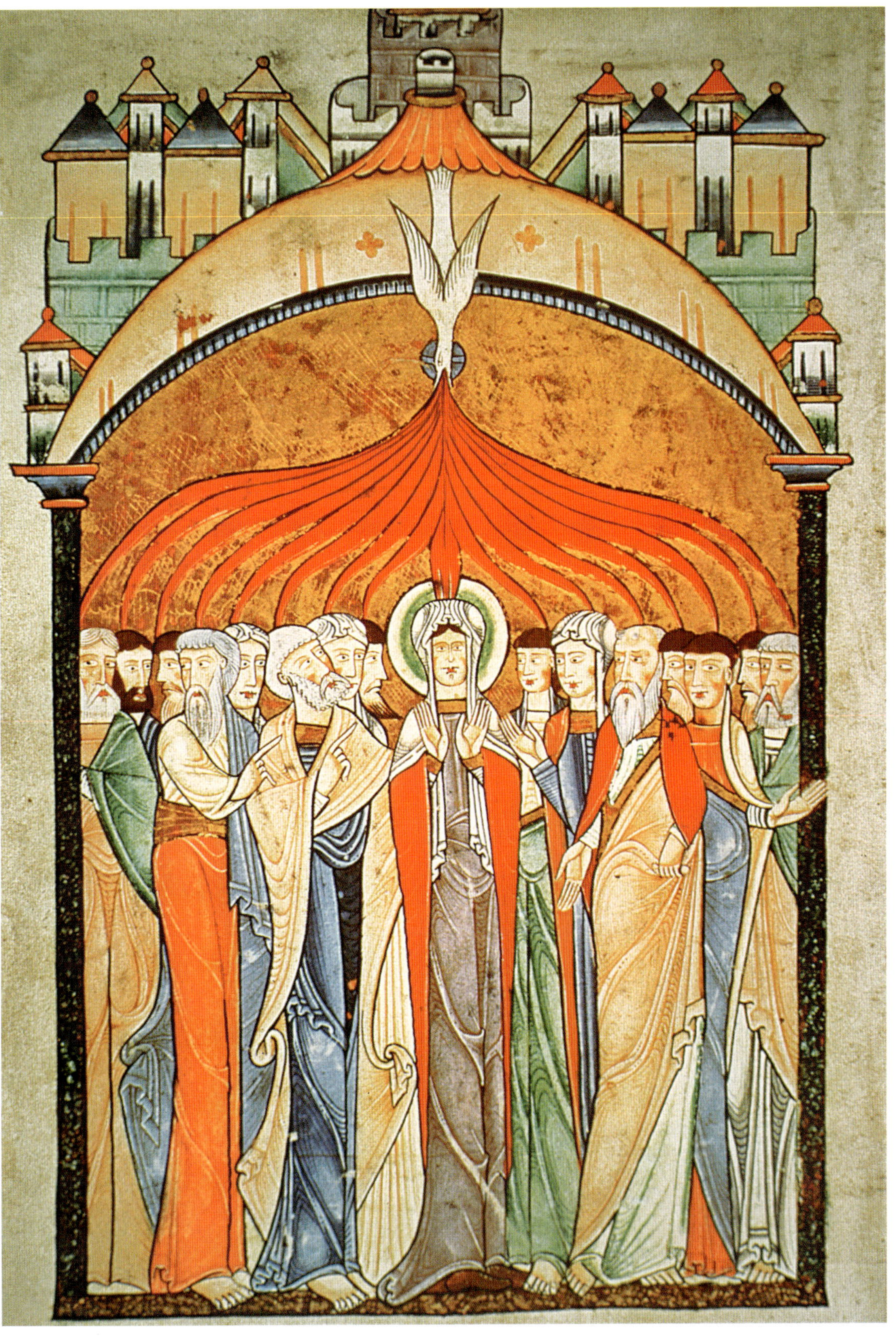

Satan Steals Job's Herds

In images, Satan is not always red, but his head is often that color, recalling the fires of hell and the crimes committed in his name.

c. 1480–85. Paris, Musée de Cluny, stained glass from the Sainte-Chapelle, reconstructed at the end of the 15th century from elements dating from the 13th century.

The Martyrdom of Saint Cyr

This altarpiece from the Hermitage of Sant Quirc de Durro, in Catalonia, presents two very different reds: the red blood of the saint suffering martyrdom and the red clothes of the torturers putting him to death. Until the modern period, executioners dressed in red or wore a piece of red clothing as a sign of their office.

c. 1140. Barcelona, Museu Nacional d'Art de Catalunya.

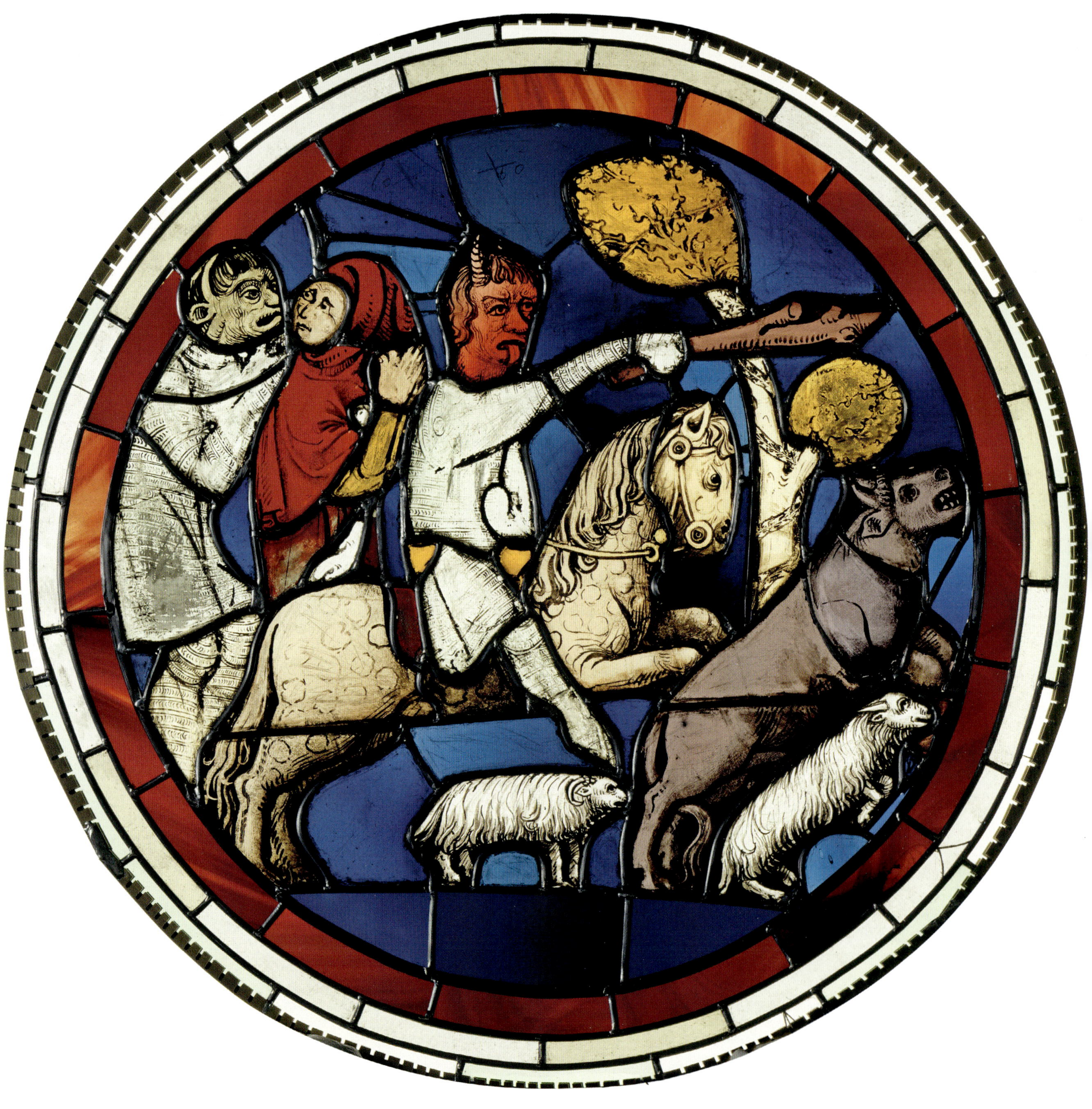

the model of the infernal fire that burned without illuminating. This red was essentially that of the Devil and demons; in miniatures and wall paintings from the Romanesque period, demons often have red heads. It would also be the color of traitors, who, a bit later and in the image of Cain, Judas, and Reynard the hypocrite fox, would be given a red coat or head of hair, blazing and dangerous as fire. We will return to this subject.

Taken as good, this same red of fire marked the intervention of God. In the Old Testament, Yahweh often appears through the intermediary of fire, as in the seminal episode of the burning bush (Exod. 3:2) or when the Hebrews fleeing Egypt were guided through the night by a column of fire (Exod. 13:21). In the New Testament, the same red of fire, divine in origin, represents the Holy Ghost, which, according to the words of the Credo, "gives life." It was both the light and the breath of life, powerful and warm. On the day of Pentecost, it descended on the apostles in the form of "tongues of fire" (Acts 2:1–4). Such a red shines, animates, regenerates, assembles, fortifies, and purifies. It was the red of divine love, the red of *caritas*, a very significant term in medieval Latin designating both the love that Jesus came to provide on earth ("I came to cast fire upon the earth, and would that it were already kindled everywhere")[6] and, among good Christians, the love that all felt toward their neighbors.

But the red of the Church Fathers was not associated only with fire; it was also the red of blood. Taken as evil, the red of blood was linked to all discourse on violence and on impurity. It was a red inherited from the Bible, the red of sins and crimes of blood, the red of revolt against God. Blood was indeed the symbol of life, and life belonged to God. For a human, to spill the blood of another human was to strike a blow against what was God's possession. Forgiveness was possible, but repentance and obedience were required. Addressing the warlike and idolatrous Jerusalem of that time, the

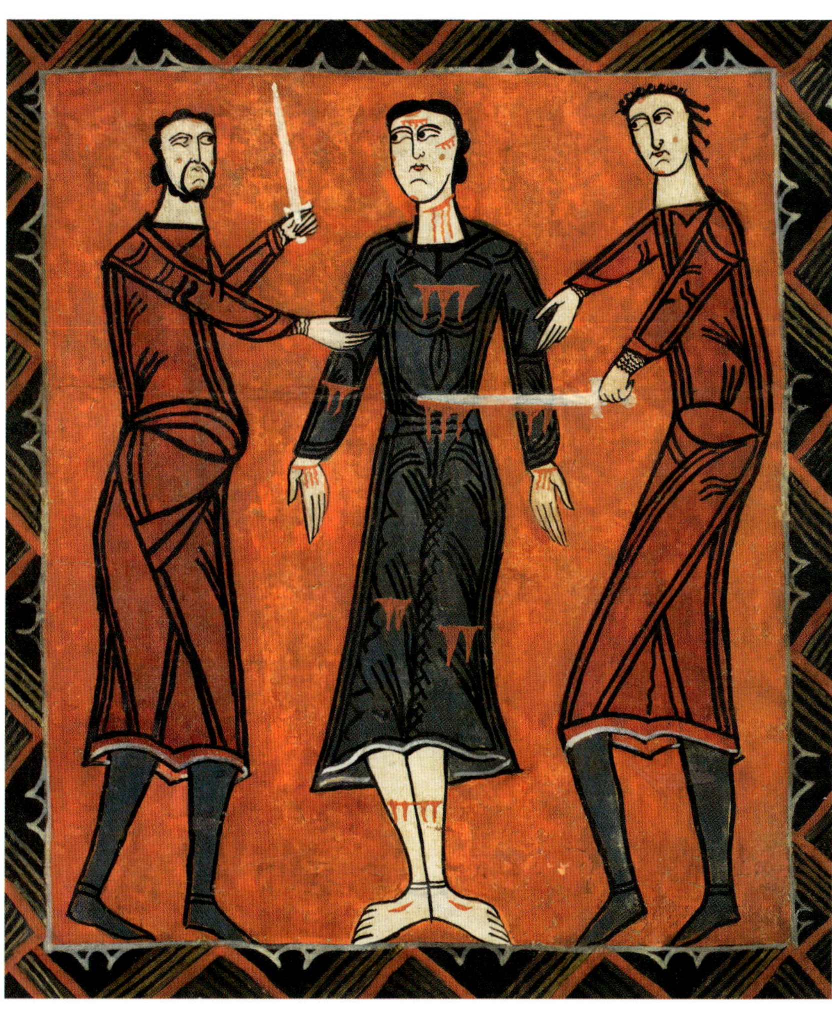

prophet Isaiah proclaims it loud and strong: "Your hands are full of blood, wash yourselves, pacify yourselves . . . then, though your sins are like scarlet, they shall become white as snow" (Isa. 1:15–18). All the same, this detestable red of blood was not only biblical, it was also inherited from pagan antiquity, notably when it concerned menses, which ancient societies did not regard as a mysterious life-giving power but as one of the most obvious symbols of human corruption. Menstrual blood was the object of many superstitions. Let us read Pliny once more, whose *Natural History* was one of the texts most read, copied, quoted, and commented upon by the Christian authors of the Middle Ages:

> But nothing could easily be found that is more remarkable than the monthly flux of women. Contact with it turns new wine sour, crops touched by it become barren, grafts die, seeds in gardens are dried up, the fruit of trees falls off, the bright surface of mirrors in which it is merely reflected is dimmed, the edge of steel and the gleam of ivory are dulled, hives of bees die, even bronze and iron are at once seized by rust, and a horrible smell fills the air; to taste it drives dogs mad and infects their bites with an incurable poison. . . . Not only does this pernicious mischief occur in a woman every month, but it comes in larger quantity every three months.[7]

Commenting on this passage, many theologians made a comparison with original sin and saw in women's menstruation the continuation of a punishment imposed by God on Eve. Urged by the serpent, she picked the forbidden fruit and led Adam into the Fall. God

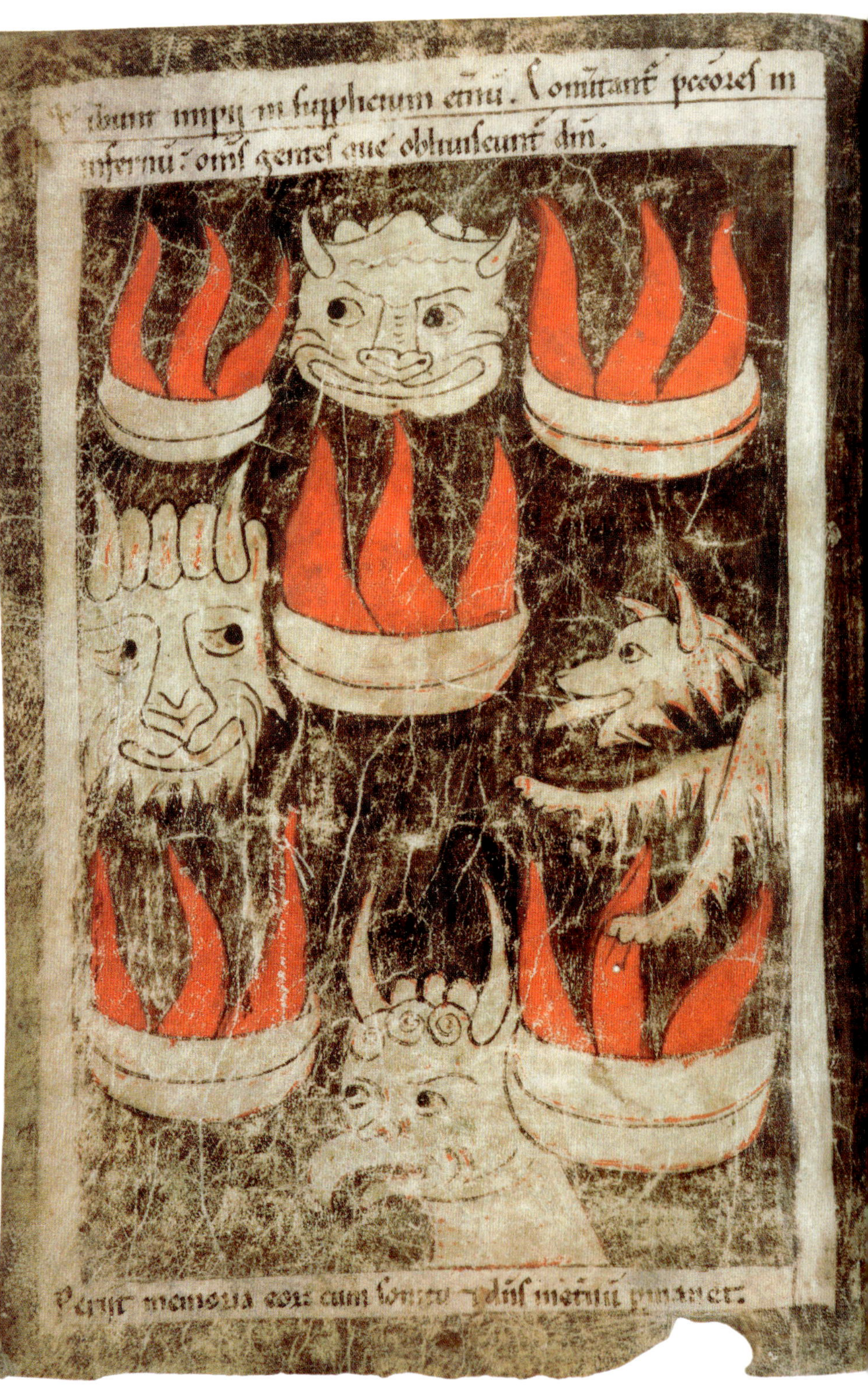

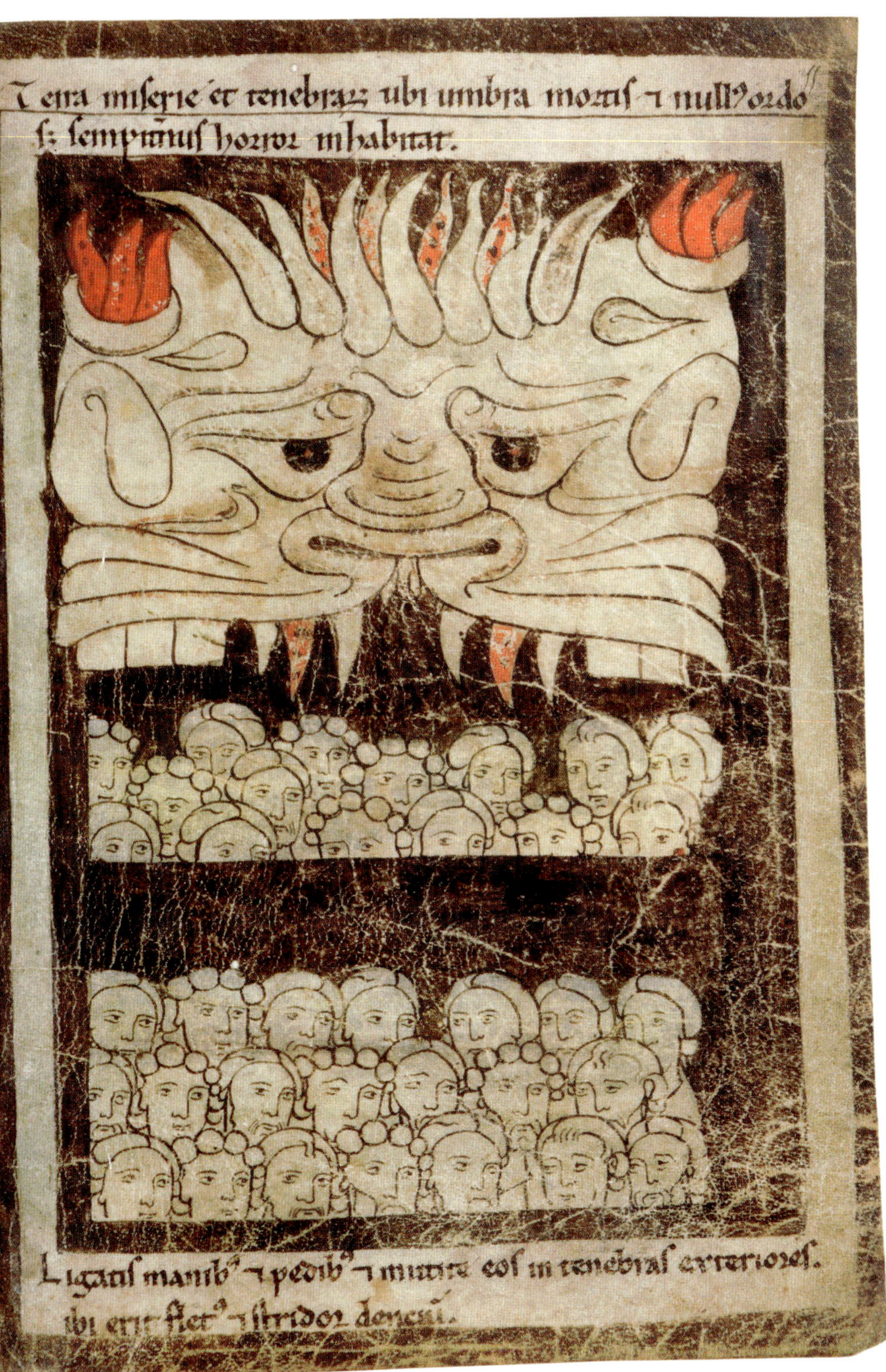

punished her and condemned her daughters—that is to say, all women—to be stained with red each month in memory of this sin. Other authors, especially in monastic circles, used it to underscore how the female body was full of filth; under her apparent beauty, the woman harbored only rot, mire, and excrement.[8]

At the opposite extreme from this particularly unwholesome—and totally fantasized—menstrual flow, there existed for the Church Fathers and their followers a beneficial, fertile red, a red that sanctified and gave life: the red of the blood that Christ spilled on the Cross. Beginning in the twelfth and thirteenth centuries, it could be found on crusaders' banners and on liturgical cloths for the Masses of the Cross and the martyrs. Thanks to the sacrifice of those martyrs, the Church "changed color," as Saint Cyprian of Carthage proclaimed already in the third century: "Blessed indeed is our church. . . . In the past she was clad in white through the good works of our brothers; now she is arrayed in crimson through the blood of her martyrs."[9] This glorious "crimson" of Christ the Savior and all those who died for their faith constituted the supreme Christian red. It is worth pausing here to consider it.

Hell

Hell is a place of darkness with burning fires that do not provide light. Its colors are red and black, as in this great painting from a Bible produced in Pamplona for the king of Navarre, Sancho VII, the Strong.

Bible Historiée, Dite de Pampelune, 1197. Amiens, France, Bibliothèque Municipale, manuscript 108, folio 254v and 255.

The Blood of Christ

The words of Saint Cyprian correspond to a reality of the earliest days of the Church, a period of major persecutions. But they also have prophetic value; the more Christianity advanced in time, the more it seemed to become a religion of red and of blood. There is one main reason for this: the increasingly frequent representation of the crucified Christ and the exaltation of his Passion, with the worship of the Holy Blood developing as a consequence.

For the medieval theologian, the blood of Jesus was not like any other. Although the son of God was made man, his blood could not be identical to that of mere mortals. It was redemptive, salvific blood, spilled as ransom for the sins of humanity. Some authors described it as a lighter, clearer red than the blood of men and women, necessarily defiled by their sins. A few artists tried in their images to make it so and to distinguish through various shades of red the blood that flowed from wounds of the Savior or the martyred saints and the blood of ordinary individuals: clear and luminous for the first, cloudy and dark for the second. That

was especially true in the panel paintings of the late Middle Ages.

Beginning in the twelfth century, the blood of Christ constituted an eminently precious relic that many churches were proud to possess: the Abbey Church of the Holy Trinity in Fécamp, Normandy; Norwich Cathedral in England; the Basilica of Sant'Andrea in Mantua, Italy; the Basilica of the Holy Blood in Bruges, and a few others in Spain, Portugal, and Germany. Increasingly, as time went on, this relic seemed to multiply. Among these churches, the question became which could boast of possessing it the longest and create the most astonishing legend to explain its provenance. Most of them explained that the blood of Jesus had been gathered by Nicodemus or by Joseph of Arimathea when the Cross was lowered, but others located the event earlier; when Jesus was still on the Cross the centurion Longinus, the sponge bearer Stephaton, or even Mary Magdalene herself (often dressed in red in the images) received the precious liquid. After which, sealed in a vial, flask, vase, or simple lead box, this blood, after many journeys, was supposedly rediscovered at some given place or offered to some given church.[10]

At the turn of the twelfth century to the thirteenth, the blood of Christ became so precious and was the object of such devotion that a significant change took place in the Christian liturgy. Ordinary followers, who until this time usually received Communion under both kinds to be united with God, were now invited to receive Communion under only one kind: bread. Communion wine, turned into the blood of Christ through the mystery of transubstantiation, was henceforth reserved for the

The Mystic Winepress

Likened to a cluster of grapes, the Savior appears under the vise of a winepress; his redemptive blood is collected in a vat, like wine from the vineyard. This iconographic theme, linked to the cult of the Holy Blood, appeared in the twelfth century and became very popular in the late Middle Ages, especially among the brotherhoods. It echoes back to the passage from the Old Testament in which the Promised Land of the Hebrews is compared to a fertile and nurturing vineyard.

Bible Moralisée, completed in several stages (14th–15th centuries), late 15th century. Paris, Bibliothèque Nationale de France, French manuscript 166, folio 123v.

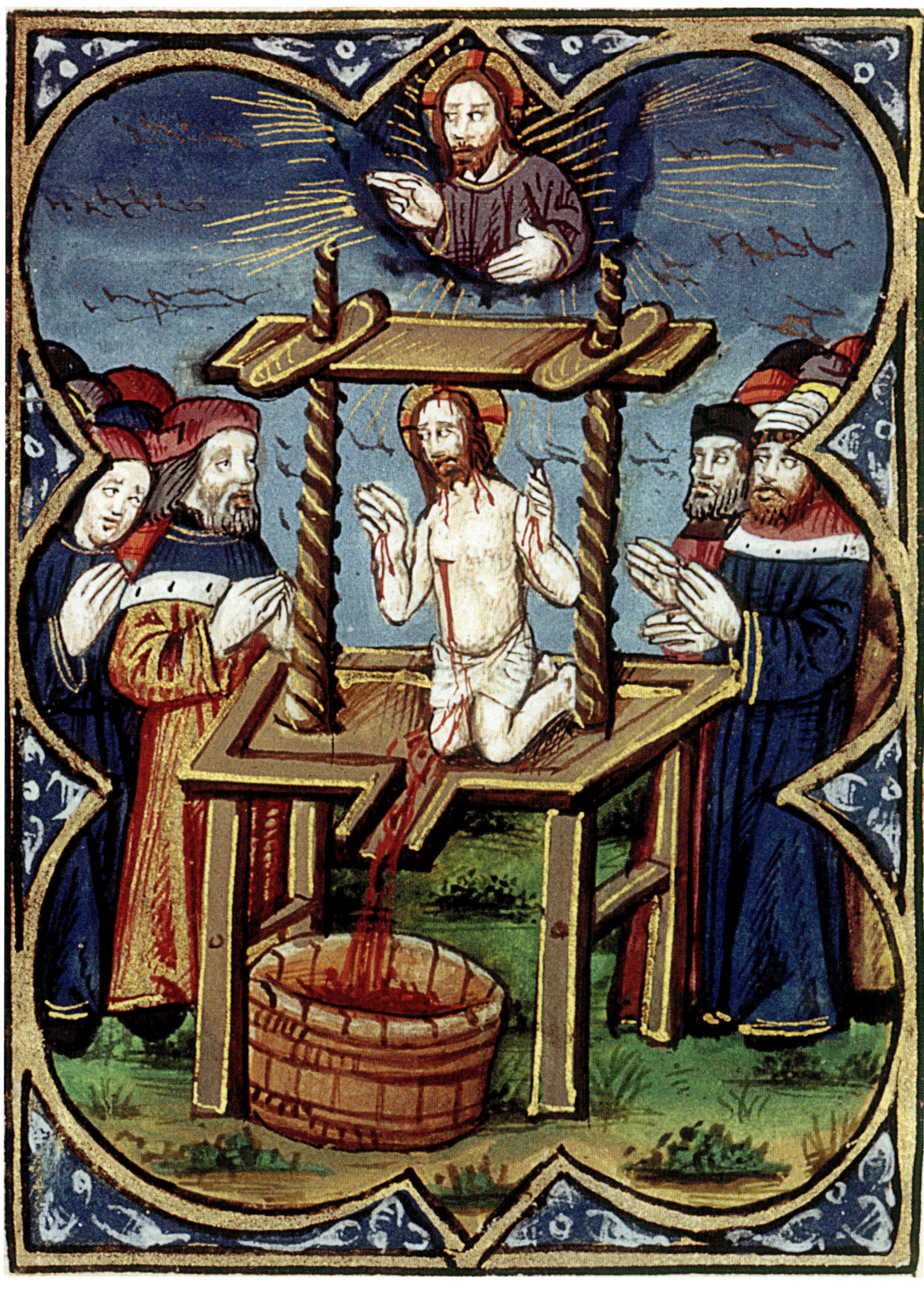

Banner and Arms of the Church

Medieval theology and iconography sometimes compare the army led by the White Knight of the Apocalypse, who vanquished Satan and his worshippers, to that of the militant Church, triumphant over the forces of evil. Its banner is white with a red cross, like the one carried by the crusaders beginning with the Third Crusade.

Apocalypse en Français, copied and painted in Paris about 1310–15, early 14th century. London, British Library, Royal Manuscript 19 B. XV, folio 37.

officiating priests and members of the clergy present in the church. The faithful no longer had a right to it, except during a few holidays and particularly formal ceremonies. That restriction, definitively confirmed by the Council of Constance in 1418, encountered its share of resistance and revolt from partisans for Communion under both kinds. The most famous and violent of them remains the revolt of the Hussites of Bohemia at the beginning of the fifteenth century, whose spectacular rallying sign was a large chalice of the color red. But there were others, earlier but more limited. Such a restriction of the Eucharist was in fact contrary to the very words of Christ, pronounced during the Last Supper and reported by the three Synoptic Gospels. Taking a cup of wine, Jesus gave thanks and passed it to his disciples, saying, "Drink of it, all of you, for this is my blood, the blood of the new covenant, which is poured out for the many for the forgiveness of sins" (Matt. 26:27–28). Drink of it, all of you . . .

This link between blood and wine raises the question of the color of the latter. What was that wine consecrated by Jesus at the Last Supper? And what color should the communion wine be that the priest transmutes into the blood of Christ in memory of this event? The answer from the Church Fathers and the liturgists was unanimous: red. In fact, for ancient societies as well as for medieval cultures, the archetypal color of wine was red, even though in the Middle Ages, until very late, white wine was more often consumed than red wine, and even though, as an actual liquid, Communion wine was always mixed with water in the chalice and took on lighter, colorless shades. In reality, its color was hidden from the faithful and barely visible to the officiates; it hardly counted. But symbolically, it could be only red. Otherwise, how to bring about transubstantiation; how to change wine into blood? Moreover, in medieval images, wine is always represented as red in color, no matter what its provenance or use, secular or sacred. Wine that was not red could not truly be wine.

A popular iconographic theme in the late Middle Ages and the early modern period, the mystic winepress, which offered artists the opportunity to present streams of red liquid, clearly underscores this link between wine and the blood of Christ. Its origin is found in several passages from the Old Testament in which the land promised to the Hebrews is compared to a thriving vineyard, and in two sermons by Saint Augustine in which the body of the crucified Christ is compared to a cluster of grapes. Capturing this almost literally, artists beginning from the late twelfth century invented a surprising image: Jesus bearing his Cross is represented seated or kneeling under the vise of a great winepress that is crushing him as though it were a matter of fruits of the vine. His blood flows out from all sides, and the faithful—even the apostles themselves—come to drink this blood or bathe in it in order to wash away their sins. Unusually bloody, such an image did not experience immediate success, probably because it pushed the limits of sacrilege. But reservations gave way beginning in the fourteenth century. Brotherhoods of the Precious Blood had it depicted on their banners, and wine growers and wine merchants incorporated it in the stained glass windows they provided for their chapels. As for painters and glass artists, they tried to outdo one another in giving the

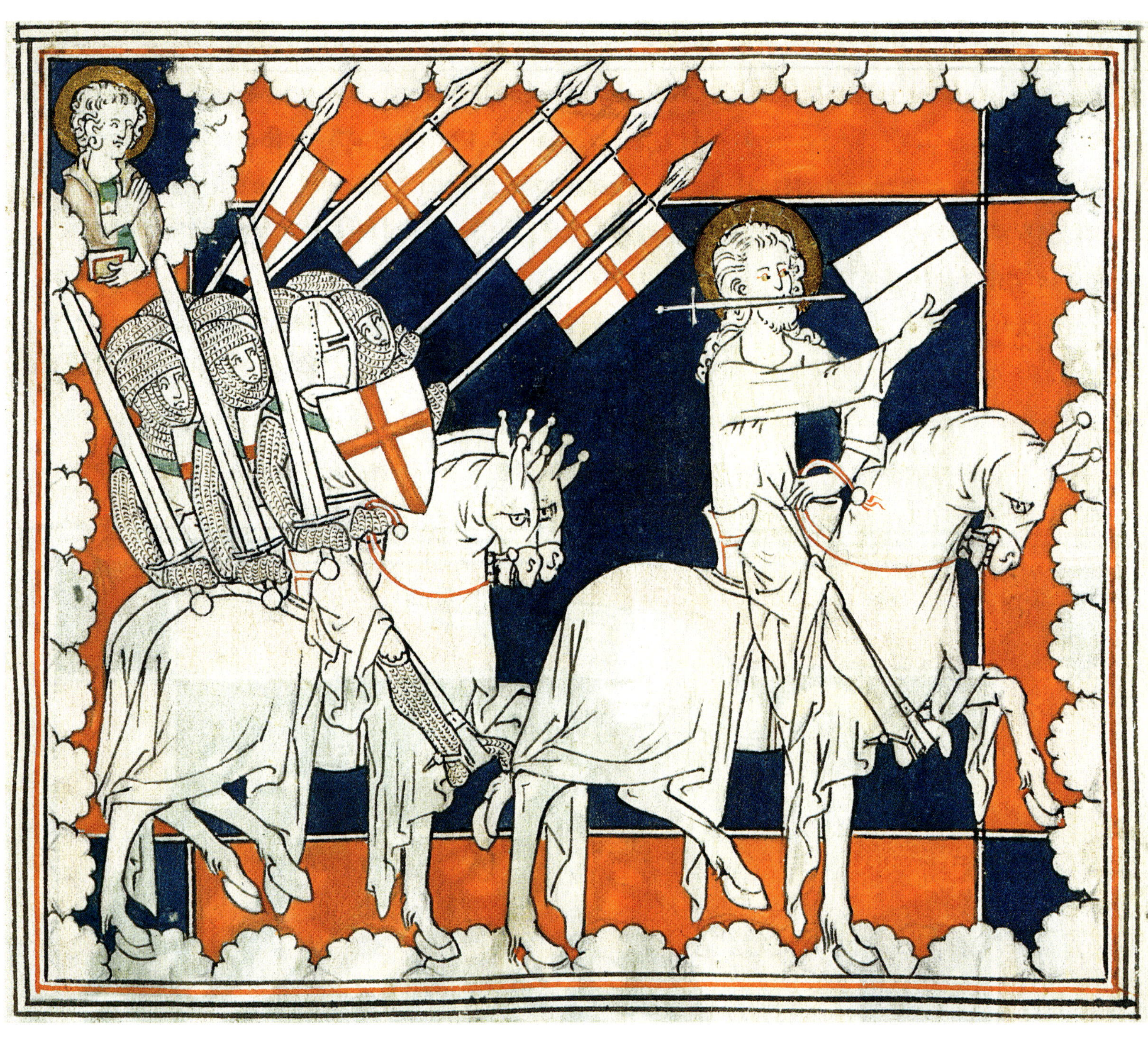

blood of Christ, redeemer or nourisher, their most beautiful red: vivid, clear, and luminous.[11]

Let us look back a bit further and consider a banner of a different nature, that of the Crusades, white with a red cross. Through that form and color, the blood of Christ was also symbolically represented, but associated here with the soldiers of the faith, ready to spill their own blood to free the Holy Lands. Much in evidence during the Third Crusade (1189–92), led by Richard the Lionheart and Philip Augustus, this banner was undoubtedly absent from the First Crusade (1095–99), which ended with the taking of Jerusalem, and the Second Crusade (1147–49), which was a total failure. Both would have been too early for a true heraldic image to be displayed on a banner. What is well documented as early as 1095, however, is "taking the cross," which involved sewing a cloth cross onto an article of clothing. In his appeal to the crusade launched at the Council of Clermont in that year, Pope Urban II himself urged such a procedure and gave the reason for it: "It is Jesus Christ who today leaves his tomb and presents you with his cross. . . . Bear it on your shoulders, let it shine on your banners and your flags. It will become the pledge of victory for you and the crown of martyrdom."[12] A bit unsystematic at first—crosses in all shapes, sizes, and colors, sewn on anywhere—this custom gradually became institutionalized and the object of a well-established ritual during the Second Crusade, thanks to Saint Bernard. Distributed during his sermons, the cross was small in size and cut from a piece of red cloth; it was always placed on the left shoulder of a tunic or cloak in memory of Christ bearing his cross. It never appeared on the crusader's chest, even when he himself took the initiative for making and positioning it. Such a placement was the invention of Romantic imagery in the nineteenth century.[13]

Beginning in the mid-thirteenth century, soldiers of Christ of another kind adopted the color red as an emblem: the cardinals. Like the crusaders, they were ready (theoretically) to give their lives in defense of the faith and the Church. Small in number at first, and usually chosen from among the clergy of the Roman diocese, they only really gained importance beginning in the eleventh century when, among their various assignments, they were given that of electing the pope, or at least of having the influence to do so. Two centuries later, during the First Council of Lyon in 1245, Pope Innocent IV bestowed on them a specific insignia to distinguish them from other prelates: a hat the color of red. It evoked the blood spilled by Christ and incited the cardinals to be the "first soldiers of the faith," ready to spill their own. But the color also evoked the ancient Roman Senate, where a toga embellished with purple was one of a senator's emblems and privileges. The cardinals did indeed gather around the pontiff like a kind of senate. Later, a robe, cap, and mantle in the same color would be added to the hat, making cardinals extraordinary individuals, actors dressed entirely in red. This incredibly garish costume was not worn daily but only during the Church's highest holidays, as well as for councils and conclaves. Beginning in the sixteenth century, when a bishop or archbishop was promoted to a cardinal, he was said to "don the purple." This noun no longer described a dye but the entire red garment or fabric that symbolized rank and power, as it had in antiquity.

The Red
of Power

Pope Clement IV

In this mural painting from the Ferrande Tower in Pernes-les-Fontaines, near Carpentras, Pope Clement IV grants the realm of Sicily to Charles of Anjou, youngest brother of Saint Louis. The pope wears a red vestment and a tiara with a single crown; Charles, already crowned, wears an armorial vestment on which the Capetian fleurs-de-lis can be discerned, with the heraldic charge of a label, marking the youngest son. The key, an attribute of papal dignity, and the lead seal of the papal bull of investiture are deliberately enlarged to emphasize their importance.

c. 1270–75. Pernes-les-Fontaines, Vaucluse, France, Tour Ferrande, third floor.

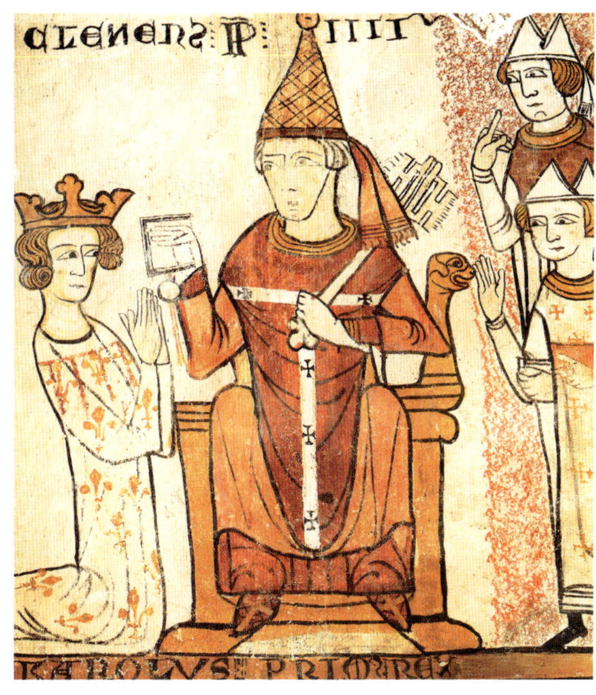

ike the cardinals, the pope himself was a figure dressed in red, or at least in red and white. Until the late Middle Ages, and in some cases even later, during formal ceremonies he wore a long red robe, a white pallium decorated with small crosses, and depending upon the circumstances, a cap (when he was not wearing the papal tiara), a cloak (when he was traveling), and slippers; all these attributes were red. Here again, the color simultaneously evoked the blood of Christ, the universal Church (whose early banner was red with a white cross), and the ancient purple of Rome. Nevertheless, as time went on, pontifical red lost ground to white. Paintings from the sixteenth and seventeenth centuries often show the pope dressed in a long white robe decorated with a pallium of the same color and wearing a white tiara with three crowns of gold; only the cloak remains red.

Today this color has practically disappeared from papal dress; only the slippers, rarely visible, are still red. Why? Out of humility and a desire to shun the splendor of purple? As a rejection of a color too politically and ideologically charged? Or, on the contrary, is the wearing of white meant to fully flaunt the pope's superiority over the council, a polychromatic assembly of dignitaries dressed in red, purple, black, and even green? It is hard to say, as each pontiff has his own motives, habits, sensibility, and nature.[14]

Let us return to the Middle Ages. In texts and images as early as the Carolingian period, the emperor seemed more devoted to red than the pope, at least on the emblematic level, if not the symbolic one. Through that color, he became the true heir of the ancient Roman emperors and the alter ego of those in Byzantium, all dressed in purple. Thanks to his biographer Einhard, we know what Charlemagne wore daily: a tunic and short cloak in

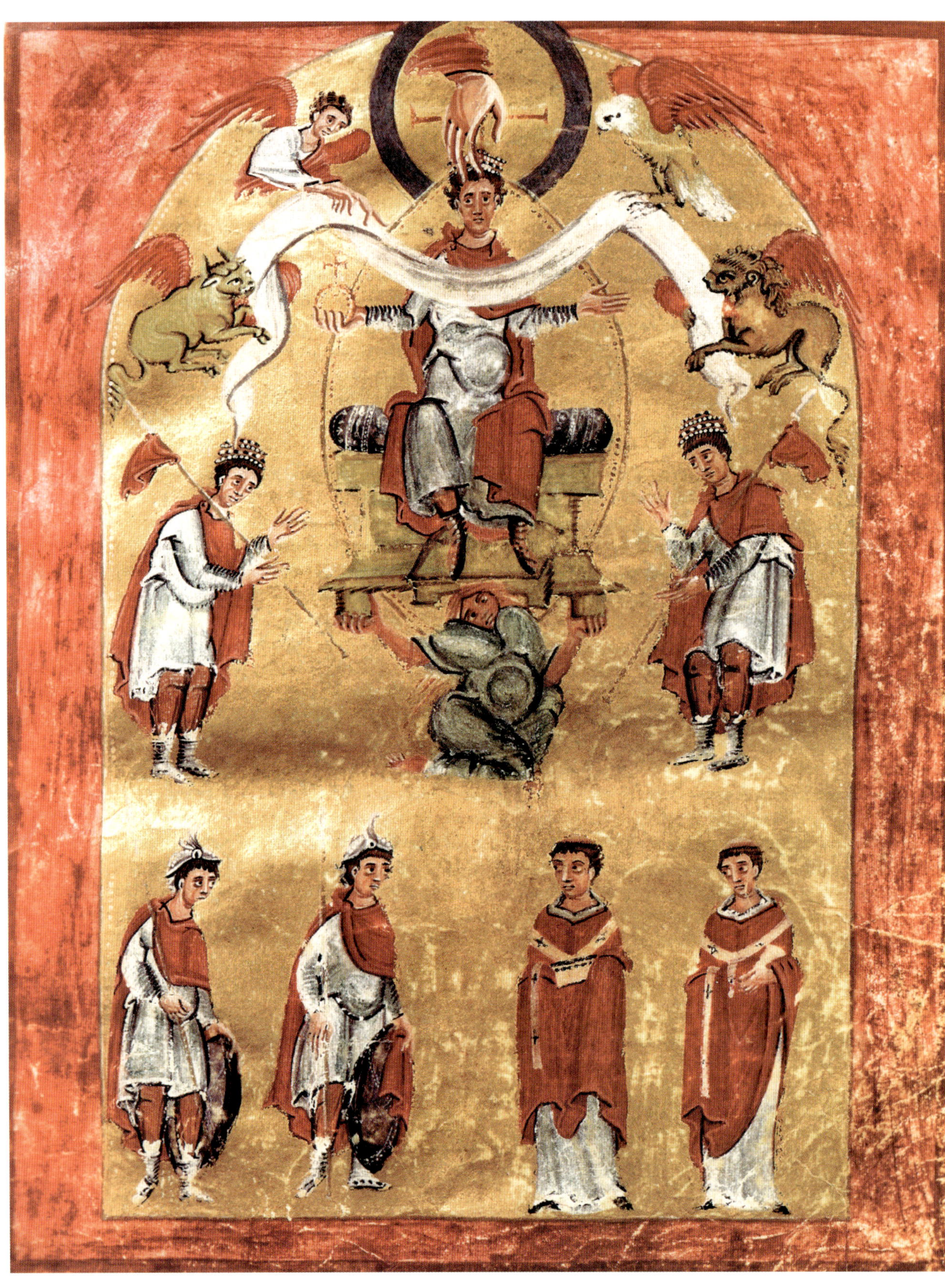

Emperor Otto III

Red, the imperial color descending from antique purple, is everywhere in this great painting from the *Liuthar Gospels*, an evangelistary copied and painted in the workshop of Liuthar, a monk in the Reichenau monastery. Enthroned in a mandorla and surrounded by the tetramorph as though he were Christ, the future emperor Otto III, crowned king of the Romans in 983, receives divine benediction and investiture.

Évangéliaire de Liuthar, copied and painted in Reichenau about 983–90, late 10th century. Aachen (Aix-la-Chapelle), Cathedral Treasury.

the Frankish style, leg wrappings, and simple sandals—a rejection of "foreign clothes whatever they were." But Einhard tells us nothing of colors. On the other hand, he notes that on the particular occasion of his coronation in Rome on Christmas in the year 800, Charles appeared before Pope Leo III dressed entirely in red—tunic, cloak, and shoes, all in the Roman style—and that the pontiff gave to him a *vexillum* (gonfalon? standard?) of the same color, with a pattern of blue and gold floral motifs.[15] Einhard wrote his *Vita Karoli* about ten years after the great emperor's death, but he had been his daily companion in the Palais d'Aix-la-Chapelle (Palace of Aachen) and had had his complete confidence. There is little reason to doubt his testimony.

The simple red cloak worn by Charlemagne at his coronation would subsequently become a heavy mantle of great size, the required attribute of imperial power. His grandson Charles the Bald would receive it ceremoniously, along with other insignia, from the hands of Pope John VIII during his own coronation in 875. The same would be true for all his successors, first Carolingians, then Ottonians, Salians, Hohenstaufens, Habsburgs, and Luxembourgs. By the year 1000, the mantle was part of the *insignia imperialia*, along with the globe, sword, scepter and holy lance. And like the banner of the Germanic Holy Roman Empire, it was red, originally plain red and then, beginning in the twelfth century, with the charge of a white cross.[16]

However, the emperor was not the only sovereign in feudal Europe who took the color red as an emblem. It was taken by many kings who received a garment or banner of that color during their coronations. Thus we still have a splendid semicircular mantle undoubtedly woven for Roger II of Sicily, crowned king in Palermo in December 1130. It is in red silk, embroidered with gold and silver thread and decorated with almost five thousand pearls, an eminently precious design that takes the surprising form of two lions back to back.

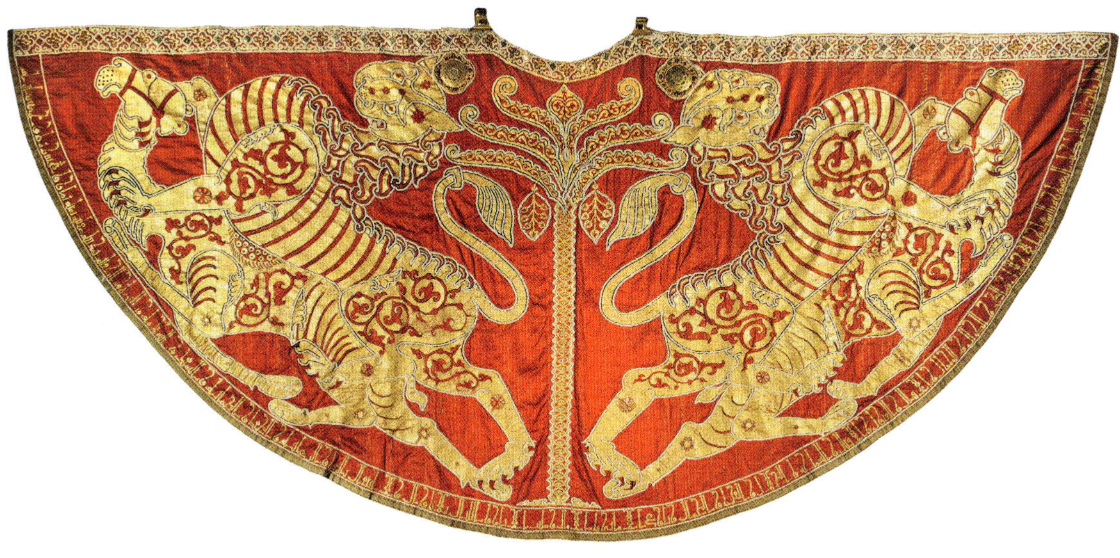

Mantle of Roger II of Sicily

According to medieval tradition, this ceremonial cope, each half of which shows a lion bringing down a dromedary, supposedly belonged to Charlemagne. In fact, it is more recent, produced in Palermo for King Roger II of Sicily soon after his coronation in 1130.

1133–34. Vienna, Kunsthistorisches Museum, Imperial Treasury.

Adam and Eve Driven from Paradise

In medieval images, the angel that expelled Adam and Eve from paradise after they picked and ate the forbidden fruit is often dressed in red. This is the red of justice, which we find again in other images on the robes of judges and sometimes on the clothes of executioners.

Stained glass by Hans Acker, 1461, mid-15th century. Ulm, Germany, Ulm Münster, Besserer Chapel.

In 1194, Emperor Henry VI had this mantle transported to Germany, and from then on it was used at the coronation of all his successors to the imperial throne until the end of the eighteenth century.[17] At various times in their histories, the kings of the Iberian Peninsula, of Scotland, of Poland, and especially of England also had coronation mantles in the color red, a symbol of their power and prestigious inheritance of antique purple. Only the kings of France, who were always asserting their difference from other monarchs, never wore such a mantle. We do not know in exactly what attire the first Capetian kings were coronated, but beginning with Philip Augustus, crowned in 1179 while his father, Louis VII, was still alive, and until Charles X, lavishly crowned in 1825 according to the ritual of the Ancien Régime, that mantle was always *d'azur semé de fleurs de lis d'or*. The azure, moreover, which was a relatively light blue in the seventh and eighth centuries, tended to become darker over the course of time and sometimes to take on purplish or crimson shades.[18]

If French kings never wore red copes or mantles like the emperor and most other sovereigns, they did, on the other hand, make use of a red ensign for more than three centuries: the oriflamme. The legend of its origin makes it Charlemagne's standard, "of a vermilion color as sparkling as gold," *The Song of Roland* tells us.[19] According to a more modest version, it was a matter of a simple feudal banner, cut from plain red cloth and belonging to the abbey of Saint-Denis. As the abbey could not wage war, it was represented in battle by an "avowed," the Count of Vexin, who, in rallying his troops, came to the abbey itself where the banner was kept to collect it. Philip I inherited the Vexin countship in 1077, and henceforth it was the kings of France who had the honor of bearing the oriflamme of Saint-Denis into battle. It seems that Louis VI, son of Philip I, was the first to actually do so, in 1124, and Louis XI did so for the last time during the Battle of Montlhéry in July 1465. A simple monochrome gonfalon of the feudal period, the oriflamme seems to have been given long flying tails during the Hundred Years' War and sometimes to have been decorated with flowers, rings, flames, or small crosses.[20] All these materials, objects, and practices underscore how the color red maintained direct ties with power in the medieval West, with sovereign power but also feudal power and representative power. Not only did important feudal figures—dukes, counts, great barons—turn to red to present themselves, so did representatives of the emperor or the king, and minor lords who imitated them in their own way. Thus dukes and margraves on the borders of the Holy Roman Empire bore banners and coats of arms in which red dominated. And at the other extreme but still within the empire were those punctilious officials in the late Middle Ages who tried in vain to prohibit common mortals from wearing red clothing or using wax seals of that color, supposedly reserved for the emperor and the dynasties. And farther east and even more astonishing, there were those great Polish lords who demanded of their vassals or peasants feudal payments in the range of reds: pieces of red fabric, stained glass, cochineal "seeds," red fruits and berries, cattle with red coats, and even "well-fatted roosters whose crests are a

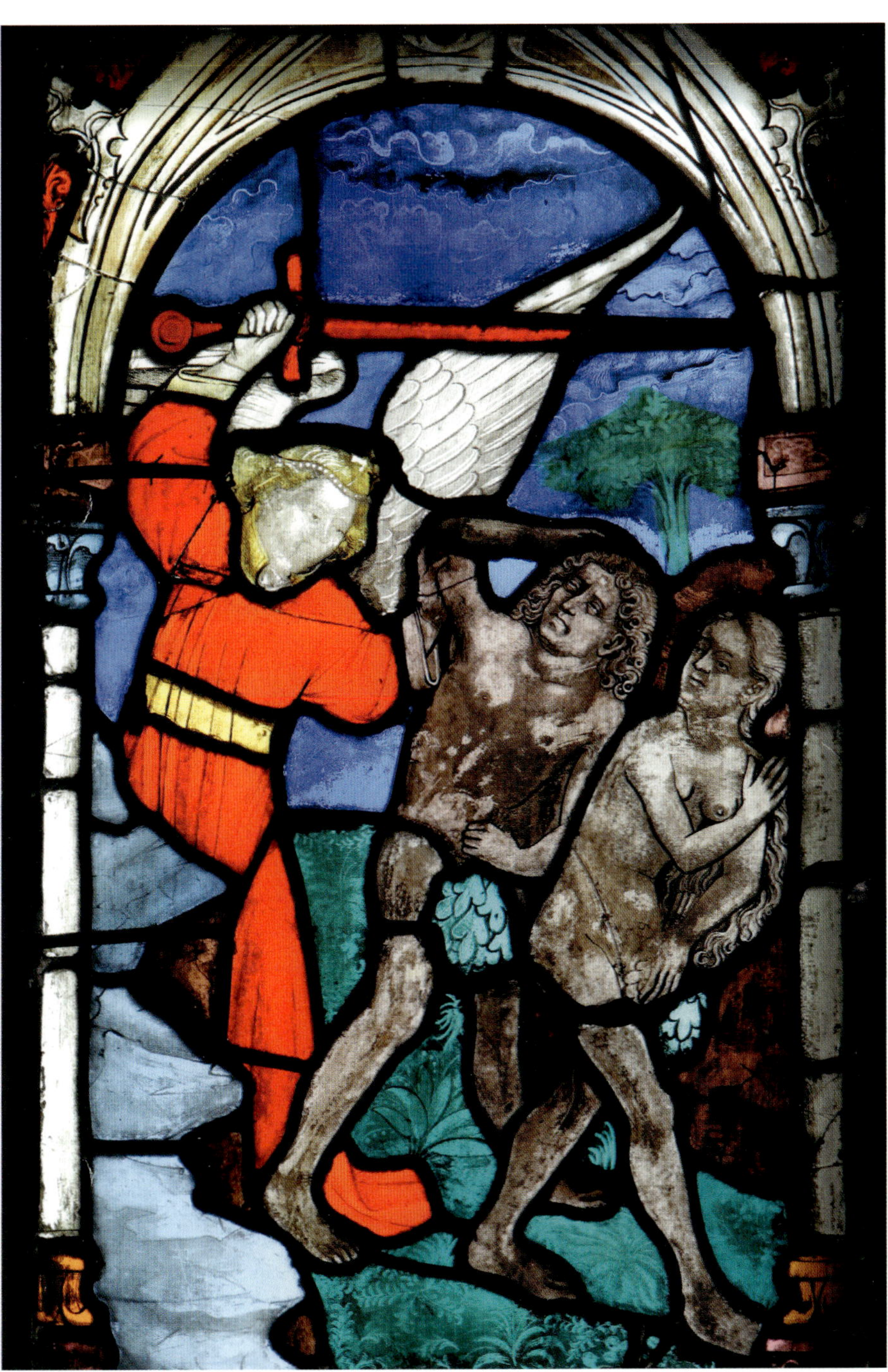

beautiful, fiery red."[21] In the Middle Ages, to display, receive, control, or forbid the color red, in whatever form, was to manifest one's power.

Red was also worn to exercise power on behalf of a third party. That is why judges, in actual courts, as in the iconography of miniatures, were inevitably dressed in red, the color of their delegated power and their function: to state the law and render judgments in the place of the king, prince, city or state. But it was also, more generally, the symbolic color of Justice, whether the justice of God or of men.[22] The angel who expelled Adam and Eve from Paradise after they had disobeyed the Lord and eaten of the forbidden fruit is a red angel in the imagery, an angelic dispenser of justice. Similarly, in a more secular manner, any executioner wore a cap, gloves, or piece of clothing of this color, as an attribute of his office.

The red of power, the red of sin, the red of punishment, the red of blood to be shed: we will find this symbolism for the color lasting well into the modern period.

The First Color of Heraldry

Papal, imperial, royal, governmental, or judicial, red is also fully aristocratic. It was the favorite color of great and minor nobility, who valued all things red: fabric, clothing, finery, jewels, precious stones, flowers, decoration, emblems. Coats of arms perhaps constitute the area where that preference is most obvious because, for the feudal period, it is possible to enact statistical studies.[23] On the scale of Western Europe and for the period extending from the mid-twelfth century to the early fourteenth century, we are aware of about seven thousand different coats of arms with their colors.[24] These are almost all noble coats of arms, and more than 60 percent of them include red. Thereafter, that percentage declines to 45 percent around 1400, 35 percent around 1600, and only 30 percent in the second half of the 1700s.[25] It is true that over the course of time the number of coats of

arms continually increased (more than twenty million European coats of arms are recognized for the sixteenth to eighteenth centuries) and that their use expanded to all social classes and categories. As signs of identity—or heredity, like family names—as well as marks of possession and decorative elements, they appeared on a great number of objects, images, artworks, furnishings, and property.

In the twelfth and thirteenth centuries, the first coats of arms were composed of two elements, figures and colors, appearing most often in the shape of shields because of their origins on battle and tournament fields. The figures formed an open repertoire, consisting of animals, plants, and many geometric shapes. The colors, on the other hand, existed only in a limited number and bore specific names in the French language of heraldry: white (*argent*), yellow (*or*), red (*gueules*), blue (*azur*), black (*sable*), and green (*sinople*).[26] These six colors were absolute, conceptual, almost immaterial; their shades did not count. For example, the red used by English kings in their coats of arms since the reign of Richard the Lionheart—*de gueules à trois léopards couronnés d'or*—could be light, dark, medium, or tending toward orange or purple; its shade had no importance or significance. What counted was the idea of red and the colored materiality of the field of the shield. For the historian, this constitutes a huge advantage over all the other color documentation the Middle Ages left to us. For regarding painted coats of arm, the historian does not have to take into account the work of time (chemical changes in pigments, transformation of shades) and can engage in statistical

Omnipresence of Red in Heraldry

Gueules, the name of red in the French language of heraldry, is the dominant color in medieval coats of arms. In this folio from a European armorial, copied and painted in Lille about 1435, only one of the twenty-five coats of arms represented does not include this color. Next in order of frequency are white, yellow, blue, and black. Green, absent here, is always rarer. (English and Dutch coats of arms are shown.)

Armorial de la Toison d'Or et de l'Europe, copied and painted in Lille, c. 1435. Paris, Bibliothèque de l'Arsenal, manuscript 4790, folio 80v.

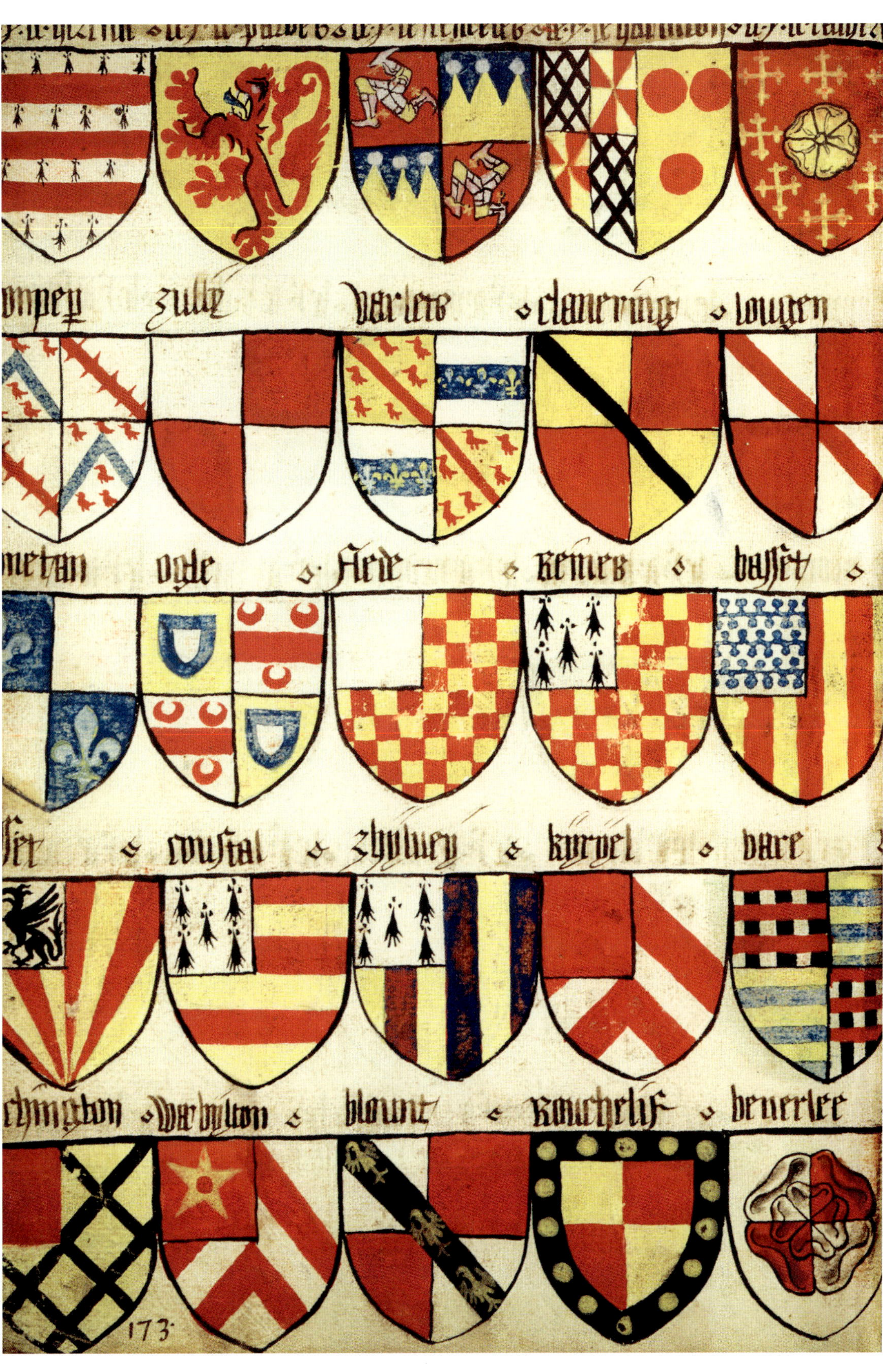

List of Zurich Arms

Four hundred and fifty coats of arms are painted on the two sides of this narrow parchment scroll (four meters long by thirteen centimeters wide), a masterpiece of medieval heraldry. Red is the dominant color here, present in almost two-thirds of the shields. The first of them, to the far left in the upper row, displays a figure in this color: *d'or à un chameau de gueules*. As might be expected, this is the imaginary coat of arms for Prester John.

Die Wappenrolle von Zürich, c. 1335–40. Zurich, Switzerland, Musée National Suisse, AG 2760.

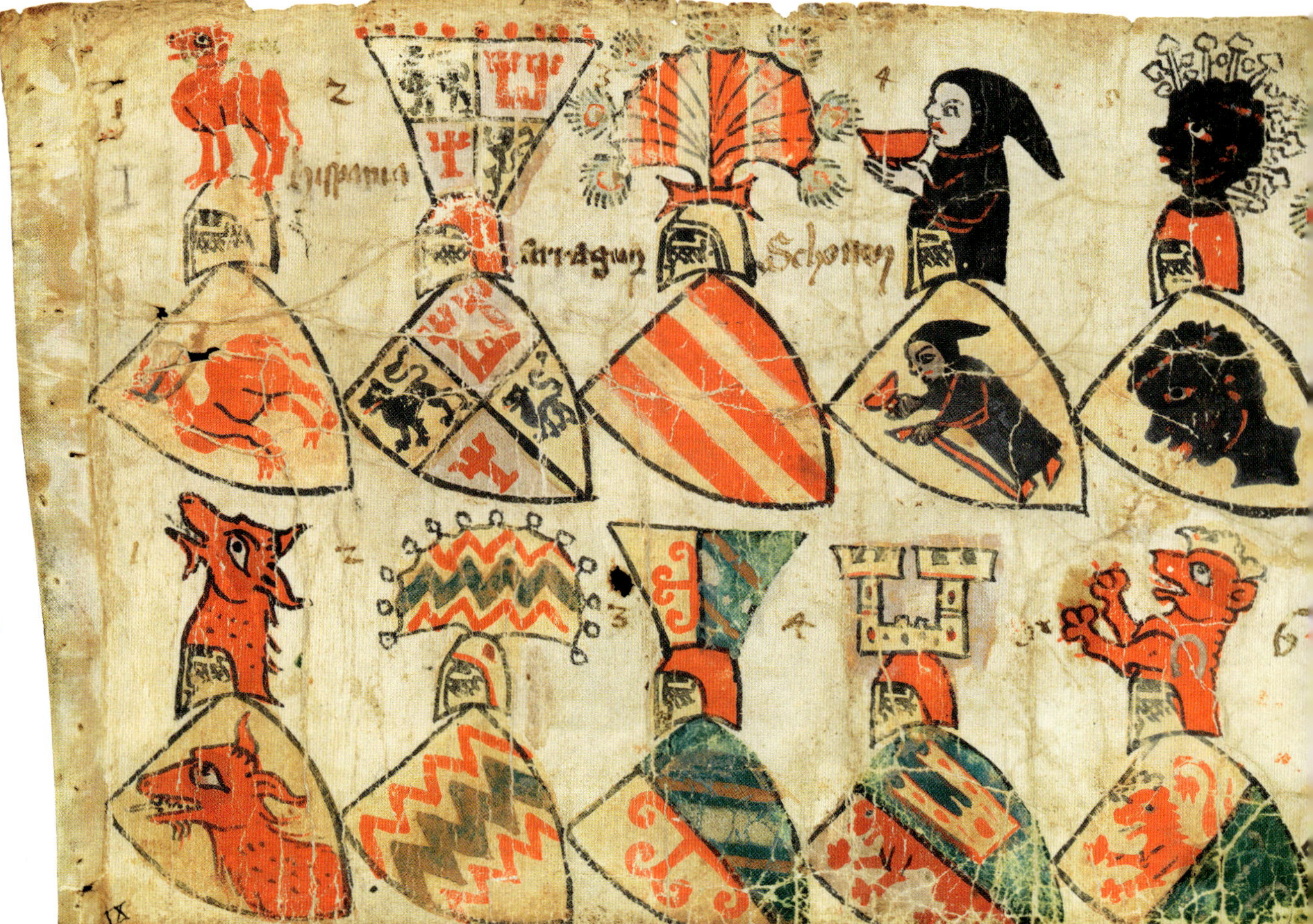

analyses of all kinds regarding the use of these six colors in time and place.

Among the noble class until the mid-fourteenth century, *gueules* was by far the color most used, which underscores the very marked taste of feudal aristocracy for all things red. Even in France where the king bore coats of arms with a field of *azur*—the only Western royalty to do so—red easily outstrips blue.[27] With this red originated many legends, under the Ancien Régime and even into the nineteenth century, explaining how this or that family came to bear *gueules* in its coat of arms in memory of an ancestor who died heroically in the Crusades, spilling his blood for Christ. The Crusades had absolutely nothing to do with the appearance or composition of coats of arms, but until recently they have inspired much rambling from amateurs in heraldry and the public at large.

Other ramblings come from philologists explaining the origin of the heraldic term *gueules*, designating the color red in French since the twelfth century. Most refuse to see it as a simple allusion to the *gueule* or throat of an animal; instead they diverge in deciding

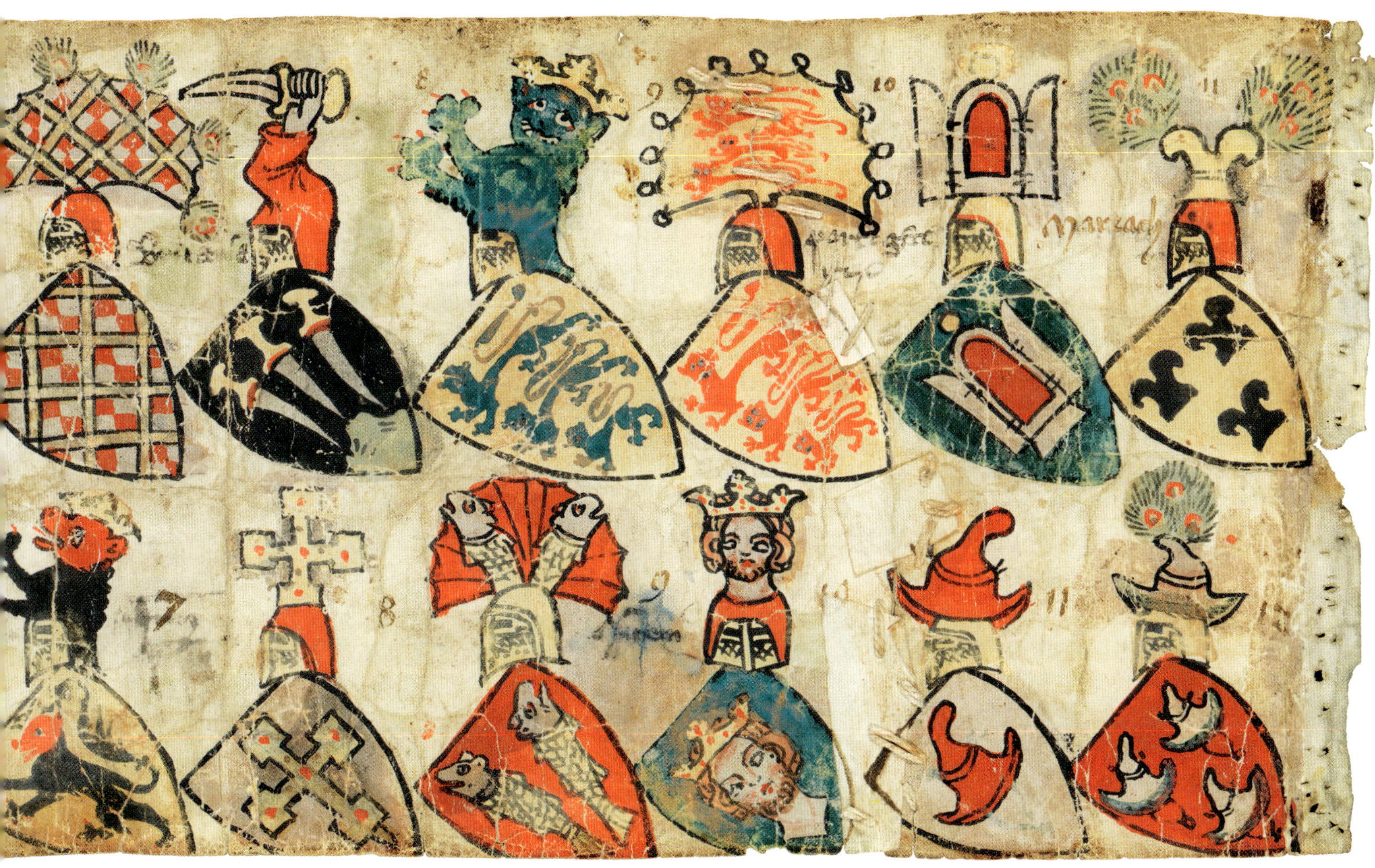

whether to seek its etymology among the Gallic, Persian, Arabic, or Frankish languages. These are very shaky, if not to say unfounded leads.[28] Latin would undoubtedly offer less extravagant possibilities, but for the time, the wisest choice is to recognize that the word *gueules* is of unknown origin and thus acquires all the richer poetic and oneiric power. Moreover, the same holds true for the other heraldic terms designating colors, even if their origins are less obscure.[29] These are powerful terms whose semantic import puts the emphasis as much on symbolism as on coloration.

Let us take, for example, the coat of arms of a favorite literary hero for medieval audiences: Perceval, a figure who appeared for the first time about 1180-85 in Chrétien de Troyes's *Le Conte du Graal*, and who later became one of the three victors in the quest for the Holy Grail. In doing so, he took a place among the principal knights of the Round Table, ranking with Lancelot, Gawain, Tristan, and a few others. Thirteenth-century literary texts and fourteenth-century miniatures attribute to him a coat of arms that is unusual in being monochrome, a simple field entirely red in

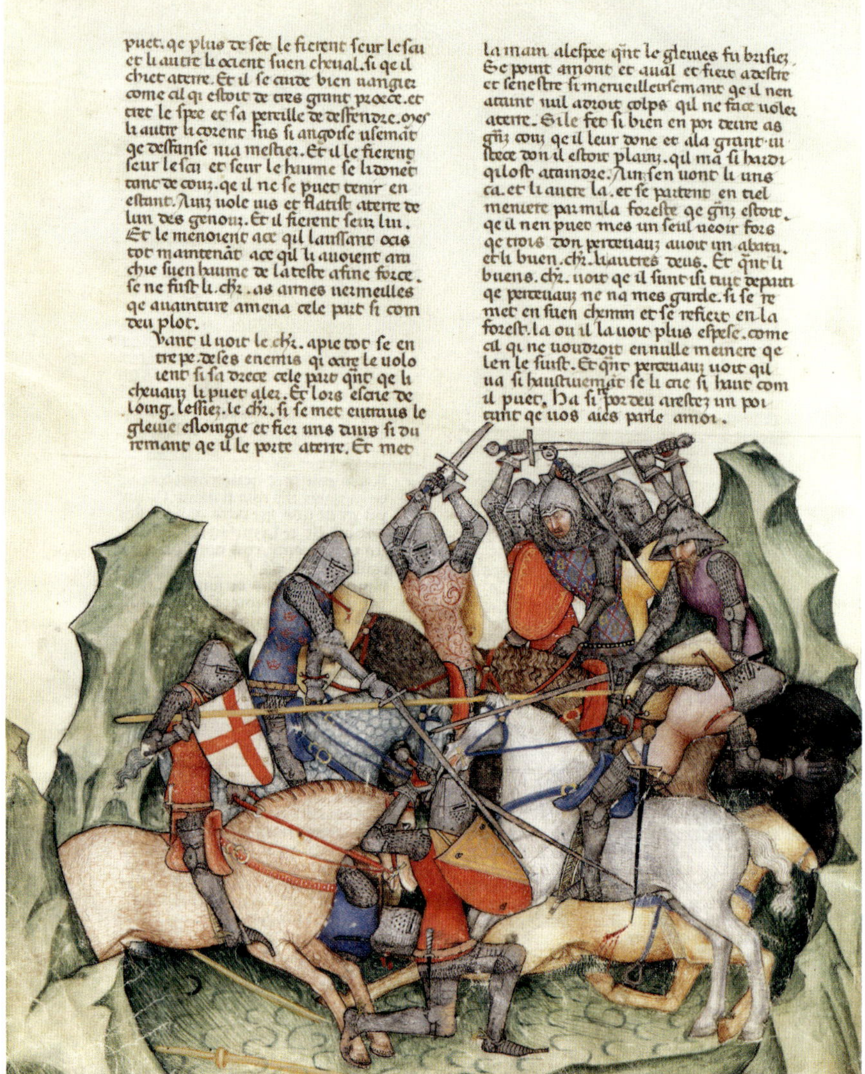

plain, his shield and his character would take on even greater symbolic power. Through this mysterious blazon, through this matchless coat of arms, conquering an evil and redoubtable knight, Perceval appears as a young man of high birth, attributed with every virtue and destined for an extraordinary fate.[30]

Red's prestige becomes very apparent in the treatises on heraldry from the fourteenth and fifteenth centuries. They go on at length about the symbolism and hierarchy of colors, not only within the area of heraldry itself but also on a more general level, thus constituting a rich source for identifying the value systems that underlie the chromatic codes of the late Middle Ages, notably those involving clothing practices. According to their authors, *gueules* often occupies first place among the colors because it is a sign of nobility, beauty, and courage. Here, for example, is what a Norman herald wrote sometime before the 1430s:

> The first color is vermilion, which, in coats of arms, is called *gueules*. It is compared to fire, which is the most brilliant and most noble of the elements. Among minerals, it is associated with rubies, a particularly rich and precious stone. That is why no one must wear this color who is not noble, a powerful lord and valiant in combat. But if it is worn by a man of very noble lineage and if he proves worthy of it and behaves daringly in battle, it is a sign of all virtues.[31]

Half a century later, an anonymous author, who may have been from Lille or Brussels, said the same thing when he compiled the second part of a work destined for fame: *Le

color. If Perceval's shield was said to be "all red," that would be accurate but poetically lacking. On the other hand, if it was said that he bore a "vermilion shield," like those strange *chevaliers vermeils* (vermilion knights) that appear from time to time in Arthurian romances, the metaphoric and oneiric possibilities would already be greater. But if his coat of arms was described in terms of heraldry, *de gueules

Blason des couleurs en armes, livrées et devises. To the discourse of his predecessors he added a few points on the symbolism of dress:

> Red, said Aristotle, is located halfway between white and black, the same distance from one as from the other. But we can see that it goes together better with white than with black because of its strong light, similar to that of fire.... Among the virtues, red signifies noble birth, honor, valor, generosity, and daring. It is also the color of justice and charity, in memory of our Lord Jesus Christ. Among man's temperaments, it is sanguine; among the ages of life, it is man's prime, among the planets, Mars, among the signs, the Lion.... Combined with other colors, red ennobles them. On a piece of clothing, it gives great courage to the one who wears it. Paired with green, red is beautiful and signifies youth and joie de vivre. With blue, wisdom and fidelity. With yellow, avarice and greed. Red does not go well with black, but with gray, it is the sign of great hopes. And with white, these are two very beautiful colors, signs of the highest virtues.[32]

This *Blason des couleurs* enjoyed considerable success. In most of the surviving manuscripts and printed copies, it follows a small manual on heraldry attributed to a famous herald Jean Courtois, known as the Sicily Herald. First printed in Paris in 1495, it was reprinted in 1501 and then six more times until 1614. Meanwhile, it was translated or adapted into various languages (first Italian, then German, Dutch, and Castilian).[33] It had great influence in various domains, notably literary and artistic ones. Rabelais alludes to it four times in his *Gargantua,* and many sixteenth-century Venetian painters borrowed from its codes for dressing in one color or another the figures they presented.[34]

Until very late, sometimes well beyond the Middle Ages, red remained the favorite color of the aristocracy in the West. This was so not only among noble women, who found in it the color of beauty and love, but also among men, because it simultaneously symbolized courage, power, and glory. As an eminently feminine color in many areas, red was also a male color, worn into war, at tournaments, for the hunt: three terrains where it was necessary to make an appearance, be seen, recognized, feared, and admired. How better to achieve this than by dressing in red? In fact, over the long term, that color—already the color of the god Mars of the Romans—clothed very many soldiers, recognizable from a distance and sometimes the victims of their too visible uniforms, like the French soldiers in autumn 1914 with their disastrous "madder red" trousers.

All the same, it may be with the hunt that this proud, undaunted, masculine red experienced its greatest, if not its longest, history. In the Middle Ages, and continuing into the early modern era, a king, prince, or great lord had to hunt; if he did not hunt, he was not worthy of his rank. For hunting he almost always dressed in red, as did his huntsmen, all ready to fight and kill animals that were fawn-colored (various kinds of deer), red (fox, young boar) or black (bear, old boar) as their packs flushed them out and chased them. The red of the hunt was simultaneously glorious, resonant, violent, savage, and bloody.

Galahad, Knight of the Grail

Son of Lancelot, Galahad was the most virtuous of the knights of the Round Table. With Bors and Perceval, he led to its conclusion the quest for the Holy Grail, a blessing denied his father because of his adulterous love affair with Queen Guinevere. As the perfect Christian knight, Galahad bore on his shield the arms of the Church and the crusaders: *d'argent à la croix gueules.*

Collection of Arthurian romances in prose (*Lancelot, Queste del Saint Graal*), copied and painted in Pavia or Milan, c. 1380–85. Paris, Bibliothèque Nationale de France, French manuscript 343, folio 25v.

Love, Glory, and Beauty

et us leave the huntsmen to their hunt and remain with the ladies. The special attribute of medieval red, as we have noted, was to be both masculine and feminine, virile and full of grace. Any pretty woman maintained close relations with this color, whether it was a matter of her body, clothing, finery, or the passions of her heart. Red was the color of love, radiance, and beauty.

Twelfth- and thirteenth-century tales of chivalry give us an idea of what then defined feminine beauty among the seigniory. A beautiful woman had to have a fair complexion, oval face, blond hair, blue eyes, thin, arched brown eyebrows, small, high, firm breasts, slender waist, narrow hips, and a slim figure. The physical ideal was that of the *pucelle* (young nubile girl) described many times in Arthurian legends.[35] Obviously these were clichés—which would change moreover at the end of the Middle Ages—but they corresponded to a certain reality. Courtly literature was both the reflection and the model of feudal society and, provided we remember literary texts never directly "photograph" the societies they talk about, for the historian it constitutes a first-rate source for value systems and modes of sensibility.

The face especially held the attention of poets and romancers. They emphasized the color of the eyes—blue, but all shades of blue, which they specified: *azur, pers, vairet, inde, sorinde*.[36] They also emphasized the radiance of the complexion and the contrast between the white of the skin and the red of lips and cheeks. If necessary, that red could be heightened through various kinds of makeup that ladies of good society made great use of, despite repeated condemnations by clergy and moralists. For the Church, using makeup was a deception, a sin, an attack on the natural state desired by the Creator. Only red for the cheeks, with a hematite-powder base, was sometimes tolerated because it could be "a sign of modesty." Red for the lips, on the other hand, was an abomination, transforming women into witches or prostitutes.

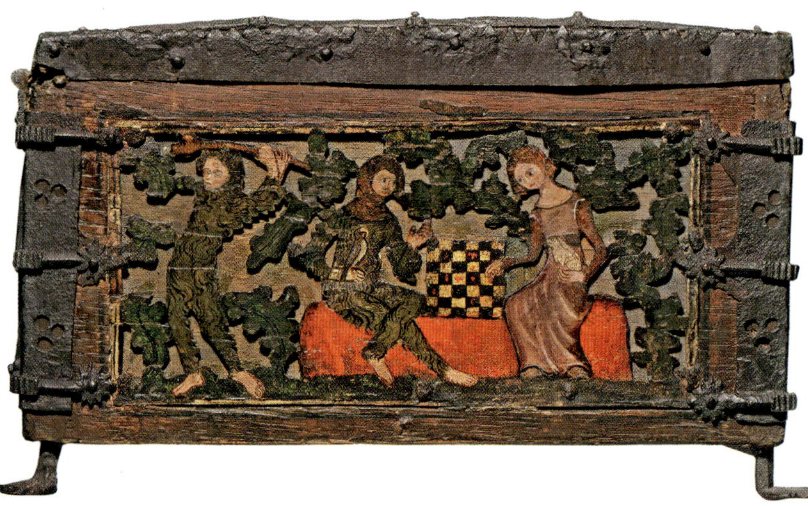

Red and Green, Two Courtly Colors

Refugees in the wood of Morrois, Tristan and Isolde play chess, a scene often represented on the Germanic *Minnekästchen* (medieval coffrets) from the thirteenth and fourteenth centuries.

mid-14th century. Cologne, Museum für Angewandte Kunst.

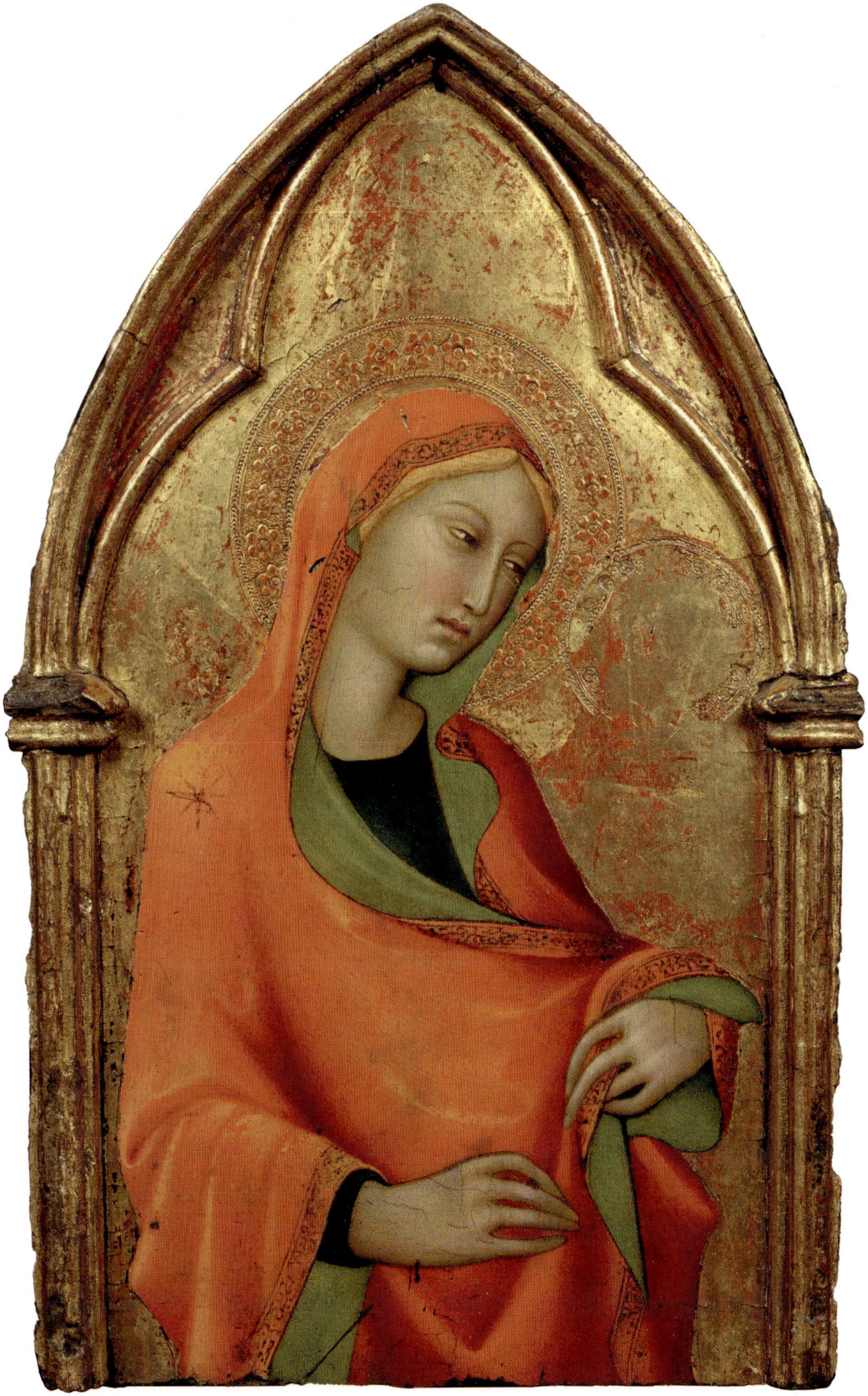

Mary Magdalene

In the iconography of the late Middle Ages and early modern period, Mary Magdalene often wears a red robe or cloak, an ambivalent color that evokes her former status as a prostitute even as it emphasizes her love for Christ.

Lippo and Federico Memmi, *Mary Magdalene*, Siena, c. 1325. Avignon, Musée de Petit Palais.

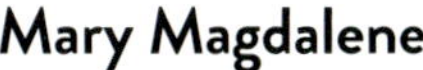

The Holy Grail

A somewhat mysterious object, the Holy Grail is mentioned for the first time by Chrétien de Troyes in his unfinished romance *Perceval ou le Conte du Graal* (c. 1180–85). His successors made the Grail out to be the goblet from the Last Supper or even the vessel in which Joseph of Arimathea supposedly collected the blood of Christ descending from the Cross. That is why in images the Grail often takes the form of a red vase or chalice.

Manessier, *Troisième Continuation du Conte du Graal*, manuscript copied and painted in northern France, c. 1270. Paris, Bibliothèque Nationale de France, French manuscript 12576, folio 261.

Nevertheless various recipes have survived, based on beeswax or goose fat, colored with kermes or madder, and scented with honey, rose, rosemary, or apple. The fashion was for bright, vivid red lips, contrasting with white cheeks, which were themselves accentuated with a light coat of ceruse. The blackish and purplish reds that Roman women of the late empire used to excess were considered vulgar. To be beautiful, noble ladies dyed their hair (blond) and their eyebrows (brown), and if they paid little attention to their eyelids or lashes, they carefully removed hair from the nape of their necks, temples, and especially the *entroeil*, the area between the eyes, which had to be smooth and wide in order to enhance the forehead. Generally speaking, body hair, a symbol of animality, was banished, as was reddened skin, which transformed a princess into a peasant.[37]

What mattered more than anything else was radiance, of complexion, eyes, lips. Lips were easy to compare to jewels, since the fashion was for mouths that were small, plump, and bright red. A large mouth had something bestial or immoral about it; thin, pale lips were a sign of disease or deceitfulness. The rounder, fuller, and more radiant the mouth, the more attractive it was and the more it resembled a ruby, a stone especially admired, which was called an *escarboucle* (carbuncle) when it was an unusual cut. Some poets enjoyed rhyming *boche* (*bouche*—mouth) with *escarboche* (*escarboucle*—carbuncle); others explained that the ruby was called by this name when it shone with a particular brilliance; still others placed an *escarboucle* at the center of the shield or the top of the helmet of some particularly virtuous knight. That red stone, which seemed to glow like burning coals (hence its Latin name, *carbunculus*), guided the knight through the darkness, protected him from the forces of evil, and ensured him a kind of invincibility. The bestiaries teach us that many formidable animals, notably dragons, possessed a similar stone just behind their foreheads; vanquishing them to seize it was a justly rewarded exploit.

One mythical object produced a red glow comparable to that of the carbuncle: the Grail. Like Perceval, it appeared for the first time in the unfinished romance by Chrétien de Troyes, *Le Conte du Graal*, in about the 1180s and then enjoyed an exceptional literary career, stretching well beyond the framework of the Middle Ages alone. Defining exactly what the object is, however, is no easy task. Even if we look no further than the two or three generations that followed Chrétien, authors—and scholars commenting on them—differ with regard to whether the Grail was a large plate, chalice, ciborium, cauldron, cornucopia, or even a precious stone (that is the opinion of the German poet Wolfram von Eschenbach).[38] Most often it was a vessel, the one in which Joseph of Arimathea supposedly gathered some of the blood spilled by Christ on the Cross. Made of gold or silver, this vessel was enriched with precious stones, rubies most prominent among them. That was the reason it cast an incomparable light: red, white, and golden. Thus the Grail could simultaneously be a distinguished relic of the Passion, a sacred vase containing a nourishing host, a liturgical object, and a magical talisman. Seeing and drawing near to it was reserved for the three elect of the quest: Galahad, Perceval,

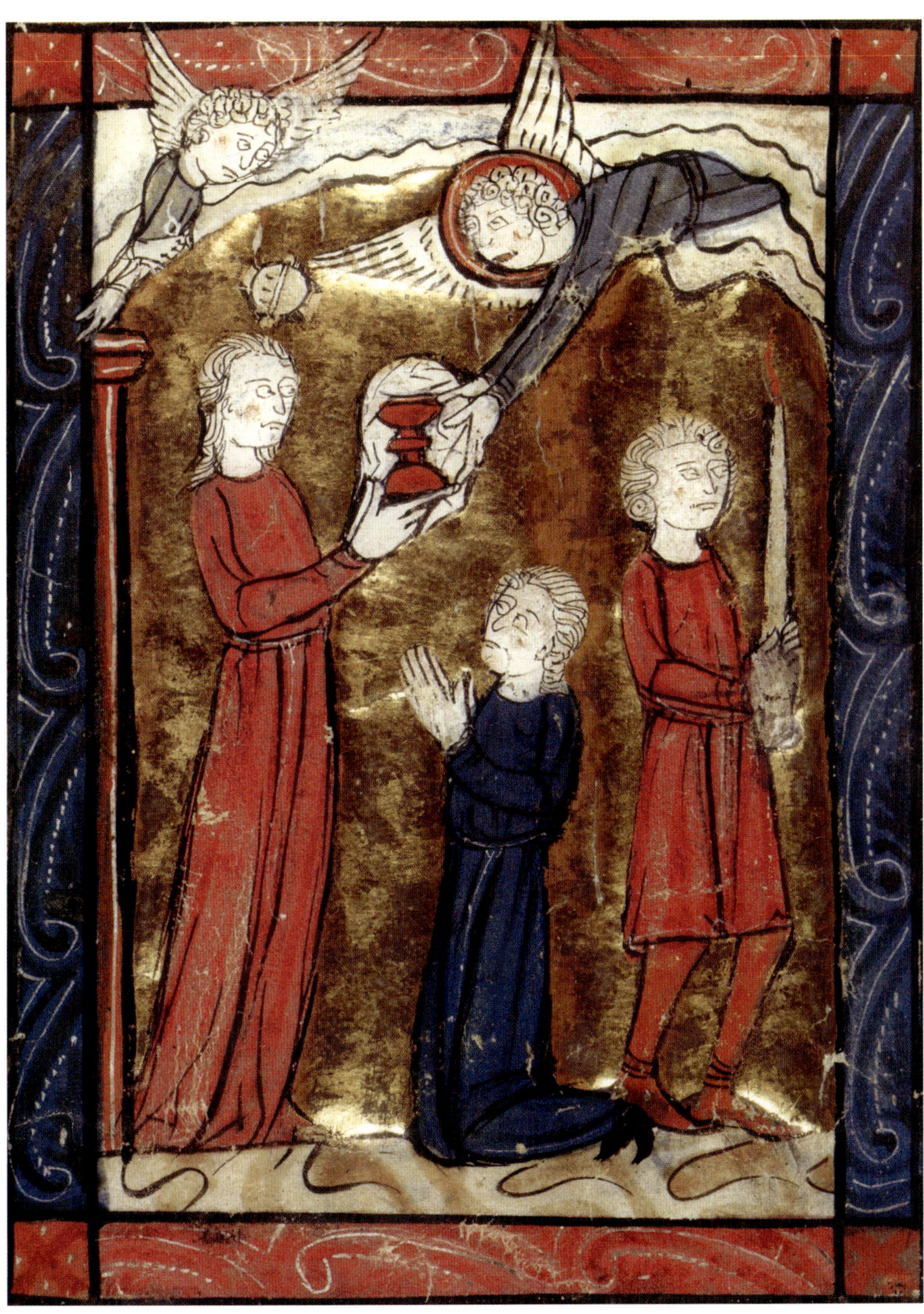

and Bors. In this it was a blessing, an authentic beatific vision, denied to knights like Lancelot, who lived in sin, discredited by his adulterous love affair with Queen Guinevere. In the twelfth and thirteenth centuries, one could be the "world's best knight" and find oneself denied access to the Holy Grail.[39]

The color of beauty and radiance, red is also and above all the color of love, whether mystical or carnal. In texts and images, we find it associated as much with Christ's love for men (*caritas*) as with the affection that tenderly binds two spouses (*dilectio*), the carnal intercourse between lovers (*luxuria*), and even the most extreme debauchery (*fornicatio*). Medieval red possessed a very wide symbolic field and expressed love in all its forms.

We have already noted how divine love and charity contributed to the exaltation of the blood of Christ (Crusade banners, cardinals' hats, worship of the Holy Blood). At the opposite extreme is lust, just as red, if not more so, especially when it was a matter of prostitution. Of course brothels, *maisons lupanardes*, were not yet marked by a red lantern—that would have to wait until the nineteenth century. But by the end of the Middle Ages, some municipal regulations required prostitutes to wear a piece of clothing (dress, hood, aglet) in a garish color in order to be distinguished from honest women. Usually it was a loud red, sometimes combined with yellow (Rhenish Germany) or black (northern Italy).[40] This link between the color red and prostitution finds its roots in the Bible. In the seventeenth chapter of Revelation an angel shows Saint John the great harlot of Babylon. She is "dressed in purple and scarlet," seated on the waters, and holding a

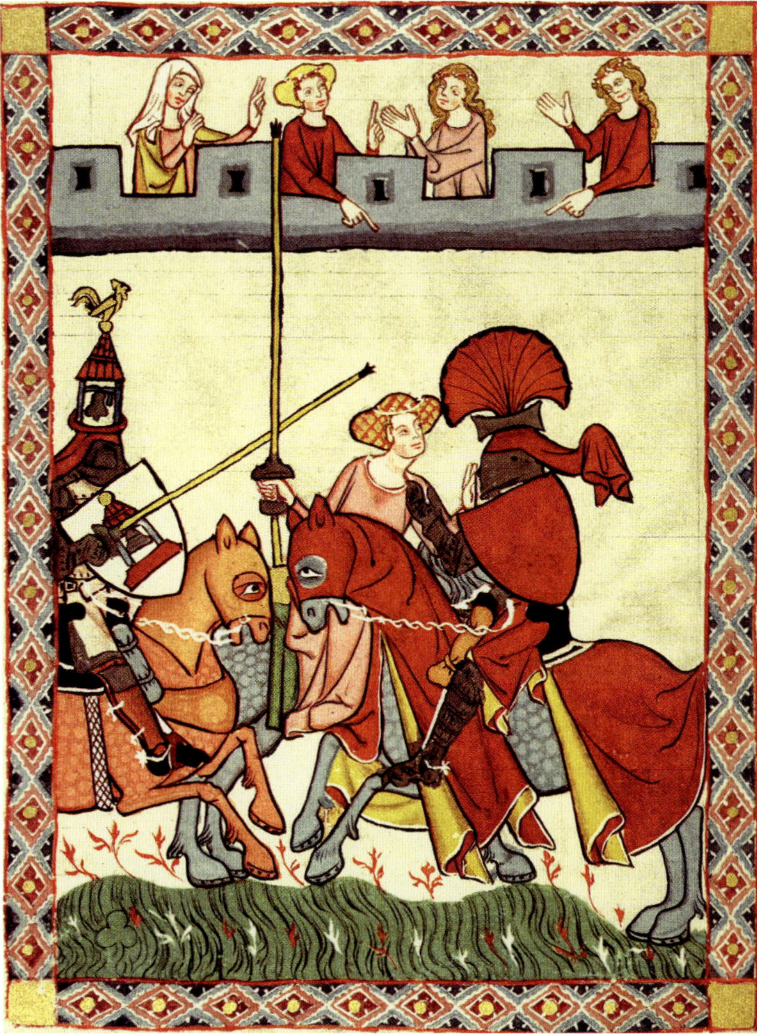

mirror (the image of lust); later, she rides a "monstrous red beast" with seven heads (the dragon).[41] Medieval artists often represented Saint John's vision and gave the great harlot a red dress, just as they often dressed Mary Magdalene in red, a holy woman, of course—and even the first to whom the risen Christ may have appeared—but a former courtesan, with long red hair and a painted face.

Without going so far as to show or suggest debauchery, thirteenth- and fourteenth-century miniatures often chose red to present the love that united two young people. It could be simple amorous banter under a rose bush with splendid red blossoms, as in many great paintings from the famous *Codex Manesse* (Zurich, c. 1300–1310).[42] Or it could be tender kisses exchanged between two lovers dressed in red or red and green (the color of youth), as we see in various examples in the illuminated manuscripts of the Arthurian romances. But it could also be actual carnal intercourse, in a bed draped with red, witnessed or unwitnessed. Generally speaking, a red dress is never neutral; it is almost always an appealing dress, meant to attract or to convey the passions of the heart. At tournaments, when a lady gave the sleeve of her dress to her escorting knight, or even when she promised it to the future victor, it was almost always a red sleeve. So that it would fly in the wind, the knight attached it to the shaft of his lance or tied it around his helmet. That red sleeve was not a trivial piece of clothing; it was the mark of a victory, achieved or anticipated. When a lady offered her sleeve, she often offered much more. In sports, we still use the expression, "*remporter la manche ... et la belle*" (win the round ... and the lady).[43]

The Red Sleeve of Love

The lady who gives her sleeve to her escorting knight is not an invention of the Romantic period; it is well attested in medieval romances. It was a red sleeve, the color of love and the color of the costly gowns ladies wore to attend tournaments. The knight attached it to the top of his lance or, as here, to his helmet.

Der Dürner (unknown Swabian poet and knight), *Codex Manesse*, Zurich or Constance, c. 1300–1310. Heidelberg, University Library, Cod. Pal. Germ. 848, folio 397v.

At the end of the Middle Ages and the beginning of the modern era, red fruits could also constitute symbolic attributes of love, especially cherries. For the timid, offering cherries was a way of declaring one's love without having to use words. Cherries symbolized youth and springtime; the "time of cherries" was the time of love. The apple, an autumn fruit, is not always red, but it sometimes played a similar role when it was offered by a man. If it was offered by a woman, on the other hand, it often constituted a poisoned gift, in the image of Eve offering Adam the forbidden fruit. As for figs, with purple rather than red exteriors, they were charged with strong erotic connotations and directly evoked the female genitals. In the same vein, the pear, no matter what color, could symbolize male genitals. Lexical and language events provide a range of evidence for this until well into the nineteenth century; if a man was an exhibitionist he "showed his pear" (and that did not mean his face).[44]

Nevertheless, in the Middle Ages red could be less carnal and, like blue—the color of tenderness and fidelity between spouses—express forms of love that were more delicate, even romantic, if we may risk such an adjective for the feudal period. Used in this fairly rare way, red was combined with white. Once again, Chrétien de Troyes's *Le Conte du Graal* provides us with a magnificent example in one of most famous passages in all medieval literature. Sad and alone, Perceval is crossing a snowy plain one day and pauses to contemplate three drops of blood on the ground, shed by a goose whose neck has been pierced by a hawk. The red of this blood against the white of the snow reminds him of the bright young face and vermilion cheeks of his beloved Blanchefleur, whom he has left behind to seek adventure. That memory plunges him into a state of such deep melancholy that no companion can cure him.[45]

Red and white are presented together here; no combination of colors forms a more potent contrast for the medieval sensibility.

Blue versus Red

Dyers at Work

In order to dye in red, whether with madder, brazilwood, orcein, or kermes, the water in the vat had to be boiling hot and mordants had to be used abundantly.

Bartholomaeus Anglicus and Jean Corbechon, *Le Livres des Propriétés des Choses*, manuscript copied and painted in Brussels, 1482. London, British Library, Royal Manuscript 15 E. III, folio 269.

As the favorite color, admired and celebrated without peer for centuries, even millennia, red, in its full glory, was suddenly confronted with an unexpected competitor over the course of the twelfth century: blue. Disliked by the Romans, who saw it as the color of barbarians, blue remained inconspicuous during the early Middle Ages. Of course it could be seen here and there, especially on fabric, but it was not an important color, either on social and artistic levels or on religious and symbolic ones.

And then everything began to change. Between the mid-twelfth century and the first decades of the thirteenth century, blue experienced a remarkable quantitative and qualitative advance. It became a fashionable color, first in art and images, then later in dress and life at court. Henceforth blue dominated in enamel work, stained glass, and illuminated manuscripts, and served as the background color for coats of arms for the king of France and the legendary King Arthur. In the lexica of romance languages, its transformation was spectacular. Although it was very difficult to name blue in classical Latin, two words of non-Latin origin emerged for designating this color now gaining prominence. One was Germanic (*blau*/blue), the other Arabic (*lazurd*/azure). In all areas of social, artistic, and religious life, blue gradually came to be valued and began to compete with red, the first of the colors and the most beautiful until that time.

For the historian, the question is whether those changes were the result of technical progress in the area of pigments and dyes, or whether ideological changes brought about blue's spectacular rise. For centuries European dyers had been incapable of producing beautiful blue tones—that is, pure, dense, luminous tones that deeply penetrated the fabric fibers—all qualities they could easily obtain in the range of reds. Now, in a matter of two or three generations, they succeeded. Where do we find the origins and the causes of this change? Do they lie in the chemistry of pigments and dyes or rather in the new social and symbolic status of the color blue? How did blue's advancement begin?

Upon close examination, it seems that theological and ideological stakes preceded chemical and economic changes. The example of the Virgin, the first "person" in the West to appear frequently clothed in blue in images, constitutes important evidence. Until the eleventh century Mary could be dressed in any color, but it was almost always a dark shade: black, gray, brown, purple, dark blue, or green. The main idea was that it should be a color of affliction, a color of mourning, appropriate for the Virgin in

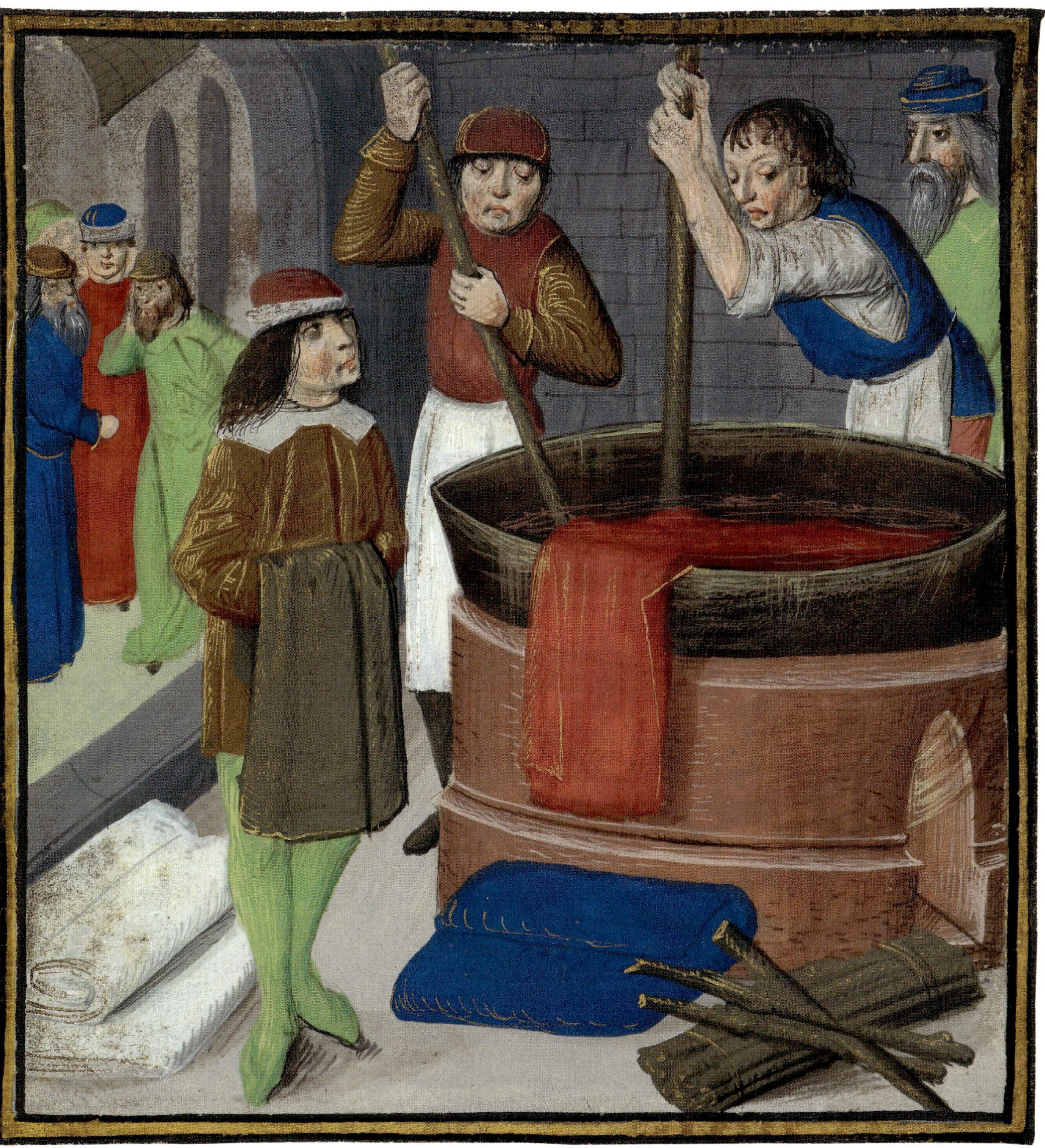

mourning for her son, dead on the Cross.[46] But after the year 1000, this palette shrank, and blue alone tended to fill the role as the attribute of mourning. Moreover, it became lighter and more attractive; from dull and dark it became purer, more luminous, and more saturated. This was the period when glass artists perfected the famous blue (with a cobalt base) for which the abbot Suger paid so dearly for the stained-glass windows of his new church in Saint-Denis, and which was used again a few years later at Chartres.[47] Similarly, in miniatures illuminators began systematically to paint the sky blue, which they had not always done before this time (far from it, in fact).

By appearing dressed in blue in images, the Virgin, queen of heaven, contributed to the advancement of this color. Kings began to imitate her, first the kings of France—Philip Augustus hesitantly, Saint Louis throughout the last part of his reign (1254–70)—then other kings of Western Christendom. Gradually, great lords and wealthy patricians did the same, in France, England, and the Iberian Peninsula. Only Germany and Italy resisted this new fashion, for the time being.

I have examined at length this "blue revolution" of the twelfth and thirteenth centuries elsewhere and do not wish to linger on it here.[48] Nevertheless, it must be noted how the dyeing trades were transformed by this change in taste and demand. For urban drapers, the new fashion helped to distinguish two different trade guilds henceforth: the dyers of red, who also dyed in yellow, and the dyers of blue, who also dyed in black and green. The two were now rivals. Similarly,

rich merchants of madder and kermes worried about the growing fortunes of woad merchants, a plant that grew in many areas and whose leaves had blue dyeing properties. Cultivating woad became a veritable farming industry in some regions (Picardy, Thuringia, and later Languedoc).[49] Local tradition maintains that the woad merchants of Picardy entirely financed the new cathedral in Amiens, rebuilt beginning in the 1220s. That is an exaggeration, but it underscores the fortunes to be made henceforth in the trading and manufacturing of blue.

One document is particularly revealing in the new economic war between red and blue: a contract signed in Strasbourg in 1256 between madder merchants and two glass masters from France. For a window to be placed in one of the cathedral chapels, the merchants ordered stained glass that told the edifying story of Theophilus, a monk who sold his soul to the Devil (after which the Virgin bought it back), and specified that the Devil be represented in blue on the glass in order to discredit the color. Their effort was in vain; the glassmakers obeyed, but their rendering was not enough to stimulate the madder trade or to slow the new rage for blue that was beginning to reach Alsace.

In the same period, a little farther east, in Thuringia, the cultivation of woad was in full expansion, so heavy was the dyers' demand for blue colorant. Woad merchants made fortunes to the detriment of madder merchants, whose revenues were declining everywhere. Madder merchants again tried to curb the new fashion by discrediting the color blue. Thus in Erfurt in 1265, they ordered a large

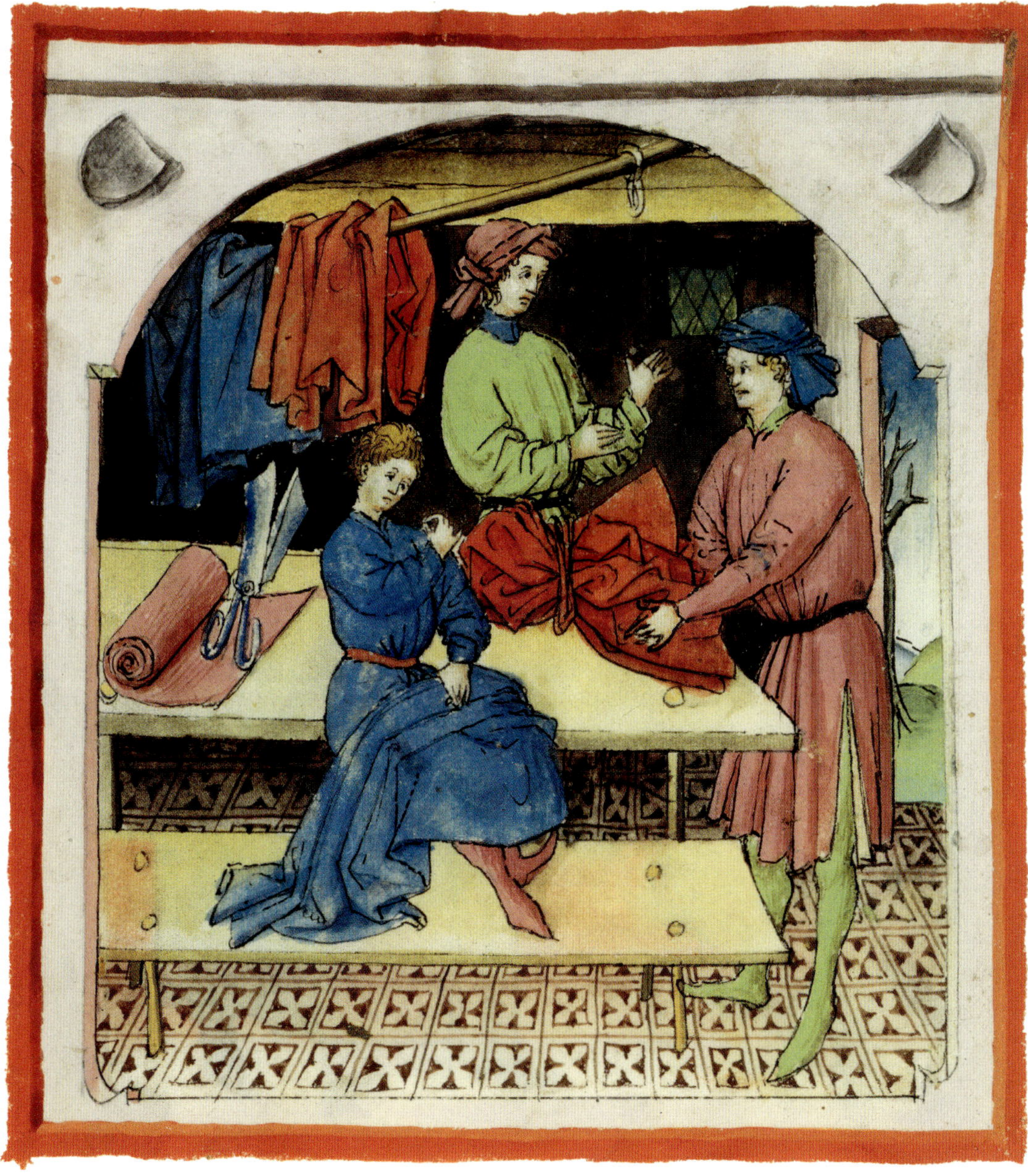

Tailor's Workshop

In fifteenth-century Germany, red clothing remained the most prized among the noblemen and patricians. But in France and Burgundy, as in Italy, blues and blacks began to compete with red.

Rhenish manuscript of a *Tacuinum sanitatis*, copied and painted mid-15th century, c. 1445–50. Paris, Bibliothèque Nationale de France, Latin manuscript 93333, folio 103.

mural for their chapel depicting the Devil tempting Christ; at their request, the Devil was painted blue.[50] The Devil would remain blue until the time of Martin Luther, but it seems to have done the new color more service than disservice. Henceforth, a blue devil was much less cause for fear than a red, black, or green devil.

The Wardrobes of Beautiful Florentine Ladies

Despite the rise in blue shades in royal and princely clothing throughout the thirteenth century, the taste for beautiful red fabrics did not disappear in France, England, or elsewhere. Competition between the two colors stimulated demand and production. In Germany and northern Italy, the preference for red lasted even into the early modern period among the nobility and patrician classes.

In the textile domain, beautiful reds were not called "vermilion," the term used for flowers, stones, and faces, but "scarlet." They were obtained not from madder, but from kermes, a very expensive dyestuff that we have already discussed with regard to dyeing in antiquity. This very costly product was of animal origin, but in the Middle Ages many dyers and most of their clients did not know that and believed it came from a plant.[51] Hence its common designation as a "seed" (*grana*, *granum*), referring to the dried insects, resembling cereal grains, that provided the dyestuff.

The etymology of the word *écarlate* (scarlet) remains much debated. Should it be seen as a word coming from the Persian and appearing in Western languages through the intermediary of the Spanish Arabic *saquirlat*? Or rather, more simply, as a translation of the Latin *sigillatus* (sealed), which became *sagilatus* and then *scarlatus*, describing the luxury woolen cloth bearing the seal of an authority that supervised and guaranteed the way it was produced and dyed? It is difficult to say, especially because the Arabic could itself have come through the Latin. What is clear, on the other hand, is that the term *escarlate* originally described all expensive fabrics of any color woven from very beautiful wool sheared many times.[52] But since those luxury fabrics were almost always red, *escarlate* and *rouge* became synonymous over the course of the thirteenth century, first in French and then in other languages (Spanish and Portuguese: *escarlat*; Italian: *scarlatto*; German: *scharlach*). *Écarlate* became a color adjective reserved for the most beautiful and expensive red textiles: pure, vivid, luminous, solid, saturated. In the Middle Ages this color could be obtained only with kermes; neither madder nor orcein, effective and desirable dyestuffs though they were, could achieve it.[53]

In order to appreciate the enduring taste for red tones in Italy among the highest classes, let us look at the example of Florence, a great city for cloth where all kinds of dyestuffs were

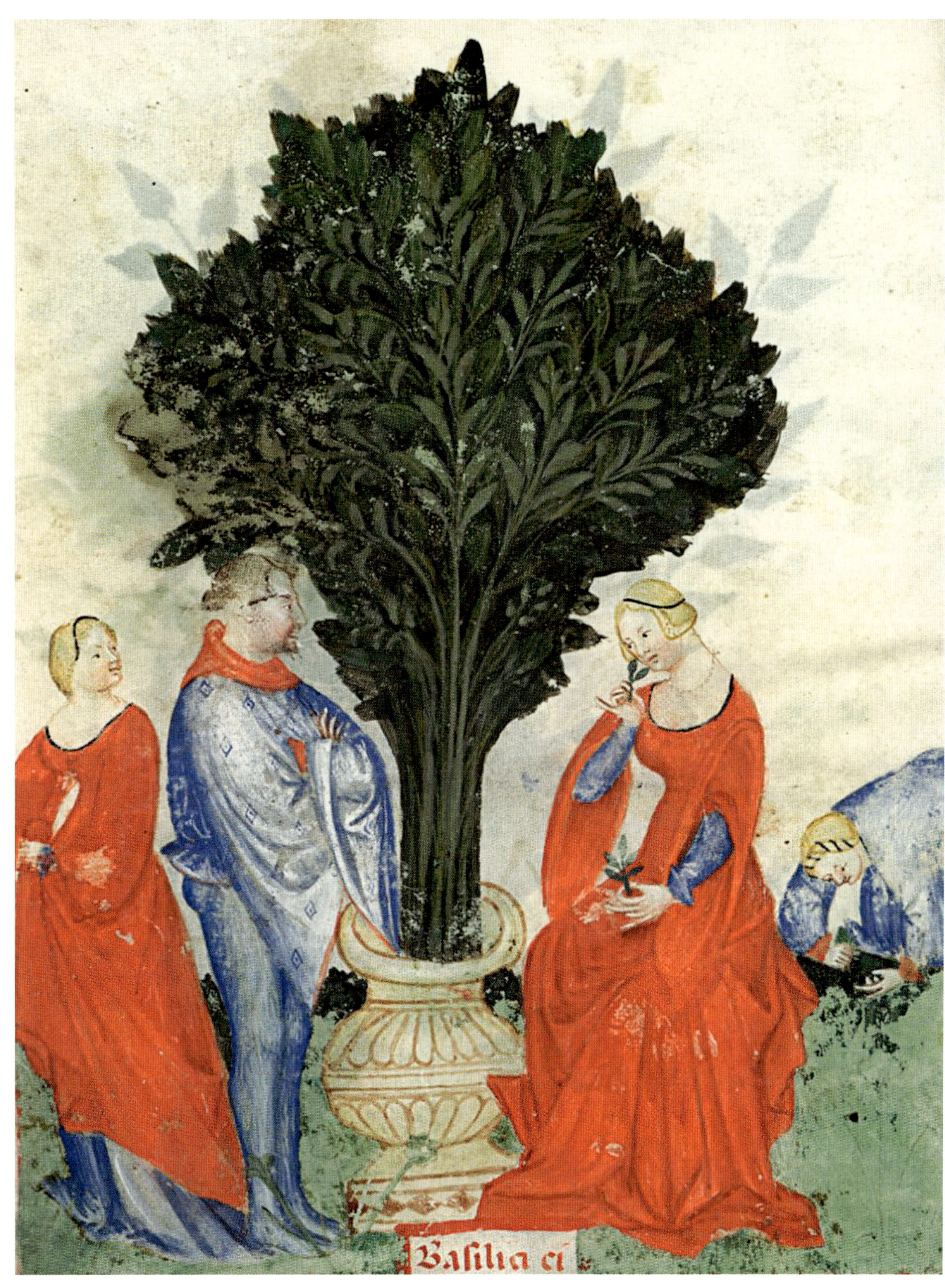

Elegant Young Women Dressed in Red

Despite the new fashion for blue and then black shades, in fourteenth-century Italy a beautiful dress remained a red dress. For any young woman, it was the color of elegance, love, and beauty. She wore red for every joyous or festive occasion and was often married in that same color.

Milanese manuscript of a *Tacuinum sanitatis*, **copied and painted late 14th century, c. 1390–1400. Paris, Bibliothèque Nationale de France, new Latin acquisitions manuscript 1673, folio 22v.**

Titian's Reds

Like Raphael, Titian was a great painter of reds, which he knew how to break down into very subtle shades, from purplish crimsons to the most delicate pinks, and including all the tones imitating flowers and stones. Even more than Rome, Florence, or Milan, at the beginning of the modern period Venice remained the European capital of red, in dyeing as well as painting.

Titian, detail from *The Miracle of the Speaking Infant*, 1511. Padua, Scuola del Santo, fresco of the Life of Saint Anthony of Padua.

used. Dyers there were strictly specialized, by colors, by textiles, and by dyes. The dyers in red, who were very dependent on mordants, were not licensed to dye in blue or black. Moreover, for the most part, they worked in different facilities according to whether they used madder or kermes. As for those who dyed silk, they owned their own workshops. The trade was compartmentalized and strictly regulated, but that did not prevent fraud or conflict, especially with regard to waters of the Arno River. If the red dyers went first, the river water became reddish and dirty, to the great fury of the blue dyers. But the opposite could also be true, making it necessary for municipal authorities to establish a calendar and a schedule organizing access to the river water. Other trades (tanners, washerwomen, fishermen) needed it as well, and wanted it to be clean, which was rarely the case.

What were the most popular colors for clothing in Florence and Tuscany in the period that concerns us? Reds and blues, of course, but especially reds, at least for women. Fortunately, an exceptional document has survived that gives us a good snapshot of the wardrobe of Florentine ladies in the years 1343–45, just before the Black Death eliminated three-quarters of the city's one hundred thousand inhabitants. This document, copied in a manuscript that was damaged when the Arno flooded in 1966, is entitled *Prammatica del vestire*.[54] What is it? A kind of general inventory of the wardrobes of Florentine women, or at least of those belonging to nobility, the patrician class, and the *popolo grasso*; an inventory carried out by many lawyers in order to implement recent sumptuary laws and to tax all

those who must be taxed.[55] The authorities did indeed want to reduce luxury expenditures (clothing, fabrics, jewels, dishes, furniture, equipment), because these were investments they considered unproductive. With regard to clothing, they also wanted to combat the new fashions, which they deemed indecent or outlandish (brightly colored dresses with low necklines, especially those that were too tight fitting). And finally, they wanted to maintain boundaries between the various social classes and categories; each should remain in its place and dress according to its condition, rank, fortune, and reputation. As always, these sumptuary laws were moralizing, reactionary, segregationist, misogynistic, and anti-youth.[56]

From autumn 1343 until spring 1345, all upper-class Florentines had to present their trousseaux before the lawyer for their district, who counted, named, and described the various pieces they contained. In their effortful, faltering, tortured Latin, these authorities provided maximum detail: textile materials (wool, silk, samite, velvet, cotton, canvas), shapes, cuts, dimensions, colors, decorations, linings, and accessories. This information was transcribed into various notebooks, now gathered into a single volume, in handwriting that was not very neat and, with the notations highly abbreviated, is difficult to read. In total, 3,257 notices inventoried 6,874 dresses and coats, 276 head ornaments, and a large number of accessories of all kinds, all of which belonged to more than 2,420 women, some of whom appeared multiple times. The whole thing constitutes a document unique in every way, not only for the history of clothing and society, but also for the history of vocabulary and description that it provides. Thanks are owed to the Italian State Archives for bravely undertaking to publish it in its entirety.[57]

Let us take advantage of this publication of nearly seven hundred pages to examine colors. They are many and various, but red shades clearly dominate, sometimes alone, sometimes combined with another color (in vertical halves, checks, stripes of all kinds), including yellows, greens, sometimes whites, more rarely blues or blacks. The great fashion for blacks, then beginning in Milan, would not reach Florence until the end of the century. With the help of a varied lexicon that mixed Latin and vernacular words, dialectical and technical terms, convoluted wording and neologisms, the lawyers strove to name with precision the different nuances of all those reds. There was a wide palette: light and dark reds; drab and bright reds; plain and mixed reds; faded, graying, desaturated reds; reds tending toward pink, orange, purple, russet, fawn, brown. Florentine dyers seemed to be able to make everything in the range of reds and to offer their clientele a much more diverse chromatic repertoire in this color than in any other. However abundant they were, blues and yellows were far from being so varied. It is a short step from there to the idea that supply responds to demand; the beautiful ladies of Florence loved red, all reds, on the eve of the Black Death.

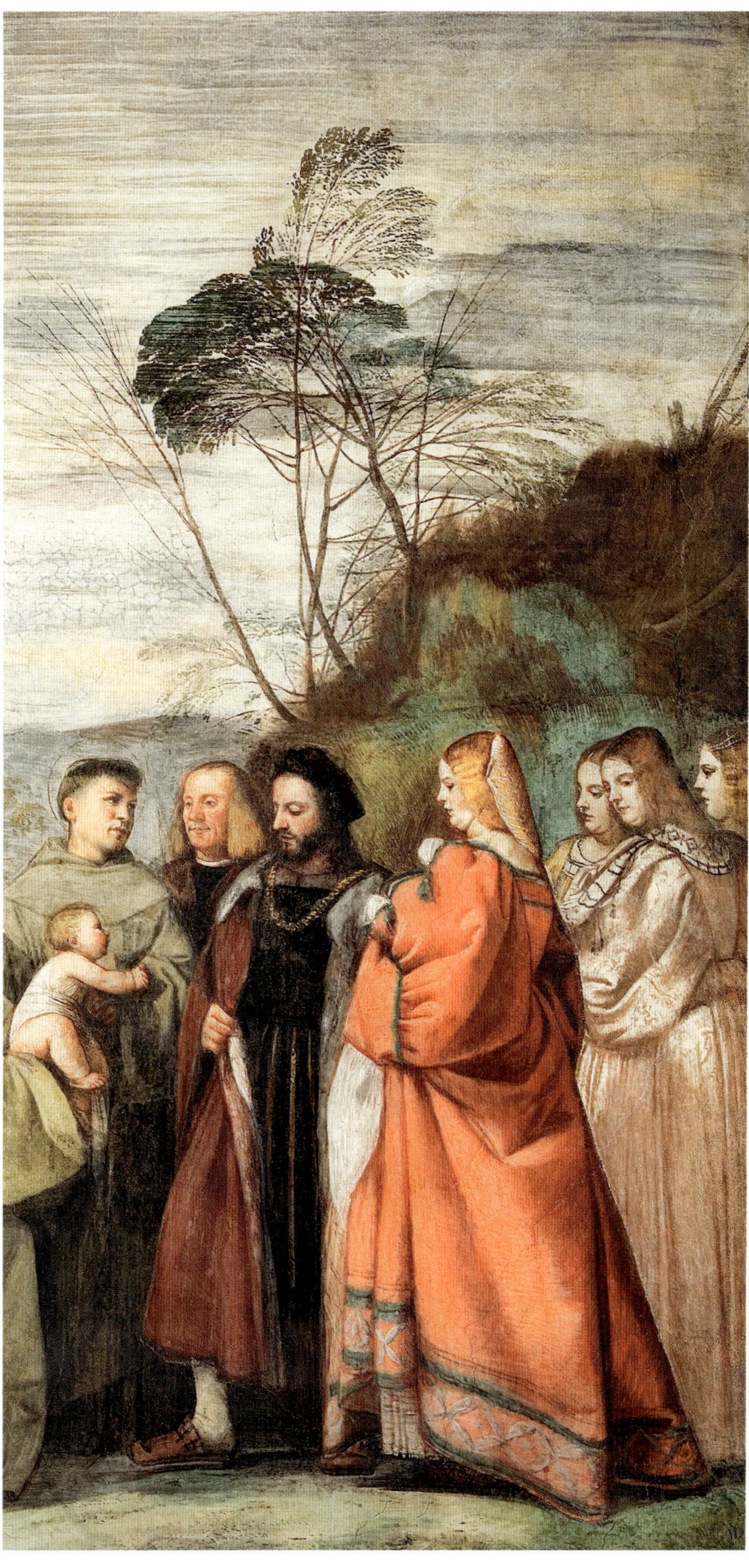

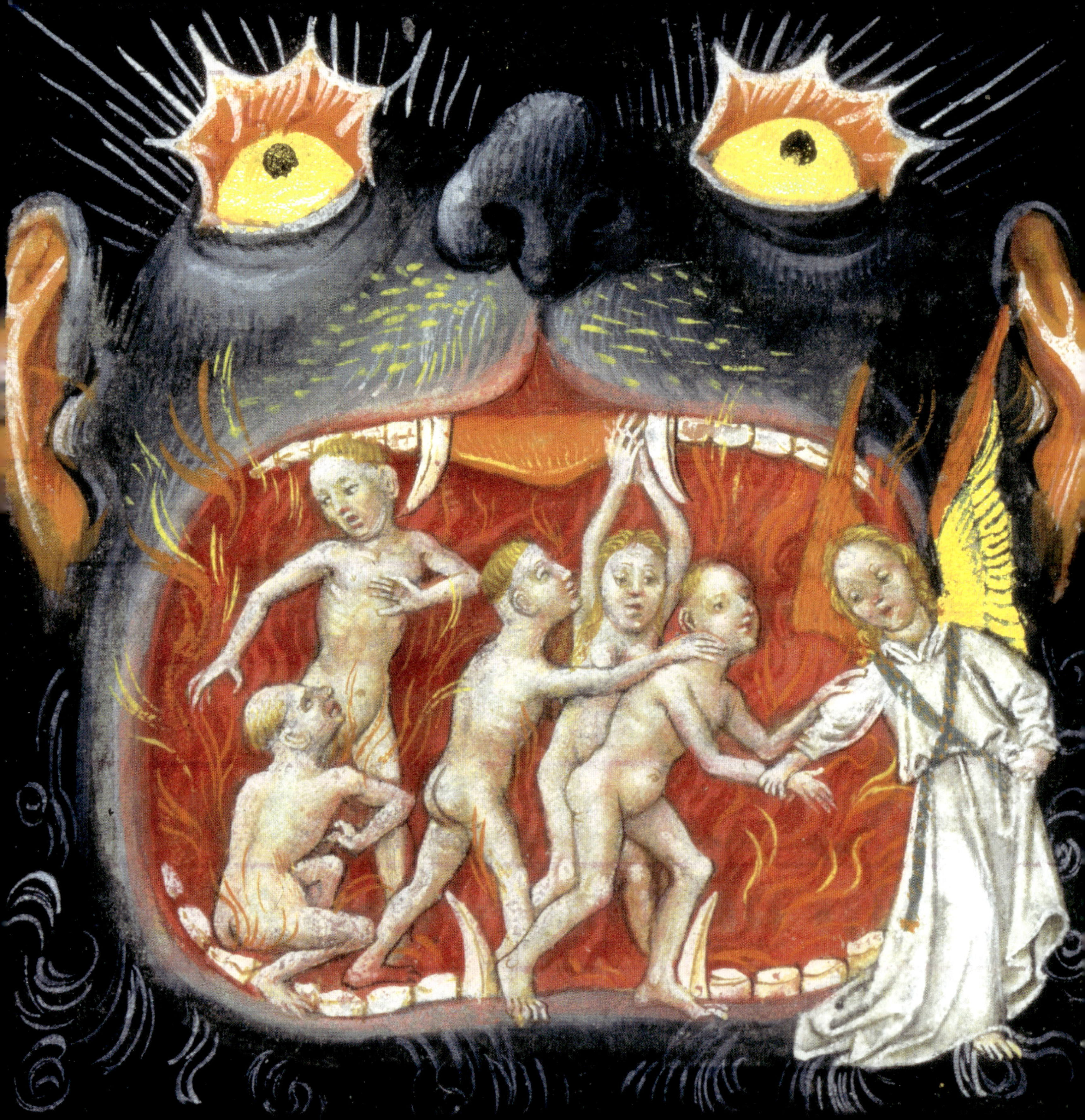

A CONTROVERSIAL COLOR

FOURTEENTH TO SEVENTEENTH CENTURIES

At the end of the Middle Ages, red entered a period of turbulence. Its status as the first color, the color par excellence, was beginning to be disputed and would be increasingly undermined in the centuries that followed. Not only was red facing competition in many areas from blue, a color henceforth more admired and favored, it also had to confront the rise in black tones, which were very much in vogue in courtly circles, where they embodied luxury and elegance in clothing for many long decades. In the area of dress, red was in decline, even if fabrics dyed with kermes and later with cochineal retained their prestige. The fashion was no longer so much for bright, pure, luminous reds, as it was in the feudal period, but for darker shades (crimson) or shades only bordering on red (pink, purple). Alternatively, certain red shades tending toward yellow or brown were rejected and associated with whatever evoked the flames of hell, original sin, and a whole parade of major vices, among them pride, falsehood, and lust. This was especially true for *roux* (russet), which seemed to combine into a single shade the worst of red and the worst of yellow, and even more so for *tanné* (tanned), a kind of brownish red or dark russet that many texts from the 1500s offer as "the ugliest of all the colors."[1]

Nevertheless the principal danger for red was not competition or changes in taste and sensibility. Essentially it lay in the new color codes propagated by sumptuary laws and the Protestant Reformation. According to those ethical standards, red was too garish and costly a color, indecent, immoral, depraved. Hence, by the end of the sixteenth century, it entered a phase of decline in various aspects of material culture and daily life, a trend that was reinforced by the Catholic Counter-Reformation, which tended to adopt a share of Protestant values in matters of everyday morality. At a time when the pope increasingly wore white, red hardly held the place of honor for a good Christian anymore.

A bit later, science itself came to confirm red's decline. With Isaac Newton's discovery of the color spectrum in 1666, a new classification system that the physics and chemistry of colors still relies upon today, red lost its place at the center of the chromatic scale, where it had been throughout antiquity and the Middle Ages. Now it was located at one end: an inglorious position for the former queen of colors, which seemed to have lost a share—but just one share—of its symbolic powers.

PAGE 94

The Souls of the Righteous Snatched from the Jaws of Hell

In the depths of hell, a place where red and black dominate, "a blazing furnace and an ocean of fire" (Rev. 20:10–15) burn perpetually. But that fire does not illuminate or consume human bodies; like salt, it preserves them in the darkness where their torments are eternal.

Hours of Catherine of Cleves, Utrecht, c. 1440. New York, Morgan Library and Museum, Manuscript 945, folio 107.

A Fire

When it is supposed to be more realistic, iconography diversifies the colors of fire and adds orange, yellow, white, and sometimes blue or even black to the red.

School of Hieronymus Bosch, detail from *Tondal's Vision*, c. 1520–25. Madrid, Museo Lázaro Galdiano.

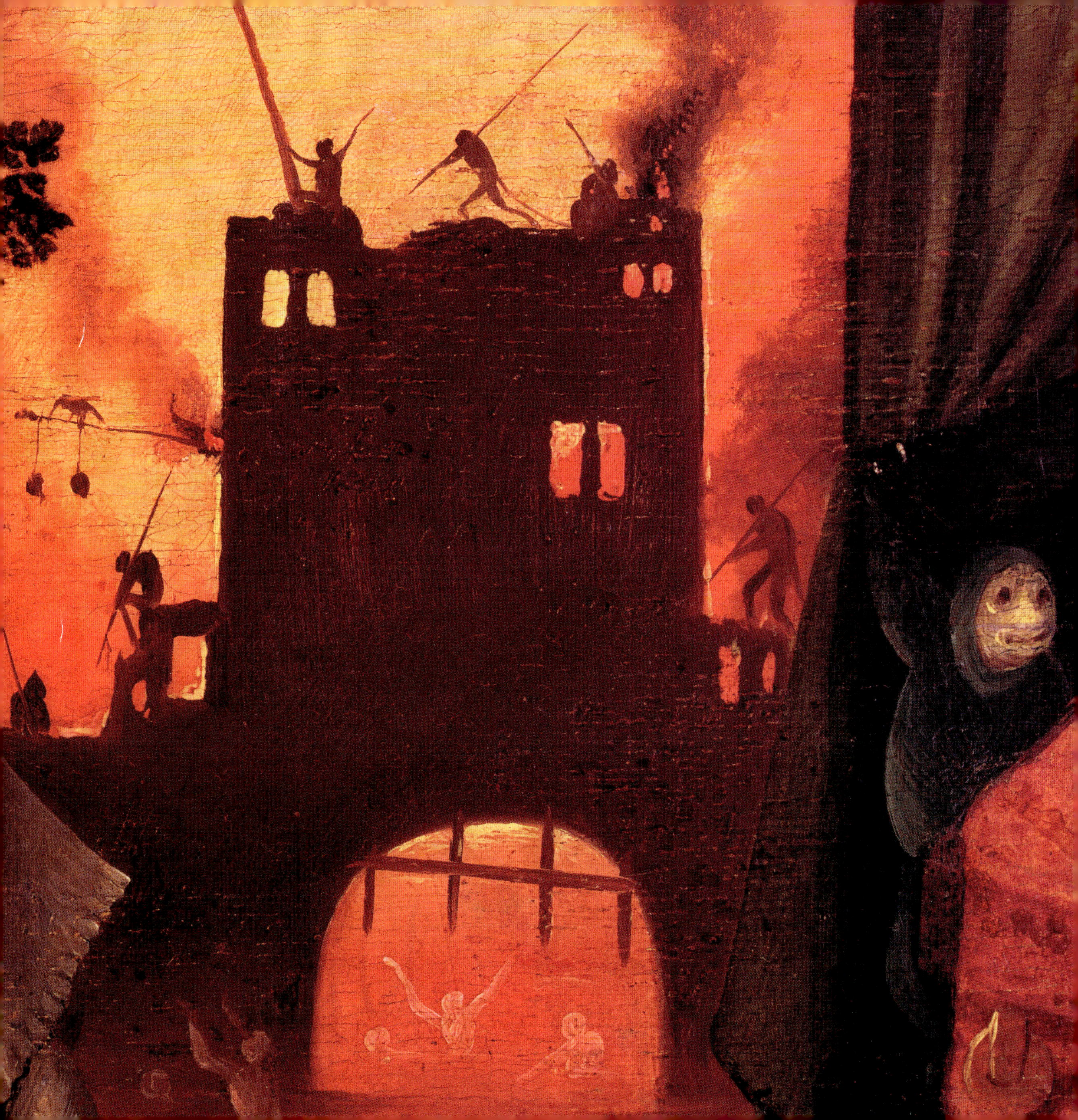

In the Flames of Hell

When it was seen in a bad light, Christian red was almost always associated with crimes of blood and the flames of hell. The Church Fathers devoted many commentaries to it, and the theologians who followed them associated it with many vices. When, over the course of the thirteenth century, the system of the seven deadly sins and their correspondences was definitively established, red was linked to four of them: pride (*superbia*), anger (*ira*), lust (*luxuria*), and sometimes gluttony (*gula*).[2] In the palette of vice, red was very much the dominant color. Only avarice (*avaritia*) and envy (*invidia*) escaped its grasp; green was the color for the first, yellow for the second. As for sloth, some considered only moral laziness (*acedia*) to be a deadly sin, others added physical idleness (*prigritia*) as well. Hence, authors wavered regarding the associated color: sometimes it was red, sometimes yellow, more rarely blue. Beyond this scholarly system of correspondences, whose influence on artistic and literary creation was not inconsiderable, red was more commonly associated with everything that evoked violence, debauchery, treachery, and murder.[3]

When they died, sinners went to hell, a place of terror located at the center of the earth, and a place entirely red and black, if we are to believe the increasingly numerous images representing it that way after the year 1000, when the theme of the Last Judgment flourished. The black was that of the darkness that reigned there permanently; the red evoked "the ocean of fire and the blazing furnace" (Rev. 20:10–15) that occupied most of the space. Fires burned there perpetually without giving light; they did not reduce the bodies of the damned to ashes, but smoked and preserved them so that their torture would be eternal. In the Romanesque period, punishments for two sinners in particular were presented by artists: the miser, hung by the purse to which he is forever bound, and the adulteress, whose breasts and vulva are devoured by snakes and toads. Subsequently, the various sins were all represented, and the forms of torture became diversified. In miniatures, even if hell was sometimes polychromatic, red and black remained the dominant colors.[4] They were found on the bodies of the demons who tortured the damned and hurled them into a boiling cauldron, and on the body of the Devil himself. The Devil was most often black, or black with a red head, or greenish, although that came later. For all authors, his eyes were small and red like burning coals and his hair stood on end like the flames in the infernal furnace. In all domains the Devil maintained obligatory ties with red.[5]

For medieval culture, the combination of red and black was particularly negative. That is why it was found on the body of Satan and in that sort of abyss that represented hell, such as the immense maw of the monster Leviathan, evoked in the Bible in the book of Job (Job 41:19). Elsewhere, the combination of red and black was avoided, a pairing of colors that the medieval eye seems to have found intolerable. In clothing, it was rare before the fifteenth century and considered ugly and a bad omen.[6] In coats of arms, it was forbidden. Heraldry divided the six heraldic colors into two groups: in the first appeared white and yellow; in the second, red, blue, green, and black. A strict and restrictive rule that existed from the time coats of arms appeared (that is, by the mid-twelfth century) forbade the juxtaposition or superimposition of two colors belonging to the same group. This rule probably resulted from issues of visibility, as coats of arms originated on the battle and tournament fields and were made to be seen from a distance. Subsequently, no matter what their use, violations never exceeded 1 percent of cases.[7] Putting red (*gueules*) over or beside black (*sable*) was forbidden and thus never encountered in actual coats of arms. Only a few particularly negative literary figures (traitorous knights, cruel and bloodthirsty lords, heretical prelates) might be given coats of arms with these two colors overlapping. Such a combination would highlight their evil natures.

Nevertheless, it is undoubtedly in the game of chess that this refusal to combine red and

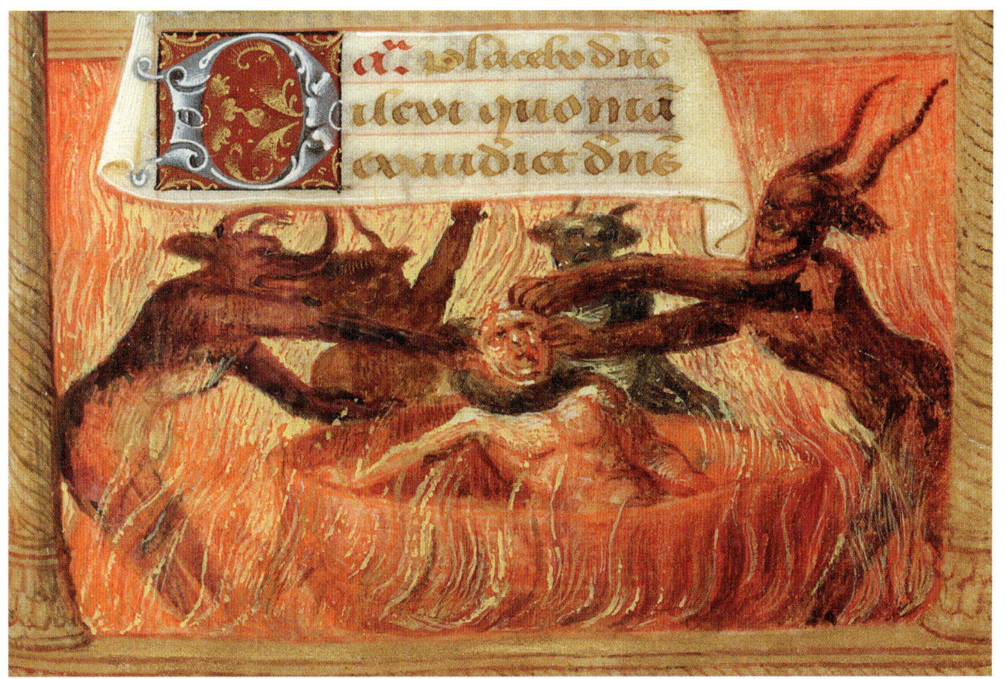

The Fiery Furnace

According to medieval beliefs, the tortures suffered in hell corresponded to the sins committed on earth. Here, the evil rich man in the flames seems to be strangled by his purse string.

Heures Dites de Jules II, detail, late 15th century. Chantilly, Musée Condé, manuscript 78, folio 130.

Game of Chess

For a long time, the Western game of chess pitted a white side against a red side. At the end of the Middle Ages, the red side began to be replaced gradually by a black side. The scene represented in this *cassone* panel corresponds to a period of transition: the chessboard squares are still white and red, but black pieces have already made their appearance. A *cassone* is an Italian wedding chest meant to adorn a marital chamber; the groom had it decorated by an artist before giving it to his bride, so that she could fill it with items from her dowry.

Painted *cassone* attributed to Liberale da Verona, c. 1470–75. New York, Metropolitan Museum of Art.

black appears earliest and most obviously. When the game was created in northern India about the sixth century CE, it featured a red side and a black side, a strong and significant opposition throughout Asia, where red was the main counter to black. Two centuries later, the Arabic Islamic culture retained those two colors when it adopted the game and then spread it throughout the Mediterranean world; making red and black confront one another on the chessboard was relevant and consistent for that culture. On the other hand, when the game arrived in Europe just before the year 1000 it had to be Westernized: not only did the nature and the movement pattern of each piece need to be reconsidered, but so did the colors of the two sides. Red against black did not in the least register as a pair of opposites in the feudal Christian mind. Here were two colors that maintained no relationship with each other, not even one of opposition; combining them, even if only on a game board, had something diabolical about it. Over the course of the eleventh century the black was thus changed to white, and on the chessboard a red camp and a white camp confronted each other, as those colors were then considered to be most in opposition, both on the material and the symbolic levels. That was the case until the fifteenth century, when the modern game gradually developed, opposing a white side to a black side.[8]

The red charged with punishing crimes and making sinners atone was not only present in hell's furnace. It was also there in judicial rituals. In the last chapter we mentioned the red of the judge's robes, common in medieval images, and the red of the cap and gloves of the executioner. Both correspond to very real dress practices that extended well beyond the framework of the Middle Ages. In fact they can be linked in the modern period to the red clothing and headgear worn by the condemned, galley slaves, convicts, and deportees until well into the nineteenth century, as well as the wheelbarrows and carts, symbolically painted red, that carried the guilty to their place of torture. Red was the color of both the offense and the punishment. Both usages of red were common in all countries, but especially in France at the time of the Terror, in 1793–94. We find it again in branding practices that consisted of marking with hot iron, as for livestock, convicts who escaped the death penalty but whose bodies had to retain a trace of their felony; or even more simply in the sole fact of having one's name written in red letters in a trial book, thus signifying that one has been found suspect and thus condemnable. Examples in central Europe abound beginning in the seventeenth century.

All these practices associating red with punishment by appealing to fire and bloodshed have a long history. Many examples can already be found in the Bible, and we can observe them extending into the most contemporary of our own practices, certainly less radical and bloody but continuing to make red the color of punishment. Hence, schoolchildren's exercises are corrected in red ink, and warning notices or threats of punishment posted in red letters. And in certain cases, a "red list" catalogs those prohibited from writing checks, using credit cards, fulfilling civic duties, or performing certain jobs.[9]

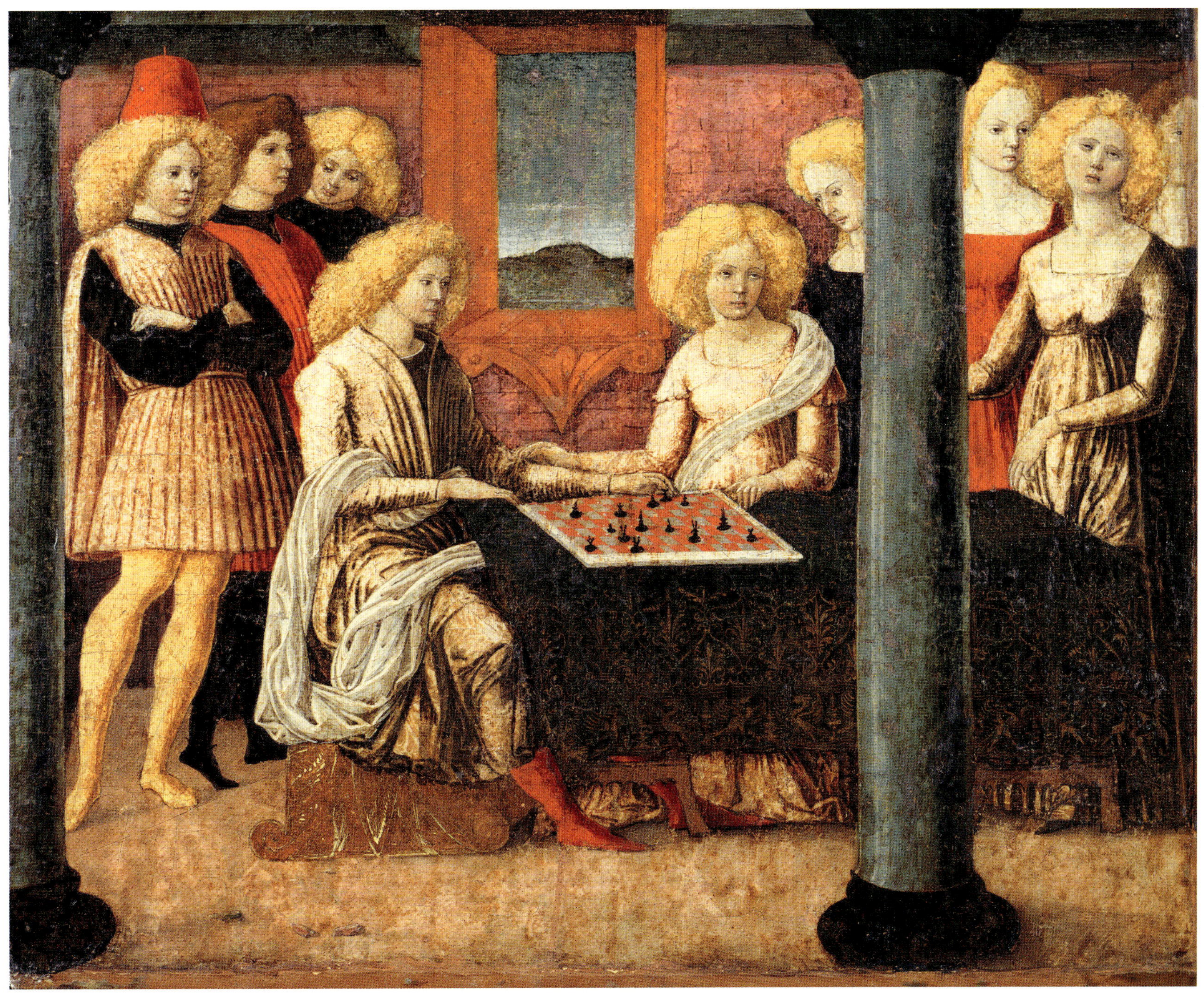

Judas,
the Redhead

Cain Killing Abel

Perpetrator of history's first murder, Cain is sometimes given red hair, a recurrent attribute of traitors, apostates, and criminals.

Detail from mid-12th century *Parc Abbey Bible*, Louvain, 1147–48. London, British Library, Manuscript Add. 14788, folio 6v.

Let us remain with the Middle Ages and shift from red to russet. This particular shade of the color, which today we would say tends toward dark orange, underwent a considerable loss in status beginning in the twelfth century, eventually embodying a great number of vices all on its own. In texts and images, one figure became the incarnation of that infamous russet color: Judas.

Not a single canonical text from the New Testament, or even from the Apocrypha, tells us about the physical appearance of the traitor apostle. Hence representations of him in early Christian and medieval art are not characterized by a single specific trait or attribute. In depictions of the Last Supper, however, efforts were made to distinguish him from the other apostles, differentiating him somehow by his position, height, or attitude. It was not until after the year 1000 that his red hair and beard appeared and slowly took hold, first in miniatures, then in other visual mediums. Originating in the countries of the Rhine and Meuse, this iconographic custom gradually swept a large part of Christian Europe. By the end of the Middle Ages and the beginning of the modern period, Judas's red hair and beard had become his most commonly recurring attributes.[10]

Even so, Judas's attributes were many: short in height, contorted or brutish masklike features, dark skin, hook nose, thick mouth, dark lips (because of the kiss of betrayal), halo absent or dark in color, yellow robe, secretive or awkward gestures, left hand holding the stolen fish or purse with the thirty silver pieces, demon or toad entering his mouth, later a dog at his side. Like Christ, Judas could not *not* be identified. One after the other, each century provided him with his retinue of attributes, within which each artist was free to select those most in keeping with his own iconographic concerns, artistic ambitions, or

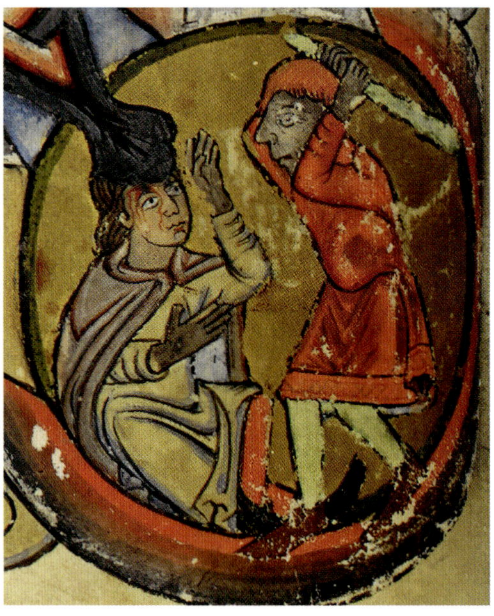

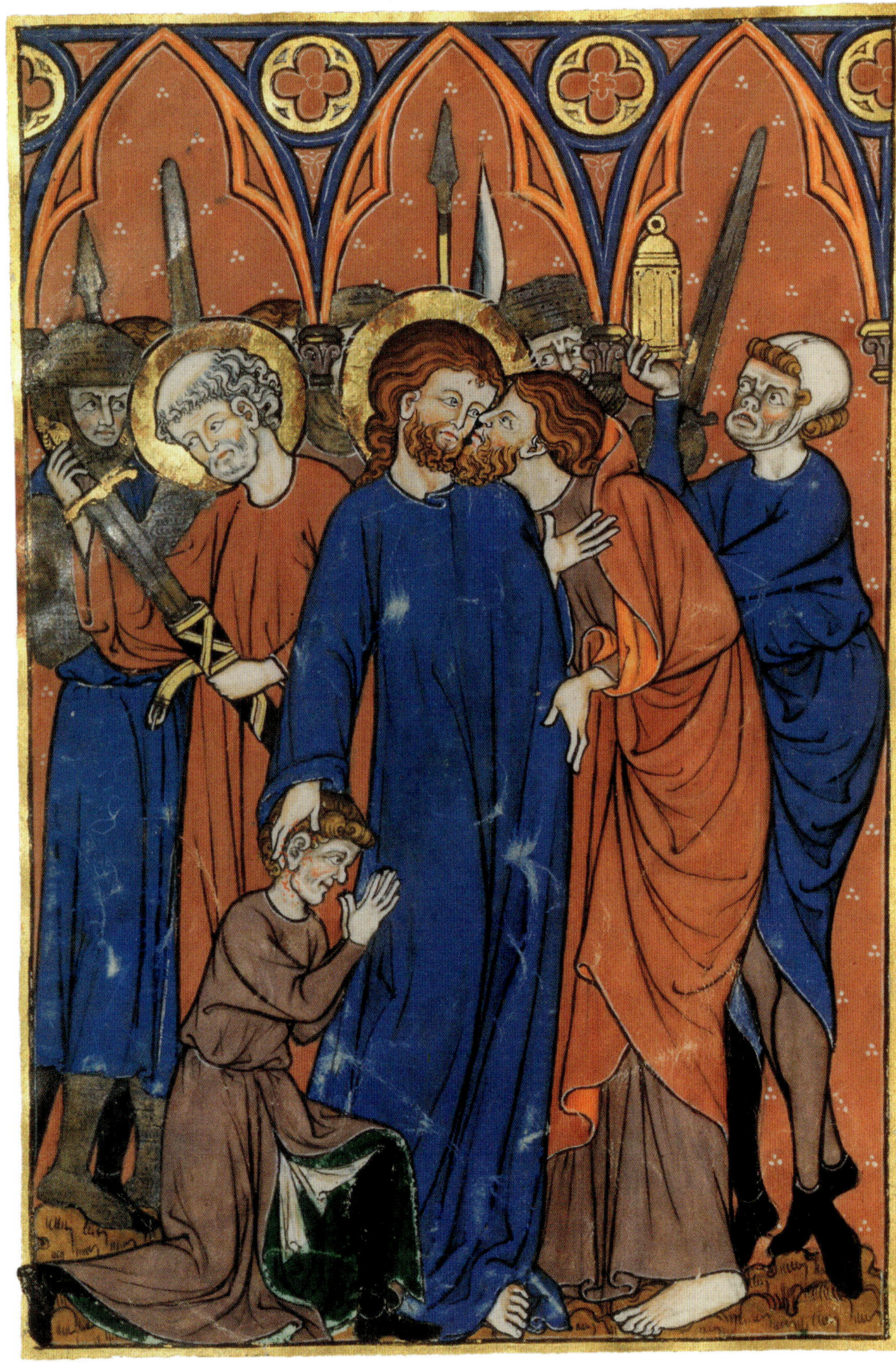

The Kiss of Betrayal

Medieval images often attribute red hair to Judas, a sign of his evil nature. In the scene of the kiss of betrayal, it is not unusual for a kind of chromatic osmosis to take place between the treacherous disciple and his victim; on the eve of his arrest, Jesus himself is shown with red hair and beard.

Le Livre d'Images de Madame Marie, Hainaut, c. 1285–90. Paris, Bibliothèque Nationale de France, new French acquisitions manuscript 16251, folio 33v.

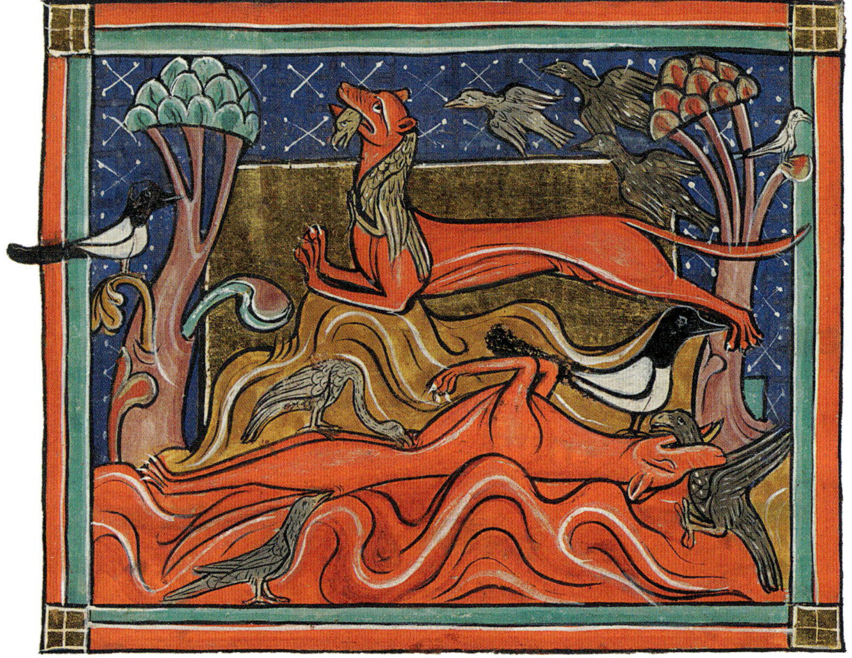

Wily Fox

With its red coat, the fox is the animal that most embodies trickery and deceit. Here we see it playing dead and letting the birds approach its body, so it can more easily seize one of them in its jaws and carry it off to devour it.

Latin Bestiary, c. 1240. Oxford, Bodleian Library, Bodley Manuscript 764, folio 26.

symbolic intentions.[11] Nevertheless one attribute is nearly always present from the mid-thirteenth century on: red hair.

Judas did not have a monopoly on this trait however. In the art of the late Middle Ages, a certain number of traitors and rebels could also be redheads. One example is Cain, who murdered his brother Abel: in the symbolic typology drawing parallels between the New and Old Testaments, he is presented as a pre-figuration of Judas.[12] Another is Ganelon, the traitor in *The Song of Roland*, who, out of vengeance and jealousy, willingly sends Roland (his own relative) and all his companions to their deaths.[13] And Mordred, the traitor in the tales of the Round Table: King Arthur's son through incest, he betrays his father, and this

act of treachery prompts the collapse of the whole Arthurian universe. The same trait represents rebel sons, disloyal brothers, usurping uncles, adulterous women, and all those who engage in dishonest or criminal acts.[14] To this list we must add two animal figures, literary heroes of the tales named after them: Reynard, the rebellious and quarrelsome fox, and Fauvel, the crowned horse embodying all the vices.[15] Both of them have red coats, a sign of their hypocrisy and treachery.

Of course, in the thousands of images left to us from the thirteenth, fourteenth, and fifteenth centuries, all these figures are not always redheads, far from it. But having red hair constitutes one of their most remarkable iconographic features, to the point that gradually this red hair was sometimes extended to other categories of outcasts and reprobates: heretics, Jews, Muslims, Cagots (a persecuted minority from the French-Spanish border region), lepers, cripples, beggars, vagrants, the poor and displaced of all kinds. In images, red hair color joins the red or yellow (or even red and yellow) clothing marks and insignia that individuals of those same social categories were actually obliged to wear in certain cities or regions of Western Europe beginning in the thirteenth century.[16] It seems to be the first sign of exclusion or infamy.

The shameful nature of redness was not a medieval creation however. It came to the Christian West by way of a triple heritage: biblical, Greco-Roman, and Germanic. In the Bible, if neither Cain nor Judas are redheads, other figures are, and, with perhaps only one exception, they are negative figures in one way or another. First there is Esau, the twin

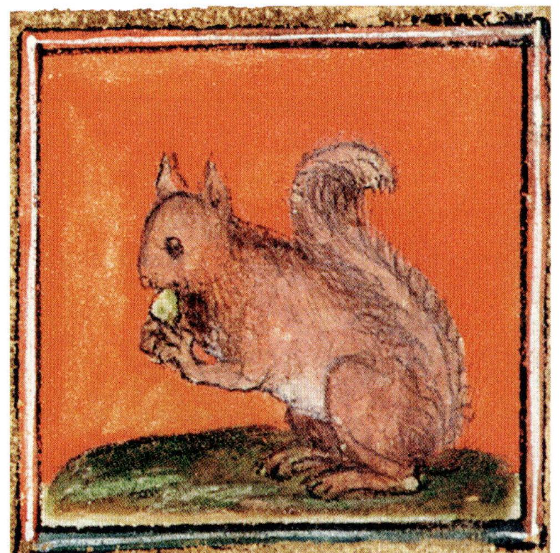

brother of Jacob, who from birth was "red and hairy as a bear," Genesis tells us (Gen. 25:25). Crude and impetuous, Esau willingly sells his brother his birthright for a dish of lentils, and despite his repentance, he finds himself excluded from his father's blessing and forced to leave the Promised Land.[17] Then there is Saul, the first king of Israel, the end of whose reign is marked by a morbid jealousy toward David, a jealousy that leads to madness and suicide (1 Sam. 9:2–3).[18] Finally there is Caiaphas, the high priest of Jerusalem who presides over the Sanhedrin during the trial of Jesus and who is as red as the creatures of Satan are red-haired or red in the Apocalypse.[19] The only exception is David, described in the book of Samuel as "red-haired, with a bright look and beautiful bearing" (1 Sam. 16:12).[20] This is a case of the transgression of a value scale, as we encounter in all symbolic systems; for the system to function effectively there must be a safety valve, an exception. David is that exception.

In Greco-Roman traditions, red hair was also seen in a bad light. Greek mythology, for example, places it on the head of Typhon, a monstrous creature, rebel son of Earth, enemy of the gods and of Zeus in particular. Diodorus Siculus, Greek historian from the first century BCE, tells how "formerly" redheaded men were sacrificed to Typhon to assuage his anger. This legend may perhaps have come from pharaonic Egypt, where Seth, a god often likened to the principle of Evil, was also considered to be redheaded and to receive sacrifices of young men with the same color hair, according to Plutarch.[21] Religious cults were less bloody in Rome, but redheads were no less maligned. Thus the word *rufus*, as we have seen, was both a nickname tinged with ridicule and one of the most common insults. It remained so throughout the Middle Ages, especially in monastic circles, where it was commonplace for monks to call each other *rufus* or *subrufus* (reddish).[22] In Roman theater, red hair or red wings attached to masks denoted ugly men and buffoons. Having red

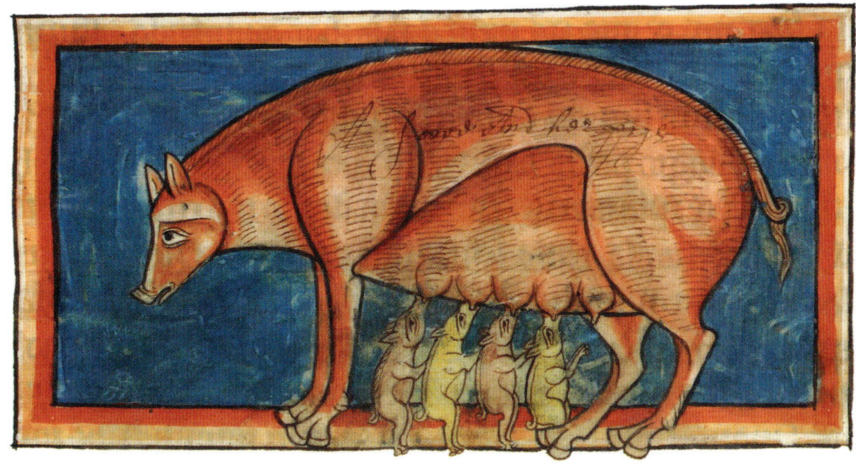

Red-Haired Witch

According to the traditions of the late Middles Ages and early modern period, witches had green teeth and red hair. They created all kinds of potions to help them bewitch the men they wanted to lure to the sabbat. In medieval recipes for love potions, as for poisons, two plants are always present: valerian and St. John's wort.

Anonymous artist, *Love Potion*, lower Rhine valley, c. 1470–80. Leipzig, Museum der bildenden Künste.

hair was degrading or ridiculous, as the poet Martial recalls toward the end the first century in two of his *Epigrams*:

> Red-haired, black-faced, short-footed, box-eyed, it's a great achievement, Zolius, if you're a good fellow.

> I am a jest of the potter, mask of a red-haired Batavian. The face you mock, a boy fears.[23]

Ancient and medieval treatises on physiognomy—mostly inherited from a fourth century BCE text attributed to Aristotle—make similar remarks but often go further than physical disgrace and ridiculous appearance. They present redheads as cruel and hypocritical beings, a tradition that would continue in the West until the modern period. When a comparison with an animal is proposed, it is always the fox, the most treacherous of all animals, to which the redheaded man is compared:

> Blonds are proud and magnanimous because they take after the lion. Brunets are strong and solitary because they take after the bear. Redheads are cunning and wicked because they take after the fox.[24]

In the Germano-Scandinavian world, where a priori one would expect that redheads, more numerous there than elsewhere, would be better respected, it was very much the same story. The most violent and formidable god, Thor, had red hair, as did Loki, the demon of fire, a destructive and evil spirit, father of the most horrible monsters. The German imagination—like that of their cousins the Celts—did not differ in the least from the Hebrew, Greek, or Roman one: to be redheaded was to be full of vices and cruelty.[25]

Inheriting this same tradition from all sides, the Christian Middle Ages could only embrace and intensify it. Nevertheless, its originality seems to lie in the special association of red hair with lying and betrayal. Of course, as in antiquity, to be redheaded was still to be cruel, vicious, or ridiculous; but over the course of the centuries during the Middle Ages, it came to mean especially being false, cunning, dishonest, deceitful, disloyal, treacherous, or renegade. This is echoed in many proverbs that offer warnings about redheaded men and women: "in them, there is no faith" (it is impossible to trust them).[26] And that is to say nothing of the superstitions that, by the end of the Middle Ages, deemed it a bad omen to cross the path of a redheaded man and took all women with red hair to be witches or prostitutes.[27]

For a long time, historians, sociologists, and anthropologists have tried to explain this rejection of redheads in Western traditions. To do so, they have proposed various hypotheses, including very debatable ones, such as calling upon biology to present red hair and freckles as an accident of pigmentation tied to a form of "ethnic degeneracy." What is "ethnic degeneracy"? Historians remain perplexed by such falsely scientific explanations.[28] For them, red hair's disrepute is a social attitude; in every society, including the Celtic and Scandinavian ones, the redhead is first of all someone unlike others (blonds and brunets), someone who belongs to a minority and who causes disorder, anxiety, or scandal.[29] Being different always comes with the risk of exclusion.

Judas, the redhead par excellence, combines in his person the negative aspects of two colors: red and yellow.[30] He was the red of the blood of Christ, whom he betrayed, as this etymological word play, popular in Germany in the late Middle Ages, reminds us: his nickname *Iskariot*—"the man from Cairoth"—could be understood as *ist gar rot*, "who is all red." But through his treason he was equally permeated with yellow, the usual attribute for dishonesty and disloyalty. That is why in images he is wearing a yellow gown or piece of clothing, as all traitors do. Over the course of the centuries, yellow continued its decline. Whereas in Rome it played an important role in religious rituals and was a valued color in both masculine and feminine clothing, during the Middle Ages it was gradually abandoned, disparaged, and eventually condemned. Renegades, apostates, relapsed heretics, and falsifiers of all kinds were regularly dressed in yellow at the stake. Even their houses were symbolically painted that color.

Yellow is still disliked even today, and always comes in last among the six basic colors (blue, green, red, white, black, yellow) in opinion polls of favorite colors.[31] That rejection dates from the Middle Ages; Judas, the false apostle, was its principal agent and first victim.

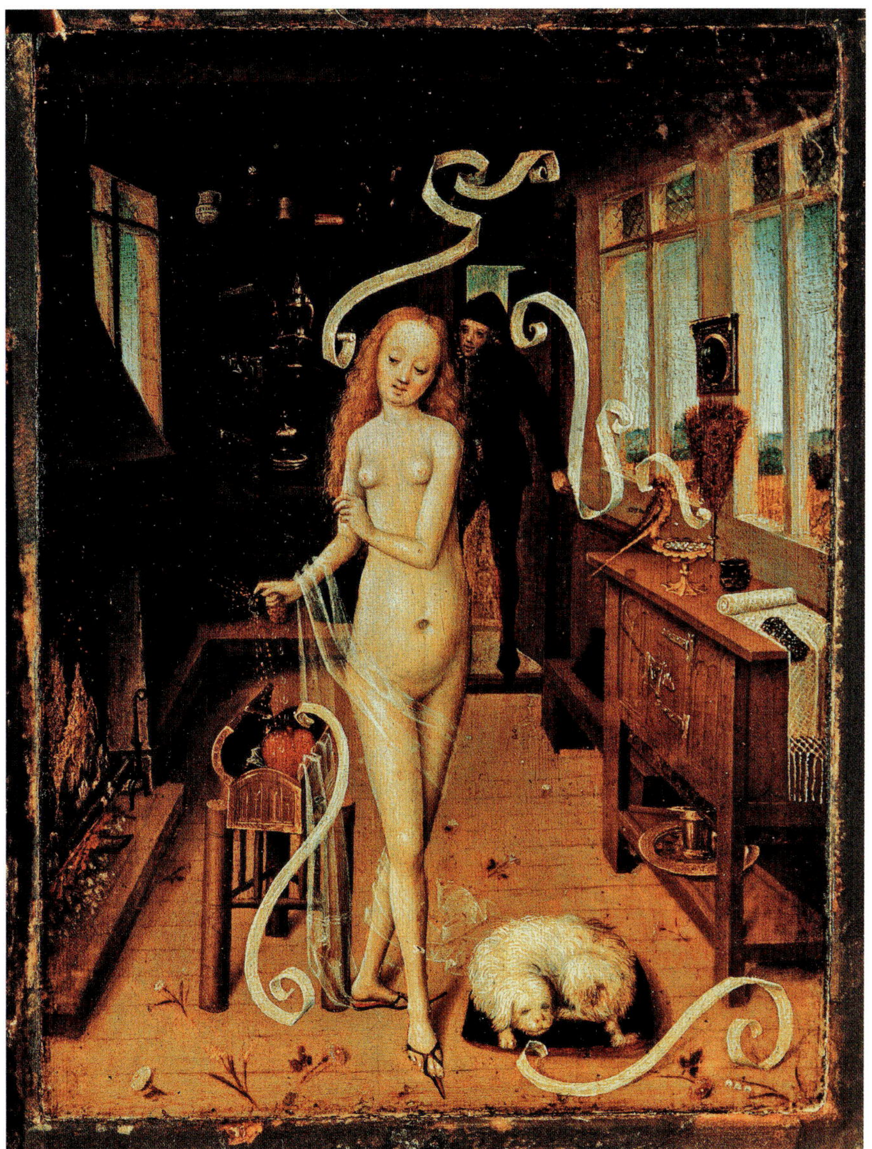

Hatred of Red

At the dawn of the modern period, sumptuary laws and decrees on dress issued by civil authorities proliferated, notably in Germany and Italy. Like the aforementioned *Prammatica del vestire* of 1343, regarding the rich patricians of Florence, those laws and decrees fulfilled a triple function, economic, moral, and social.[32] First they aimed to combat luxury expenditures and nonproductive investments. Second they sought to fight new clothing fashions considered frivolous, scandalous, or indecent. Finally and most important, they undertook to reinforce barriers between the different social classes and make sure that each, in appearance and lifestyle, remained in its place.

Colors were of great importance with regard to clothing. Some were forbidden to certain social classes or categories, while others were mandated. In both cases, red came at the top of the list. The color was often imposed upon those who practiced professions or occupations that relegated them to the margins of the social order. That was the case with prostitutes, who, from the fourteenth to seventeenth centuries in many Western cities, were required to wear a piece of clothing (dress, hood, scarf, aglet) in a garish color to distinguish them from honest women. That color was often red; the oldest example dates from 1323 in Milan.[33] But at one time or another and in one town or another, other professions and social categories were affected by such measures and required to identify themselves through a red insignia. As we have already discussed, this list included butchers, executioners, Cagots, lepers, simpletons, drunks, various kinds of convicts and outcasts, and non-Christians: Jews and Muslims.[34]

When red was not required but rather forbidden, it was not because it was too vivid or immodest a color but because of the dyestuff that produced it. Fabric and clothing dyed with the most expensive kermes (*granum preciosissimum*) were reserved for high nobility or the upper patrician classes. Other social classes had to make do with less costly dyes, such as madder, brazilwood, orcein, various lichens, or "common seed" (lesser-quality kermes). The distinctive and prestigious kermes red has a long history, from the Paleolithic to the contemporary period.

In the sixteenth century, the Protestant Reformation establishment declared war on colors, or at least on those it considered too vivid or garish. Hence it became heir to the sumptuary laws and religious codes of the late Middle Ages. Gradually, in all domains, it gave priority to the black-gray-white axis, more dignified than "papist polychromy" and more in keeping with the culture of the printed book and engraving, then coming into

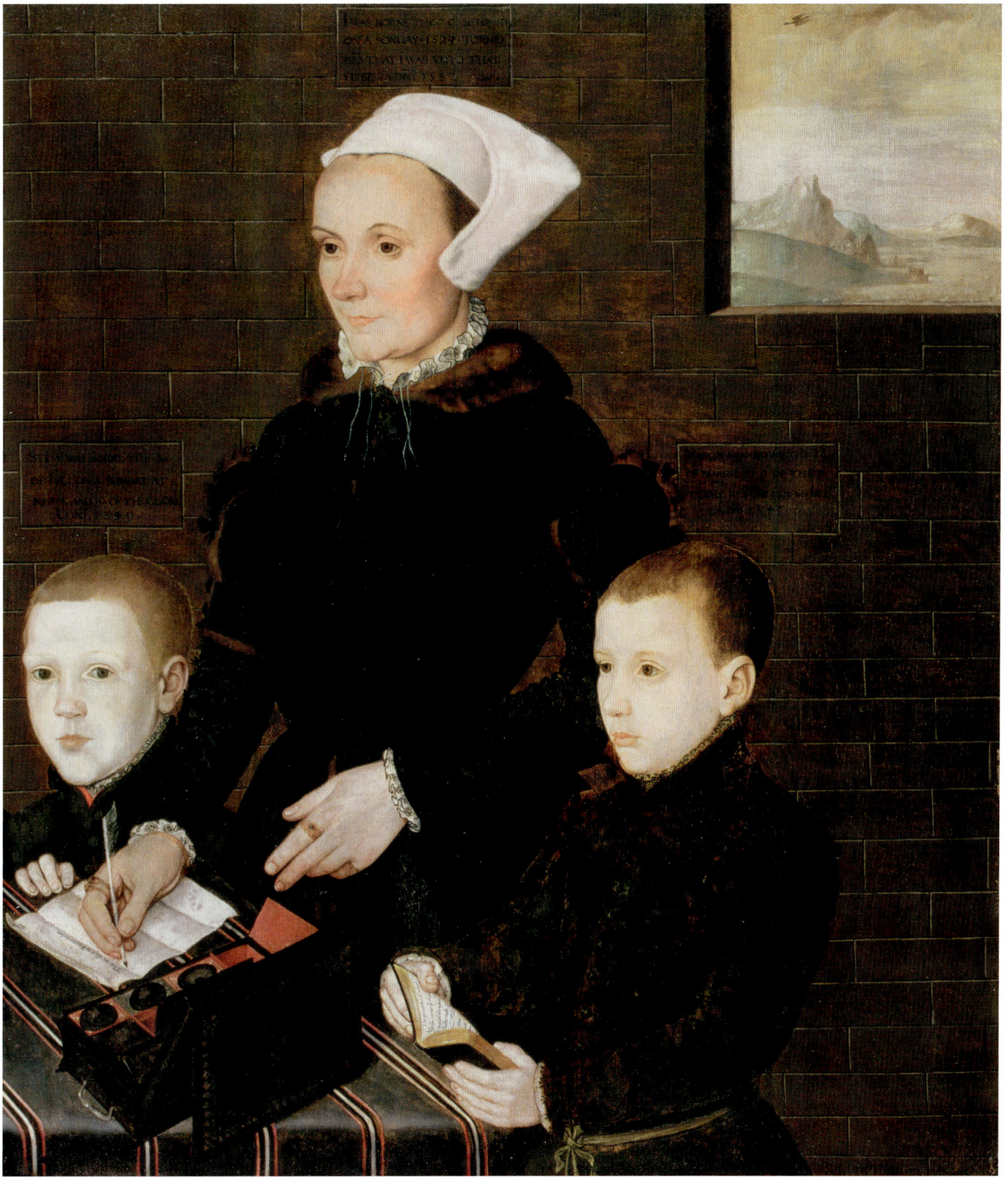

its own. I have examined the "chromophobia" of the great reformers at length elsewhere, notably in my work *Black: History of a Color*.[35] I will refer readers there and limit myself here to a summary of the major points, emphasizing the fate reserved for red, the principal victim of this war waged on colors.

Protestant chromoclasm, whether Lutheran or Calvinist, involved first of all the church and the church service. For the great reformers, the presence of color was excessive there; it had to be reduced or eliminated. In their sermons, they repeated the biblical words of the prophet Jeremiah, railing against the luxury flaunted by King Joachim and against "the princes who build magnificent temples, like palaces, cutting out windows, arraying

Two Chromophobic Reformers: Luther and Melanchthon

Enemies of lively colors that "clothe men like peacocks," the great reformers of the sixteenth century were always portrayed in black clothing.

Lucas Cranach the Elder, *Martin Luther and Philipp Melanchthon*, 1543. Florence, Galleria degli Uffizi.

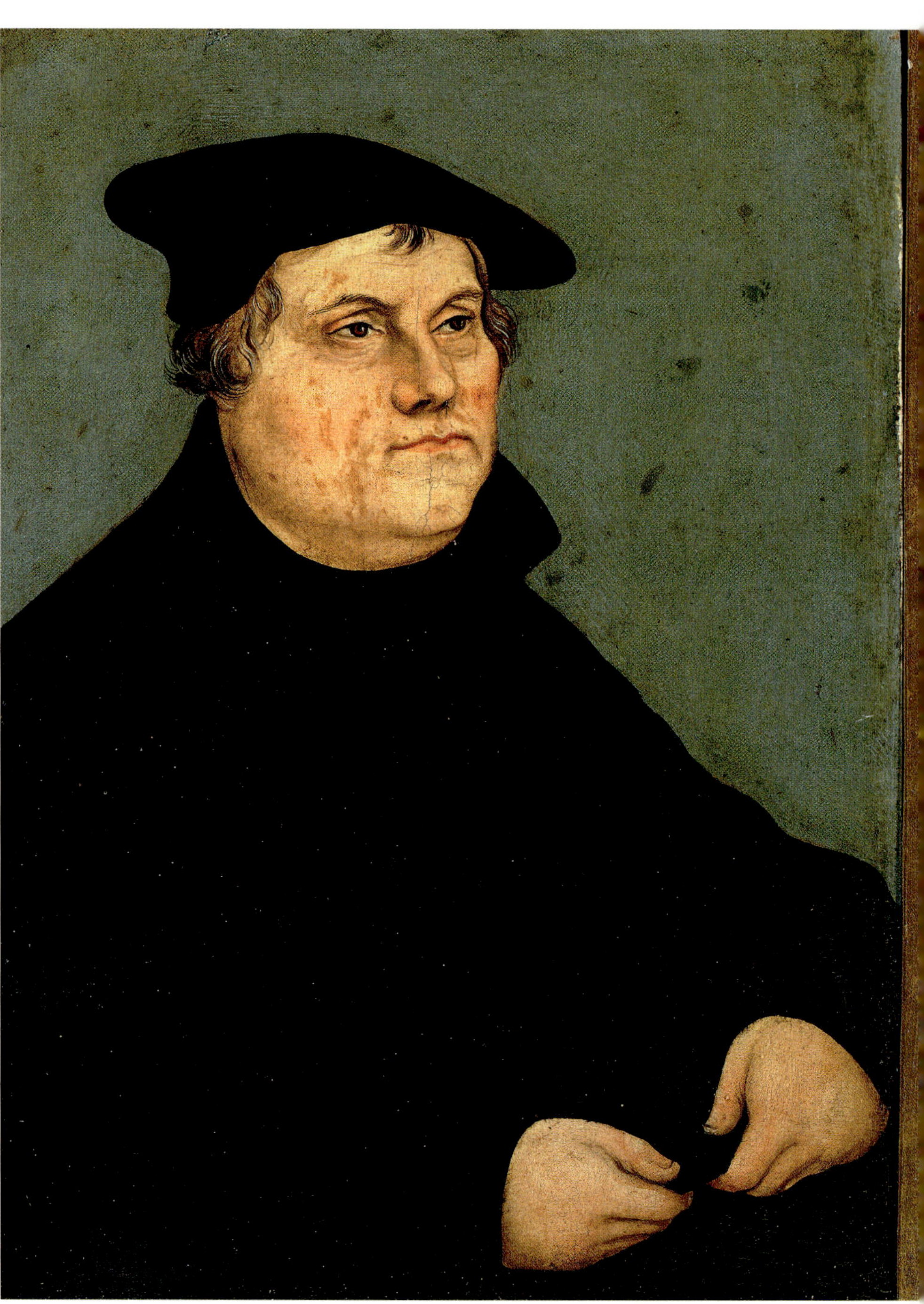

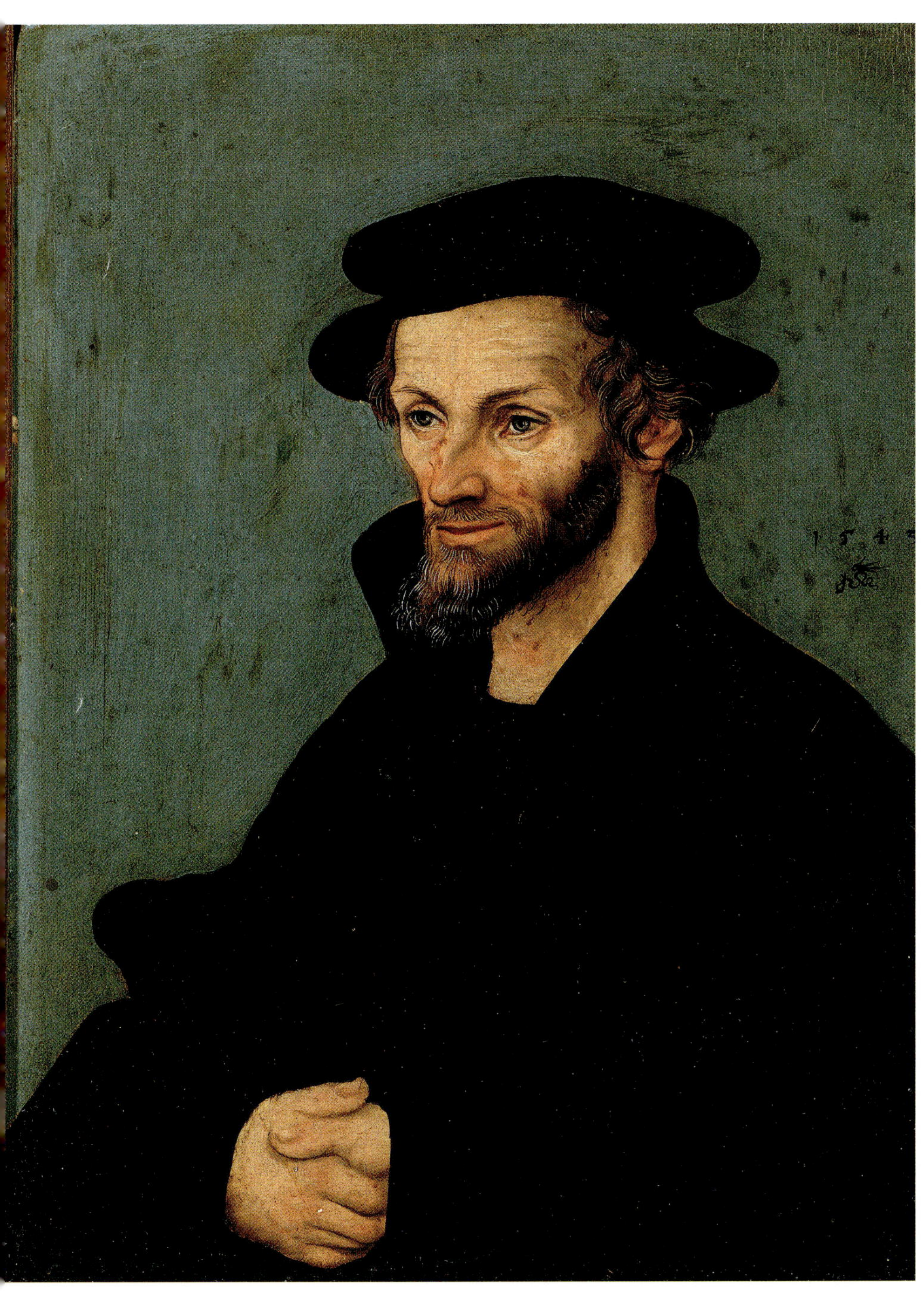

them in cedar and vermilion" (Jer. 22:13–14).[36] The color red—for the Bible, the richest color, and for the sixteenth century, the color that symbolized the height of luxury in the Roman Catholic Church—was the principal target, followed by yellow and green. They had to be driven from the temple. Hence the violent destruction—against stained glass in particular—and strategies for removing color from the walls, such as stripping or whitewashing them and using monochromatic black or gray hangings to hide the paintings and images. Chromoclasm went hand in hand here with iconoclasm.[37]

Just as extreme was the Reformation's attitude toward liturgical colors. In the rite of the Catholic Mass, color played an essential role; objects and vestments of the worship service were not only coded by the calendrical color system, they were also combined with light, architectural and sculpted polychromy, painted images in the holy books, and precious ornaments in order to create a veritable theater of color. Red was especially featured during the celebrations of the Holy Spirit (Pentecost is one immense red holiday), the Holy Cross, and the martyrs. In the eyes of the great reformers, all that had to disappear: "the church is not a theater" (Luther); "pastors are not players" (Melanchthon); "rituals that are too rich and colorful falsify the sincerity of worship (Zwingli); "the most beautiful ornament of the church is the word of God" (Calvin). The palette and code of liturgical colors was thus abolished and replaced by white, black, and gray.[38]

Although churches gradually became as stark as synagogues, it was nevertheless probably in customs of dress that Protestant

Lutheran Anti-Papist Print

Lutheran propaganda often used engravings to ridicule the pope and the Roman Catholic Church. In this print, we can recognize Pope Leo X (the lion) surrounded by four Catholic theologians, all with heads of animals: Thomas Murner (cat), Hieronymus Emser (ram), Johannes Eck (pig), and Jakob Lemp (dog). The addition of color seems to emphasize the scandalous excesses of the church of Rome.

Anonymous wood engraving, 1521. Paris, Bibliothèque Nationale de France, Department of Prints and Photography.

chromophobia exerted its most severe and lasting influence. During the Reformation, clothing was always a sign of sin and shame because it recalled the Fall; Adam and Eve lived in earthly paradise naked until, having disobeyed God, they were expelled and then given clothing in order to hide their nudity. That clothing was the symbol of their sin, and its first function was to remind man of his fall from grace. For that reason, all clothing had to be somber, simple, modest, and adapted to climate and occupation. To draw attention to oneself through one's clothing was a grave sin. Protestant morals dictated a profound aversion to luxurious clothing, makeup and jewelry, costumes, and changing or eccentric fashions. This resulted in extreme austerity in dress and appearance, and the abolishment of all useless accessories and artifices. The great reformers set the example, both in their personal lives and in the painted or engraved representations that they left of themselves. They are all portrayed in severe, monochromatic dark or black clothing.

Considered immodest, bright colors—red and yellow primarily, but also pinks, oranges, greens, and even purples—were absent from the Protestant wardrobe. Conversely, dark tones were commended—blacks, grays, and browns most importantly. As a pure color, white was advised for children's and sometimes women's clothing. Blue was tolerated insofar as it remained drab and somber. If clothes were multicolored, if "men dressed like peacocks"—the expression Melanchthon used in a famous sermon in 1537—they were severely condemned.[39] Red was the particular target; it was the color of papist Rome, likened to the great whore of Babylon discussed in the book of Revelation. Various engravings circulated showing the pope riding an ass or a pig, or sometimes a dragon, and dressed like a debauched woman. His attire was often accentuated with red gouache or watercolor, the red of all the vices, as sometimes was the three-tiered tiara that he wore and that served to identify him.

In this war against the colors some cities proved more radical than others. In Geneva under Calvin, as in Florence under Savonarola a few decades later, anything related to frivolity, pleasure, and ostentation was condemned and prosecuted. Private lives and practices were under surveillance, attending church services was mandatory, going to the theater or places of pleasure was forbidden. Also forbidden were dancing, games, makeup, costumes, and excessively loud colors. Calvin wanted to make Geneva a new Jerusalem, an exemplary city with new ways of life and belief. Any moral infraction was not only an offense against God but also an actual social crime. Appearance and attire were especially targeted. Outward signs of wealth, jewelry, belts, useless accessories and ornaments, low-cut dresses, slashed sleeves, and anything that could incite licentiousness and "bawdiness" were banished. In sermons, some words of the prophet Ezekiel were often quoted as an example to follow: "Then they stripped off their many-colored clothes" (Ezek. 26:16). In 1555–56, a veritable crusade began against colors deemed too rich or garish, especially red, a color that the Reformation pastors abhorred. In 1558, a dress ordinance prohibited the color's use, for men as well as for women.

But it was especially following Calvin's death in 1564 that decrees and regulations proliferated; by the end of the century the hatred for red seems to have reached its height.[40]

A similar rejection of red and strong colors can be found again in artistic creation, especially painting, not only in Geneva but throughout reformed Europe. Henceforth the Protestant palette differed from the Catholic one; it adapted to the discourse—sometimes contradictory—of the great reformers and the instructions of pastors. Here again, it is with Calvin that we find the first considerations and recommendations regarding art and colors;

they would be followed by many Protestant painters until the nineteenth century. Calvin did not condemn the plastic arts but insisted that they be exclusively secular and strive to be instructive and to honor God. They were not to represent the Creator (which was an abomination) but Creation. The artist had to reject artificial or gratuitous subjects that invited intrigue or lasciviousness. Therefore the painter was to work with moderation, seeking harmony in forms and tones, taking his inspiration from God's creation and representing what he saw. The most beautiful colors were those of nature, such as the blue shades of the

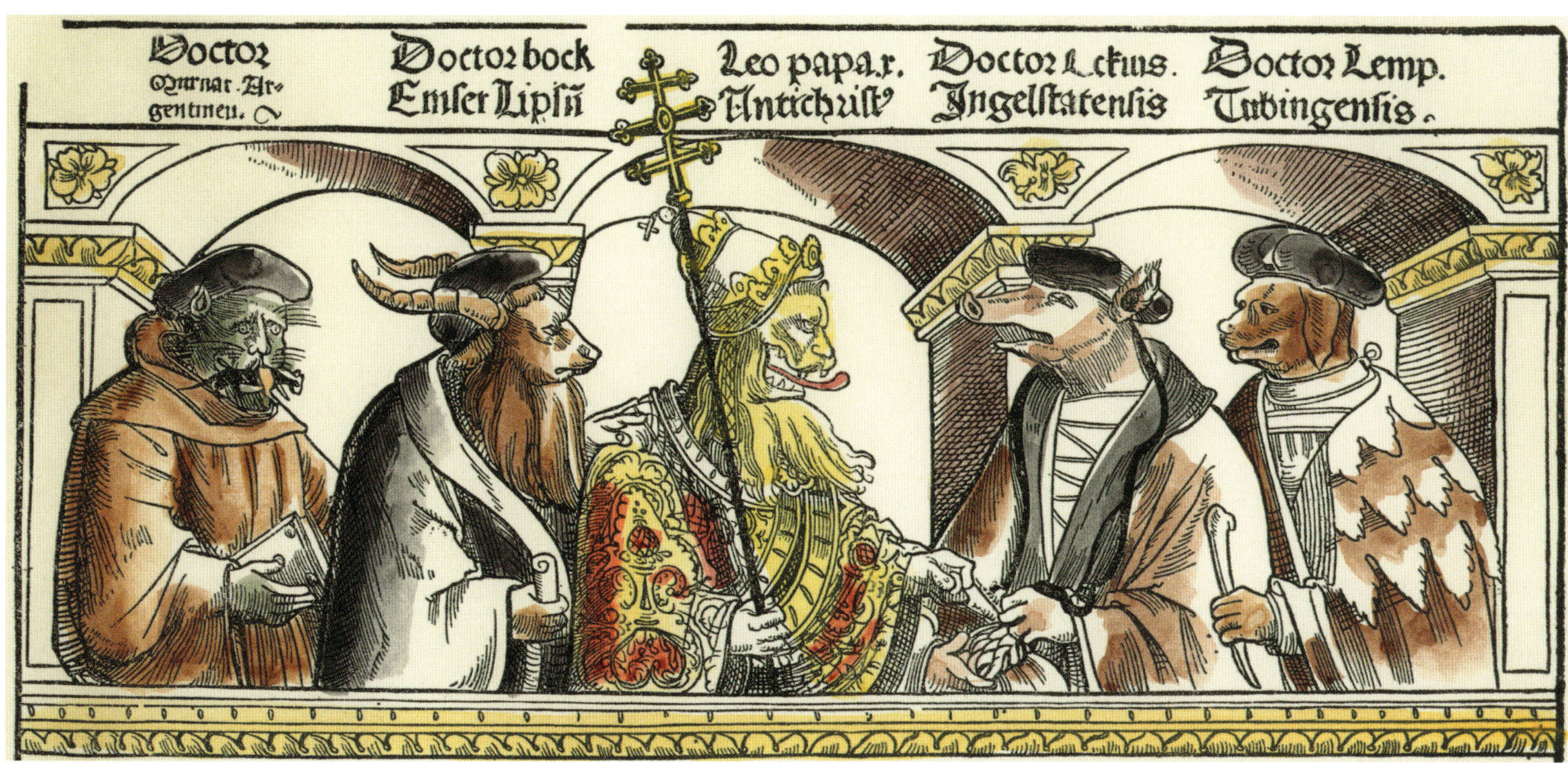

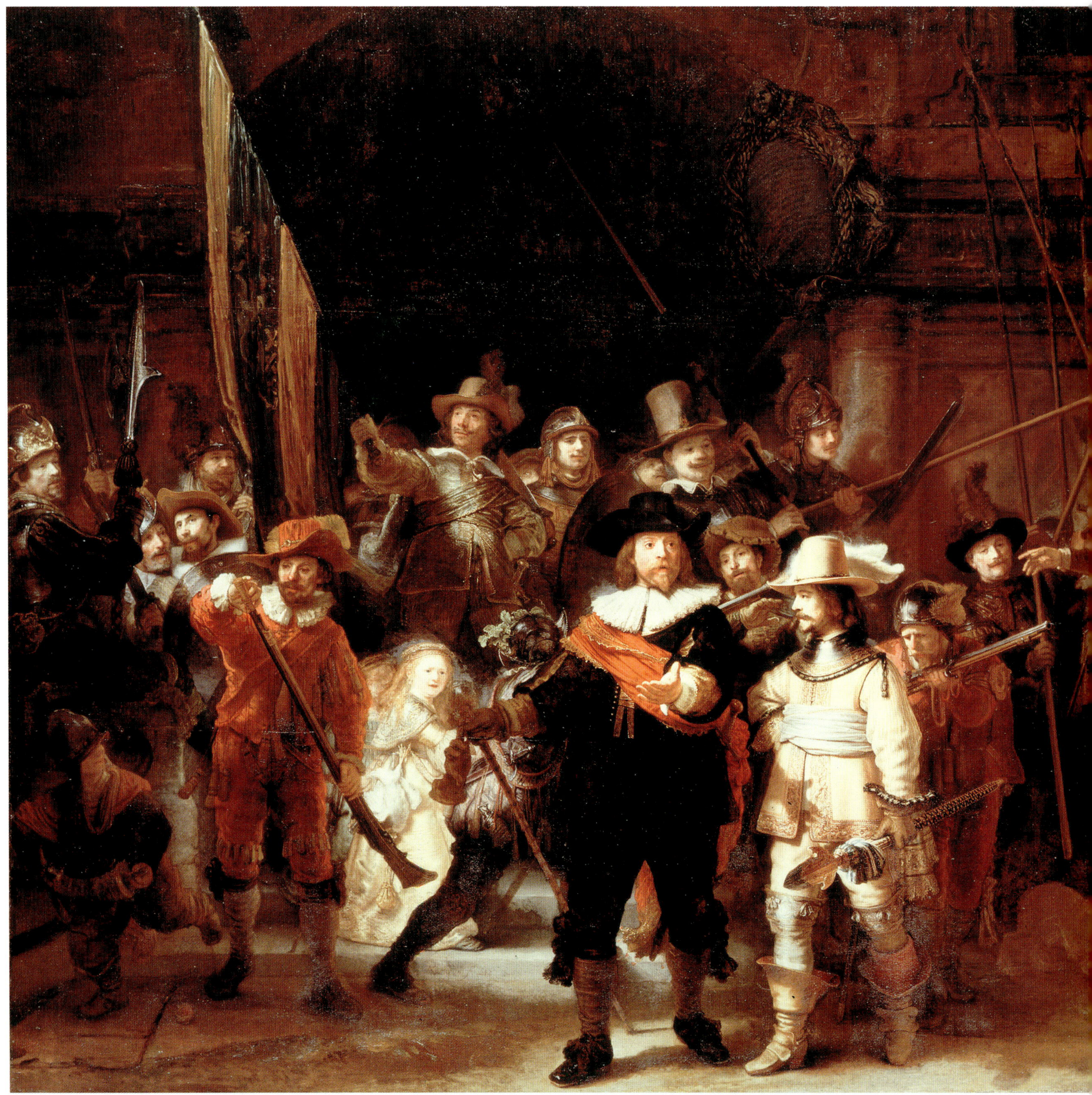

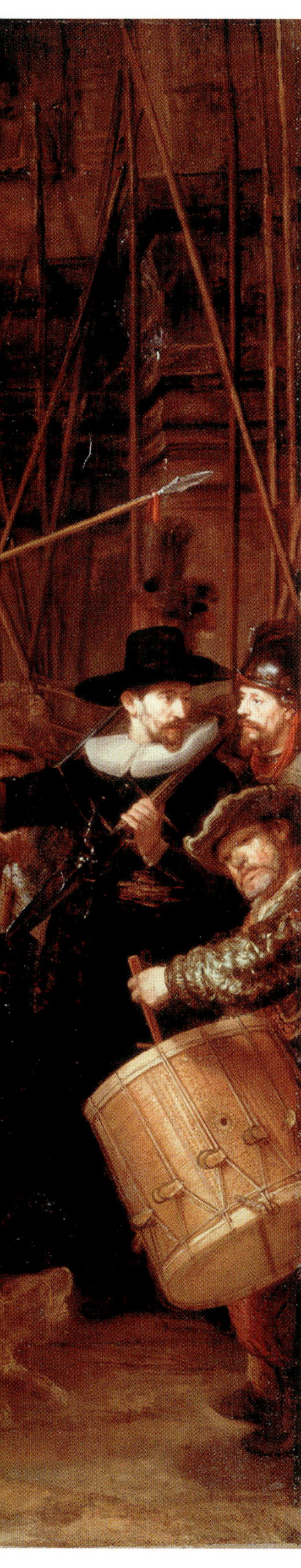

The Night Watch

Commissioned by Amsterdam's wealthy militia musketeers, this painting by Rembrandt was given its current title only in the nineteenth century; the darkening of the bitumen glaze gave the impression of a nocturnal scene, which was not at all the case. With his sash of violent red, an unusual color for Rembrandt, the captain of the militia, Frans Banning Cocq, is clearly given prominence at the center of the painting.

Rembrandt, *The Night Watch*, 1642. Amsterdam, Rijksmuseum.

sky and the green tones of plants; as works of the Creator, "these tones have more grace."[41] Banished from the Church and forbidden for clothing and everyday life, red was detestable and had to be rejected.

Generally, the Calvinist painters, who avoided mixed and multiple colors, sought dark shades, chiaroscuro, monochromes, and even the vibratory effects of grisaille. In the seventeenth century, Rembrandt is one of the most perfect examples. Touches of vivid colors in his paintings are rare. When red is present, its function is to create a discrepancy and emphasize a clothing detail that makes a figure conspicuous. Thus in Rembrandt's famous *The Night Watch* (1642), a simple red sash is enough to highlight, at the center of the canvas, Frans Banning Cocq, mayor of Amsterdam and captain of the company of militia guards. As a Calvinist painter and enemy of unrestrained palettes, Rembrandt is at the opposite extreme from another artist of genius who lived in Antwerp hardly a generation earlier: Rubens, a fervent Catholic, tremendous colorist, and lavish champion of all the shades of red.

The Red
of Painters

Rubens is by no means an isolated case. For the most part, painters have always loved red, from the Paleolithic period to the most contemporary. Very early on, red's palette came to offer a variety of shades and to favor more diverse and subtle chromatic play than any other color. In red, artists found a means to construct pictorial space, distinguish areas and planes, create accents, produce effects of rhythm and movement, and highlight one figure or another. On walls, canvas, wood, or parchment, the *musica* of reds was always more pregnant, more cadenced, and more resonant than others. Moreover, painting treatises and manuals are not mistaken; it is always with regard to red that they are most long-winded and offer the greatest number of recipes. For a long time, it was also the chapter on reds that began the exposition on pigments useful to painters. That was already the case in Pliny's *Natural History*, which had more to say on red than on any other color.[42] And the same is true for the collections of the medieval recipes intended for illuminators and in the treatises on painting printed in Venice in the sixteenth and seventeenth centuries. It was not until the century of the Enlightenment that in certain works—most often written by art theoreticians and not painters themselves—the chapter on blues would precede the one on reds and offer a greater number of suggestions.

For now, let us open those recipe collections from the end of the Middle Ages, called *réceptaires* by scholars. These are difficult documents to date or study, not only because they were all copied by hand, each new copy offering a new account of the text, adding or omitting recipes, altering others, changing a product's name or designating different products by the same name, but also because practical advice and methods continually appear side by side with allegorical or symbolic considerations.[43] The same sentence may contain obscure annotations on the symbolism of colors and practical recommendations on ways to fill a mortar or clean a container. Moreover, notes on quantity and proportion are often imprecise, and cooking, decoction, or maceration times are rarely indicated. As was often the case in the Middle Ages, the ritual seems more important than the results, and numbers, when they are given, seem to have more to do with qualities than quantities. The wording is sometimes surprising. A recipe from Lombardy from the 1400s intended for illuminators begins with this sentence: "If you want to make a bit of good red paint, take an ox . . ." Surely the author is having fun here when he calls for an entire animal of enormous size to transform a few drops of blood

Giovanni Arnolfini

A rich merchant from
Lucca who lived in
Bruges, Giovanni
Arnolfini wore the same
scarlet fabrics and
sumptuous furs that
his company sold. His
singular face combined
with Jan Van Eyck's talent
makes this one of the
strangest portraits in all
of Flemish painting.

Jan Van Eyck, *Portrait
of Giovanni Arnolfini*,
c. 1440. Berlin, Gemälde
Galerie.

FOLLOWING PAGE SPREAD

The Hunt by Night

Early on, red became
the color of hunters
and has remained so
to this day, at least for
hunting parties. These
events are not so much a
pursuit of game as they
are an aristocratic ritual
meant to raise a ruckus
deep within the forest,
a right reserved for the
privileged few.

Paolo Uccello, *The Hunt
by Night*, c. 1465–70.
Oxford, Ashmolean
Museum.

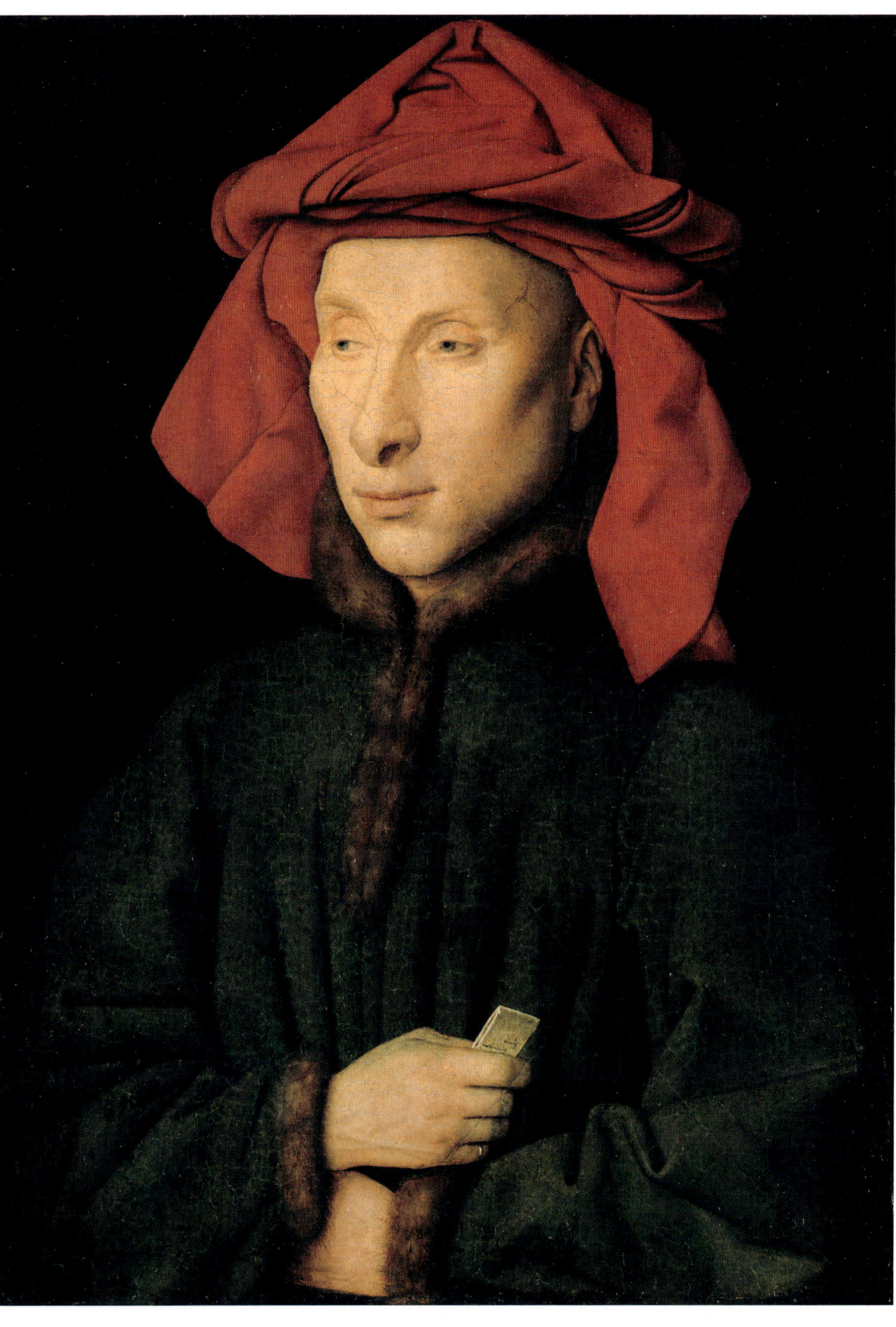

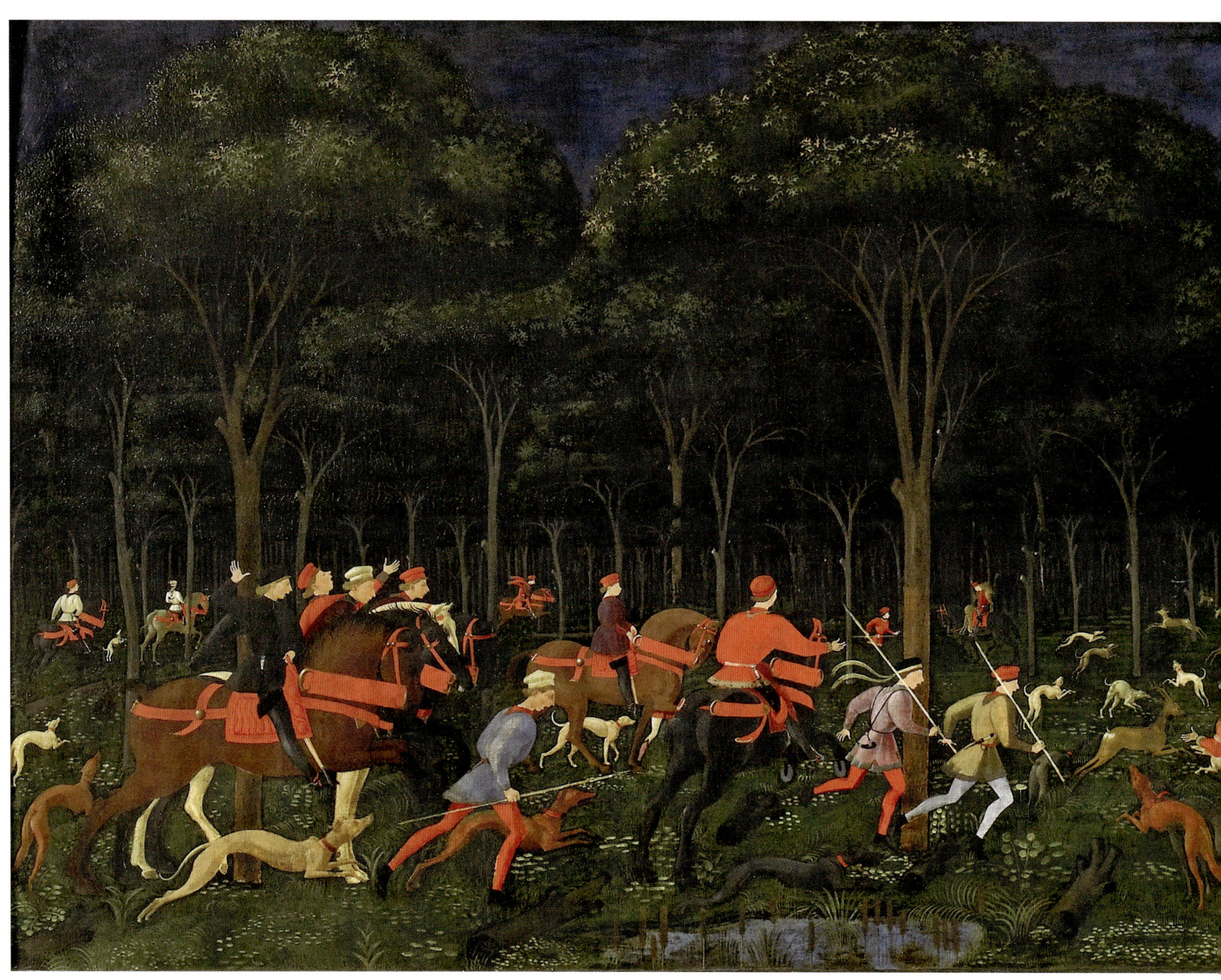

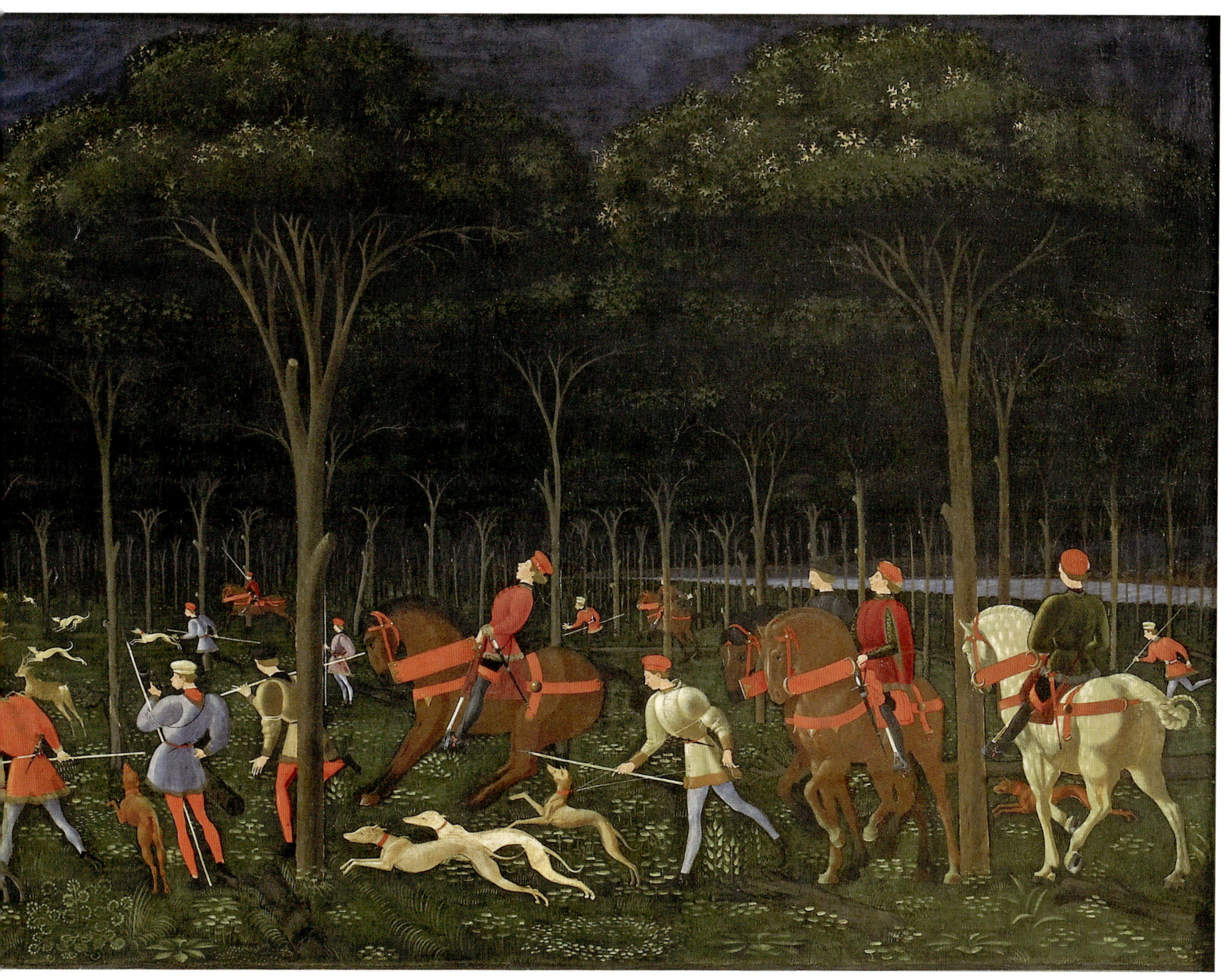

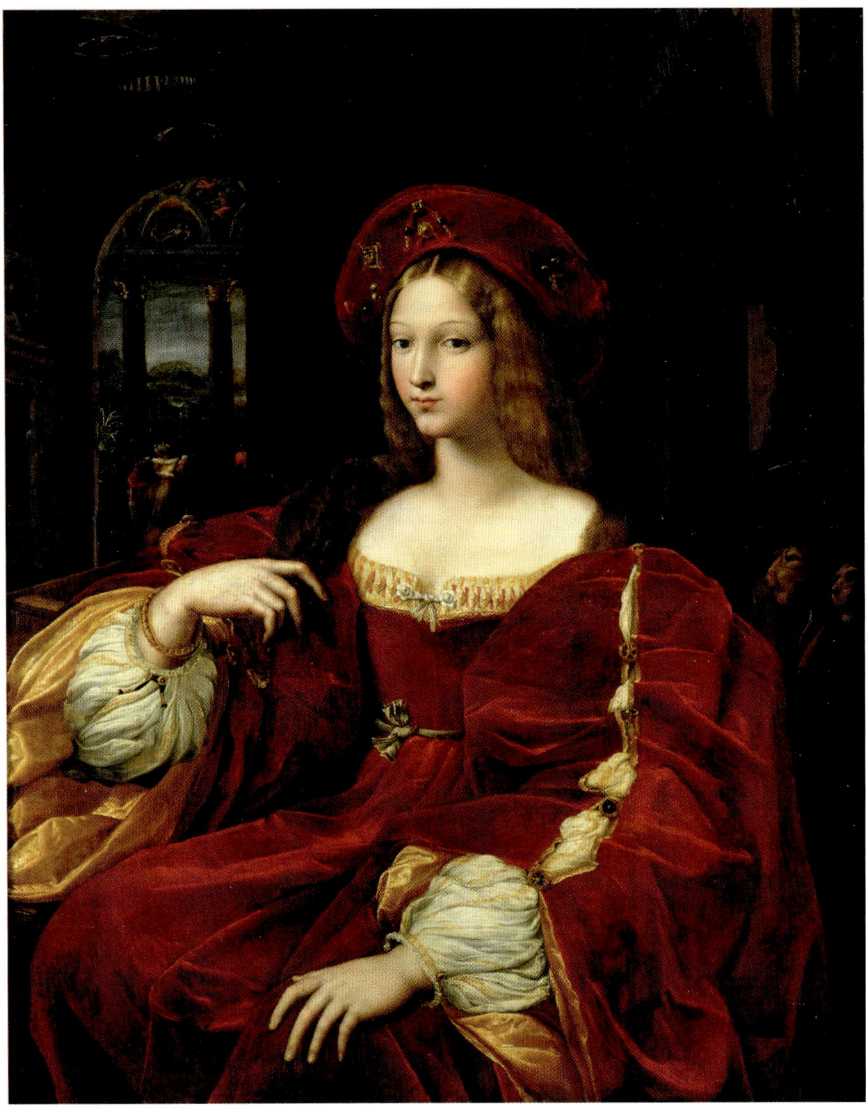

the importance of the slow work of time—wanting to speed up the process being neither effective nor honest—and the meticulous choice of containers: clay, iron, tin, opened or closed, wide or narrow, large or small, one particular shape or another, each designated by a specific word. What happened within those receptacles was on the order of metamorphosis, a mysterious and dangerous operation that required many precautions in the selection and use of the container. All the collections intended for painters pay attention to the issue of mixing and the use of different materials: mineral was not vegetable; vegetable was not animal. One could not do just anything with anything: vegetable was pure, animal was not; mineral was dead, vegetable and animal were living. For making a pigment, often the essence of the operation consisted in making a material considered to be alive act upon a material considered to be dead: fire on iron; madder or kermes on aluminum salts; vinegar or urine on copper.[45]

Thanks to recipe collections in manuscript form, the first printed manuals, and analyses done in laboratories, we have good knowledge about the materials involved in the composition of pigments used by illuminators and painters in the late Middle Ages and the early modern period. For reds, the list is long but the materials hardly differ from those in use in ancient Rome: cinnabar (natural mercuric sulfide, rare and costly), realgar (natural arsenic sulfide, unstable and even more rare), minium (white lead artificially heated, very commonly used), and, especially for mural painting, clays rich in iron oxide, either

into a red pigment that will probably be used to paint a tiny surface.[44]

In a general way, whether they are addressed to painters, illuminators, dyers, or even doctors, apothecaries, cooks, or alchemists, all these recipe collections appear to be as much speculative texts as practical works. They share the same sentence structures and vocabulary, especially with regard to verbs: take, choose, gather, crush, grind, mill, boil, mix, stir, add, filter, steep. They all stress

A Princely Color: Crimson Red

Although Raphael was commissioned to paint this portrait, it was executed mostly by Giulio Romano. But the sumptuous red of the clothing is faithful to the color used by the master, a tremendous painter of reds.

Raphael and Giulio Romano, *Portrait of Isabel de Requesens, Vicereine of Naples*, formerly *Portrait of Giovanna of Aragon*, 1518. Lens, France, Musée du Louvre-Lens.

A Fashionable Color: Purplish Red

Like Raphael, Rubens was a great painter of reds. He excelled in the dark tonalities of the color, very much in fashion in the early seventeenth century.

Peter Paul Rubens, *Portrait of Susanna Lunden*, or *Le Chapeau de Paille*, said to be the portrait of the painter's sister-in-law, c. 1625. London, National Gallery.

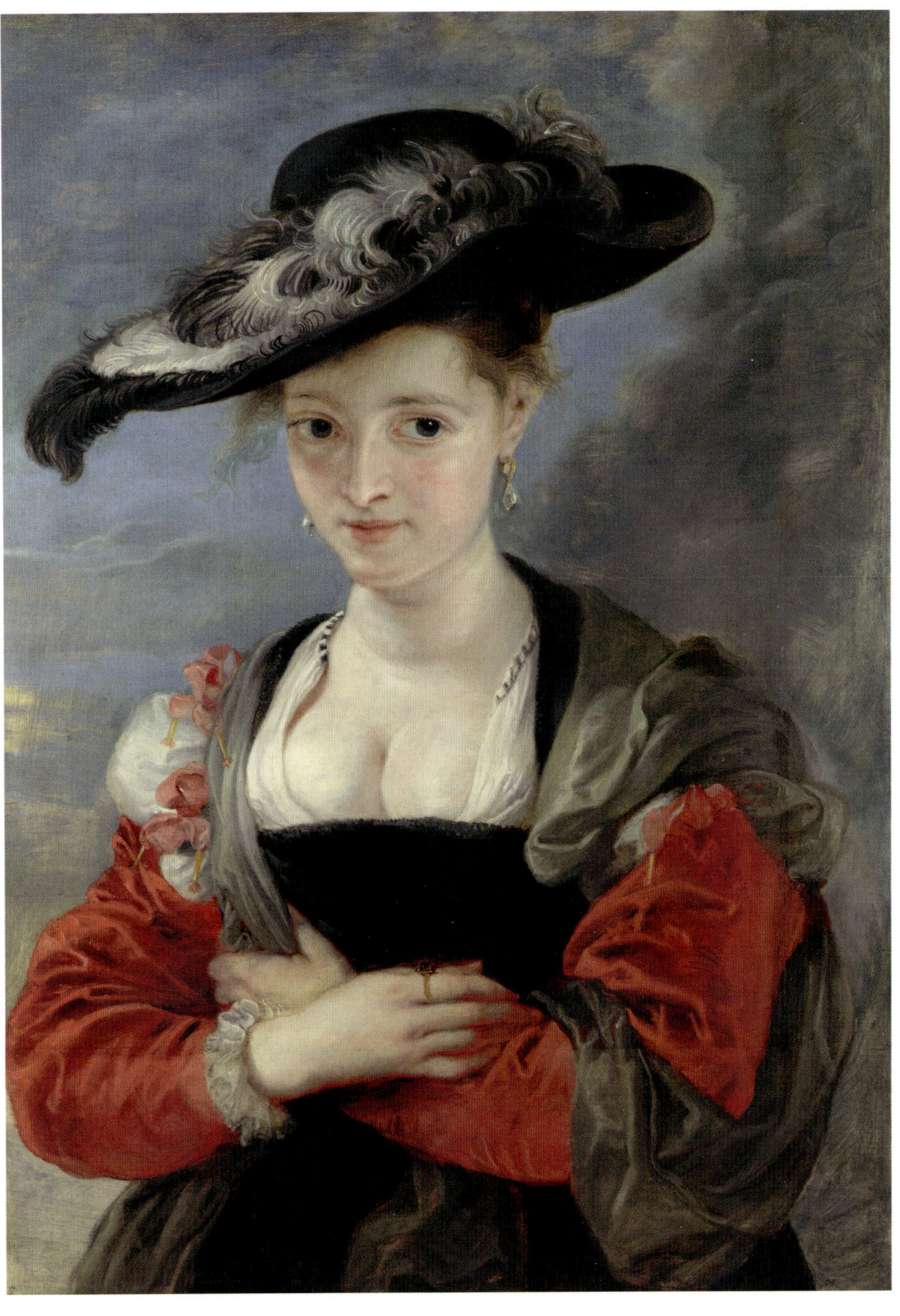

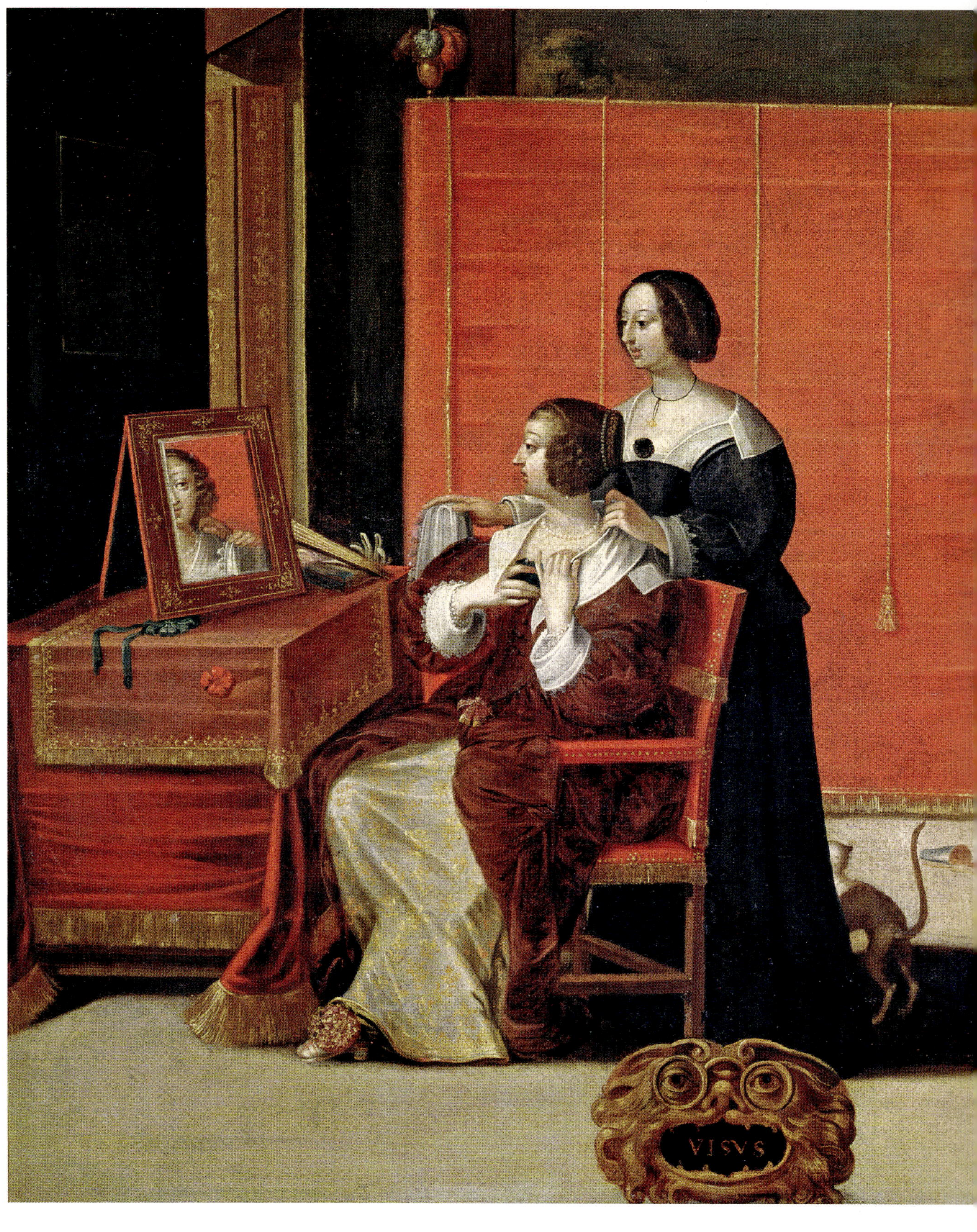
VISVS

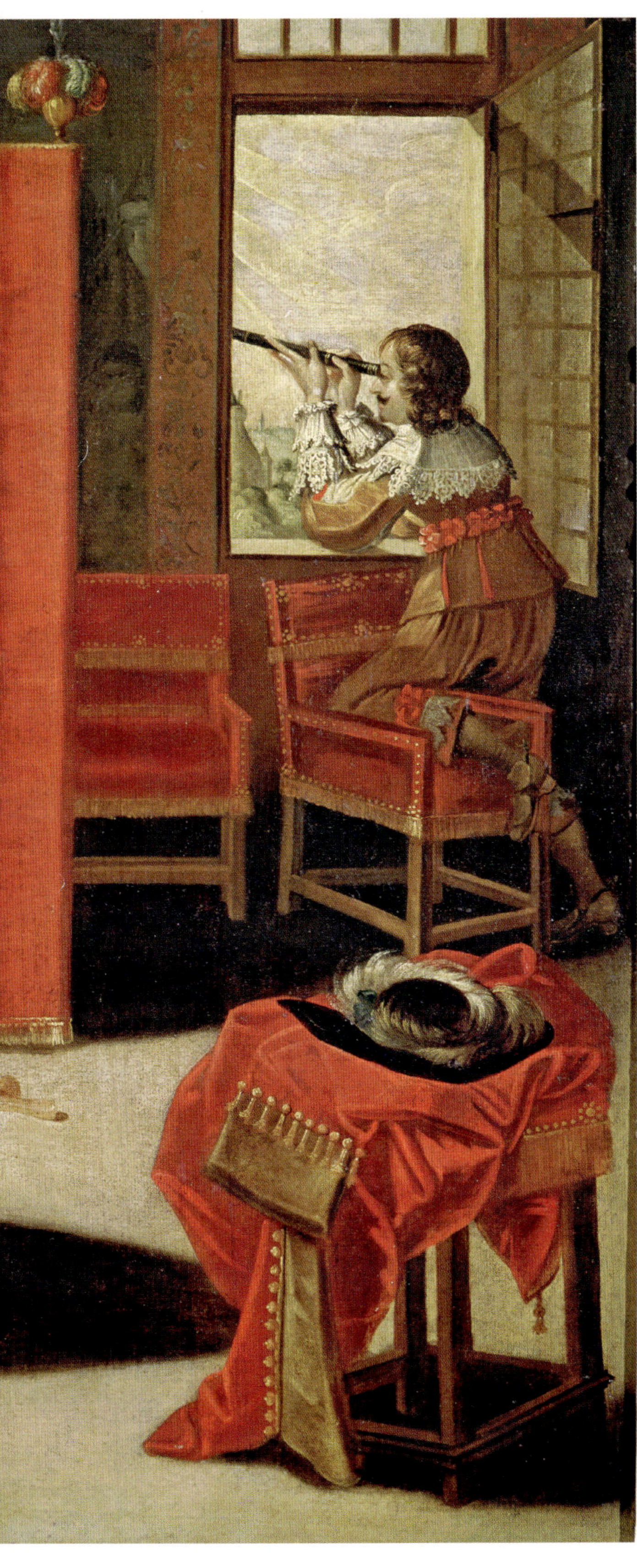

Woman at Her Toilette

Seventeenth-century doctors distrusted water and recommended that it not be used excessively for cleansing the body. Hence, washing was essentially a dry affair, involving powders and makeup. And it was rarely private, as seen in this painting, which clearly emphasizes the social stakes of the toilette and its setting—note the richness and "modernity" of the furniture, the abundance of luxurious red fabrics—over hygienic concerns.

Anonymous, in the style of Abraham Bosse, *The View*, c. 1635–37. Tours, Musée des Beaux-Arts.

naturally red (hematite) or heated to transform yellow ocher into red ocher. To this list of mineral pigments were added pigments of vegetable or animal origin: dyeing lacquers (madder, kermes, brazilwood) that painters liked because, like clays, they were very resistant to light; and sandarac, a reddish resin obtained from an Asian palm, the rotang.[46] In the end, the Middle Ages added only a single red pigment to this list: vermilion, an artificial mercuric sulfide, obtained through the chemical synthesis of sulfur and mercury. Like natural cinnabar, this was a very toxic pigment, perfected in China, familiar to Arab alchemists, and arriving in the West between the eighth and eleventh centuries. It provided a beautiful orange-red, but had the disadvantage of darkening in the light of day.

The late Middle Ages and the modern period have left us works by great painters that are particularly remarkable for their range of reds. Let us mention Van Eyck, Uccello, Carpaccio, Raphael, and later, Rubens and Georges de La Tour. But all artists seemed to love this color and tried to draw various tonalities from it. Accordingly they chose their pigments, taking into account not only their physicochemical properties, their ability to cover or make opaque, their resistance to light, and how easily they could be worked or combined with other pigments, but also their price, availability, and—what is most disconcerting to us—the name they went by. Indeed we can observe in the laboratory that in panel paintings from the late Middle Ages, symbolically "negative" reds—those coloring the fires of hell, the face of the Devil, the coat or feathers of infernal creatures, and all impure blood of one kind or another—were often painted with the same pigment: sandarac, a resin lacquer more commonly called "cinnabar of the Indies" or "dragon's blood."[47] Various legends circulated in workshops regarding this pigment, a relatively expensive one because it had to be imported from far away. It was believed to come not from a plant resin but from the blood of a dragon, gored by its mortal enemy, the elephant. According to medieval bestiaries, which followed Pliny and the ancient authors here, the inside of the dragon's body was filled with blood and fire; after a fierce struggle, when the elephant had punctured the dragon's belly with its tusks, out flowed a thick, foul, red liquid, from which was made a pigment used to paint all the shades of red considered evil.[48] Legend won out over knowledge in this case, and painters' choices gave priority to the symbolism of the name over the chemical properties of the pigment.

Unlike the dyers, the painters of the modern period hardly profited at all from the discovery of the New World or the settling of Europeans in the Americas. No truly new colorants resulted from these events. But Mexican cochineal, transformed into lacquer, allowed them to perfect a subtle, delicate pigment in the range of reds, superior to earlier lacquers from brazilwood or kermes for fixing a glaze over vermilion. Beginning in the sixteenth century, vermilion experienced a steady rise in popularity and its production became something of an industry, first in Venice, the European capital of color, and then in the Netherlands and Germany. It was sold in apothecaries, hardware shops, and paint stores, and even though it was more expensive and less stable than minium, it eventually contributed to that pigment's decline.

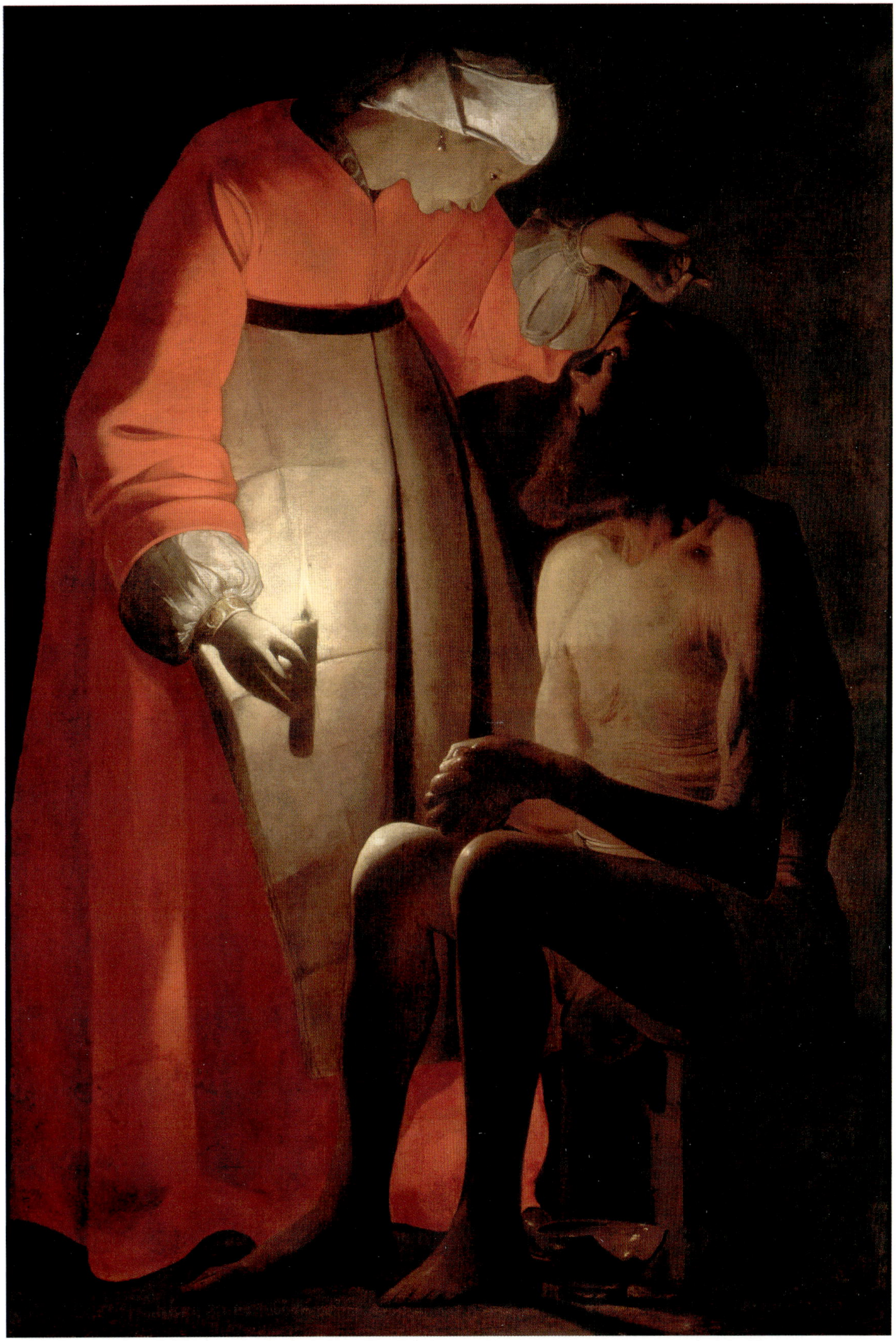

Red Brought
to Light

The palette of Georges
de La Tour is restrained
and homogeneous:
whites, browns, and reds,
admirably set off by the
play of chiaroscuro, which
often adds nocturnal
effects to the scene. The
date of this wonderful
painting is debated,
but the geometric
composition and the
strict centering suggest a
mature work.

Georges de La Tour, *Job
Mocked by His Wife*,
c. 1650. Epinal, France,
Musée Départemental
d'Art Ancien et
Contemporain.

A Primary Color

When Science Took Over Colors

Newton's discovery of the spectrum opened the way to much speculation on the optics, physics, and chemistry of colors, leading in 1720 to Jacob Christoph Le Blon's invention of color engraving, perfected a few years later by Jacques Gautier d'Agoty.

Jacques Fabien Gautier d'Agoty, *Observations sur l'Histoire Naturelle, sur la Physique et sur la Peinture*, vol. 1, Paris, 1752, plate 2.

On the scientific level, the seventeenth century constitutes an important period of changes for colors. Inquiries evolved, experiments multiplied, and new theories came to light. Even before Newton discovered the spectrum in 1666, scholars and scientists implemented new classification systems and called into question the old Aristotelian order of colors—from the lightest to the darkest—an order that, for almost two millennia and in every domain, had constituted the normal and normative sequence for classifying colors: white, yellow, red, green, blue, black.

The physical sciences were first to call this chromatic axis into question, especially the science of optics, which had hardly progressed since the thirteenth century. Beginning in the 1600s, there were numerous new speculations on light, and as a result, on the colors, their nature, origin, hierarchy, and perception. Nevertheless the spectrum was still far off at that time: white and black remained full-fledged colors, and red retained its place at the center of the axis, side by side, as ever, with green. Still, a few theoreticians proposed replacing this linear axis with a circle; others with branching patterns of sometimes unexpected complexity. One of the most audacious diagrams was reproduced by the famous Jesuit Athanasius Kircher (1601–1680)—a prolific writer interested in everything, including colors—in his great work on light, *Ars magna lucis et umbrae*, published in Rome in 1646. It is not clear whether he was its author, but this diagram is very ingenious. Constructed from many connecting arcs, it tries to convey visually the whole set of relationships that colors form among themselves.[49] Red is at the center, enthroned at the junction of the arcs and their offshoots.

More pragmatically or concretely, other men of science observed and theorized about the know-how of artists and artisans. The Parisian doctor Louis Savot, for one example, questioned dyers and glass artists and began constructing his chromatic classifications from their empirical practices.[50] The Flemish naturalist Anselme De Boodt, frequent guest at the court of Emperor Rudolph II, with his cabinets of curiosities, placed at the center of his studies not only red—"the color of colors" (*color colorum*)—but also gray, obtained both by mixing black and white and by mixing all the colors.[51] But most important was François d'Aguilon, Jesuit priest and regular visitor to Rubens's studio—which was a veritable laboratory for all inquiry regarding color—who formulated the clearest theories, beginning in 1613, those that would have the greatest influence on the following two generations. François d'Aguilon distinguished "extreme"

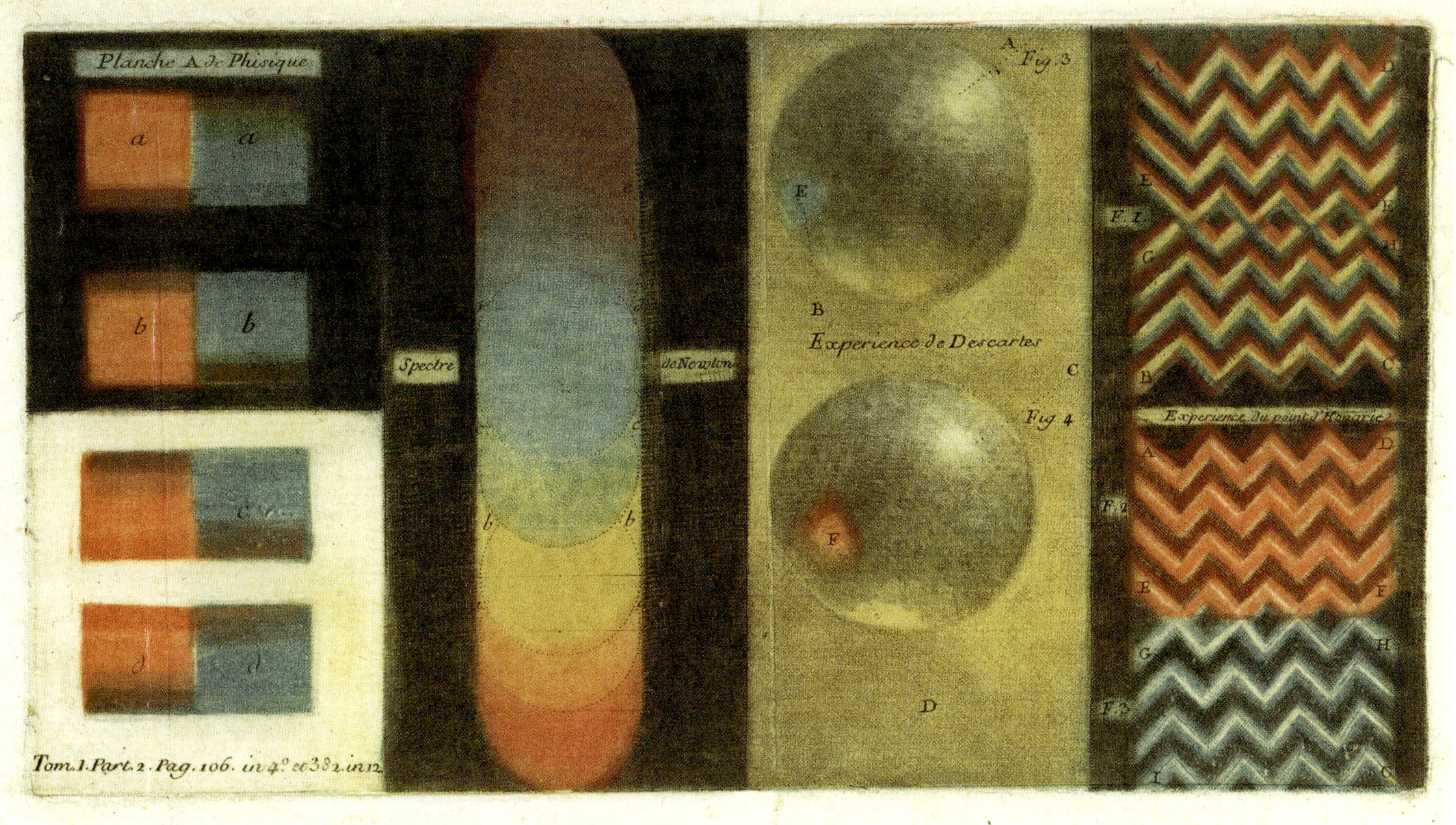

colors (black and white), "medium" colors (red, blue, yellow), and "mixed" colors (green, purple, and orange). In an elegant diagram similar to those of musical harmony, he showed how the medium colors combined to engender others without the intervention of the extreme colors. Here again, red (*rubeus*) was located at the heart of the chromatic process.[52]

In the same period, many painters, both famous and unknown, were using their palettes in experimental ways. Even while they used the same pigments as their predecessors, they tried to obtain the greatest number of tones and shades by employing only a small number of basic colors, either by mixing them before applying them, or by superimposing or juxtaposing them on the medium, or by resorting to a colored medium. Actually, none of this was truly new, but in the first half of the seventeenth century, among artists as well as artisans, inquiries and experiments flourished.

Throughout Europe, painters and dyers were asking the same questions as men of science. How to classify, combine, and mix colors? How many "basic" colors were necessary for creating all the others? And what name should be given to those colors not produced by mixing but rather that played the role of matrix themselves? On this last point, the proposed vocabulary varies: "primitive," "first," "principal," "simple," "elementary," "natural," "pure," "capital." In Latin, the expressions *colores simplices* and *colores principales* are most frequently used. In French, the lexicon is more inconsistent if not more ambiguous.[53] The adjective "primary," eventually accepted for describing the basic colors, did not emerge until the nineteenth century.

And how many basic colors were there? Three? Five? More? Here as well, opinions differed. A few authors looked back very far and followed the ancient tradition, notably Pliny's *Natural History*, which cites only four: white, red, black, and the enigmatic *sil* (*silaceus*), identified sometimes as yellow, sometimes as blue.[54] This inconsistency explains why many other authors did not refer back to the ancient texts but rather to the experience of contemporary painters and maintained that there were five "first" colors: white, black, red, yellow, and blue. A bit later, after Newton had scientifically eliminated black and white from the color order, most scholars came to accept only three: red, blue, yellow. This was not yet the theory of primary and complementary colors formulated later by chemists and physicists, but it was already the modern subtractive triad that would allow Jakob Christoffel Le Blon to invent color engraving in 1720–40.[55]

Let us remain for the moment with the seventeenth century. Whether there were three primary colors or five of them, red, blue, and yellow were always among them. Green, on the other hand, which many painters and dyers henceforth obtained by mixing blue and yellow, was reduced to the second rank, among the "mixed" colors (the expression "complementary color" did not make its appearance until the nineteenth century), in the same category as purple and orange. This was a whole new development, contrary to all earlier classifications and social uses of color that put red, blue, yellow, and green on the same plane. In *Experiments and Considerations Touching Colours*, a book published in 1664 that was simultaneously practical and theoretical, Robert Boyle (1626–1691), the Irish chemist with many varied interests, expressed the hierarchies of this new classification system very clearly:

There are very few simple or "primary" colors, the various combinations of which somehow produce all the others. Because even though painters can imitate the shades—but not always the beauty—of the countless colors one encounters in nature, I do not believe that they need to use colors other than white, black, red, blue and yellow to bring out this extraordinary variety. Those five, variously combined—and also, if I may say so, uncombined—are sufficient for creating a considerable number of colors, a number that those unfamiliar with the painters' palette cannot even imagine.[56]

If red retained its position as first in this new distinction between primary and secondary colors, that was no longer the case in the spectrum discovered by Isaac Newton two years later, in 1666, which has remained to the present day the basic scientific classification system for arranging the colors. For Newton, colors constituted "objective" phenomena. That was why it was necessary to put aside questions regarding vision, as too linked to the eye ("uncertain and deceiving"), and those regarding perception, as too subject to different cultural contexts. It was necessary to concentrate on the problems of physics alone, which he did by returning to earlier experiments involving light passing through a glass prism. Indeed, the young English scientist thought that color was nothing other than light subjected to various physical changes as it moved or encountered matter, changes that had to be observed, defined, studied, and measured. By doing multiple experiments, he discovered that the white light of the sun was neither subdued nor darkened by passing through a glass prism; on the contrary it created a colored, elongated patch as it exited, inside of which it was dispersed into many colored rays of unequal lengths. Those rays formed a chromatic sequence that was always the same: violet, blue, green, yellow, orange, red. Newton first distinguished six rays but later added a seventh one in order to form a set of seven. Henceforth, the colors that compose light were identifiable, reproducible, controllable, and even measurable.[57]

Newton's discoveries constituted a decisive turning point, not only in the history of colors but also in the history of science. It took a certain amount of time, however, for them to gain recognition. Newton kept them secret for many years and then only partially revealed them, in several stages, beginning in 1672. It was not until his general survey on optics was published in English in 1704, then translated into Latin three years later, that all his theories on light and color were finally made known to the scientific world.[58] But what impeded the reception of his discoveries and caused a certain number of misunderstandings for many subsequent decades was his vocabulary. He used the vocabulary of painters, although he thought like a physicist. For example, "primitive" colors had a very specific meaning for him and were not limited to red, blue, and yellow, as for painters. Hence arose the confusions and quandaries that lasted well into the eighteenth century and were echoed in Goethe's *Theory of Colors* more than a century later. Red's location, no longer at the center of an axis or diagram but at one end of a continuum seemingly formed from various rays, aroused the suspicion of many artists as well as Goethe. How could a color recognized as "principal" or "primary" have become so marginal? How could physics have so rearranged the color order and banished the queen of colors to its borders? "Newton," Goethe would say, "is definitely mistaken."

Fabric and Clothing

Harvesting Cochineal

In Mexico after the Spanish conquest, growing the nopal cactus and raising the cochineal insect that fed on it became an industry. Despite the Atlantic crossing, Mexican cochineal was less expensive than European cochineal because the harvesting was done by slaves.

José Antonio de Alzate y Ramirez, *Memoria sobre la Naturaleza, Cultivo y Beneficio de la Grana*, manuscript copied and painted, 1777. Chicago, Newberry Library, Ayer Collection, Manuscript 1031.

n the seventeenth century, these new classifications in chemistry and physics that sometimes made red a principal color and sometimes a marginal color paralleled what was happening in everyday life. On the material plane, red was everywhere in decline; on the symbolic plane, it retained its first place and all its signifying power.

It was perhaps in dress and the home that red's decline was most apparent. The Protestant Reformation had transpired and had judged this color as too vivid, too rich, and too "dishonest," as Melanchthon said. All good Christians had to keep their distance from it. The most astonishing thing was that the Catholic Counter-Reformation adopted a share of the Protestant ethic in this regard. Although for church decor, worship, and the liturgy, for holidays and artistic creation, Catholicism took exactly the opposite position from the great reformers' chromoclasm, indulging in debaucheries of vibrant colors for which the baroque period offers the most striking examples, with regard to everyday dress and life, it seemed to submit to the Protestant

dictate. Tones darkened, harmonies were more muted, and black, gray, and brown triumphed; garish colors, polychromy, and silver and gold were hardly used. Of course we must distinguish between the common people and the most privileged classes: drab colors for the first, bright colors for the second. But even with regard to the wealthy middle classes and the aristocracy, there was a great difference between daily life and holiday or ceremonial occasions. Only at these times did one dress in bright and costly colors. The splendor of Versailles and the courts give an inaccurate image of the colorful atmosphere of the *grand siècle*. Actually the seventeenth century was a very somber one, as much on the chromatic as on the economic and social levels. European populations had probably never been so destitute. Wars, famines, epidemics, and natural disasters raged throughout the century and lowered life expectancy dramatically.

In such a context, red was hardly fashionable anymore. And when it was present, it was darker. Gone were the bright reds tending toward orange; the style was now for crimson and wine shades, more or less brown or purple. Nevertheless new dyestuffs imported from the New World provided dyers with the means to diversify their red palettes. To the traditional madder and kermes were now added annatto, or American brazil, a more solid and dense red than Asian brazil, from the tropical American achiote tree (*Bixa orellana*), whose fruits contained seeds with dyeing properties; and especially Mexican cochineal, a parasitic insect found on many varieties of nopal cacti, which, like its cousin the Mediterranean kermes, provided a dye with rich and vivid tones that evoked antique purple. Only the female was collected, at the time when she was bearing eggs. Once she was killed and dried, a juice rich in carminic acid was extracted that was transformed into a saturated, luminous red colorant. But as with kermes, an enormous quantity of insects was needed to produce a little dyestuff: about 150,000 to obtain the equivalent of one kilogram of dye. That is why fabric dyed with cochineal commanded a very high price.

Nevertheless, beginning in 1525–30, dried cochineals, which the Aztec were already trading, were exported to Europe, where the beauty, solidity, and intensity of the dyes they yielded were admired. The government of New Spain quickly understood what profits could be made and decreed the creation of cultivated nopal cactus farms in Mexico, where cochineals were raised as an industry. The insects, which fed on the flesh of the cacti, were harvested just before laying season, then killed, steamed, and dried. In comparison to the wild cochineal, the domestic cochineal was twice as fat and provided steadier and more significant yields.[59] In the mid-seventeenth century, the quantity of cochineals exported to Europe was estimated at 350 tons per year, providing revenues almost equivalent to those of mineral resources. But crossing the Atlantic was perilous, and it was not unusual for Spanish ships carrying the precious cargo to be attacked, especially by the English or Dutch, or even pirates, who resold their plunder.[60]

For a long time the Spanish guarded the secrets of their methods for cultivating nopal and raising cochineals, which led to jealousies

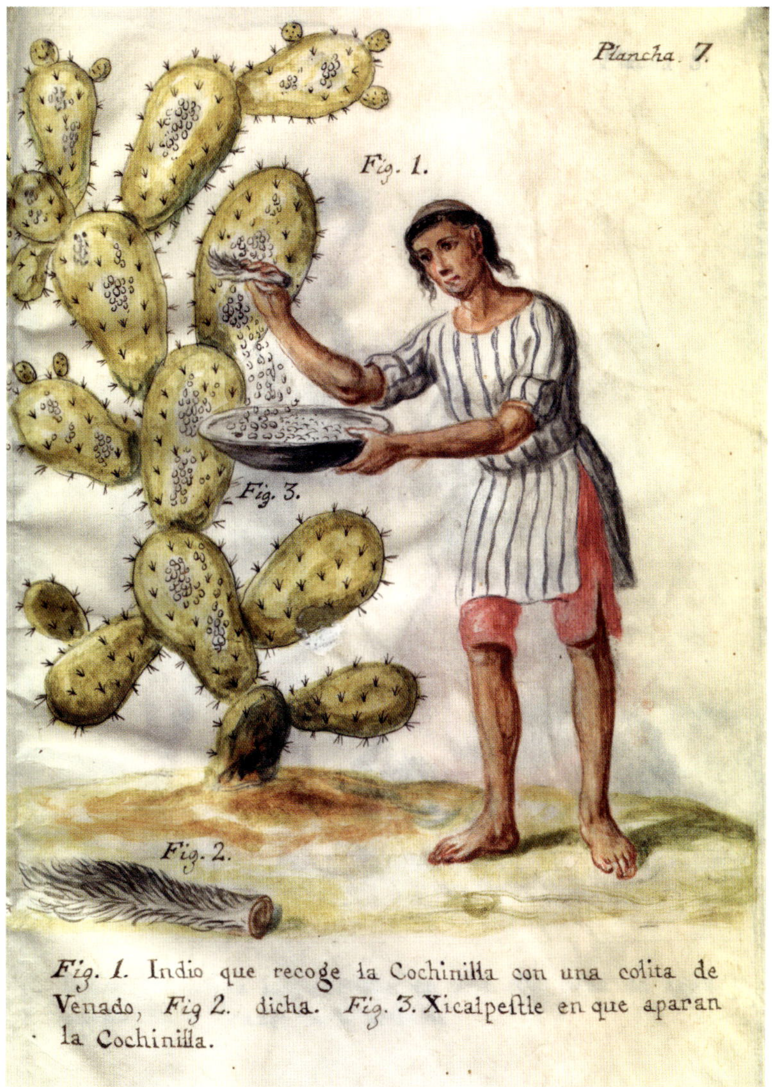

Fig. 1. Indio que recoge la Cochinilla con una colita de Venado, *Fig 2.* dicha. *Fig. 3.* Xicalpeſtle en que aparan la Cochinilla.

and attacks. Before the 1780s, when those secrets were uncovered, other European nations trying to compete with Mexican cochineal produced red dyes that could more or less rival it. In the Dutch Republic research was done to produce a better quality madder,

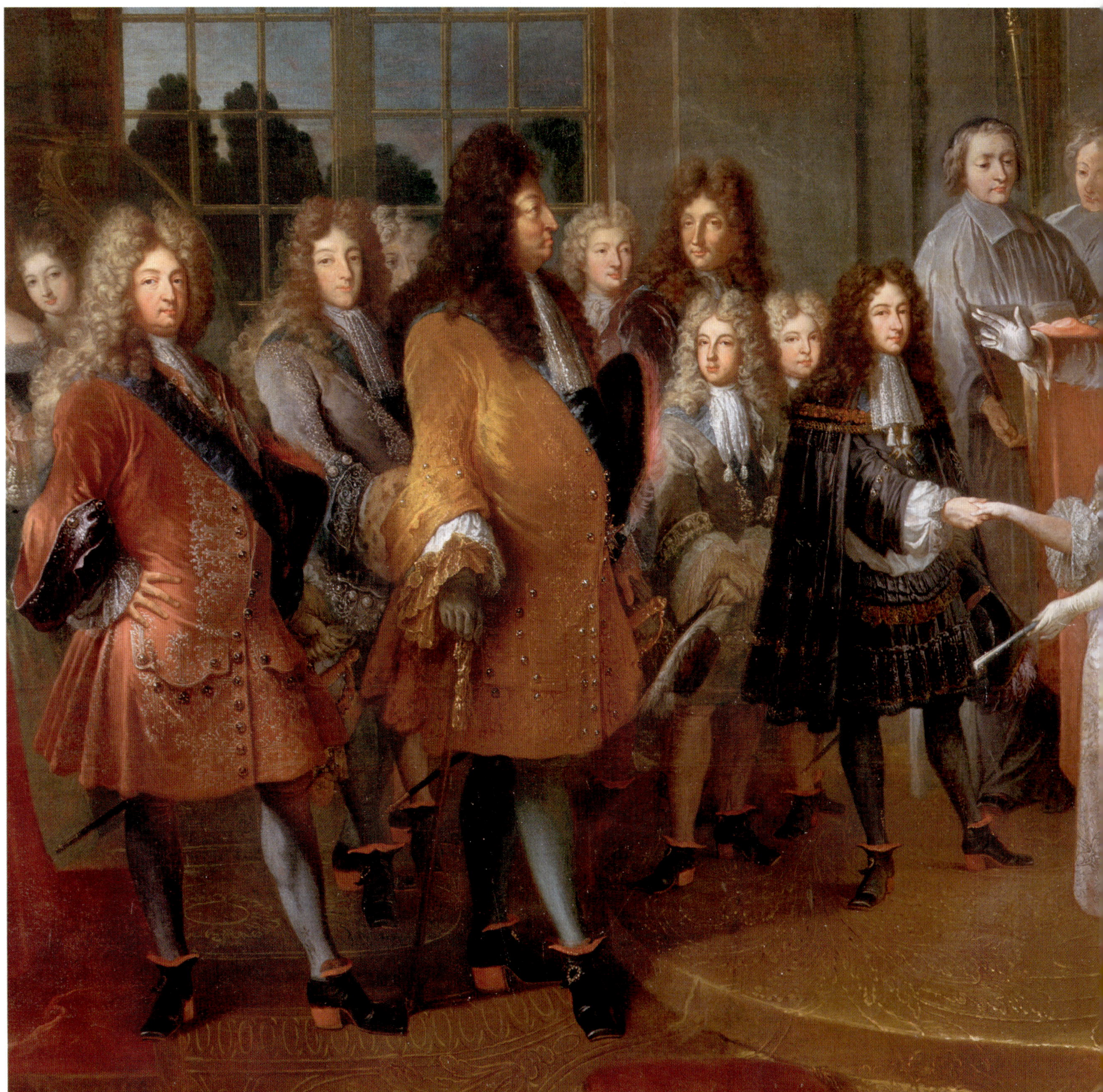

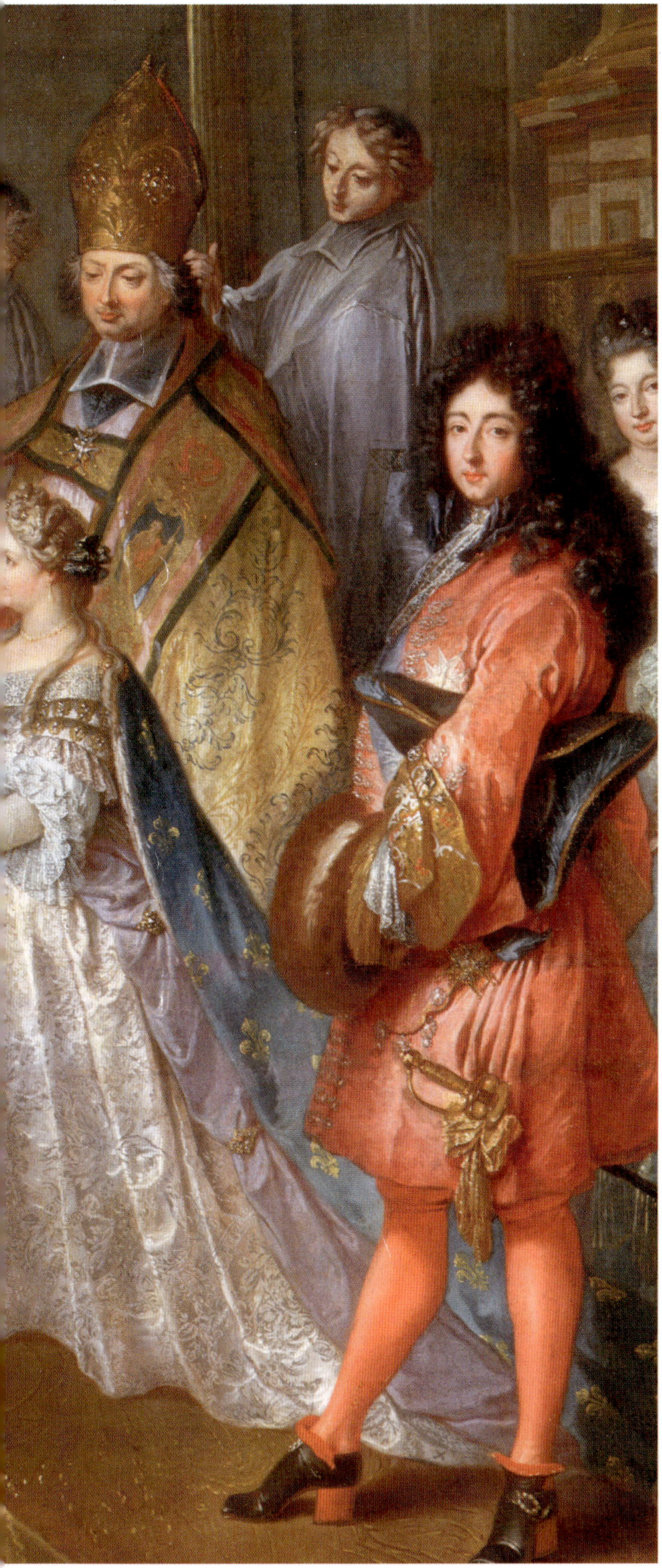

The Aristocracy's Red Heels

Red heels appeared at Versailles in the 1670s–80s. An enduring legend attributes the courtly fashion to Philippe II, Duke of Orléans, who, like his brother Louis XIV, was short. The expression *talons rouges* (red heels) became popular in the nineteenth century to describe the aristocracy and the nouveaux riches imitating the habits of the nobility of the Ancien Régime.

Antoine Dieu, *Marriage of Louis of France, Duke of Burgundy, and Marie-Adelaide of Savoy, 7 December 1697*, 1698. Versailles, Palace and Trianon collections.

which was then exported to France and Germany. In England and Italy, a dyestuff particularly effective on cotton was imported in huge amounts from Turkey: "Turkish red," later called "Andrianople red," after the major city (present-day Edirne) in the region where it was produced, now on the border between Turkey and Greece. Here again, production secrets were well guarded—mordants of animal fats, plant oils, and excremental matter were added to the madder—but by the end of the eighteenth century, reds in the "Andrianople style" were produced in Germany (Thuringia) and then in France (Alsace, Normandy) for use on furniture fabrics. These reds remained the fashion for a long time. Marcel Proust refers to them in 1920 in a description of a somewhat dilapidated sitting room:

> As for the tapestries, they were by Boucher, bought in the nineteenth century by a Guermantes with a taste for the arts, and hung, interspersed with a number of mediocre sporting pictures which he himself had painted, in a hideous drawing-room upholstered in "adrianople" and plush.[61]

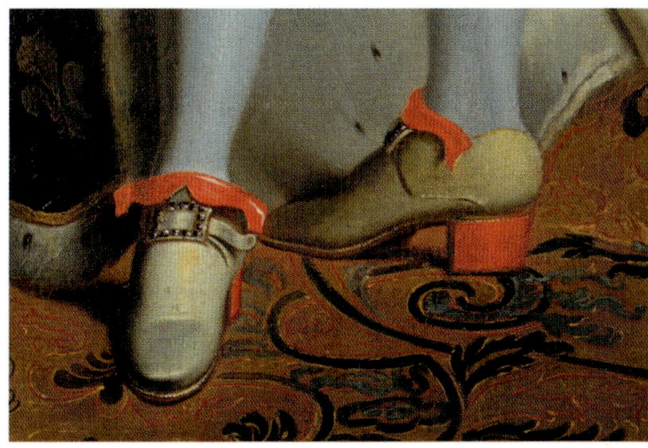

After Hyacinthe Rigaud, *Louis XIV at 63 Years of Age in Ceremonial Robes*, detail. Versailles, Palace and Trianon collections.

All these dyes were expensive. That was why red remained an aristocratic color for clothing. The famous *talons rouges* (red heels) of the French aristocracy constituted a kind of symbol here. The fashion began in Versailles in the 1670s and gradually spread to all the courts of Europe. One legend holds that it was accidentally started by the Duke of Orléans, brother of Louis XIV, one day when he soiled his shoes walking in ox blood, but that is only a legend related to court mythology. In French, the expression *talons rouge* survived until the early twentieth century to designate the aristocracy or the nouveaux riches imitating the nobility of the Ancien Régime.[62]

In the middle classes, red was rarer and obtained with less costly colorants. Similarly, among the peasant class, men's red pants and jackets were dyed with local madder, giving a solid but matte and fairly drab color. In general such clothing was reserved for special circumstances, holiday celebrations, or ceremonies. For example, on their wedding days, young women put on their most beautiful dresses, which were often red, because country village dyers obtained their best results with that color. It was not until the late nineteenth century that villages first witnessed their brides dressed in white.

Throughout the sixteenth and seventeenth centuries, red gradually became more rare in the spectacle of everyday life. Henceforth it constituted a disparity, a signal, or an accent, and in so doing became all the more noticeable. The notions of brilliance, love, glory, and beauty were still associated with it, even when it was a matter of a simple fruit or flower. That was the case, for example, with the tomato.

Originating on the Andean slopes of South America, it was introduced to Europe by the Spanish early in the sixteenth century but was not considered edible until much later. For two centuries, it was planted as an ornamental, with fruits that ripened from green to yellow, then from yellow to red, an earthy, sensual red that dyers tried to imitate. Many authors praising its smoothness and beauty considered it a marvel and gave it the name "apple of gold," or "apple of love." For example, here is what Olivier de Serres wrote in 1600 in his *Theatre d'agriculture et mesnage des champs*:

> Apples of love, wonder, and gold all require the same soil and care. Also, they all serve to cover sheds and bowers, climbing gaily over them, fastening themselves firmly to the supports. The diversity of their foliage makes the place where one assembles them very pleasant; and with good grace, the gentle fruits that these plants produce hang among their branches. . . . Their fruits are not at all good to eat; they are only useful in medicine and pleasant to handle and to smell.[63]

Little Red Riding Hood

Despite its decline in daily life, red retained all its powers of attraction into the modern period. Becoming rarer in the material culture, it even seemed to acquire greater symbolic power and a status very much its own within the world of colors. Literature and language offer a wide array of evidence for this. Hence in the French language of the sixteenth and seventeenth centuries, the adjective *rouge* (red) was used as an adverb in the same way as *très* (very): *cet homme est rouge grand* (that man is very tall); *cette robe est rouge belle* (that dress is very beautiful). The closest modern equivalent would be *fort* (strong), used as an adverb: *cet homme est fort grand* (that man is very tall). *Rouge* and *fort* can thus sometimes be thought of as synonyms, which says much about the semantic intensity of this color. The word "red" was not often used this way, of course, but in the same period the German language presents a

few similar examples of the adjective *rot* (red) being used as an adverb synonymous with *sehr* (very): *dieser Mann ist rot dick* (that man is very fat).[64] The English, Italian, and Spanish languages, on the other hand, have never used the word "red" to reinforce the meaning of an adjective or create superlative expressions.

The symbolic power of red was especially prevalent in oral literature, in tales and legends, fables and proverbs. Let us consider fairy tales, an area where color terms are not very common but always constitute highly significant touches. Statistically and symbolically, three colors outstrip all others: white, red, and black. This is a matter of a tradition going back to ancient times in which, as in the Bible, other colors are present but play a minor role. Despite the ascent of blue in the midst of the Middle Ages, despite the rich and ambivalent symbolism of green, despite the astonishing disrepute of yellow over the course of the centuries, in tales and fables in the modern period everything revolves, as ever, around the white-red-black triad.

Let us take "Little Red Riding Hood," for example, perhaps the most famous of all the European folktales. It is known especially through the versions by Charles Perrault (1697) and the Brothers Grimm (1812), but older ones exist. The first written attestation dates from about the year 1000 and comes down to us through a short poem in the form of a fable by an ecclesiastic in the service of Egbert, the bishop of Liège. Drawing on many oral traditions, he put into verse for his young students the edifying story of a little girl dressed in red who crossed through the woods and was miraculously spared from

Little Red Riding Hood

Why red? Every academic specialty can offer its own explanation: Because there was a long-standing custom of dressing children in red (historical). Because the story takes place on the day of Pentecost (liturgical). Because the little girl is pubescent and would very much like to find herself in bed with the wolf (psychoanalytical). Because fairy tales have a traditional color triad, placing the red of the hood in conjunction with the black of the wolf and the white of the butter pot (semiological).

Walter Crane, *Little Red Riding Hood*, xylographic album, London, 1875.

hungry young wolves. What saved her was her courage, good sense, and the little dress of red wool that her father had given her.[65]

Written down in the Middle Ages and given the title "The Little Red Dress," from then on the story became embellished with various episodes and adapted into multiple versions. The one Perrault drew upon at the end of the seventeenth century was the most widely known but was not yet definitive. It already bore the title we know it by, "Le Petit Chaperon rouge," and appeared in a collection of eight tales published in 1697 under two titles: *Histoires ou contes du temps passé, avec des moralités* (Stories or tales from the past, with morals) and *Contes de ma mère l'Oye* (Tales from my mother Goose). Despite his active literary and academic career, the impressive Charles Perrault—the illustrious writer of the preface for the first dictionary from the Académie Française and first among the Moderns in their quarrel with the Ancients—owes his fame to this slim volume; hardly fair but nevertheless true.

In Perrault's hands, the story of Little Red Riding Hood is cruel and ends badly. The well-brought-up, pretty little girl encounters a wolf in the forest and inadvertently shows him the way to her grandmother's house; the wolf eats the old woman and then sets a trap for the little girl, whom he ends up devouring. The story ends abruptly with the wolf's victory. The Grimm brothers' ending is happier but less probable: a hunter kills the wolf and opens its belly, from which the child and her grandmother emerge safe and sound.

The bibliography devoted to this tale is enormous. Just the piece of clothing described

as a *chaperon* (hood) alone, for example, has spawned much writing. What might it have been at the end of the seventeenth century: A simple cap? A headdress extended with a piece of cloth? A cloak with a hood? A very wide-brimmed hat? Opinions vary. Few critics, on the other hand, are really interested in the question essential to us: why red? This color returns several times in the story, and it gives the child her nickname and in turn gives the tale its title. It seems to be the story's most important element. But why red?

We may offer several answers that, far from contradicting or undermining one another, are mutually complementary and enriching.[66] First of all, red can serve a symbolic function; that is, it can characterize the whole of the story and foretell its dramatic end. This is the red of violence, cruelty, and bloodshed. Such an answer is not false, but it is not sufficient. Historical explanations seem preferable. At that time it was a rural custom to have children wear a piece of red clothing to make it easier to keep an eye on them. This old practice extended well into the present. Even into the nineteenth century in France and elsewhere, young peasant children often wore smocks in this color: "Girls, your red aprons hide away; / The bull will pass this road today," as Victor Hugo's famous poem says.[67]

Just as relevant is the custom we have already mentioned, for girls and young women to wear red dresses for holidays, because village dyers were most successful with the range of reds. In peasant circles, a beautiful dress was almost always a red dress. That may be the case with the little girl of our story; to

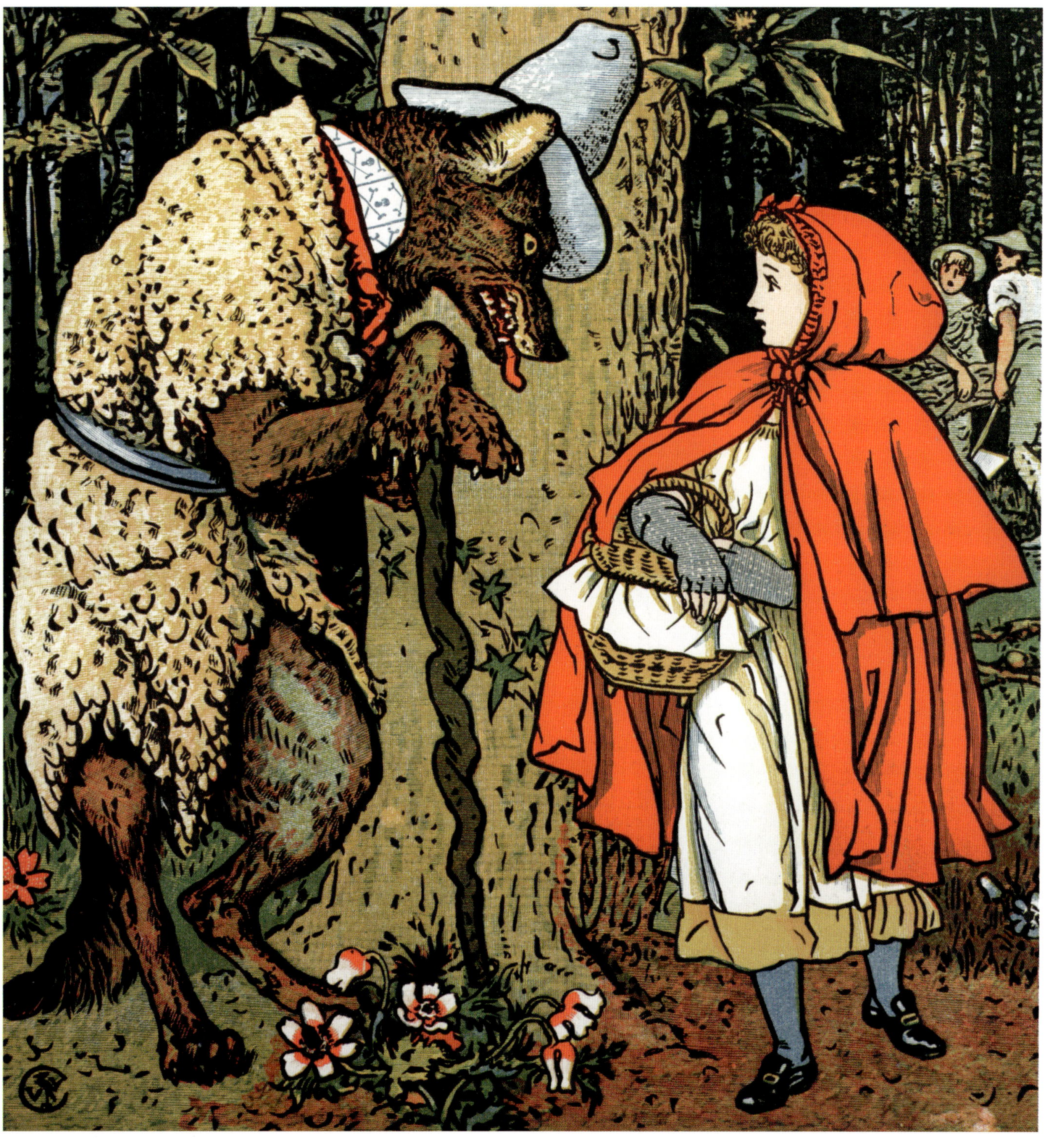

pay a visit to her grandmother, a more or less festive occasion, she wore her most beautiful clothing: a red hood.

One scholarly explanation has more solid foundation: it associates the clothing color with the red of the Pentecost. Two early versions of the story specify that it takes place the day of Pentecost, another that the little girl was born the day of Pentecost.[68] In the first case, she is simply wearing the color required for this holiday, that of the Holy Spirit: red. In the second, it is conceivable that since her birth, on a day so exceptional and auspicious, she has been devoted to red and always wears this color. Along the same lines, but without evoking the liturgical calendar, we can also imagine that this red is a protective color, a magic color, for fending off the forces of evil. European dress color customs attest to such a function from the earliest to the most recent times. Even up until World War II in certain regions of France, Germany, and Italy, it was not uncommon for young children—girls and boys—to wear red ribbons believed to protect them from misfortune.[69] Sometimes it was the newborn's cradle that was decorated with such a ribbon. This prophylactic red can be associated with other reds that function magically, abundant in mythological accounts, medieval literature, and oral traditions. Hence the good or evil red hats of dwarfs, gnomes, elves, and various forest and underworld spirits. Or again, the famous *Tarnkappe* of early Germanic legends, a kind of cloak or head covering that made the one wearing it invisible or invulnerable.[70] In its own way, the red hood of our little girl is a *Tarnkappe*, but one that, according

to Perrault at least, has lost its power; despite her clothing, the wolf devours her.

More debatable are the hypotheses advanced by psychoanalysis, notably by Bruno Bettelheim in his famous work *The Uses of Enchantment.*[71] The red of the hood supposedly has strong sexual connotations: the little girl, no longer a young child but a pubescent or prepubescent adolescent, basically "may have a deep desire to find herself in bed with the wolf," that is to say, with a "vigorous, male individual, full of desire like she is." The bloody devouring in the bed is supposedly the loss of virginity; the young girl is not losing her life so much as her innocence. Such an explanation, expanded and repeated countless times, leaves the historian perplexed. Not for its too easy appeal but because of its anachronistic nature. Since when has red been the color of sexual desire? Does such a question even make sense before Freud? There is room for skepticism here. Certainly, red has long been the color of lust and prostitution, but that is not at all a factor in this story for psychoanalysis; it is a matter of the first amorous, even carnal, feelings. In the Middle Ages, when the earliest versions of this story appeared, and even in the late seventeenth century when Charles Perrault drafted his own version of it, the first passionate impulses of the heart and feelings were associated not with red but with green, the symbolic color for nascent love.[72] If these psychoanalytic theories have their basis here—which I doubt—Little Red Riding Hood would have to be Little Green Riding Hood.

A last hypothesis may be offered to explain the red clothing worn by the little girl. But for

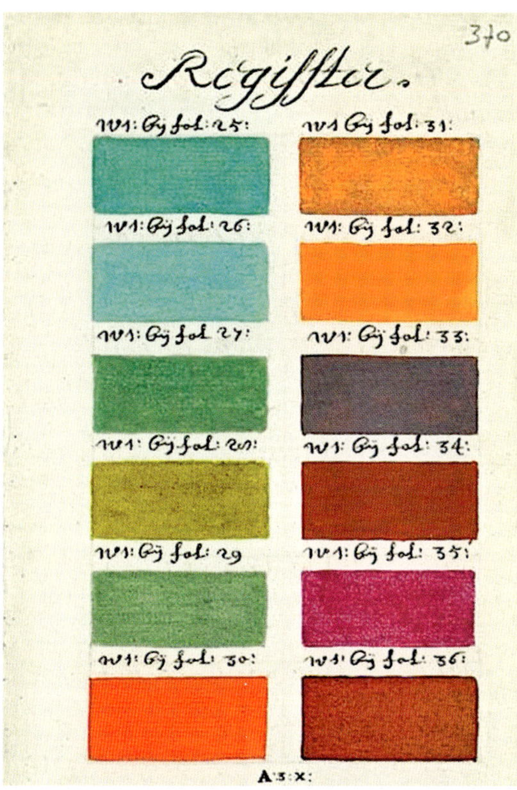

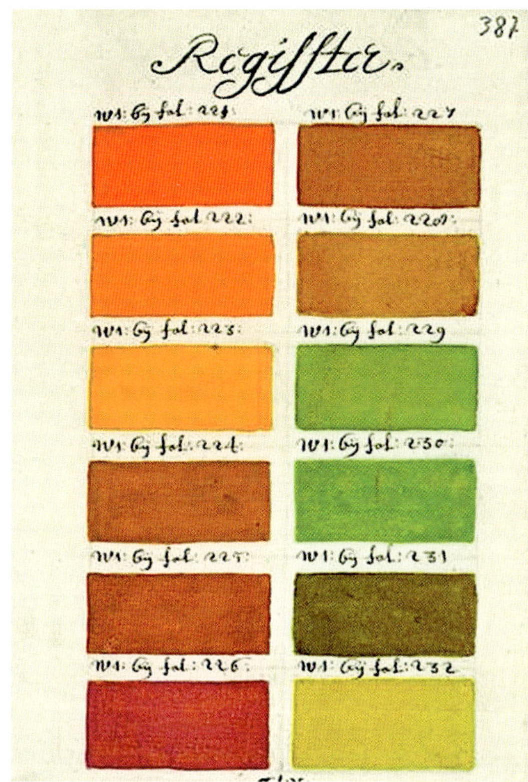

The Fashion for Color-Swatch Displays

The late seventeenth century witnessed a trend for color-swatch displays, first speculative, then practical. Their popularity grew throughout the next century. Here is one of the oldest surviving examples, painted in watercolor: colors are broken down into all their nuances (luminosity, density, tonality) for painting with water. The breakdown over the course of some 732 pages does not follow the order of the spectrum, recently discovered by Newton and still unknown to artists at the time, but the old Aristotelian order more or less modified and supplemented by painters over the centuries: white, (pink), yellow, (orange), red, green, blue, (gray), purple, (brown), black. More than five thousand shades are presented.

A. Boogaert, *Klaer Lightende Spiegel der Verfkonst*, Delft, 1692. Aix-en-Provence, Bibliothèque Méjanes, manuscript 1389.

this one, we must no longer imagine red in isolation but within the color triad it is part of, and we must do a semiological analysis. As in other tales and many fables, the account is constructed around the movement of three colors: red, white, black. In "Little Red Riding Hood," a little girl wearing red carries a small jar of white butter to a grandmother dressed in black (replaced in the bed by a wolf, which changes nothing with regard to the third color). In "Snow White," a young girl white as snow finds herself offered a poisoned red apple by an evil queen dressed in black. In "The Crow and the Fox," a black bird perched in a tree lets fall a piece of white cheese, seized immediately by an animal with a red coat. Multiply the number of examples, change

protagonists, rearrange the colors: the story is organized every time around these three chromatic poles. They form a system with narrative and symbolic powers exponentially greater than the simple sum of the meaning of each of the three colors operating alone.[73]

Here as elsewhere, in social practices as in representations, red takes on its whole meaning only insofar as it is combined with or opposed to one or many other colors.

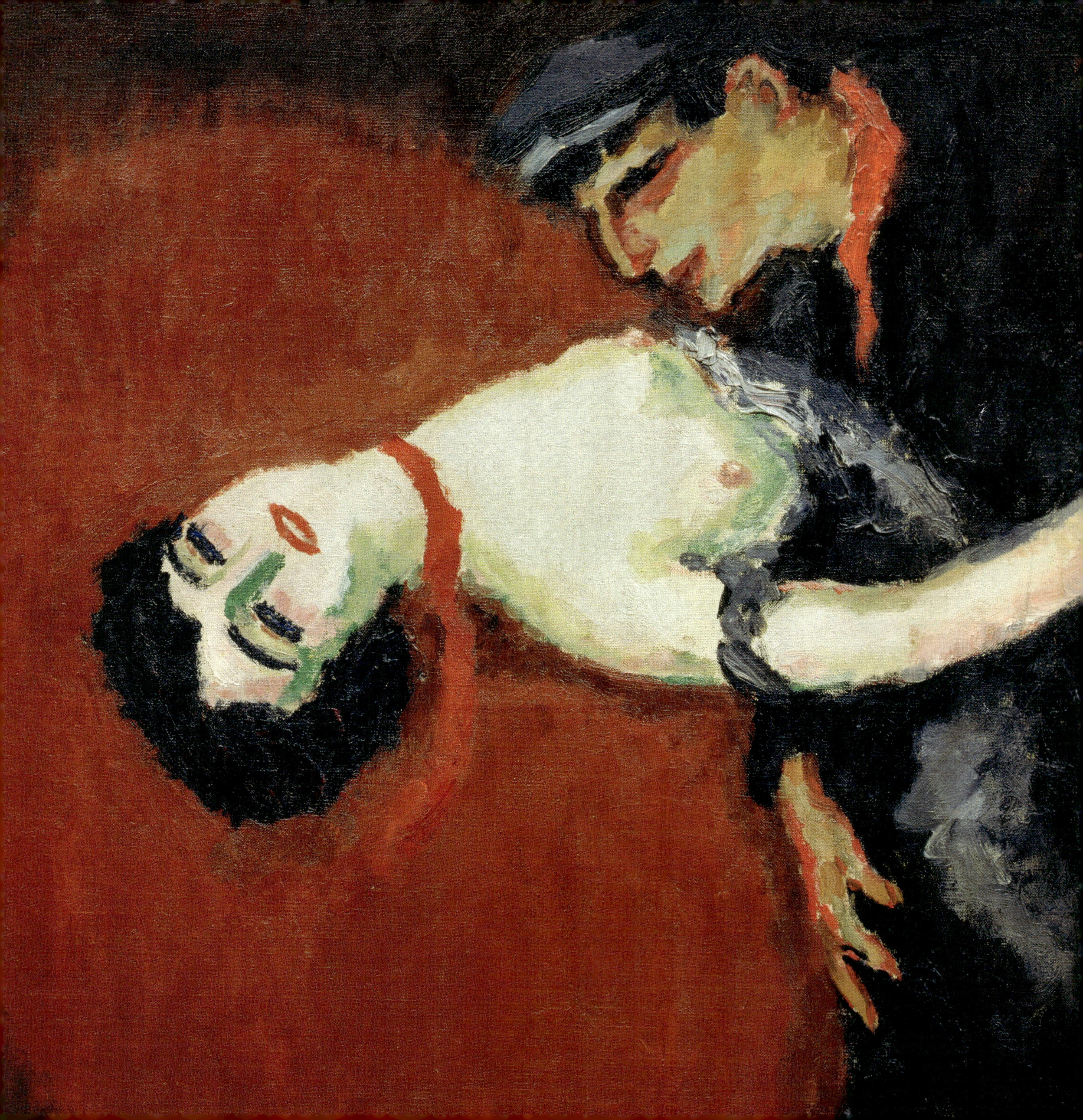

A DANGEROUS COLOR?

EIGHTEENTH TO TWENTY-FIRST CENTURIES

The splendor of life at court gave a false image to the seventeenth century. In reality it was a dark, anxious, and sometimes gloomy period, as much in its material aspects as in its attitudes and sensibilities, at least insofar as the huge majority of the European populations were concerned. There were continuous wars, shortages were rampant everywhere, the climate remained unfavorable, and life expectancy fell to very low levels. If the *grand siècle* had to be symbolized by one color, it would not be the gold of Versailles but the black of poverty.

In contrast, the eighteenth century appeared bright, luminous, and clear. It represented a sort of colorful interlude before the nineteenth century, when darkness returned once again. Beginning in the 1720s, the Enlightenment did not illuminate only the domain of thought, it also influenced the decor of everyday life. Doors and windows got bigger, and lighting options improved and their costs diminished. Henceforth, colors could be better seen and they were given more attention, especially as rapid and decisive progress was made in the chemistry of colorants, to the benefit of the dyeing and textile production industries. But all of society benefited, especially the middle classes, who, like the aristocracy, now had access to strong and vivid colors. Dull, dark tones were in decline throughout; this was the end of the muted browns, dark greens, and purplish crimsons of the preceding century. In clothing and furniture, the fashion was for light shades, gay colors, and pastel tones, principally in the range of blues, yellows, pinks, and grays.

These new styles did little to benefit to the color red however. The Enlightenment ushered in a century of blue, not of red—far from it, in fact. This was the period in which blue, long in competition with red, to the point that it was often considered one of red's opposites, seems to have become Europe's favorite color. It is still the favorite today, far ahead of all others, while red has fallen in rank, outstripped in opinion polls not only by blue but also by green.[1] The eighteenth century marks the starting point in red's slow but irreparable decline, at least in modern Western societies.

But that did not keep red from benefiting, like all the other colors, from continued advances in knowledge and techniques. Now measurable by Newtonian physics, produced and reproduced at will by the chemistry of pigments and dyestuffs, defined in all its nuances by an increasingly precise vocabulary, color gradually lost a share of its mystery. The relationships that not only artists and scientists maintained with it, but also philosophers, simple artisans, and even the common people, were gradually transformed. Attitudes changed, and dreams did as well. Certain questions debated for centuries with regard to color—about morality, symbolism, rules of heraldry—became less pressing. New concerns, new crazes claimed center stage; it was in this climate that the wave of colorimetry swept through the arts and sciences. Now colors could be broken down into displays of subtle shades to be used for painting, dyeing, decorating, or simply dreaming.[2]

Red did not escape this general trend and witnessed one of its shades, until then hardly conspicuous, become more appealing, acquire new status, be granted its own name—pink—and thereby take on a kind of autonomy. It is worth pausing here to look back and consider pink's slow emergence before celebrating its triumph in Enlightenment Europe at the time of Madame de Pompadour.

The Red of Love

Like all Fauvists, Kees Van Dongen was a great painter of reds, especially feminine reds, which are always seductive, often erotic, and sometimes dangerous.

Kees Van Dongen, *The Red Kiss*, 1907. Private collection.

Wolfgang Amadeus Mozart

Many portraits of Mozart survive, but few were painted from life. This one, largely a composite, was painted posthumously. The artist dressed Mozart in red, his favorite color.

Barbara Krafft, *Wolfgang Amadeus Mozart*, 1818. Vienna, Gesellschaft der Musikfreunde.

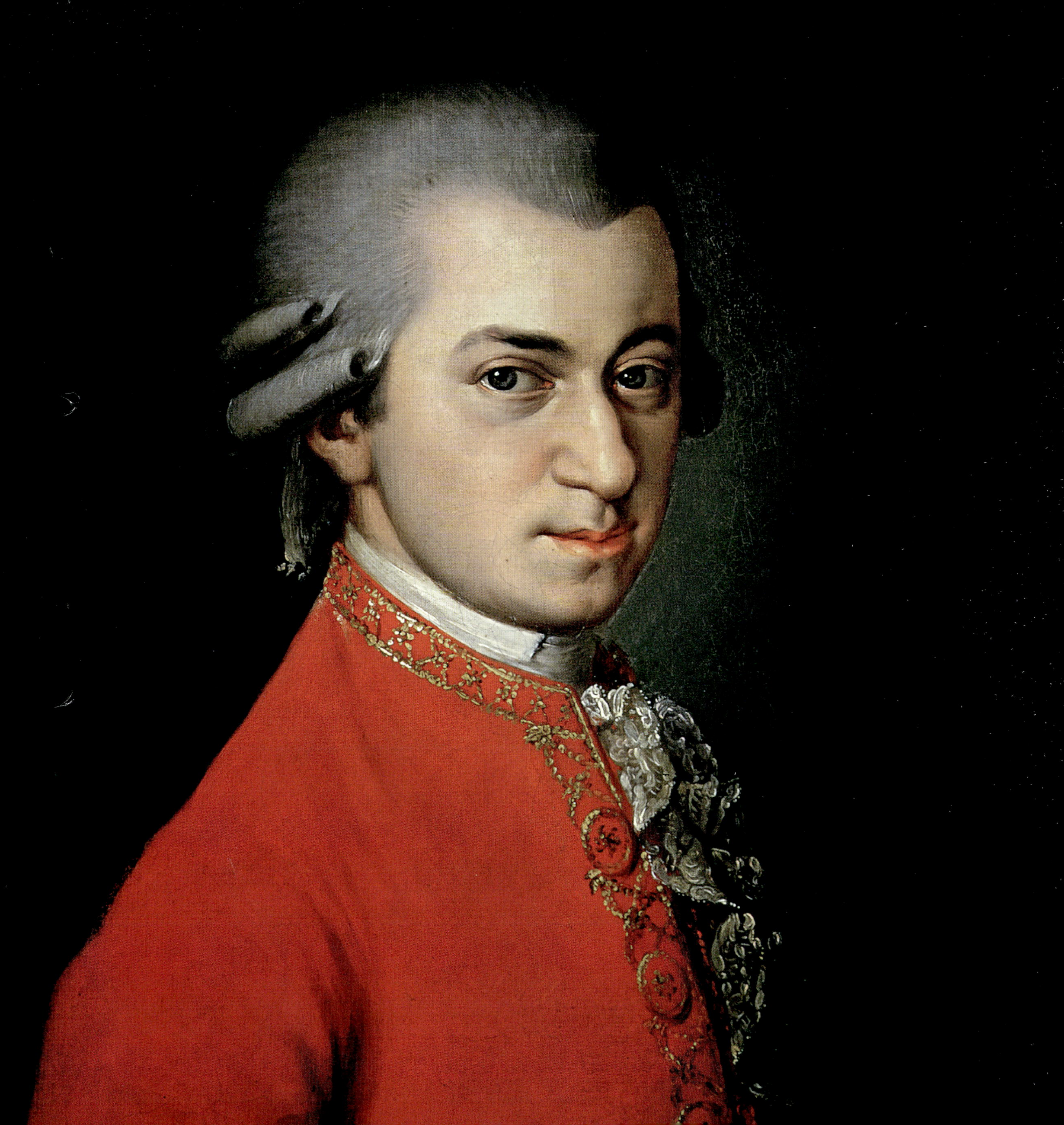

On the Margins of Red: Pink

Pink's Gentle Femininity

Prolific painter and draftsman François Boucher dabbled in all genres. His palette is very representative of French art in the century of Louis XV: luminous, transparent tones, pastel shades, subtle grays, always very light blues, and especially plenty of whites, pinks, and rosy hues. Boucher is a great painter of the female complexion.

François Boucher, *The Spoiled Child*, c. 1740. Karlsruhe, Germany, Staatliche Kunsthalle.

By the time of ancient Rome, red had been broken down into many shades that the lexicon tried to name and artists to reproduce. In Pliny's era, the Romans were already distinguishing some fifteen shades of red in their porphyry columns and purple fabrics, whereas they could name only two or three shades for green and hardly more for blue.[3] Over the course of time, a few of those red shades took on a certain independence. First came russet, which in the Middle Ages seemed to combine all the bad aspects of both red and yellow, as we have already discussed at length. Then came purple, which was long considered a mixture of blue and black, before becoming a mixture of blue and red just prior to the modern period, shortly before Newton discovered the spectrum. Thanks to its early position between blue and black, it still remains a semi-black or sub-black in two particular areas even to the present day: first,

among the liturgical colors of the Catholic worship service (purple for the times of waiting and penitence, black for funeral masses and Good Friday); second, for mourning customs in fashionable society (black for full mourning, purple for half-mourning). Finally, and most importantly, came pink, which languages long had difficulty naming and whose position on the color axis varied greatly.

Greek and Latin possessed no adjective to name the color pink, although Greeks and Romans, like all the peoples of Eastern antiquity, certainly had daily opportunities for seeing various shades of pink in nature, whether in flowers, rocks, or the sky at sunrise or sunset. If we may believe the poets, it was even a shade they seemed to appreciate. But they did not know how to define it, much less to name it. Where is our pink situated in the ancient *ordo colorum*? Between white and yellow? Between white and red? A Latin adjective *roseus* exists, of course, built upon the name of the flower (*rosa*), but it is a false friend; it does not mean "pink," but rather "bright red," "vermilion," "very beautiful red." It was often employed to describe the makeup used by women and fabrics that had been dyed with kermes (*coccum*).[4] Similarly, when Homer attributes "rosy fingers" to the dawn in his still-famous poetic phrase, it is not a matter of the flower, or of our color pink, but more simply of the splendid reddish reflections that the rising sun sometimes casts.[5] Moreover, with regard just to flowers, the roses of antiquity were never pink but almost always red, white, or sometimes yellow.[6]

Thus, whether it was a matter of nature, painting, or dyeing, the pink of ancient times

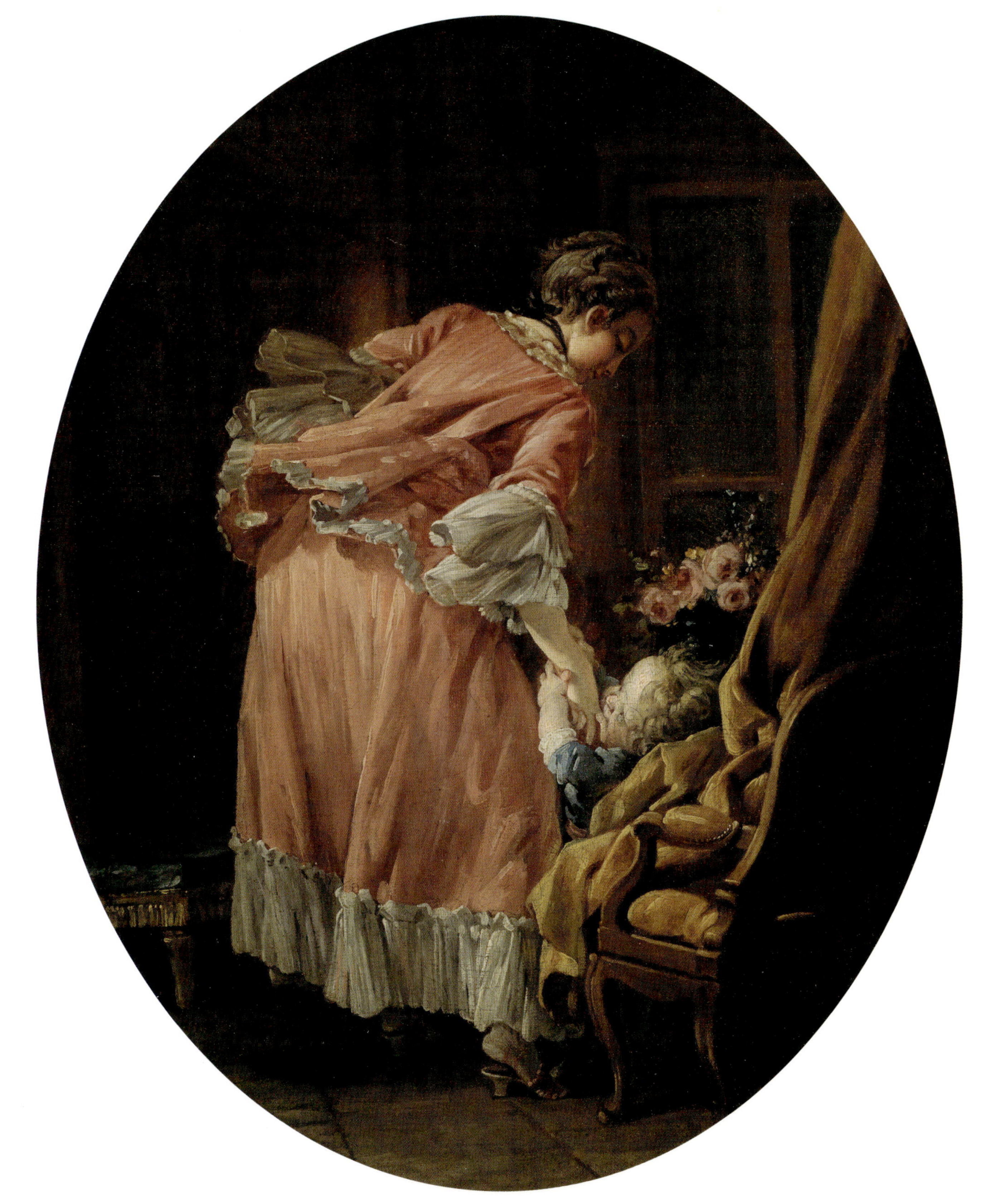

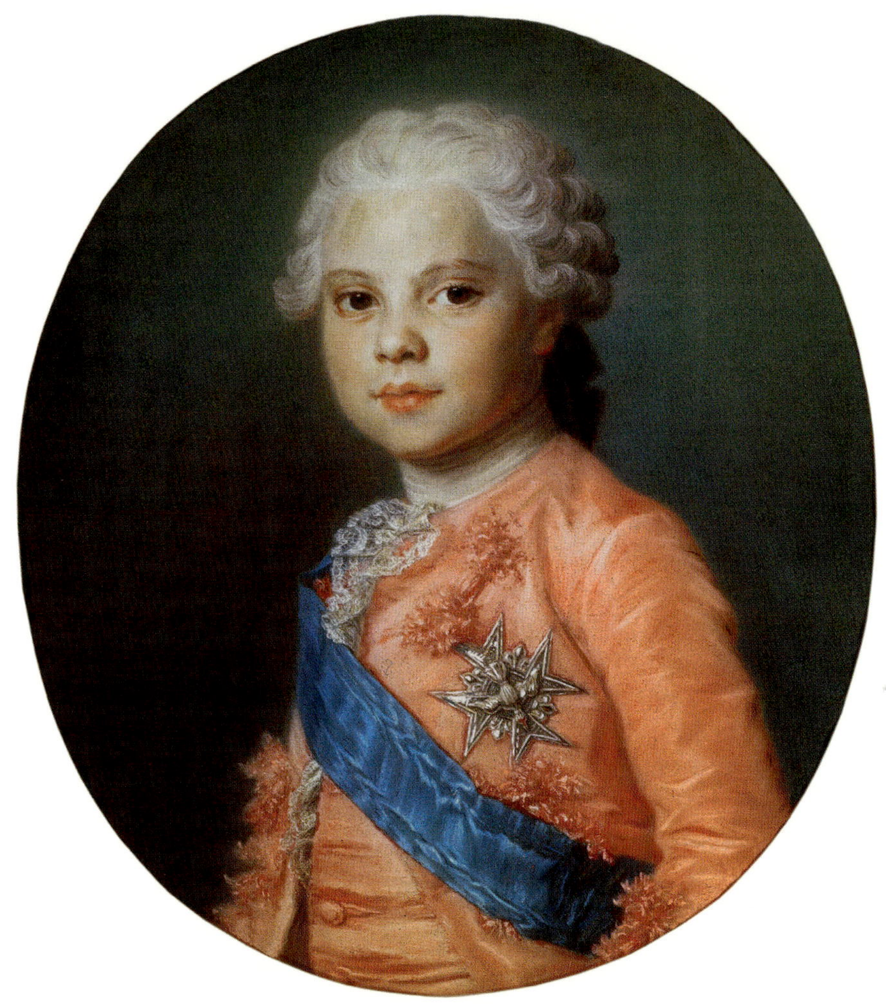

continued to mean "vermilion" and were used especially for cheeks, lips, and makeup. In Old and Middle French, *rose* (or *rosé*) did exist as an adjective, but it was rarely used. It was sometimes called upon to describe the color of the moon, or a light shade of leather or fabric, or the fur of an animal. It signified "pale," "beige," or "yellowish," more than actual pink.[8]

The first changes toward the recognition of pink took place at the turn of the fourteenth century to the fifteenth, when Venetian merchants began to import from Asia, in a more systematic fashion than previously, a dyestuff that had long been scorned: brazilwood (*brasileum*). This was a semiprecious wood, provided by many tree species from southern India and Sumatra, with dyeing properties that were well known but considered impermanent. Major dyers hardly ever used it. Nevertheless, in about 1380–1400, Italian artisans started to use new mordants and succeeded in making this dye more stable and producing new fabric colors never before seen outside of Asia; pink shades were now truly pink. They met with immediate success. In royal circles, many men wished to wear this exotic color, considered delicate and mysterious. At the French court, Jean de Berry, the great patron and lover of what we would call today "contemporary art," launched the pink craze, a fashion originating in Italy and involving not only fabric and clothing but also the pictorial arts. Very quickly the painters and illuminators were imitating the dyers. They transformed the dyestuff into lacquer and introduced various shades of this new pink into their palettes.[9]

was never given a color term strictly its own. The Latin adjective that might best describe it would be *pallidus* (pale), but that is an imprecise term with multiple meanings.[7]

The Christian Middle Ages, which sought out strong, vivid colors, made no new contributions and still could not describe our pink. The shade existed, in plant life and textiles notably, but it had less appeal than it had had in Rome and never had a name. In medieval Latin, *roseus* and its doublet *rosaceus*

One problem nevertheless remained: what to call this subtle new color, difficult to obtain but now prized throughout the West? Latin and vernacular languages had nothing to offer in this regard. Neither did Arabic, although perhaps Persian did. In the end, it was a word belonging to the Venetian dialect and to Tuscan that finally emerged: *incarnato*. Until then, *incarnato* had been used only to describe the facial complexion; from now on it would be used for all shades of pink and be translated as such into most European languages. In French, for example, *incarnat*, used as a color term, made its appearance by the years 1400–1420; in Castilian *encarnado* emerged in the same period, while *carnation* came into use in English a few decades later. Only German speakers seemed unaware of it.[10]

Finally the new color had a name. But where to locate it on the chromatic scale? The old classification system of Aristotle, which remained the standard one until Newton's discovery of the spectrum in 1666, went from white to black, passing successively through yellow, red, green, blue, and purple. Where to locate pink? If one saw it—as we do today—as a mixture of white and red, that place was already taken and decidedly so: between white and red there was yellow. On that point not only painters and dyers agreed, but so did all the authors who wrote about colors. In about 1500, for example, Jean Robertet, one of the skilled Grand Rhétoriqueurs as well as an elegant versifier, in a poem entitled "L'Exposition des couleurs," devoted a quatrain to yellow. He saw it as a mixture of red and white, and a source of joy.

Yellow
I am composed of red and white,
My coloration resembles the one of worry;
But let he who is happy in love have no worries,
Because he can wear me as seems good to him.[11]

Thus, between white and red, the space was occupied. That being the case, where to locate the new color? The only solution was to consider this beautiful new *incarnato* as a specific shade of yellow. And, in fact, that would be its status throughout Europe from the fifteenth to seventeenth centuries. All the dictionaries, color charts, and technical or professional manuals devoted to color make carnation—that is, our pink—a pale, delicate shade of yellow, not of red.[12] As for the French word *rose*, as a color adjective it never appeared in dictionaries before the middle of the eighteenth century. Diderot's and Alembert's great *Encyclopédie*, so comprehensive and knowledgeable about the colors, was one of the first to use it, but the *Dictionnaire* of the Académie Française did not include it until its sixth edition, published in 1835.

Meanwhile, in South America, Europeans had discovered an exotic wood-based dyestuff in the same family as the brazilwood (*brasileum*) they had imported from Asia but with clearly superior dyeing properties. They developed it so intensely that the name of the wood was eventually bestowed on the country that provided it, Brazil. Despite the long Atlantic crossing, the dyestuff's cost was not exorbitant, because the manpower employed in the South American forest operations consisted of slaves. Hence the fashion for pink could take off. It reached its height

Masculine Pink

In the age of the Enlightenment, pink was not at all reserved for girls' clothing. Many boys wore it and would continue to do so until the end of the nineteenth century. Here we see the future Louis XVI at ten years old.

Maurice Quentin de La Tour, *Portrait of a Child*, pastel, 1765. Paris, Musée du Louvre.

FOLLOWING PAGE

The Marquise de Pompadour

The marchioness loved pink and launched it as a fashion in the French court toward the middle of the eighteenth century.

François-Hubert Drouais, *Portrait of Jeanne-Antoinette Poisson, Marquise de Pompadour*, c. 1760. Chantilly, Musée Condé.

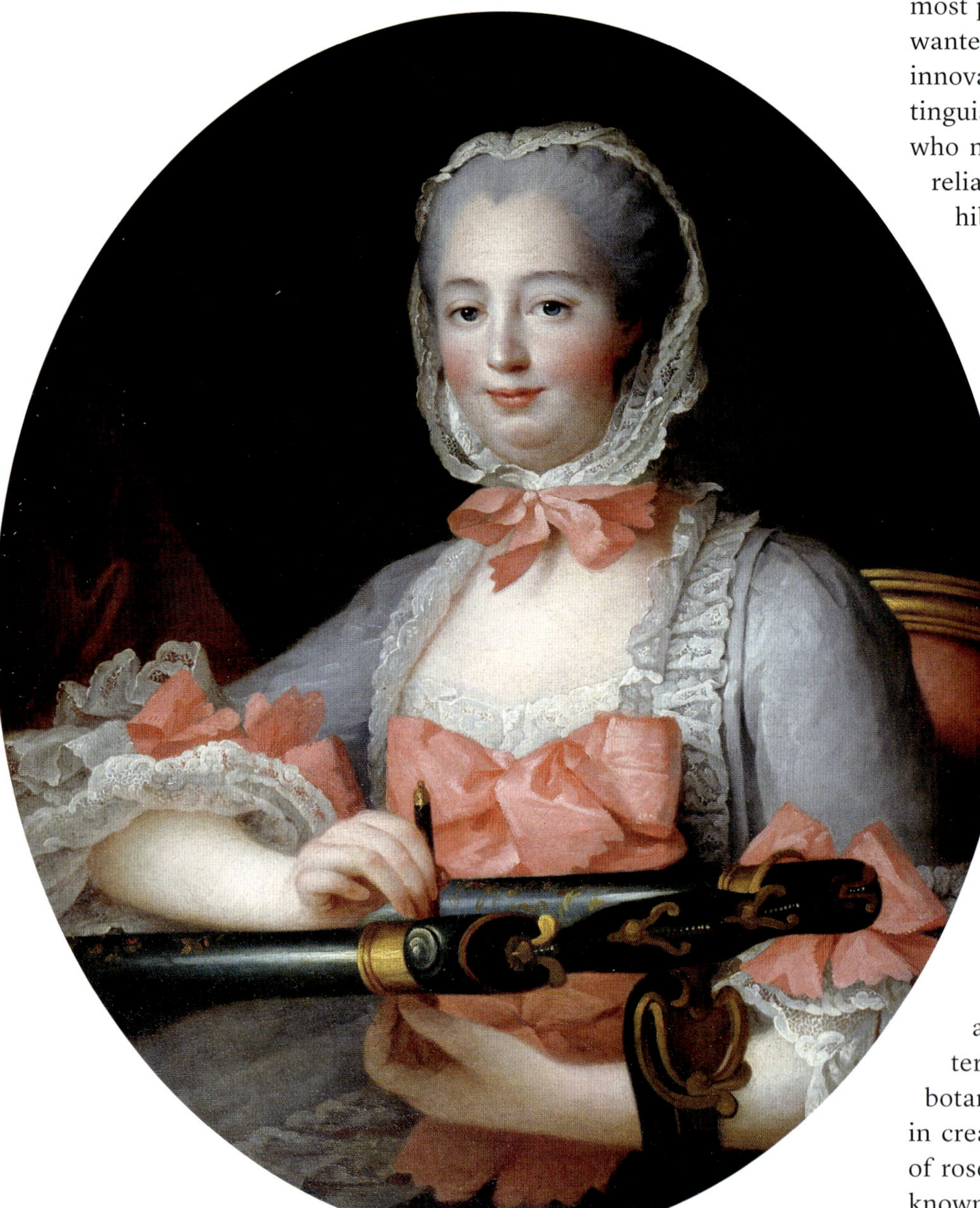

in the mid-eighteenth century, when the most privileged classes of European society wanted pastels, halftones, and the newest innovations in color shades in order to distinguish themselves from the middle classes, who now had access to bright, strong, and reliable colors that had formerly been prohibitively expensive for them.

In France under Louis XV it was Madame de Pompadour who made pink the fashion for furnishings and decor. She loved to combine it with sky blue, two tones that won her favor and that rapidly became the rage throughout Europe. But with regard to clothing, it was as much the men as the women who wore pink; that color was not in the least especially feminine yet. On the other hand, it was no longer considered a particular shade of yellow but was now finally seen as a mixture of red and white. Our modern pink was thus born sometime toward the middle of the eighteenth century. In French it was given a new name, no longer derived from the facial complexion but from the color of flower petals: the rose created the French color term *rose*. Over the course of decades, botanists and gardeners had succeeded in creating increasingly numerous varieties of roses, and roses that were truly *rose*, unknown in antiquity and the Middle Ages, had become common. These changes, however, took place very, very slowly. In the French language, the adjective and the noun *rose* were not definitively established as descriptors of the color we know by that name until the nineteenth century. The same is true in Spanish (*rosa*), Portuguese (*cor-de-rosa*), and German (*rosa*). As for the English word *pink*, for a long time it designated only the dyestuff extracted from brazilwood, before—belatedly—it came to describe the color obtained from that same wood.[13]

The fashion of dressing infants and young children in pink and sky blue does not date back to the eighteenth century. It seems to have appeared in the Anglo-Saxon world toward the middle of the nineteenth century and, contrary to what is sometimes written, seeking the Virgin's protection had absolutely nothing to do with this custom. It was a practice that developed in Protestant countries and spread slowly throughout all Western societies. Moreover, for a long time it was not divided by gender; girls and boys alike could be dressed in pink as well as blue. It even seems that male babies were more frequently dressed in pink than in blue, if we are to believe the paintings of fashionable society prior to World War I. Many examples still exist.[14] Yet this fashion was limited to the court, the aristocracy, and the upper middle class. In other social classes, infants were almost always dressed in white. It was not until the 1930s and the appearance of fabrics with colors resistant to repeated washing in boiling water that the use of pink and sky blue became more widespread, first in the United States, later in Europe. That was when a stronger gender division took place: pink for girls, blue for boys. Pink was no longer considered the child's

version of the old masculine red of warriors and hunters. Henceforth it was feminine, entirely feminine, whereas in the eighteenth century it was still very often masculine. Beginning in the 1970s, the famous Barbie doll fully embodied this feminine role and gradually extended its empire to the whole world of little girls' make-believe—which may be cause for regret.[15]

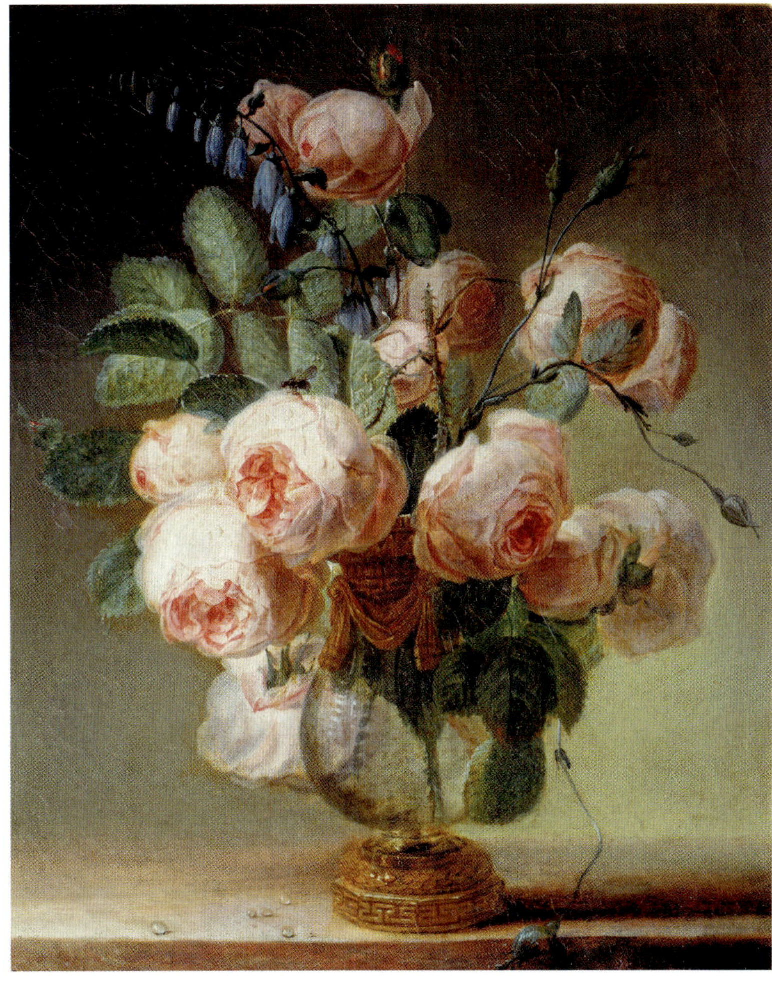

The Pink of Flowers

The rose has no monopoly on the color that goes by that name. Many other flowers assume pink shades, notably peonies.

Pierre-Joseph Redouté, *Vase of Flowers*, early 19th century. Rouen, Musée des Beaux-Arts.

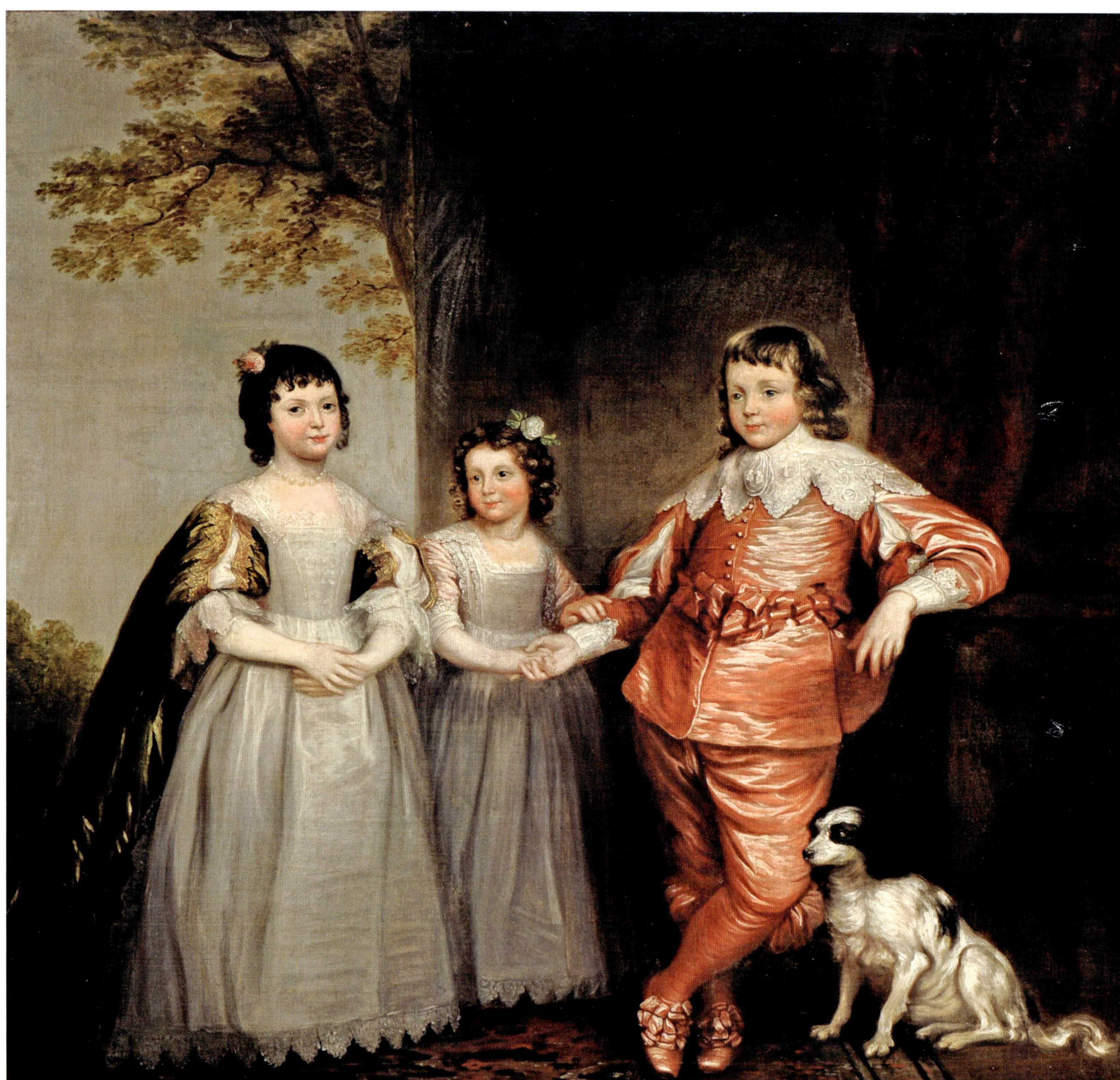

Brother and Sisters

Only his style of clothing (from the 1640s) distinguishes the boy from the girls here. Not only is he dressed entirely in pink but he is wearing his hair long.

George Romney studio, in the style of Anthony Van Dyck, *The Woolaston White Children*, c. 1780. Ormesby, Yorkshire, England, Ormesby Hall.

Little Girl in Blue

Around 1900, little girls were not at all captives of pink; blue was just as feminine as it was masculine.

Mary Stevenson Cassatt, *Sketch of Head of Margot*, pastel sketch, c. 1890. Chicago, The Sullivan Collection.

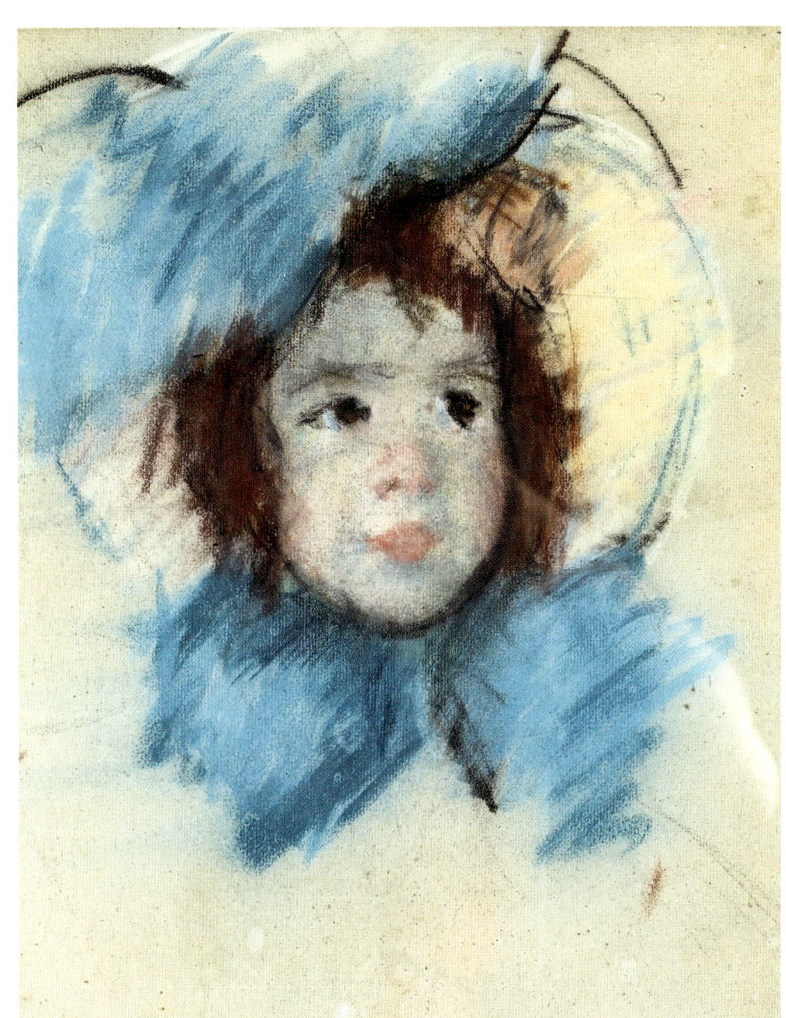

Makeup and Society Life

Courtly Feasts and Country Fashions

In the mid-eighteenth century, even while high society sought out delicate shades and pastel tones, the middle classes claimed lively, luminous colors, formerly reserved for the elite. Women in particular wore very colorful dresses, if not everyday, at least for special occasions.

Christian Wilhelm Ernst Dietrich, *Blind Man's Bluff*, 1750. Private collection.

Let us leave pink to its fate and return to red. The century of the Enlightenment, as we have said, witnessed red's decline in elegant clothing, as much in women's dresses as men's suits. It was in decline, but not absent, and even seemed to experience a short return to favor in the 1780s, first in England, then in France and Italy. On the other hand, among the peasantry, red never really went out of style. In all of rural Europe throughout the eighteenth century, it was often worn for holidays.

In courtly circles, red was especially prominent on faces. Never, not even in the most depraved and decadent Roman times, had makeup and cosmetics been used to such excess. Men and women covered their faces with white lead that they accentuated about the lips and cheekbones with cinnabar-based red products that were just as dangerous. The toxicity of the white lead in ceruse was beginning to be recognized at that time, but concern for appearances outweighed the risks. It was applied as a cream or powder, and the goal was to have the whitest possible face and neck—and for women, shoulders, arms, and throat—in order not to be mistaken for a peasant, whose skin was necessarily bronzed or reddened, or even for the provincial minor nobility living in the country, in the open air. A courtier had to have the palest face possible, if necessary supplementing ceruse by taking arsenic-based lozenges. Although still very toxic, arsenic in low doses had the power to lighten the skin to the point that veins would appear, accentuating the "blue blood" of the artificially depigmented man or woman. Additionally, light blue makeup could emphasize those veins visible through the skin at the forehead and temples. Nothing was more ennobling or status-enhancing in the second half of the seventeenth century and the first half of the eighteenth. There were many who took this mortal risk, and in fact, in the years 1720–60, very many health problems resulted from the use of white lead and arsenic lozenges.

The quest for "blue blood" seems to have started in Spain in the late Middle Ages or the early modern period. For the aristocracy, it was a matter of distinguishing oneself not only from the peasantry and the minor rural nobility but also from the descendants of the Moors, who had sometimes intermarried with the Iberians. Skin with a bluish pallor was evidence of racial purity and ancient nobility. Subsequently, this fashion for blue blood spread from Spain into France and England, and then to Germany and the rest of northern Europe. It seems to have reached

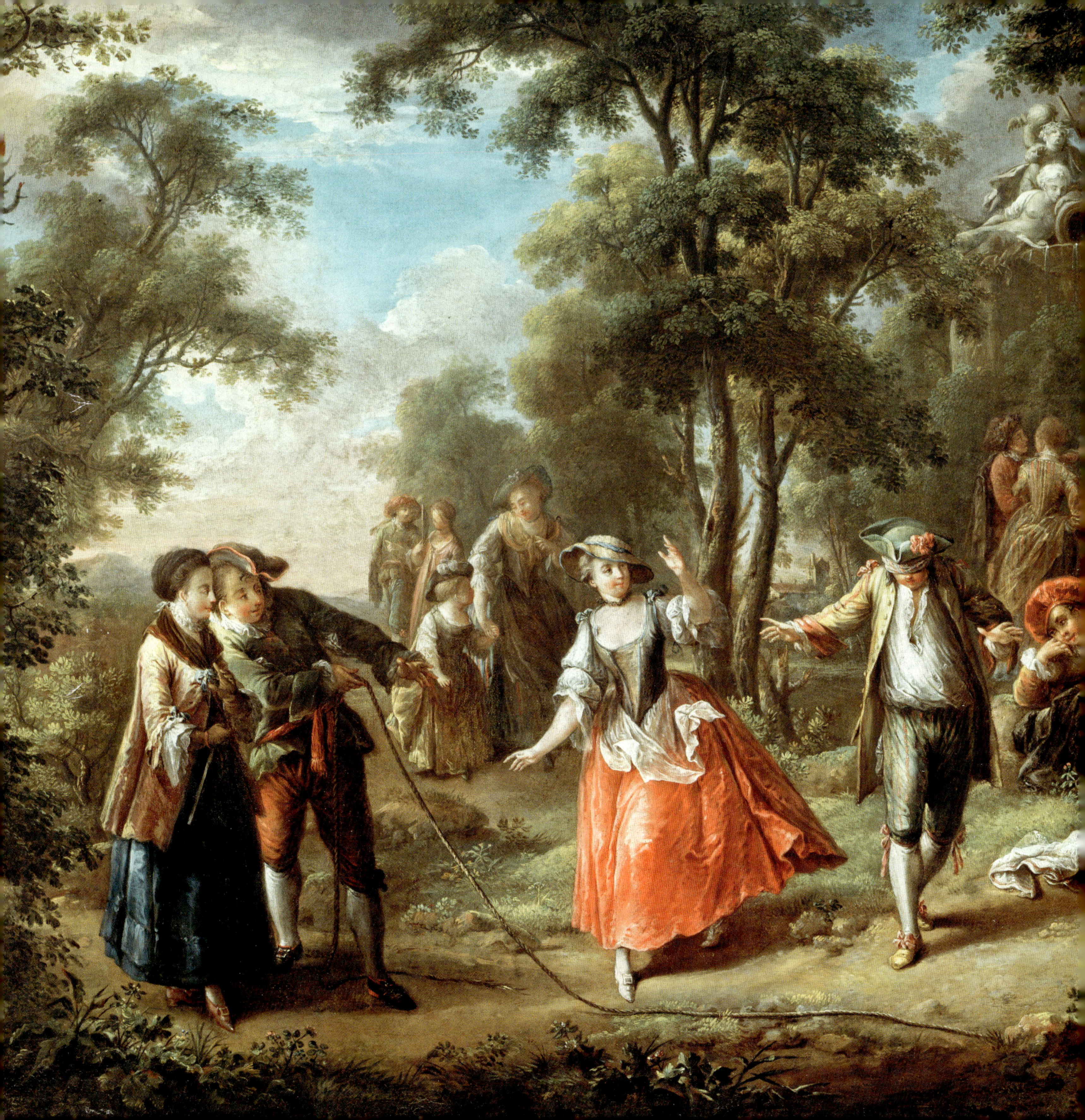

its height about 1750.[16] An aristocratic face had to take on a lunar appearance, with veins showing in the forehead and temples, and a thick layer of ceruse hiding all the imperfections of the skin and signs of aging. Men and women sometimes resembled ancient marble statues, but statues to which red had been added about the face, because fashionable society required that lips and cheeks never "be seen without rouge."

That red makeup was also dangerous, the products generally having a lead-oxide (minium) or mercuric-sulfide (cinnabar) base integrated into beeswax, mutton suet, or vegetable fats. Their use was so widespread in high society that the word "red" came to be synonymous with the word "makeup." That has not completely disappeared today; when a woman says she is going to reapply "a bit of red," everyone knows she means lipstick. Carrying

Three Marriageable Young Girls

Dressed in white and absorbed in their sewing, these three sisters are still young women, eligible for marriage. Their white skin highlights their "blue blood"—that is, the high nobility of their birth. As for the red on their cheeks, it is already a concession to society life.

Joshua Reynolds, *The Ladies Waldegrave*, 1780. Edinburgh, Scottish National Gallery.

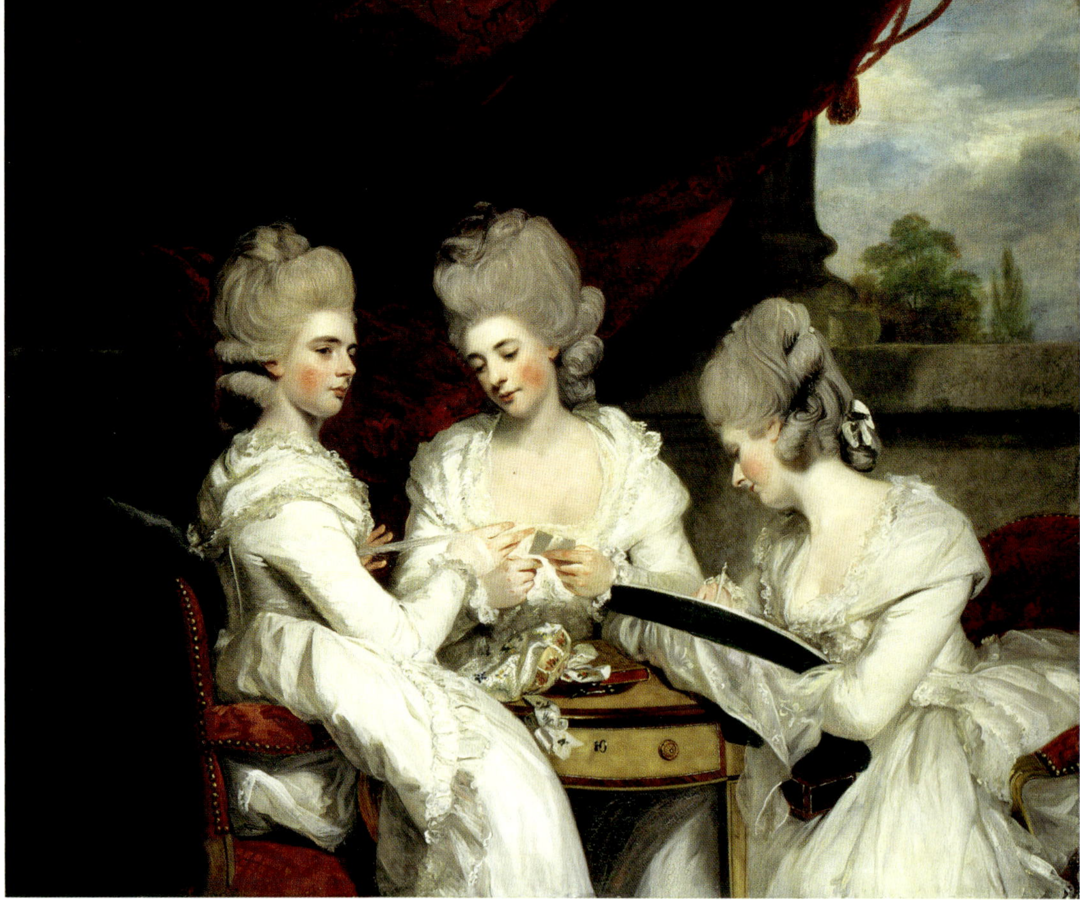

about little cases of makeup, powder, mirrors, and brushes, and not hesitating to redo one's makeup in public was a practice that already existed in the eighteenth century, not just for women but also for men. In the French court, red for lips and cheeks was almost obligatory, and the color had to be as saturated as possible. Whether its shade was light or dark varied according to the current fashion or to the rank of the one wearing it. The higher the rank, the more vivid the red. This cosmetic red was so much the symbol of fashionable society that when men or women withdrew to their estates, far from the court or the city, they were said to have "quit the red." No further explanation was needed; everyone understood, especially because many European courts imitated the court of Versailles. Not all however: when the young Marie-Antoinette, accustomed to the Viennese court, discovered Versailles in 1770, she was disconcerted if not frightened by all the "painted faces" surrounding her and immediately wrote as much to her mother. And yet, by 1770 the use of makeup at the French court was already in decline.

The white and red of makeup were often combined with the black of *mouches* (literally, "flies"), small bits of gummed cloth in the form of dots, stars, moons, or suns, meant to give one's face provocative charm or emphasize the whiteness of one's skin. They were called by different names, depending on whether they were placed at the corner of the eye (*l'assassine*, murderess), in the middle of the cheek (*la galante*, lady friend), near the lips (*l'enjouée*, cheerful one), on the chin (*la discrète*, discreet one), or on the neck or throat (*la généreuse*, generous one). As with

everything else, they belonged to the art of trompe l'oeil, an art pushed to excess by a society obsessed with its appearance and moving into a framework closer to theater. Certainly by mid-century there were growing numbers of men and women who found this excessive use of makeup indecent or ridiculous, but it took another decade for such paints, creams, powders, and other accessories to experience a true decline, first in Germany and northern countries, a bit later in Catholic Europe. The

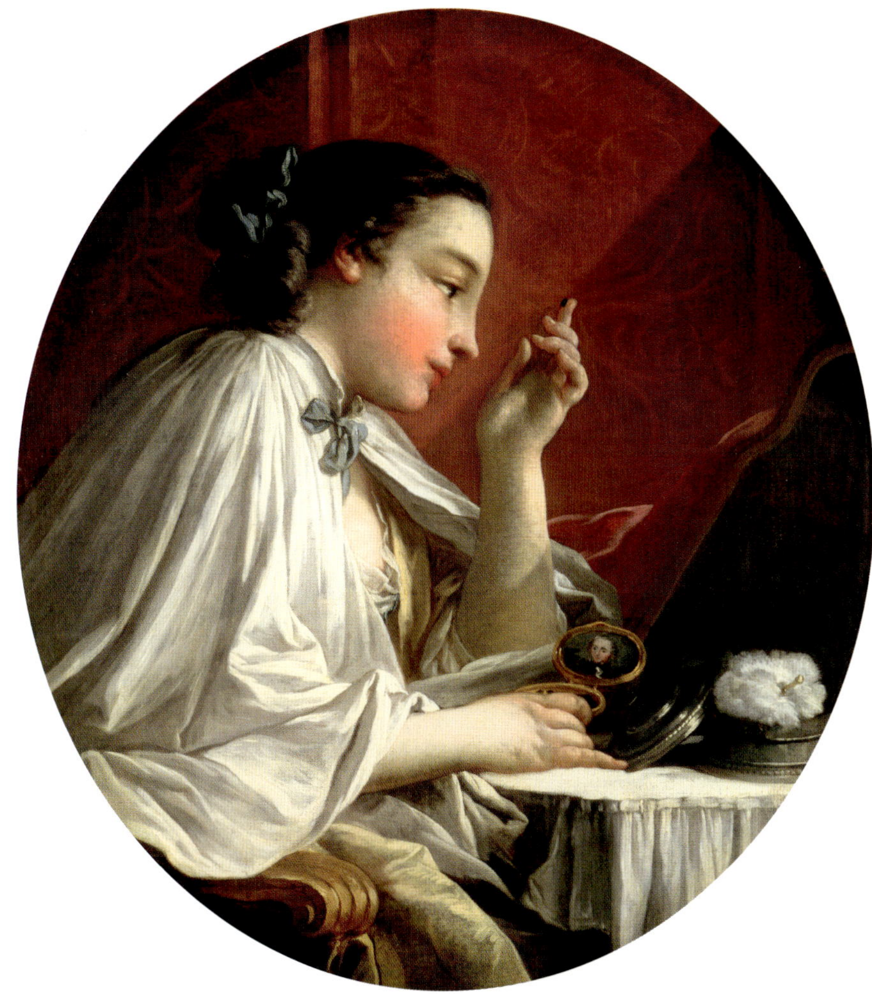

Paints, Powders, and Makeup

Society life demanded that a woman have the whitest possible face, neck, throat, and arms, and by contrast, very red cheeks, all accented here and there with black *mouches* (flies).

François Boucher, *Woman at Her Toilette*, c. 1760. Private collection.

The Red World of Prostitutes

Henri de Toulouse-Lautrec, *In Salon of Rue des Moulins*, 1894–95. Albi, France, Musée Toulouse-Lautrec.

use of red on lips and cheeks did not disappear however. In Paris around 1780, advertisements still vaunted the famous *rouge de la reine* ("queen's red," but which queen?) from Monsieur Dubuisson of the Left Bank, rue des Ciseaux, as well as another "entirely vegetal"—that is, nontoxic—red from a certain Demoiselle Latour, a red that "combined rose scent with the most brilliant of colors, available in all shades."[17]

After that, neoclassical tastes, revolutionary upheaval, and the Napoleonic Wars

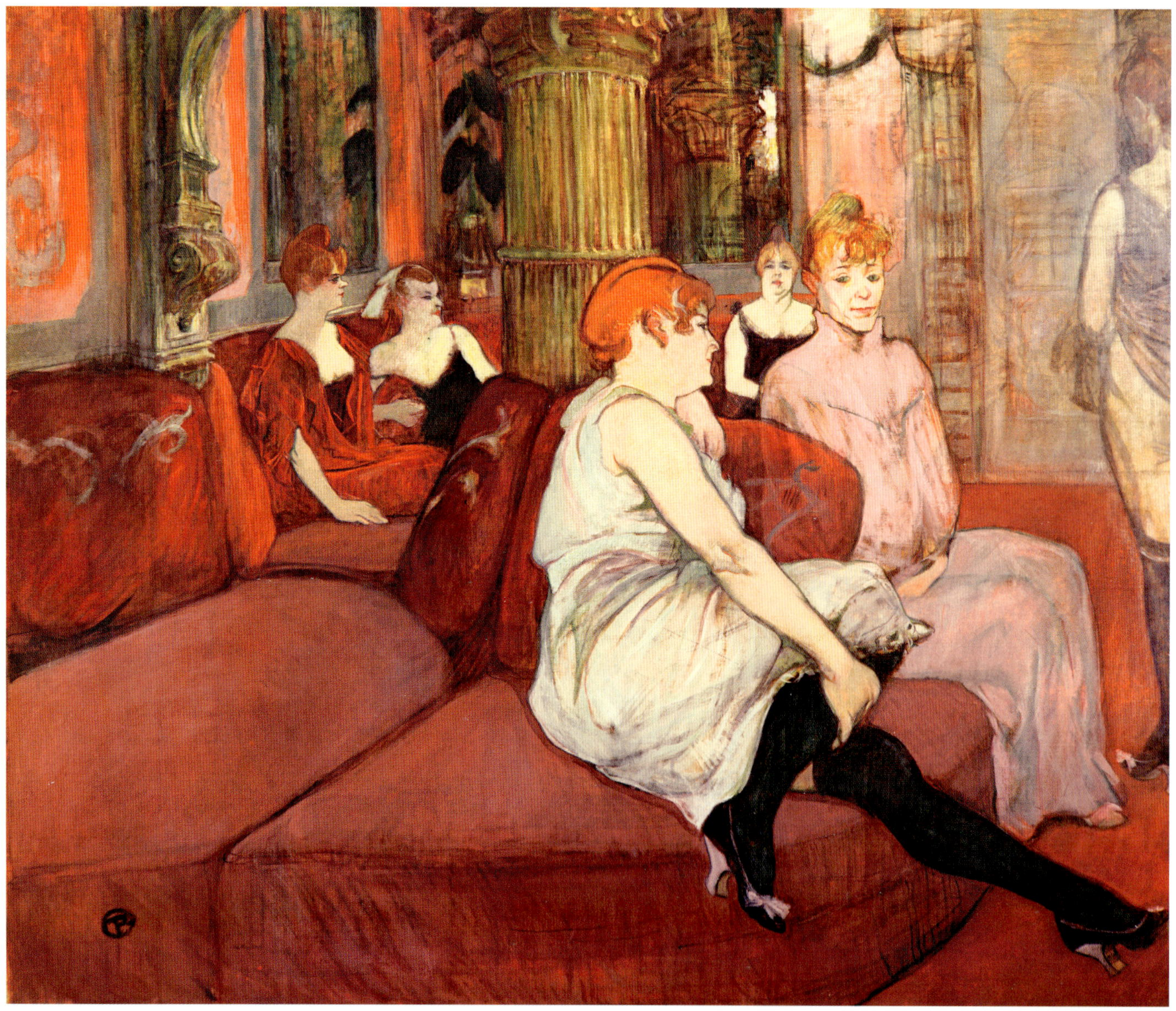

transformed fashionable society and relegated to the background the style for excessively made-up faces. It did not disappear completely, but over the course of the nineteenth century, it gradually gave way to more subtle and restrained makeup practices, in keeping with new lighting and new social codes. Only those women who made a profession of debauchery or wanted to create a scene continued to paint their faces and overuse red. Fascinated by those at the margins of the social order, many great painters

Paris Brothel

Boris Grigoriev, *Entrez!* 1913. Moscow, Pushkin State Museum of Fine Arts.

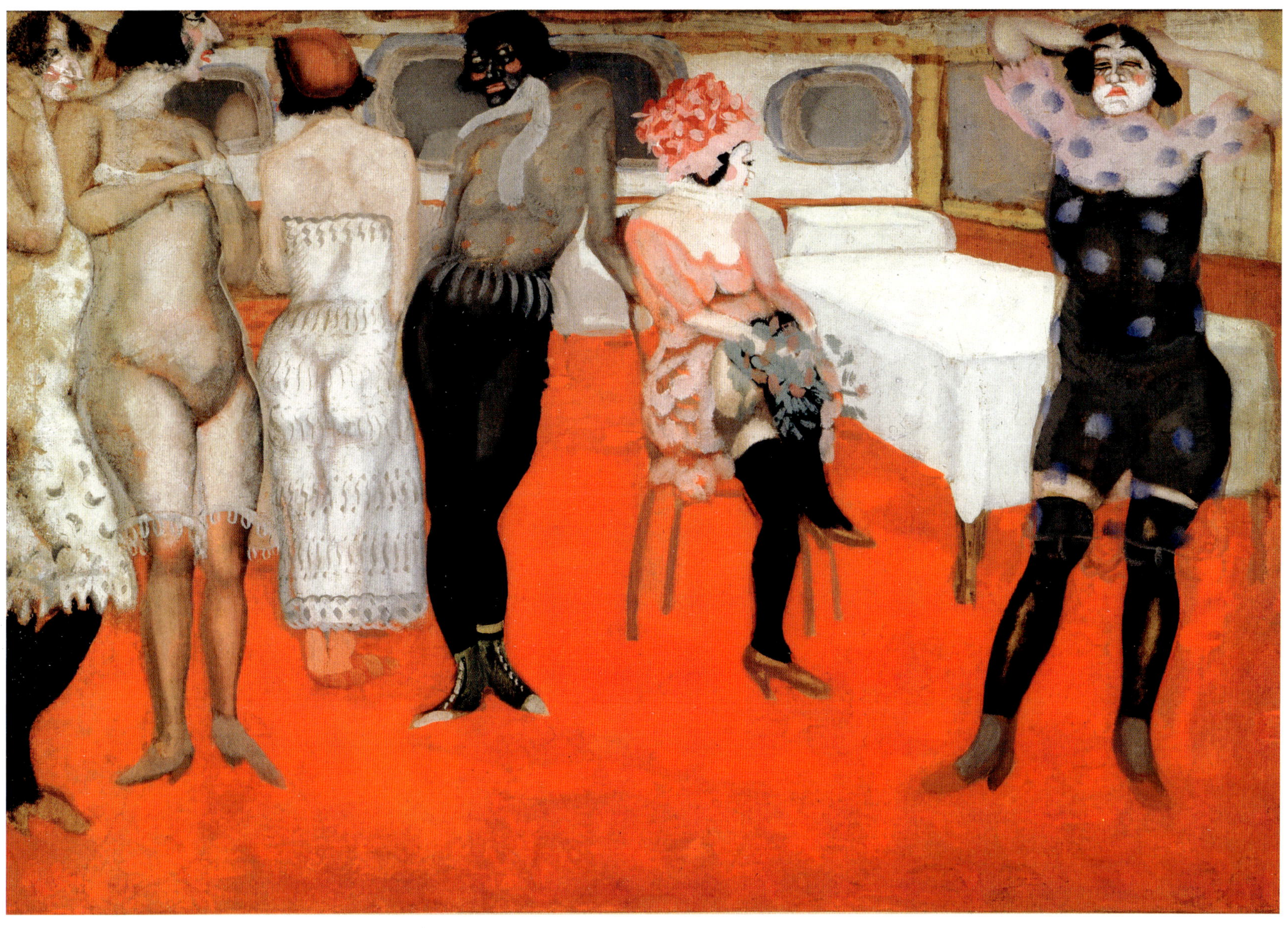

left us a few famous images of them: Manet, Toulouse-Lautrec, Van Dongen, Modigliani, Otto Dix, and others, for example.

Although they were more discreet about it, women of polite society did not give up red for

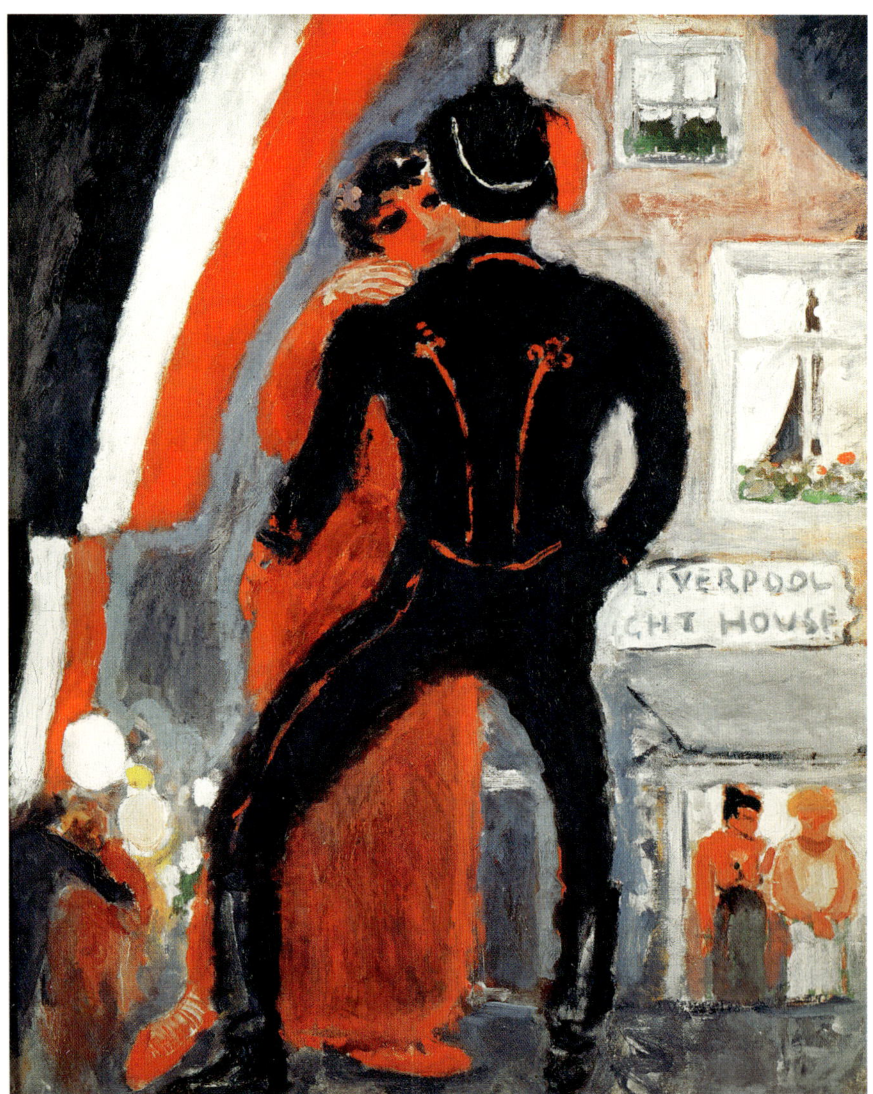

the lips, however. In fact, after World War I, its use became more democratic, and lip colorant became the object of true mass consumption. Henceforth it was sold in tubes with a turning mechanism and available in a great number of shades. In the past, names like *Carmine*, *Garnet*, *Cherry*, *Vermilion*, and *Poppy*, perhaps accompanied by a simple adjective (*light*, *dark*, *matte*, *glossy*) were sufficient. Now, red shades were indicated with phrases that were meant to be catchy or poetic, not in the least concerned with naming the exact color but rather with creating surprise, intrigue, or fantasy: *Morning Peony*, *Midsummer Night*, *Opera Festival*. Brands competed in their inventiveness, captivating female audiences with their vast arrays of shades and the quality of their new products, but also with the originality of their names. At the same time, many makeup testers were made available to serve as guides or for advertising. They constituted veritable dictionaries of red; no other color, in no other area, offered anything like this. The definitive turning point in this phenomenon probably occurred in 1927, when the chemist Paul Baudecroux invented for lips an indelible red with an eosin base, a red that topped everything by being "kiss-proof." With its bright, almost aggressive color, it was given the lovely name *Rouge Baiser* (red kiss) and enjoyed considerable success through the 1950s, vaunted by fashionable actresses such as Natalie Wood and Audrey Hepburn. After that time, women preferred products with a softer, less dense texture, but the now mythic name remains the trademark for a whole range of cosmetics even today.

Beginning in the nineteenth century, men no longer wore red on their faces (apart from clowns and certain actors) and wore it less and less in their clothing. Generally, as time went on, red became a more feminine color. When the French Army abandoned its famous madder-red trousers in spring 1915, that was the end of the masculine red of warriors that dated back to the earliest times.[18] In this area, Mars had definitely given way to Venus. Red no longer clothed men, but it continued to adorn women. For them, it remained an elegant and fashionable color, even if it was not suited for all occasion or all age groups. Although it continued to be worn by little girls, it was not considered appropriate for young or very old women, at least in high society. Marcel Proust, so attentive to colors in all domains, gives us reliable evidence of this in a famous passage from *The Captive*. The narrator, who is in love with young Albertine and wants to order an elegant outfit for her, wonders whether red is suitable. He asks the Duchess de Guermantes, whom he admires and with whom he was once more or less in love:

> But it was only in driblets that I was able to obtain from Mme de Guermantes that information as to her clothes which was of use in helping me order costumes similar in style, so far as it was possible for a young girl to wear them, for Albertine.
>
> "For instance, Madame, that evening when you dined with Mme de Saint-Euverte, and then went on to the Princesse de Guermantes, you had a dress that was all red, with red shoes, you were marvelous, you reminded me of a sort of great blood-red blossom, a glittering ruby.... Is it the sort of thing that a young girl can wear?"

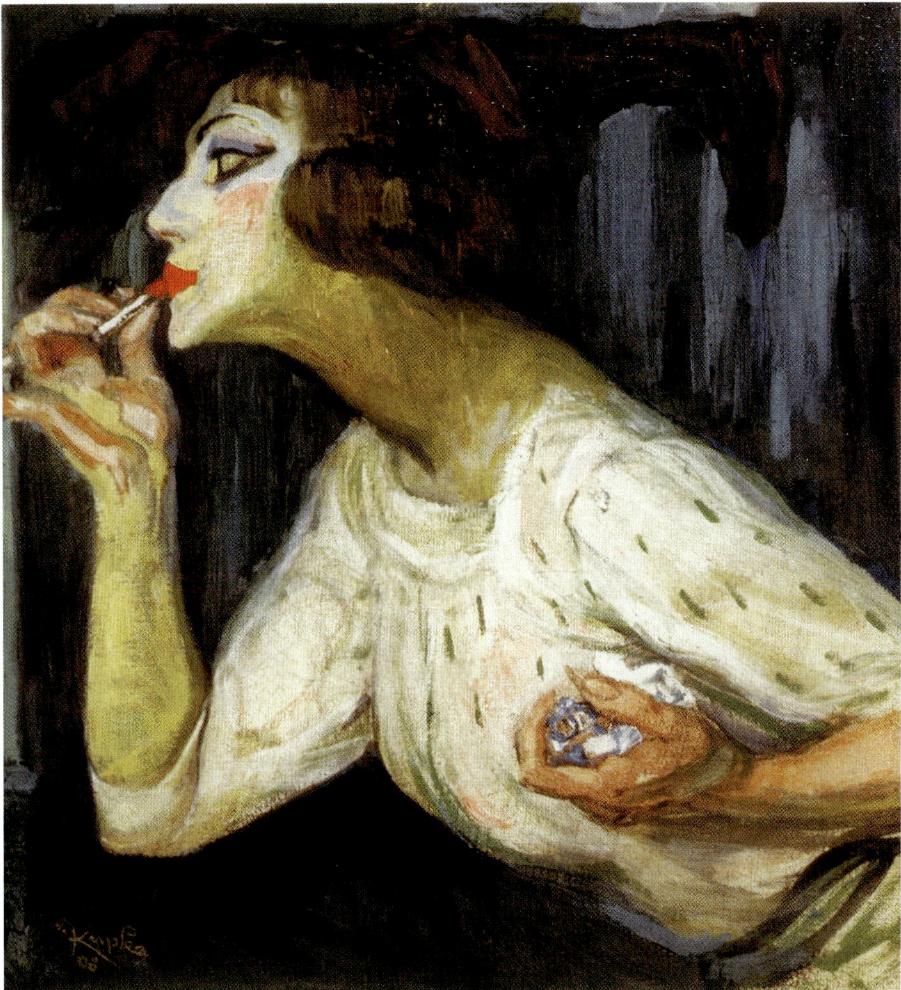

The Duchess ... quizzically and delightedly, with tears of merriment in her eyes ... appeared to be saying, "What's the matter with him? He must be mad." Then turning to me with a winning expression: "I wasn't aware that I looked like a glittering ruby or a blood-red blossom, but I do indeed remember that I had on a red dress: it was red satin, which was being worn that season. Yes, a young girl can wear that sort of thing at a pinch, but you told me your friend never goes out in the evening. It's a full evening dress, not a thing she can put on to pay calls."[19]

This passage is instructive but dated; the night in question occurs on the eve of World

A Hussar's Hired Love

This scene takes place on an infamous street in Rotterdam, not Paris. That is the Dutch flag.

Kees Van Dongen, *Le Hussard*, or *"Liverpool Light House" in Rotterdam*, 1907. Private collection.

PRECEDING PAGE

Red Lipstick

Painting their lips red is something that women have done in all periods from antiquity to the twenty-first century. Depending upon the culture, period, social class, and current fashion, the shades vary widely: purplish or blackish reds in the late Roman Empire, subtle and delicate reds in the mid Middle Ages, violent and saturated reds in the eighteenth century, all different shades today.

František Kupka, *The Red Lipstick*, 1908. Paris, Musée National d'Art Moderne.

War I, a period in which women made social calls in the afternoon and dressed differently for large evening receptions. Customs changed rapidly following the war. The Roaring Twenties soon forgot the old dress codes, and the 1960s liberated bodies from all constraints and taboos, including chromatic ones. Today, any woman can dress in red if she wants to, no matter what her age, social class, profession, or circle. Only in a few very particular circumstances—funerals, for example—might she avoid wearing that color.[20]

Madder Red Trousers

In summer 1914, the French infantry left for war dressed almost exactly like their elders in 1870. The uniform had hardly changed: heavy, impractical, and most important, too conspicuous. In autumn, their red pants, dyed with madder, were an easy target for the German army.

Arrival of a Train of French Prisoners in Germany, colored postcard, late 1914.

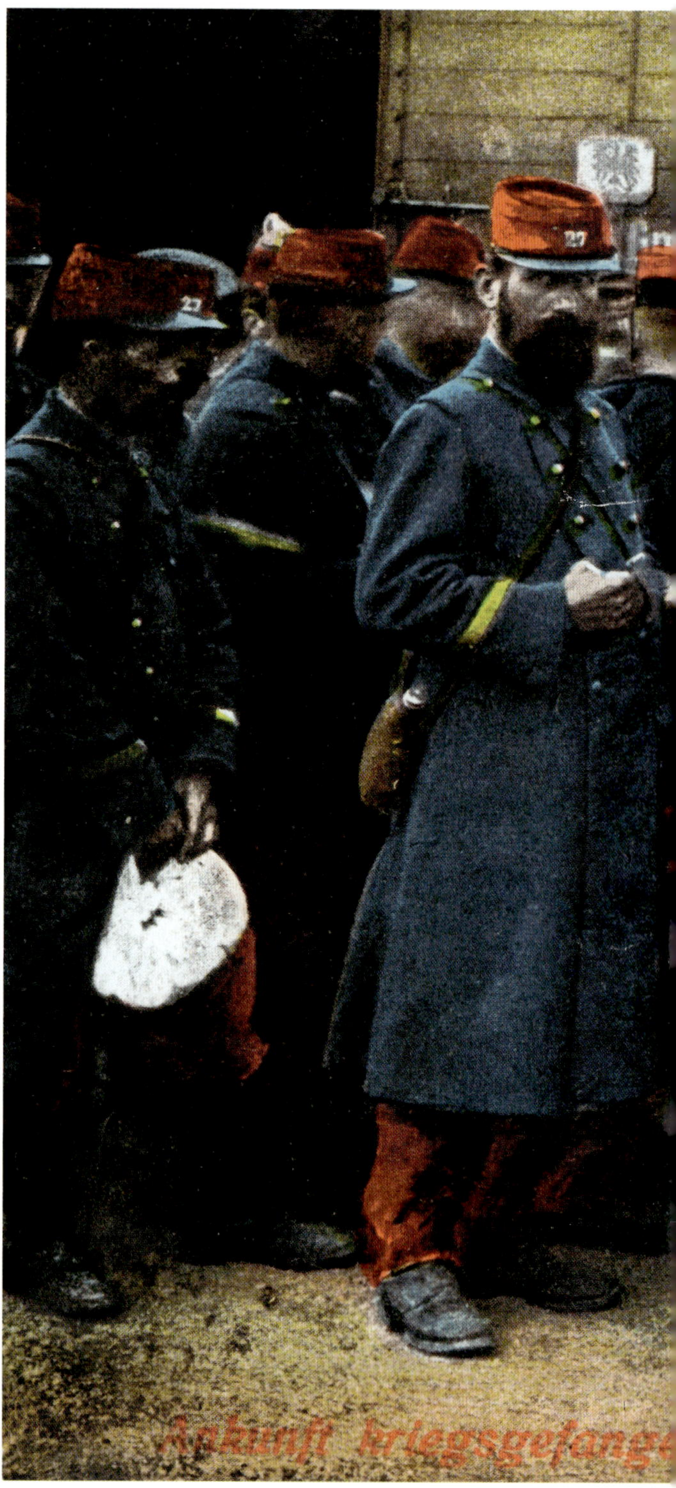

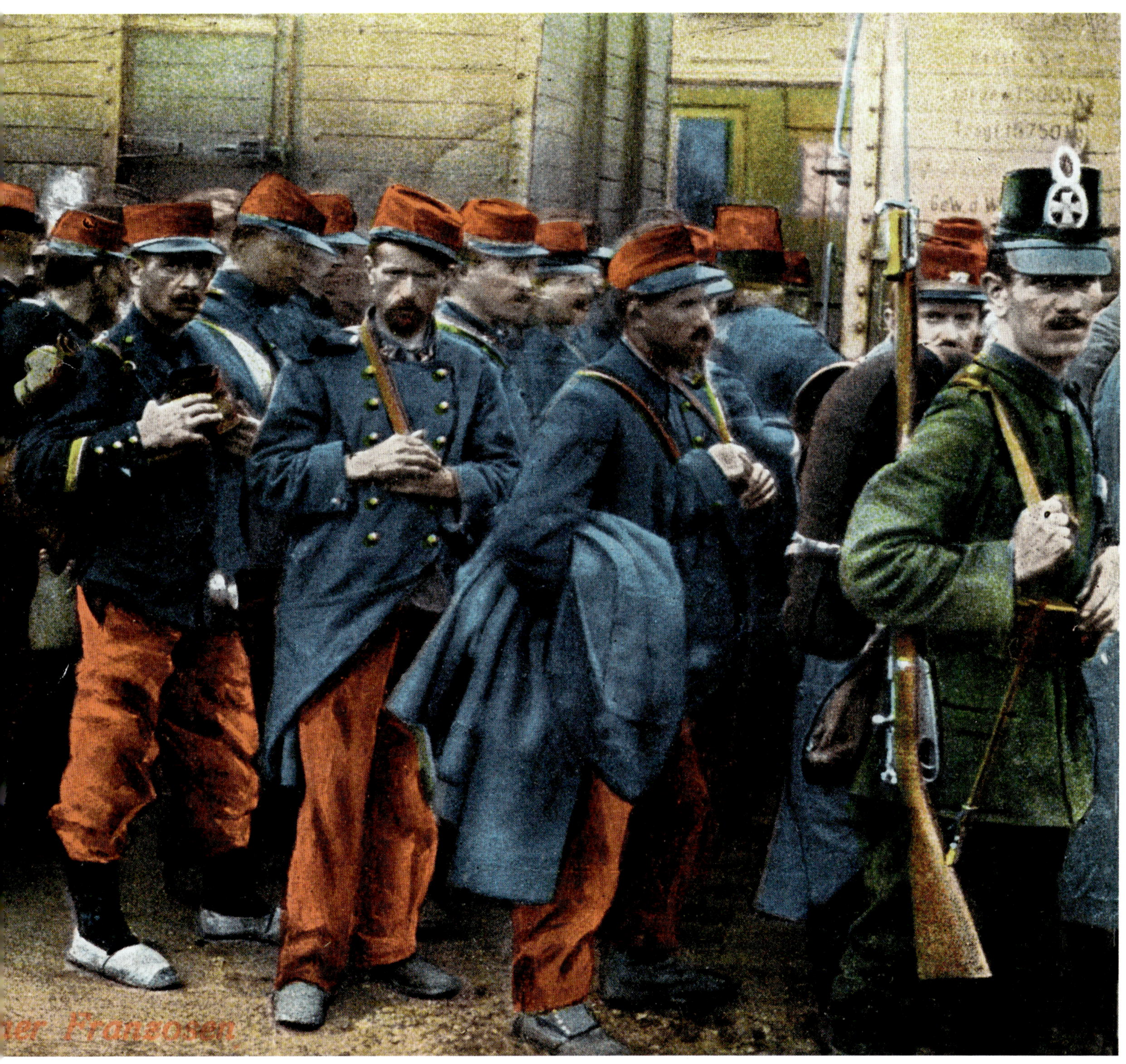
er Franzosen

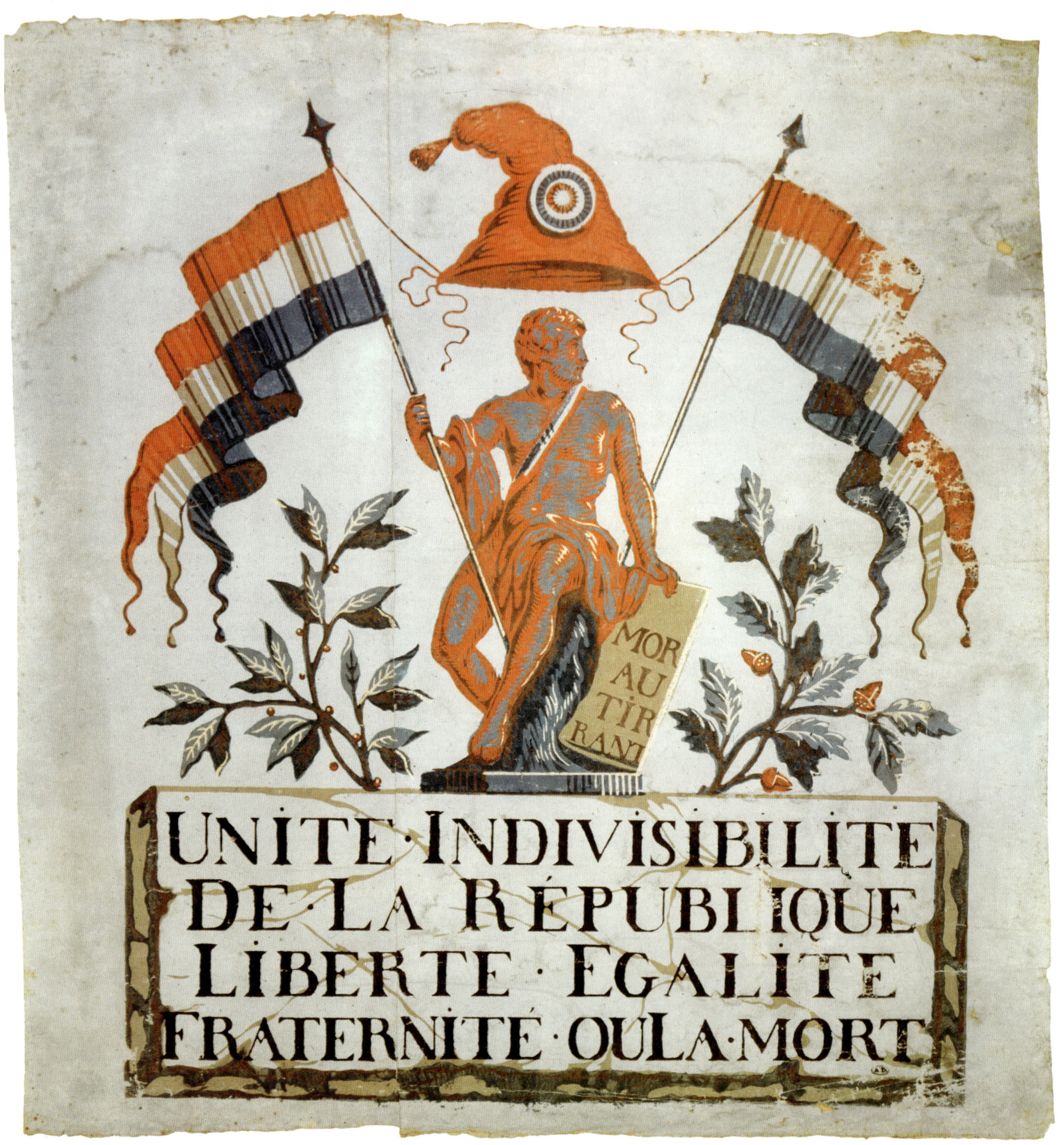
MOR
AU
TIR
RANT
UNITE · INDIVISIBILITE
DE · LA · RÉPUBLIQUE
LIBERTE · EGALITE
FRATERNITÉ · OULA · MORT

Red Caps and Flags: In the Midst of the Revolution

Emblems of the Republic

The First Republic employed many emblems. Not all of them appear on this poster: we can recognize the Phrygian cap pinned with the cockade, the motto followed by the words *ou la mort* ("or death"), and the three colors of the nation. Missing are the lictors' fasces, the pike, and especially the cock, symbol of the vigilant people.

Poster, color print, 1792.

Beginning in the late eighteenth century, the symbolism of red was enriched with a new meaning that would supplant all others over the course of several decades: political red. Emerging from the French Revolution, this red came of age in the social struggles of nineteenth-century Europe, then took on an international dimension in the following century, to the point of seizing for itself alone the symbolic import of the color. In many areas, the word "red" became a kind of synonym for adjectives like "Socialist," "Communist," "extremist," and "revolutionary." Never in the course of history had a color so embodied an ideological movement, not even in imperial Rome or early medieval Byzantium, when blue and green symbolized two particularly boisterous political factions.

The origin of this phenomenon is found in two textile objects: first, a simple cap worn by the working class that became a revolutionary and patriotic symbol for that class as France rose against its king and the privileged nobility and clergy; second, a red flag, originally precautionary and peaceful, that was dyed with the blood of the Champ-de-Mars martyrs in June 1791 and thus transformed into a symbol of the French Revolution underway. The history of these objects is worth retracing. Let us begin with the flag.[21]

Under the Ancien Régime, the red flag's connotation was neither rebellious nor violent. On the contrary, in France as in neighboring countries, it was simply a signal related to public order. A red flag—or large piece of red cloth—was displayed to warn the public of threatening danger or, in the case of gatherings, to prompt crowds to disperse. Gradually this flag became associated with various laws meant to counter the mobs that were multiplying in the 1780s and eventually with martial law itself.[22] Hence by October 1789 in France, the National Constituent Assembly decreed that in case of disturbances, municipal officers must signal imminent police intervention "by displaying in the front window of the town hall and hanging in all the streets and crossroads a red flag." When the red flag was out, "all gatherings must be considered criminal and must be dispersed through force."[23] Henceforth the flag that used to be helpful seemed much more threatening.

Less than two years later, on the revolutionary day of July 17, 1791, the flag's history

From the White Flag to the Tricolor Flag

With this composition, the painter Léon Cogniet wanted to celebrate the revolutionary days of July 27–29, 1830, and to show how the white flag of the former monarchy was transformed into the tricolor flag. In the rip of the white flag, a bit of blue sky appears, while on the other side the cloth is stained with the blood of the martyrs of the revolution.

Léon Cogniet, *Allegorical Piece on the Different Flags of France*, print, 1826–30. Paris, Bibliothèque Nationale de France, Department of Prints and Photography.

reversed directions. Louis XVI, who had attempted to flee the country, had just been arrested in Varennes and taken back to Paris. On the Champ-de-Mars, near the Autel de la Patrie, a "republican petition" was presented calling for his removal. Registers were set up, and many Parisians came to sign. The crowd was restless; the gathering seemed to be turning into a riot, and police intervention seemed imminent. Bailly, the mayor of Paris, quickly had the red flag raised, but before the crowd had time to disperse, the national guard fired, without warning. About fifty people died and were immediately proclaimed "martyrs of the Revolution." Through a kind of inversion—or even derision—of values, the red flag, "dyed with their blood," became the symbol of the people's revolt, ready to be raised against all tyranny.

From then on, the red flag played that role during all riots and popular uprisings. It was brought out each time the people took to the streets or the gains of the Revolution seemed threatened. It was a rallying sign with symbolic power that would increase throughout the nineteenth century. For the time being, in 1791, it was paired with the *bonnet rouge*, the red cap of the sans-culottes and the most extreme patriots, also called the Phrygian or liberty cap.

The *bonnet rouge* had already been in the foreground of the political scene for two years. It had made its appearance by 1789 but did not come into general use among the most ardent supporters of the new ideas until the following spring. It was especially noticeable adorning the statues of the goddesses of Liberty and Nation during the Fête de la Fédération. Soon it became the insignia worn by the most extreme factions of the Revolution. It was the symbol of the freedom to be won by men and women who wanted no longer to be subjects but citizens. The following year it became part of the regular uniform of the sans-culottes, and during the day of uprising on June 20, 1792, the mob that overran the Tuileries forced Louis XVI to don it. In the days that followed, the patriot newspaper *Les Révolutions de Paris* described the *bonnet rouge* as "the emblem of emancipation from all servitude and the rallying sign for all enemies of despotism."

After the monarchy fell in September 1792, the *bonnet rouge* was evident everywhere. Not only did it adorn the image of Liberté, seated or standing, but also pikes, flags, the fasces of Unité, the triangles of Égalité, and the beam of the scale of Justice. It appeared on most official documents and papers, especially on banknotes, in the central position, with or without other new emblems and symbols. The following year, the red cap trimmed with the tricolor cockade became obligatory attire for the assemblies of the sections of Paris. The word *bonnet* itself became a Revolutionary first name, and many French villages named for Saint-Bonnet—Bonnet was the bishop of Clermont in the late seventh century—were renamed: Bonnet-Rouge, Bonnet-Libre, Bonnet-Nouveau.

This red cap, perhaps "the revolutionary symbol most charged with meaning," was not born *ex nihilo*.[24] Prior to 1789, it already appeared in propaganda through images that accompanied the entire American Revolution, from 1775 to 1783; there it was the first attribute of Liberty. Thus, here as elsewhere,

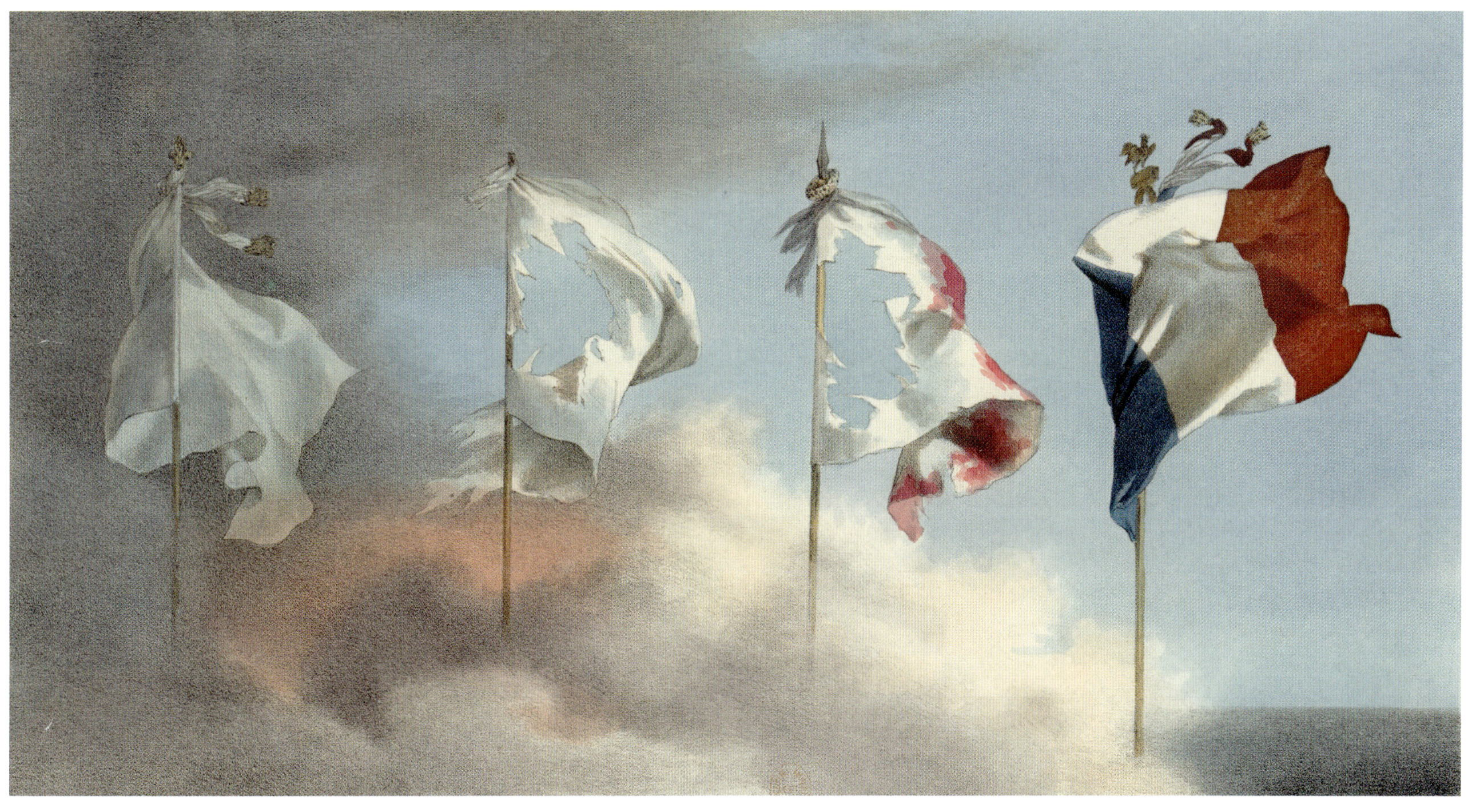

the French revolutionaries invented nothing. They expanded, adapted, and transformed earlier practices, slogans, signs, and symbols. But the American Revolution did not invent anything either. This same cap can be found as the attribute of Liberty in most iconology manuals, books of emblems, and collections of devices printed in the sixteenth, seventeenth, and eighteenth centuries. Notably, it appears in the most widely consulted of them, *Iconologia*, by Cesare Ripa, first published in Rome in 1593; its 1603 edition, featuring many illustrations, was translated into all European languages.[25] From these various collections and manuals, the image of Liberty donning a cap soon made its way into engraving and prints, and then into historical paintings and onto medals, tokens, and coins. On the eve of the Revolution, its allegorical representation hardly constituted a novelty.[26]

Sixteenth- and seventeenth-century scholars and artists saw in this cap an evocation of the so-called Phrygian cap that emancipated slaves had donned in ancient Rome. Historically that was not entirely incorrect, but we know now that in the emancipation ceremony for slaves, this cap played almost no part, and that its ties with Phrygia, a region of Asia Minor that gradually became Roman over the second and first centuries BCE, were very loose, to say the least. But that hardly matters. Symbol and legend are always more powerful than historical accuracy. And legend had it that Phrygia was a great source of slaves for the free peoples of antiquity. And once freed, these slaves readopted the cap of their ancestors, the Phrygian cap, red in color and conical in shape, the peak slightly folded forward. In images produced by the French Revolution, we can observe that the red cap, simply conical until 1790–91, became increasingly "Phrygian" over the course of events and the passing months. The peak fell forward and gave it the characteristic shape it would have henceforth.

It is not out of the question to consider two other reasons that could have contributed to the sans-culottes' adoption of the red cap between 1790 and 1792. First is the memory of the riots that broke out in Brittany in 1675 against various fiscal measures imposed by Colbert (this cap was commonly worn by peasants within Brittany). Second and most important is the fact that in the penal colonies, which had replaced the galleys of the eighteenth century, convicts wore red caps, an identifying mark and sign of infamy. The National Convention did not abolish penal colonies but it forbade the use of the red cap of infamy.

Despite its popularity, the *bonnet rouge* had many adversaries even among the revolutionaries. Although it was worn generally and especially by the Club des Jacobins by spring 1792, Pétion, mayor of Paris and an ardent Jacobin himself, condemned it because he saw it as a hat "for frightening honest people." For his part, Robespierre claimed that he liked neither the *bonnets rouges* (the sans-culottes and the nation at arms) nor the *talons rouges* (the aristocrats), a particularly interesting remark, because it underscores how in political symbolism, the two extremes very often come to meet. The members of the Convention remained faithful to the red cap nonetheless and made it a symbol of the state. By September 1792 they had it engraved, appearing at the top of a pike, on the great seal of the Republic; then in autumn 1793 they ordered that "the fleurs-de-lis be replaced by Liberty caps" on milliary columns. Under the Directory, on the other hand, the red cap was worn more discreetly. It disappeared for good in the period of the Consulate; in 1802, the prefects ordered all such caps appearing on public monuments to be removed.

A Political Color

Red caps disappeared but political red remained and even increased in scope over the course of the decades. Originally French, it became European in the mid-nineteenth century and then fully international half a century later when communism extended its reach and made red its symbolic color. Let us retrace the important steps of this movement that has deeply marked the history of colors in the contemporary period.

In France, the red flag that was rarely flown during the First Empire reappeared in the forefront during the revolutionary days of July 1830 and then on various occasions under the July monarchy during many mass riots. Thus it was present during the silk workers' revolt in Lyon in 1831 and again in Paris during the republican insurrections of June 1832 and April 1834. It was seen flying above the barricades and served as a symbol to the people revolting against both employers and an increasingly conservative government. In *Les Misérables*, Victor Hugo devotes dramatic pages to it, relating the death of the old man Mabeuf at the barricades erected in Paris in June 1832:

A dreadful explosion burst over the barricade. The red flag fell. The shooting had been so heavy and so dense that it had cut the pole. . . . [Enjolras] picked up the flag which had fallen right at his feet . . . [and said] "Who here has the courage? Who will plant the flag back on the barricade?"

Not one responded. To climb onto the barricade at the moment they were undoubtedly aiming at it once more—that meant death, pure and simple. . . . [When Enjolras] repeated his appeal, "No volunteers?" they saw the old man appear in the doorway of the tavern. . . .

He walked straight up to Enjolras, the insurgents parted in front of him with a religious fear, he ripped the flag from Enjolras, who stepped back, petrified, and then, since no one dared either to stop him or to help him, this old man of eighty, his head shaky, his foot firm, slowly began to climb the stairway of cobblestones built into the barricade. This was so grim and so grand that everyone around him cried, "Hats off!" Every step he climbed was torture; his white hair, his decrepit face, his high forehead, bald and wrinkled, his hollow eyes, his mouth gaping open in amazement, his old arm holding up the red banner, emerged from the shadows and grew bigger in the blood red glare of the torch; and it felt like they were seeing the ghost of '93 emerging from the ground, the flag of the Terror in his hand.

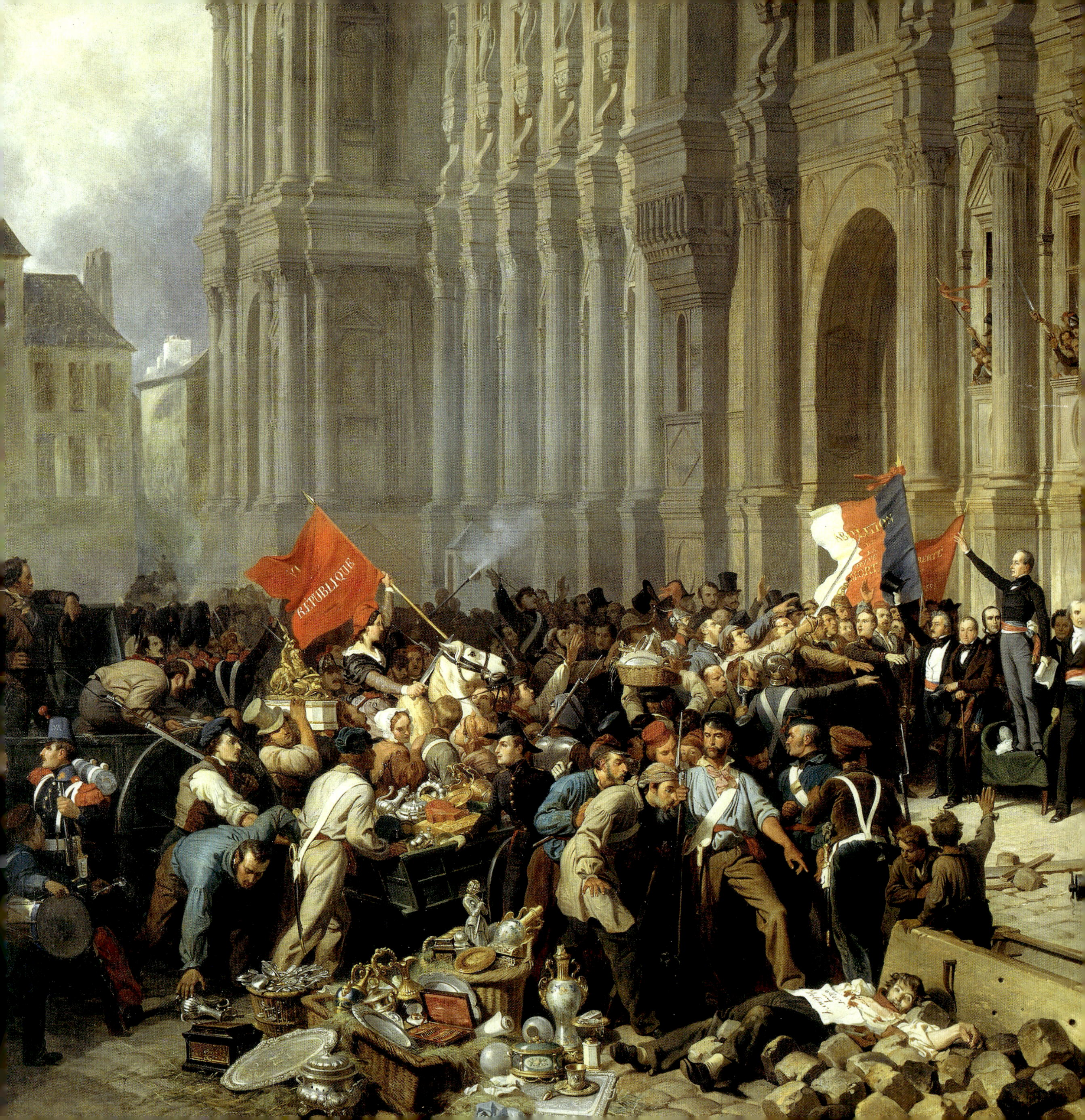
RÉPUBLIQUE
ABDICATION
LIBERTÉ

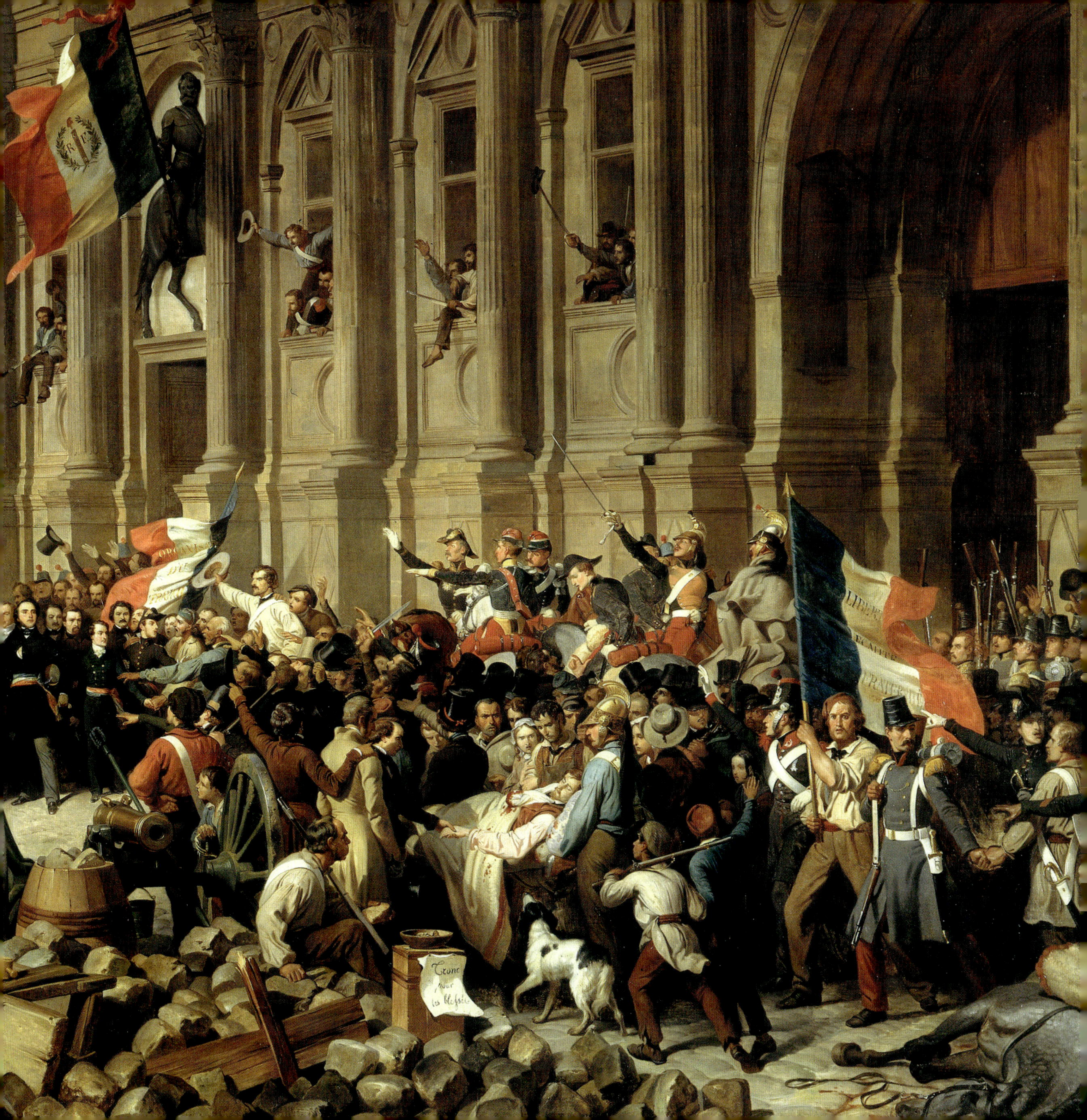

R.F.
ORGANISATION DU TRAVAIL
LIBERTÉ ÉGALITÉ FRATERNITÉ
Tronc pour les blessés

PRECEDING PAGE SPREAD

Lamartine, Savior of the Tricolor Flag

This huge painting, in which more than two hundred figures appear, represents the most famous episode in the revolution of 1848 (February 25): the poet Alphonse de Lamartine, a member of the provisional government, rejects the red flag that the insurgents want to adopt as the national flag, and turns general opinion in favor of the tricolor flag.

Henri-Félix-Emmanuel Philippoteaux, *Lamartine, before the Hôtel de Ville, Paris, Rejects the Red Flag, February 25, 1848,* 1848. Paris, Musée du Petit Palais.

When he was on top of the last step, when this trembling and terrible phantom, standing on that mound of debris before twelve hundred invisible guns, straightened up, in the face of death and as though he were stronger than it, the whole barricade took on a supernatural and colossal look in the darkness. There was one of those silences that only happens in the face of fears of wonder.

In the midst of this silence the old man waved the red flag and cried: "Long live the Revolution! Long live the Republic! Fraternity! Equality! And Death!"[27]

Later, during the revolution of 1848 that brought down Louis-Philippe, the red flag took on a new dimension. It was even on the verge of becoming France's national flag. Brandished by the Parisian insurgents who proclaimed the Republic on February 24, it accompanied them the next day to the Hôtel de Ville, where a provisionary government assembled. Speaking for the masses, one of the insurgents demanded the official adoption of the red flag, "symbol of the misery of the people and sign of a break with the past," as the national flag. In these tense times, two conceptions of the Republic confronted one another: one was "red," Jacobin, imagining a new social order so that the revolution underway not be sacrificed to the benefit of the bourgeoisie as in 1830; the other was "tricolor," more moderate, desiring reforms but not a complete upheaval of society. That was when the poet Alphonse de Lamartine, member of the provisionary government and minister of foreign affairs, made a speech, still famous, that turned opinion in favor of the tricolor flag:

The red flag that you bring to us is a flag of terror . . . that has only been around the Champ-de-Mars, dragged in the blood of the people, whereas the tricolor flag has been around the world, with the name, the glory, and the freedom of the fatherland. . . . It is the flag of France, it is the flag of our victorious armies, it is the flag of our triumphs that must be raised before Europe.[28]

Even if he more or less embellished his words in his later writings, on that day Lamartine's speech saved the tricolor flag.[29]

Twenty-three years later, in 1871, the red flag invaded the streets of Paris once again and was displayed by the Commune at the Hôtel de Ville. But Paris, red and in revolt, was vanquished by the Versailles troops of Thiers and the National Assembly. From then on the tricolor flag appeared as the one of order and legitimacy, whereas the red flag appeared as the one of oppressed and rebellious peoples. Moreover, for some time already, its history involved not only France but Europe.

During the riots that erupted throughout industrial Europe in the mid-nineteenth century, the red flag became the rallying sign of workers' movements and then of the unions or parties defending their cause, in particular the socialist parties that were created in many countries beginning in the 1850s. It was displayed as well by most of those disillusioned by the national, popular, or liberal revolutions of 1848, revolutions that had given rise to great hopes and then terrible disappointments. That was why the red flag united behind it the socialists and revolutionaries of all of Europe at the end of the nineteenth century. Its scope

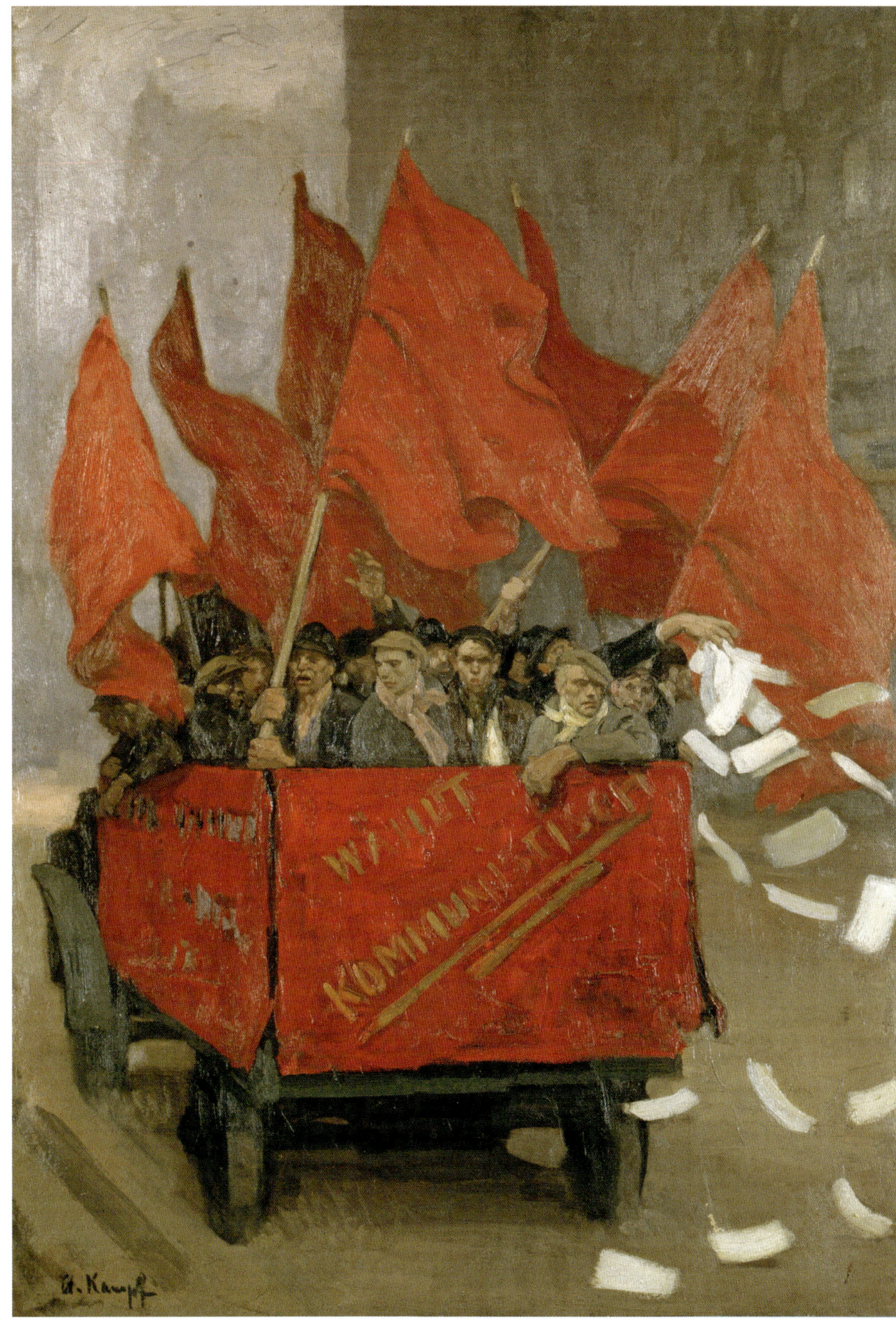

"Vote Communist!"

After the defeat of November 1918, propaganda flooded Germany in advance of the coming elections of January 1919. The elections were to make the Reich into a parliamentary democracy. Workers' organizations campaigned for a government similar to the Soviet system, established by the Bolsheviks in Russia.

Arthur Kampf, *Vote Communist!*, 1918. Berlin, Berlinische Galerie.

May 1968 Posters

In Paris, most of the May 1968 posters were conceived and printed in the "people's workshops" of the École des Beaux-Arts and École des Arts Décoratifs. The printing was done using silk-screen stencils, often on newsprint provided by the presses of the striking newspapers. The choice of red ink underscored the revolutionary nature of the protests, and at the same time it gave these posters greater expressionist force than black ink would have. That said, many so-called "May '68" posters are imitations, produced much more recently.

Paris, Bibliothèque Nationale de France, Department of Prints and Photography.

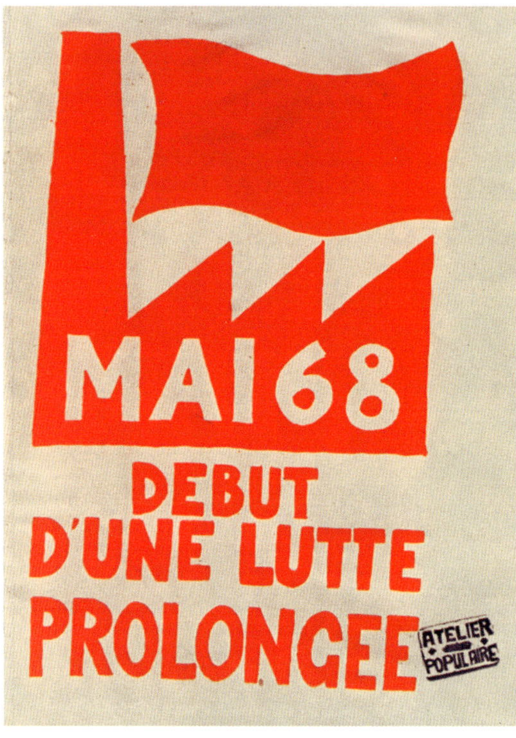

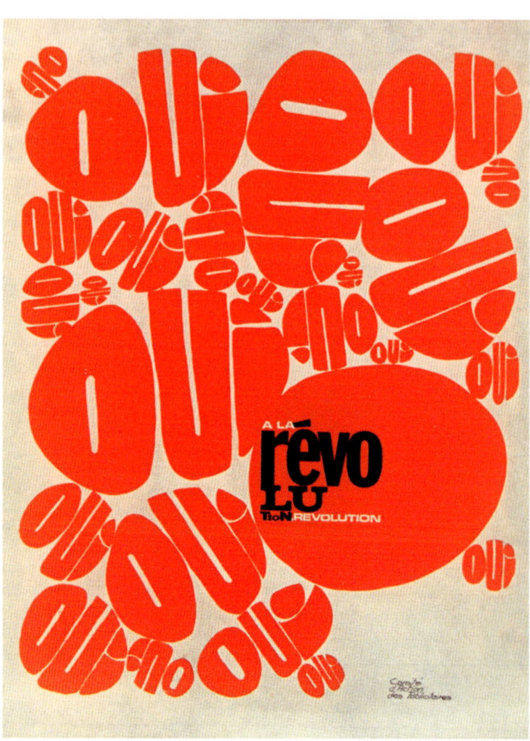

became even wider after 1889, when May 1 was chosen as International Workers' Day. Henceforth on that day, around the globe, the red flag was on display in every parade.

A final threshold was crossed following the Russian Revolution in 1917. The Bolshevik party that came into power established a dictatorship of the proletariat in the form of the Soviet regime. The red flag was adopted and became the official flag of the USSR in 1922. First it appeared with various inscriptions in Cyrillic characters before the hammer and sickle were assigned to it for good, shown in a crossed position and symbolizing the unity of workers and peasants.[30] From then on and almost throughout the world, the red flag, adorned with other symbols or not, was gradually adopted by unions, parties, and regimes adhering to communism. In 1949 it

was chosen by the new People's Republic of China, and five yellow stars—four small and one large—were added.[31]

Almost everywhere, the red flag continued to unite workers' movements, including those that remained socialist and certain small factions of the extreme left who dreamed of making the revolution permanent or extending it over the entire planet.[32] It was not until the events of May 1968 in Paris and elsewhere, in marches and on barricades, that the red flag was outflanked on its own left by the black flag, the flag of anarchists and nihilists.

In the meantime, the word "red," whether adjective or noun, had taken on great political significance in certain languages. In French by the 1840s, "*un rouge*" designated someone adhering to the most progressive ideas in political and social matters, and then more generally a revolutionary.[33] This usage was common in literature in the late nineteenth century and throughout the twentieth. Similarly, in the press and the media after the communist parties emerged and became established, one spoke more and more often of the "red vote," "red suburbs," "red municipalities," and, if one were opposed to communism, the "red peril." Through a kind of chromatic declension after 1981, when François Mitterrand came into power, pink became or once again became the color of socialism in France, and thus one spoke of the "pink suburbs" or "pink vote." This had already happened in the first

decade of the 1900s, moreover, when red still belonged solely to the socialists, and its watered-down version, pink, was assigned to the politically more moderate radicals.[34]

On the international level, in the second half of the twentieth century, communist red was especially associated with the USSR and China, as well as their satellite or allied countries. Thus in the area of sports, Eastern Europe witnessed the proliferation of clubs, often military in origin, named "Red Star of ——," paying homage to the Soviet army's insignia, adopted in 1918. In the area of publishing, the Chinese cultural revolution inundated the entire world with its *Little Red Book*, a collection of quotes by Mao Tse-tung organized into thirty-three chapters. Despite its sometimes sentimental and obscure nature, the book became one of the greatest best sellers of all time: nine hundred million copies sold worldwide. Only the Bible has outsold it.

In its political sense, the word "red" has not always been so placid. It has even embodied political forms of extreme violence. That was the case in Cambodia during the bloody regime of the Khmer Rouge, which ran the country from 1975 to 1979 and put to death more than three million people. It was the case as well as in Germany with the Red Army Faction, which engaged in bloody terrorist actions in the 1970s; and again in Italy, with the Red Brigades, who abducted Aldo Moro, the leader of the Christian Democrats, in the center of Rome in March 1978. Moro, in line to become the next president of the Italian Republic, was executed by the group two months later.

This link between the color red and political groups or parties on the left or the extreme

The Red Flag Overtaken by the Black Flag

One of the great political (and chromatic) phenomena of the events of May 1968 was the appearance on the left of an emblem even more radical than the traditional red flag: the black flag of anarchists and nihilists. Henceforth, revolutionary red was no longer the most extreme political color; through this choice of black, the extreme left and extreme right seem to merge.

Demonstration in Paris, May 13, 1968. Photograph.

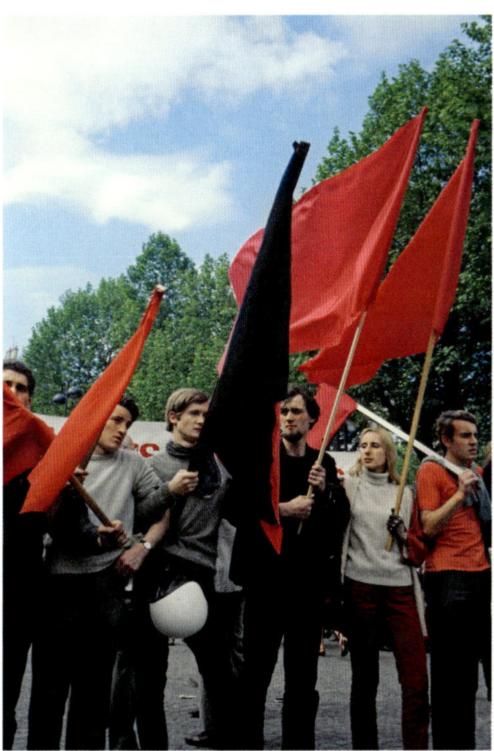

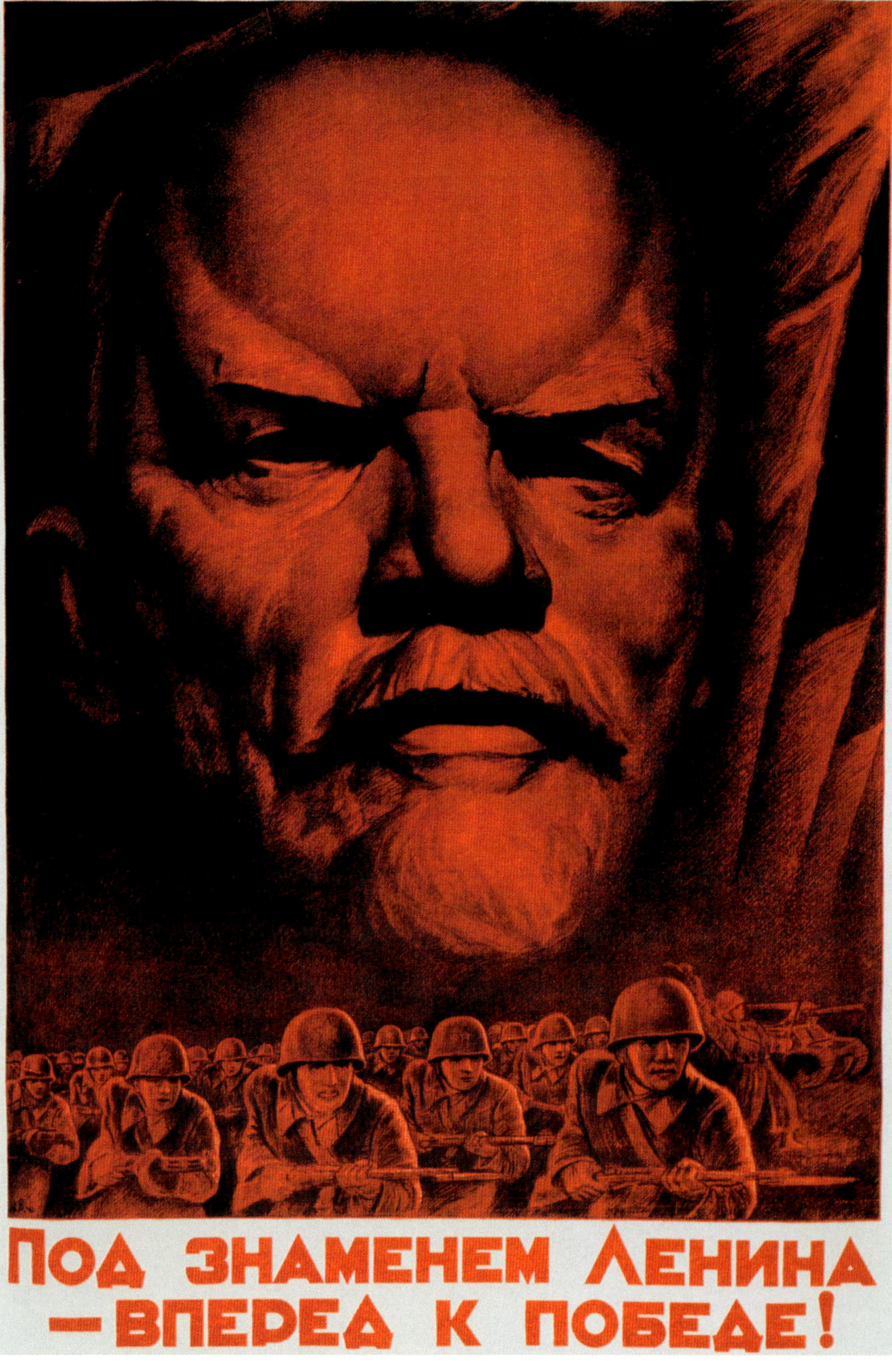

Russian Propaganda Poster

Russian Communism made red and black the two dominant colors of its propaganda. Hitler's Germany did the same, adding white, as Goebbels saw in the white-red-black triad "the power of the Aryan race displayed in color."

Follow the Flag of Lenin to Victory, Russian poster, 1941.

RIGHT PAGE

Red China

The many parades and processions in Communist China are occasions for bringing out countless red flags. Communist Party flags show a yellow hammer and sickle in the upper left corner; those of China display five yellow stars, one of them bigger than the rest.

National holiday parade, China, October 1, 1966. Photograph.

left dominated the history of this color for more than one and a half centuries, relegating to the background all its other symbolic fields: childhood, love, passion, beauty, pleasure, eroticism, power, and even justice. One current of thought seized for itself alone red's emblematic and symbolic role. Red was no longer so much a color as an ideology, to the point that only a few years ago it was still impossible to claim red as one's favorite color without immediately appearing to be a "dyed-in-the-wool" Communist. Today, since the dissolution of the USSR and the weakening of ideologies, this link has become much less strong. And among the colors, green seems to have taken over ideologically; it is hard to claim that green is one's favorite color without appearing to be an environmentalist, promoting natural energy and organic agriculture, or even an ardent radical ecologist.[35]

How do we combat such hasty and reductive categorizations that finally misrepresent the colors, stripping them of all their emotional, poetic, aesthetic, and oneiric dimensions?

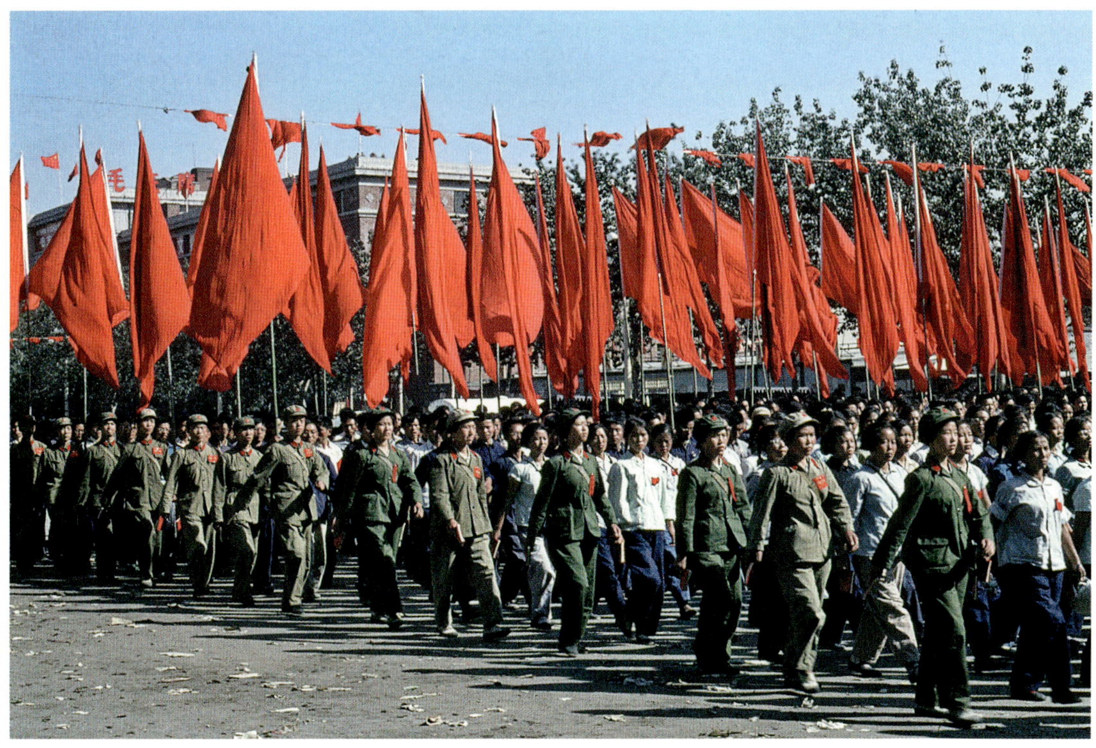

Emblems and Signals

European Flags

The flags of the twenty-eight countries belonging to the European Union use only seven colors: white, black, red, green, yellow, blue, and orange. Red is the most widely used color, displayed on twenty-three flags (82 percent).

Strasbourg, European Parliament gardens. Photograph.

Although in contemporary societies the red flag and the symbols issuing from it may sometimes give the impression that they have seized the symbolic power of that color for their purposes alone, they do not in fact have a monopoly on it. Many other emblems, insignia, trademarks, and signals have used red and continue to do so in a multitude of contexts.

Let us begin with flags of a different nature: national flags, which are hoisted and flown when they are textile objects and reproduced by the millions when they become simple images. This transition from object to image constitutes a major turning point. When and how did actual fabric, hung at the top of a pole and made to be seen from a distance, transform into a non-textile image, appearing on all kinds of mediums and meant to be seen up close? What changes brought about this transition in all domains from physical object to emblematic image?[36] These questions are still awaiting their historian; in fact, it seems they have yet to be asked. National flags in general remain understudied historical objects; it is as though researchers are afraid of them because of all the appropriations, passions, and repercussions associated with them over the course of the last two centuries. A few monographs of uneven quality on one national flag or another are available to us. But we still lack more ambitious work that would consider all aspects of flags: material, institutional, social, legal, political, liturgical, emblematic, and symbolic. Such works can only be collective.[37]

For the moment, let us be content with existing catalogs, for example those that list the flags of the countries belonging to the United Nations, to try to discern the place occupied by each of the colors appearing there.[38]

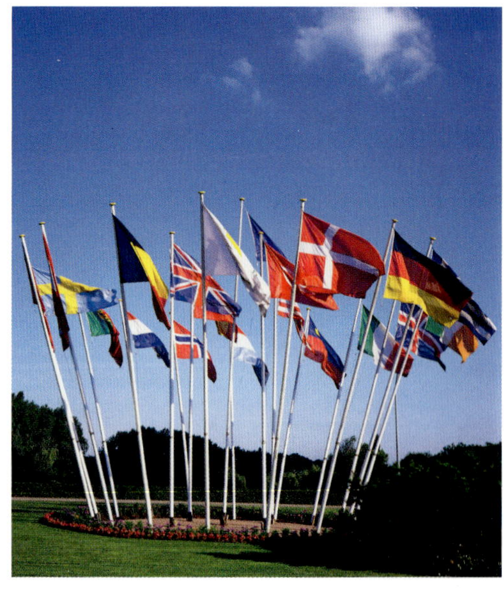

Red is clearly dominant, present in more than three quarters (77 percent) of the flags of some two hundred countries considered "independent" in 2016. That is an enormous proportion. Next come white (58 percent), green (40 percent), blue (37 percent), yellow (29 percent), and black (17 percent). Other colors are much more rare, or even absent (gray and pink for example).[39] Why is red omnipresent? It is not sufficient to say that it is a matter of the color with the most symbolic power. We must consider that the flag system now in use on six continents is a Western creation. It is built upon the codifications and sensibilities that originally belonged to Christian Europe alone and have only recently expanded to the entire world. In Europe prior to the code of flags, there was the code of armorial bearings. The line from coat of arms to flag is not direct of course, but vexillology is undeniably the child of heraldry, a system of signs in which red—*gueules* in heraldic terms—long remained the dominant color. The fundamental reason for red's omnipresence in contemporary flags lies here, no doubt, but that is not the only reason. Another important factor is that a flag never exists in isolation; it often responds to one or many other flags whose colors it adopts and reorganizes. The flag of the United States for example, originating in the years 1777–83, intentionally repeats the blue-white-red of the British flag—the enemy flag—but combines it in another way. More recently in the Communist world, many flags owe their red to the flag of the USSR and, less directly, to the mythic red flag.[40]

These heraldic, semiological, or political explanations are often the best ones for understanding the choice of one or several colors, but they are not well received generally by governments and populations: too mechanical, too obvious, too disappointing. Hence the various legends, constructed after the fact, to link the origin of a national flag with a significant or noble event or to embellish its birth through poetry or mythology. Some of these legends are ancient, like the one that makes the Danish flag—the splendid Dannebrog, red with a white cross—a sign sent from heaven in 1219 to rally the Christian troops of King Valdemar II in their battle against Livonian pagans. Or the one that sees in the large red circle of the Japanese flag an image of the rising sun, an emblem that speaks the very name of the country.[41] Tradition locates the birth of this flag in the seventh century CE, but it must be acknowledged that it is only documented beginning in the sixteenth century. Other a posteriori legends or explanations are less rich and often more recent, like those that see in the red of one flag or another the blood of the martyrs who gave their lives for their country's independence and freedom (itself embodied by green).

Another system of signs that originated in Europe and spread throughout the world gives red a dominant place: road signs. It also descends from medieval heraldry and constructs its notices like true coats of arms, even more so than flags. Indeed, almost all road signs follow the rules for using heraldic colors, and many can be described in heraldic language.[42] Let us cite two examples of French road signs: the one-way street sign, *de gueules à la fasce alaisée d'argent*; the reduced speed limit sign at school crossings, *d'argent à deux écoliers passant de sable, à la bordure de gueules*.

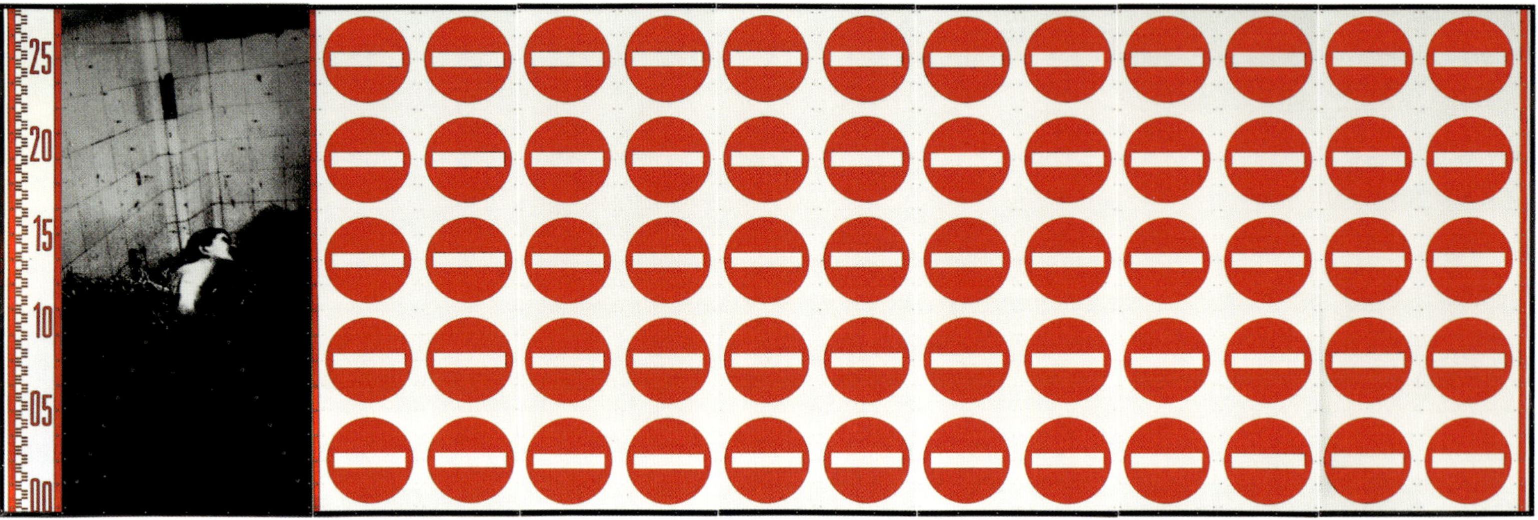

Roadway Blazons

Road signs, like railway signals before them, were very influenced by the heraldic code. Most road signs are designed like coats of arms and can be described in heraldic language. The sign for one-way streets in French heraldic terms: *de gueules à la fasce alésée d'argent.*

Jean-Pierre Raynaud, *One-Way Wall*, collage with paper and screws, 291 × 873 cm, 1970. Photographic document by Jean-Philippe Charbonnier, Denyse Durand-Ruel Archives, artist's collection.

Red light. Atlanta, Georgia, United States.

Historically roads signs evolved from maritime signs, originating in the eighteenth century, and railway signs, which came into use in the 1840s. A detailed genealogy of signs would thus be necessary to distinguish what was already in use and what was newly created when road signs appeared at the turn of the nineteenth to the twentieth century. Clearly it is not possible to provide that here.[43] Instead let us simply examine the relationship between the highway code and the world of colors.

Road signals take three different forms: horizontal (markings painted on the ground), vertical (highway and street signs), and illuminated (three-colored traffic lights, blinking or flashing lights). But in all three cases, the meanings or connotations of the various colors remain the same. Only six colors are used in France: red, blue, yellow, green, white, and black. In Europe, since the Middle Ages, these have been the six basic colors in all chromatic systems. In large road signs, the three main colors are white, red, and blue. However, white does not function alone; it is always used with the other colors. Present on the great majority of signs, it has no meaning by itself; often it simply provides the background. Red, on the other hand, is always connected to the idea of something dangerous or forbidden: danger when it surrounds a sign (countless examples), forbidden when it is paired with white (one-way, stop) or, less often, with blue (no parking). When blue is the background color—which is often the case—it can signal an obligation (minimum speed, mandatory direction, etc.) or provide simple topographical information (parking, hospital, highway), in which case it is paired with white. Yellow is mostly used for temporary signals, but it also serves as background color for certain signs that warn drivers to use caution (accident, construction, roadwork). Less frequent, green generally signifies authorization. As for black, sometimes it warns of danger, and sometimes it signals the end of something forbidden, by means of a diagonal bar.

That is the broad outline of the meanings of colors used for road signs in France and in many neighboring countries. But the code is less strict and more flexible than one would think. That is undoubtedly why it functions effectively. Each color possesses many connotations and denotations, and the same idea can be expressed through many colors. Also, variations exist from one country to another and even, in certain countries (Germany, Italy, Great Britain), from one region to another or from one category of road to another. But a

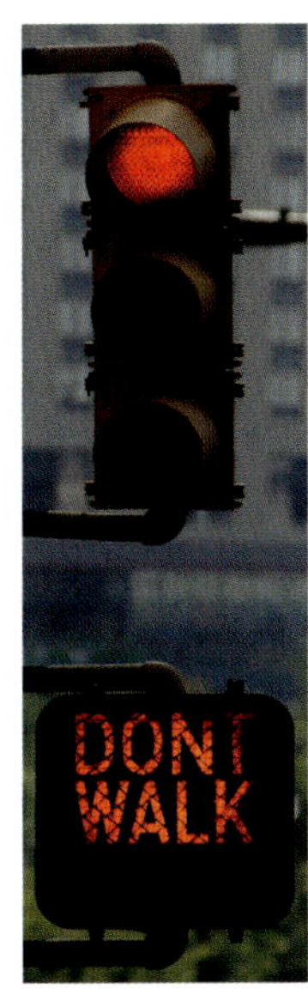

few basic ideas recur, like the one associating red with anything forbidden. In old booklets of highway code colors, there is hardly any red because hardly anything was forbidden, whereas in today's voluminous catalogs, red has become ubiquitous because prohibitions have taken over. All by itself, this difference neatly summarizes the evolution of our societies between the early twentieth and the early twenty-first centuries.[44]

One particular element in road signals constitutes a system all its own: two-color traffic lights, which gained a third color over the course of time.

Here again, road signs evolved from railway signs, which had evolved from maritime

Maritime Signals

It took a long time for an international code of maritime signs to develop. Although signal lights were first used during Roman times, it was not until the eighteenth century that a nascent code appeared, which did not become truly international until 1860. This code too was heavily influenced by heraldry and strictly adheres to the very rigid rules for using the heraldic colors.

International Code of Navigation, poster, c. 1920.

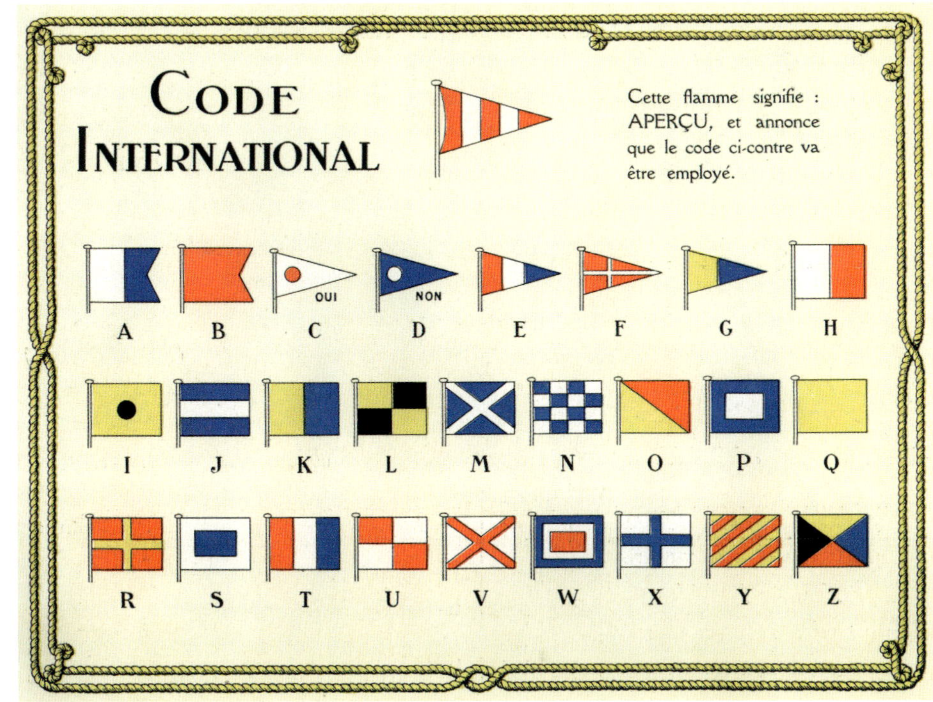

signs. On the road as on the sea, the first lights were two-color and opposed red and green. In towns the earliest traffic lights were installed in London in December 1868, on the corner of Palace Yard and Bridge Street. It was a matter of a pivoting gas lantern, operated by a traffic policeman. The system was a dangerous one; in 1869 an explosion mortally wounded the policeman lighting the lamps. Nonetheless, London proved to be the great pioneer in this area in Europe, since Paris did not follow its lead until 1923, and Berlin until 1924. The first Parisian traffic light was installed at the intersection of Sébastopol and Saint-Denis Boulevards; it was entirely red, prohibiting passing, with green making its appearance only in the early 1930s, and orange, the intermediate color, appearing later still. Meanwhile, two-color traffic lights had swept the United States: Salt Lake City, 1912; Cleveland, 1914; New York, 1918.[45]

Why were these two colors, red and green, chosen to regulate traffic flow, first at sea, as early as the eighteenth century, then on rail, and finally on the road? Red was certainly the color of danger and prohibition since earliest times (that was already the case in the Bible).[46] But for centuries green had nothing to do with permission or right-of-way. On the contrary, it played the role of the color of disorder and transgression, of all that goes against the established rules and systems.[47] Moreover, it was not considered an opposite of red, as white was from the beginning or blue was from the central Middle Ages. But color classifications changed, notably through the course of the eighteenth century, when Newton's discoveries (color classification according to the spectrum) definitively took hold and when the theory of primary and complementary colors became widespread. Henceforth red, a primary color, had for its complementary color green. The two colors began to be paired, and since red was the color of prohibition, green, its complement and almost its opposite, gradually became the color of permission. First at sea and then on land, between 1760 and 1840, it became the custom to forbid passage with red and authorize it with green.[48] A new history of chromatic codes was thus established.

Red
for the
Present Day

The Red Cross

Founded in 1863 by a group of Genevan citizens, the International Committee of the Red Cross is the oldest existent humanitarian association. Its emblem is the inverse replica of the Swiss flag: a white background with a red cross. On the field in times of armed conflict, this emblem (as well as its counterpart, the red crescent) protects medical services and installations.

Jean-Michel Folon, *French Red Cross*, poster, 1981.

This tie between red and things forbidden or dangerous can be found in many other areas. Here, contemporary society extended a symbolic function of red inherited from the Bible and medieval Christian moral codes and put it to use on a grand scale. In various roles, red warns, prescribes, prohibits, condemns, and punishes. That is one of its primary uses today when it makes itself scarce in everyday life and private space, everywhere outstripped by blue.

As it did under the Ancien Régime, a red scrap of cloth or a red mark signals danger. Hence we have the red line or icon on medications, accompanied by warnings like "do not take more than the prescribed dose" or "use only as recommended by your physician," as well as the alternating red and white lines along streets marking where spaces are reserved or access is forbidden. The firefighters'

red light is recognized worldwide, and their red truck has the right of way over all other vehicles. Although the dress uniform of these firefighters is not red, but black or navy blue, it is generally trimmed with red. As for fire extinguishers and equipment used for fighting fires, they are red throughout the world. Moreover, they are often the only objects of this color in a building, house, or premises, which allows them to be spotted easily. Similarly, along the street, red signs mark stores or offices with special status: the red *carotte*, an elongated diamond, for tobacco shops in France; the red cross for pharmacies in Italy, for example. And again, in case of armed conflict, the red cross and red crescent of the humanitarian and medical organizations with those names are easily identifiable and, appearing on vehicles or buildings, protect them against military attacks—at least in theory.[49]

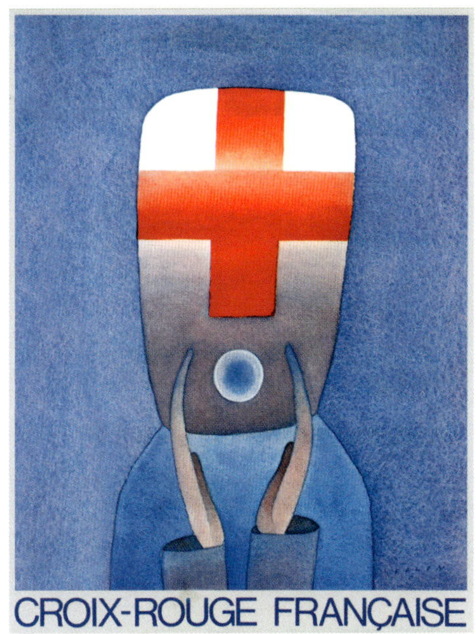

Firefighters' Red

For over a century in many countries, firefighters have worn red-trimmed uniforms and driven red fire trucks, which have the right of way over all other vehicles, including police cars. Hence, the firetruck's success as a children's toy: red first!

Citroën B 14 Pumper, wood and metal toy, 1927.

Over the course of time, language itself has created many idioms and expressions that convey the idea of things dangerous or forbidden through the word "red." Let us cite: "red alert," "red telephone," "red zone," "being in the red," "red-light district," "wave the red flag," and even "the red light is on" from radio and television or movie sets. Similar expressions exist in almost all Western languages. They echo other expressions, proverbs, or idioms that involve the human body, especially the face, and that express emotions related to dread, fear, shame, anger, or confusion: to see red, to turn red, to be red with anger, or, more simply, to be or become as red as a rooster, lobster, beet, tomato.[50]

According to a slightly different usage, red is the color that marks punishment, from the red ink used to correct pupils' papers to the red iron used to brand former criminals and convicts, and let's not forget the red robes worn by judges from the Middle Ages. Moreover, it must be noted that this red of justice is the color of both the one who pronounces the sentence and the one who serves it. Recall the ancient proverb that Victor Hugo repeats twice in *Les Misérables*: "The convict's coat is cut from the judge's robe." Both of them are indeed red.

Fortunately, this color is not always so disturbing or dangerous. In marketing practices, red is used primarily to attract attention: a price indicated in red highlights a sale or special bargain; a red dot on a product's label indicates particular sales conditions; a "red label" vaunts the superior quality of a product, better than the run-of-the-mill but inferior to those with a "black label." Similarly in advertising displays, red is used to accentuate, highlight, and capture attention, even to

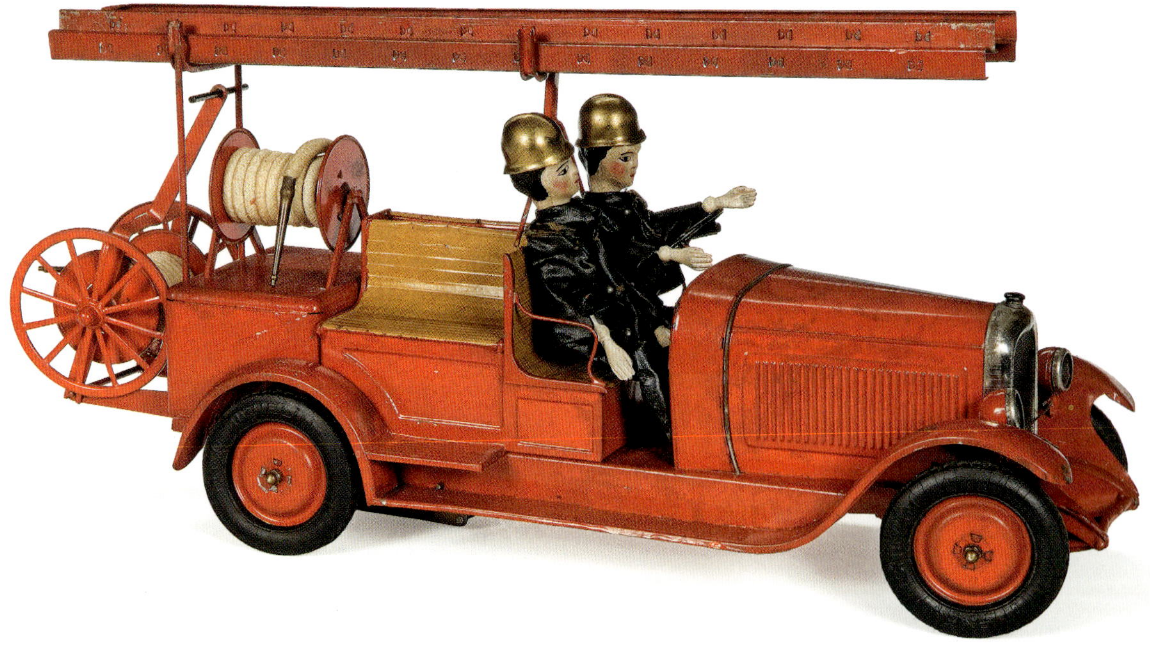

From Saint Nicholas to Father Christmas

Contrary to a widely held belief, Père Noël is not the least bit American, and his red suit has nothing to do with Coca-Cola's trademark. He descends from Saint Nicholas, bishop of Myra (in Anatolia), performer of numerous miracles and protector of children, to whom he distributes presents on December 6, his holiday. Since the Middle Ages he has been represented dressed in red. The tradition of Saint Nicholas Day was maintained in Protestant northern Europe, whereas in Catholic Europe "Father Christmas" and the holiday of December 25 gradually took hold.

American poster by John D. Kelley appearing in *St. Nicholas Magazine*, 1895, New York.

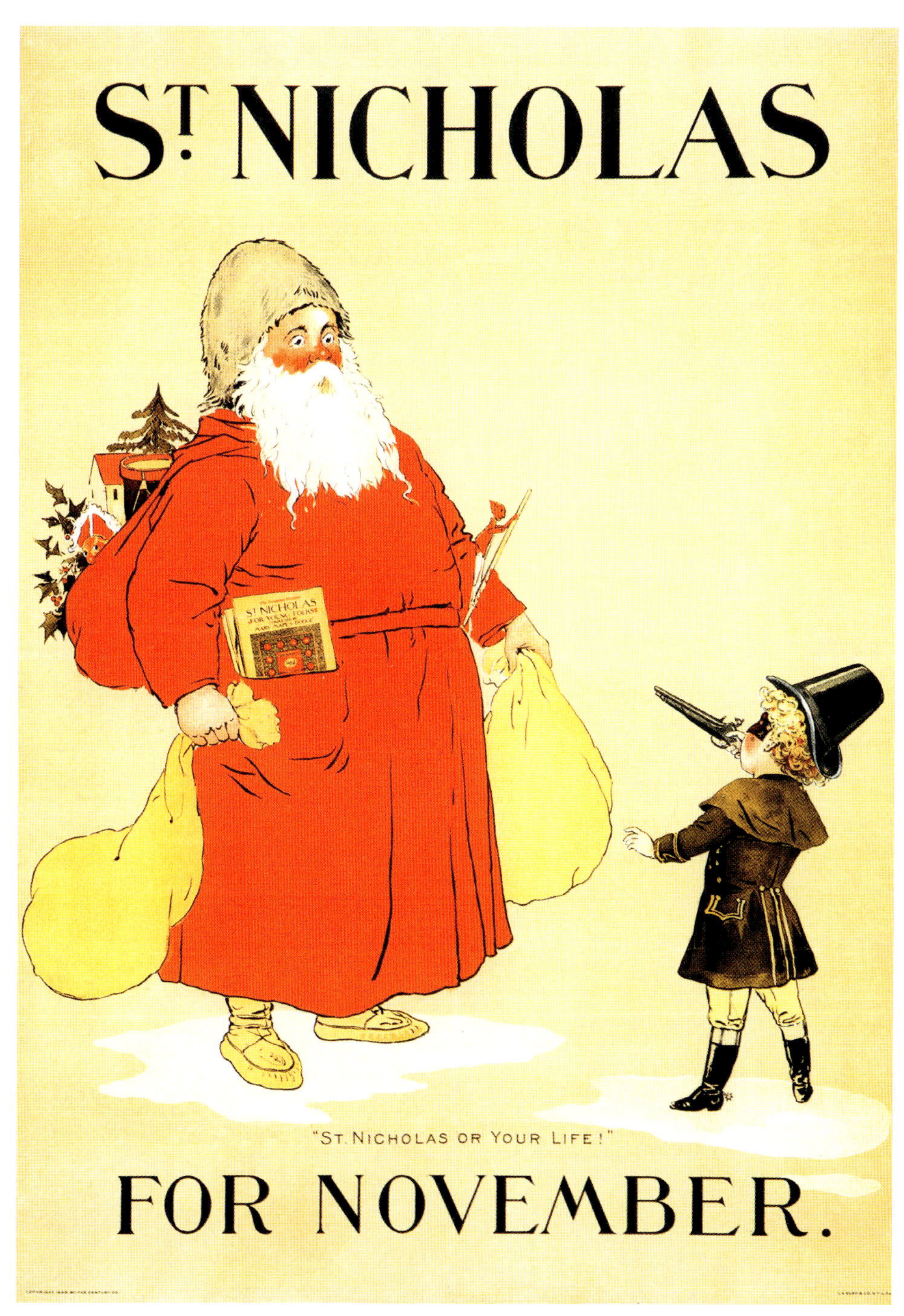

Corrections in Red

Exercise books and homework are not the only documents to be corrected in red—so are page proofs from printers, as early as the late nineteenth century, as we can see from these two pages from the famous typographical poem by Stéphane Mallarmé, *Jamais un Coup de Dés n'Abolira le Hasard* (A Roll of the Dice Will Never Abolish Chance). The very elaborate page layout and variations in type that the author desired required that six successive sets of proofs be made, all corrected with a red pencil. The poet's key work, this unusual poem is not crystal clear.

Stéphane Mallarmé, *Jamais un Coup de Dés n'Abolira le Hasard*, set of proofs, 1897. Paris, Bibliothèque Nationale de France.

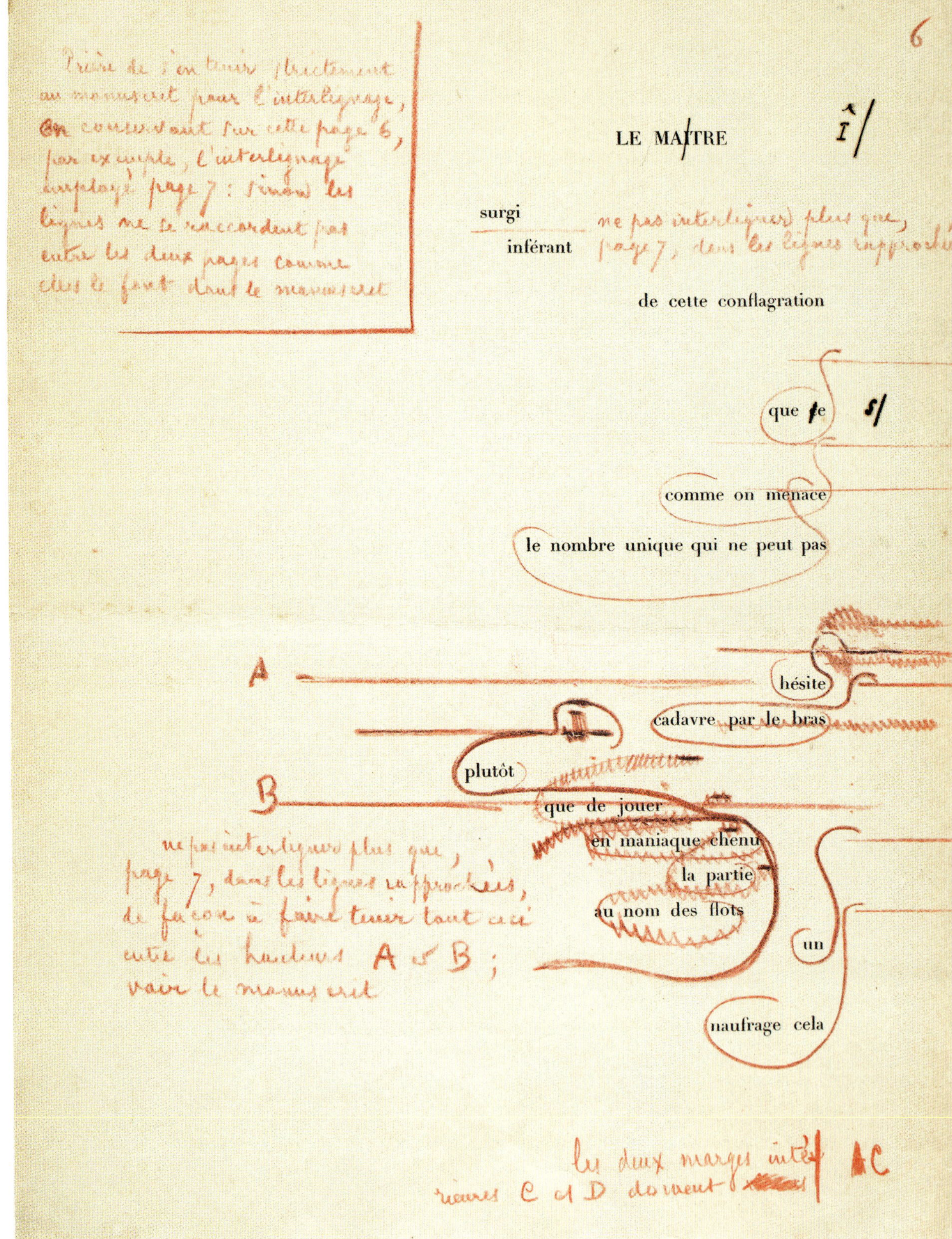

hors d'anciens calculs
où la manœuvre avec l'âge oubliée

jadis il empoignait la barre

à ses pieds
de l'horizon unanime

prépare
s'agite et mêle
au poing qui l'étreindrait
un destin et les vents

être un autre

esprit
pour le jeter
dans la tempête
en reployer la division et passer fier

écarté du secret qu'il détient

envahit le chef
coule en barbe soumise

direct de l'homme

sans nef
n'importe
où vaine

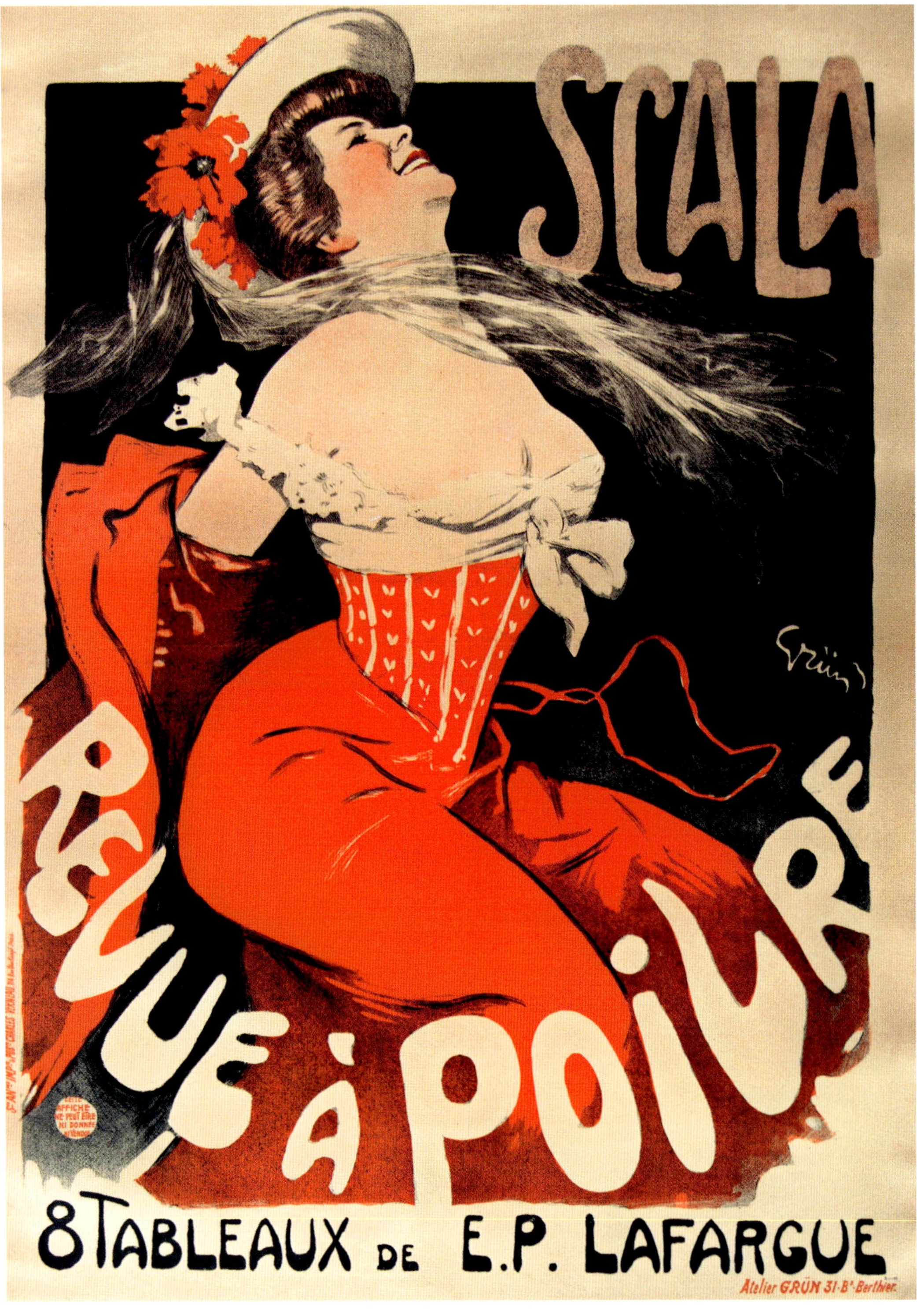

The Red of Celebration

Before World War I in Parisian cabarets—such as the Moulin-Rouge at the foot of Montmartre—upper-class audiences came to mix with the riffraff. All the social classes mingled to watch often extravagant shows: dance, operetta, vaudeville, magic, and "curiosities."

Lithographic poster, 1904. Paris, Bibliothèque Nationale de France, Department of Prints and Photography.

The Red of Seduction

Dressed in any color other than red, Marilyn would not be entirely Marilyn.

Photograph, c. 1954.

please or charm, because red has remained the color of seduction. Although it has not been the favorite color of men and women for a long time now, at least not in the Western world—blue holds that place—it is still a color often associated with pleasure, especially sensual pleasure.[51] Red candies remain children's favorites, as do red toys and red balloons; red fruits are thought to be full of vitamins and more delicious than all others; as for women's underwear, recent surveys maintain that men find red garments more attractive than black or white ones.[52] Generally speaking, although red is no longer really the color of

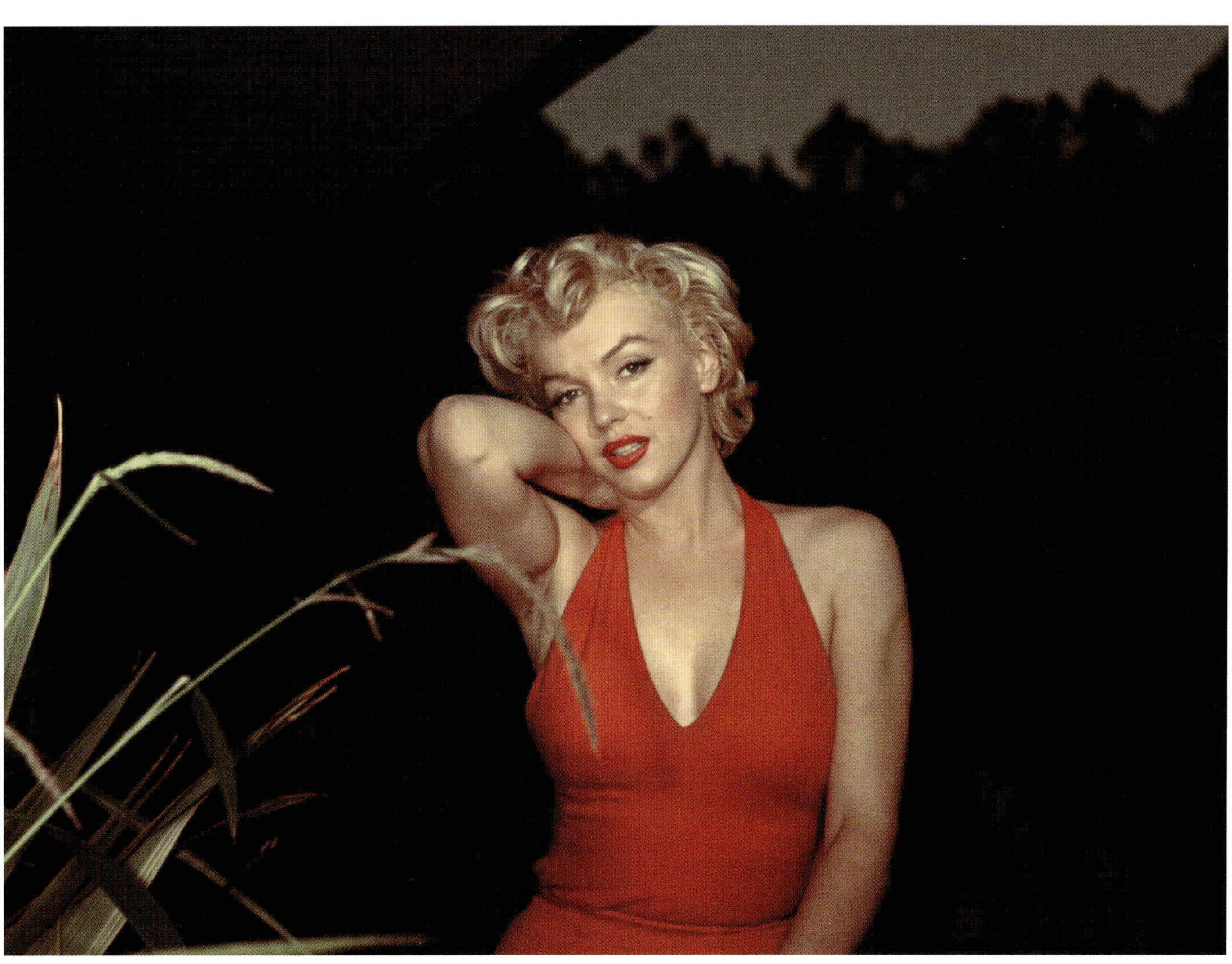

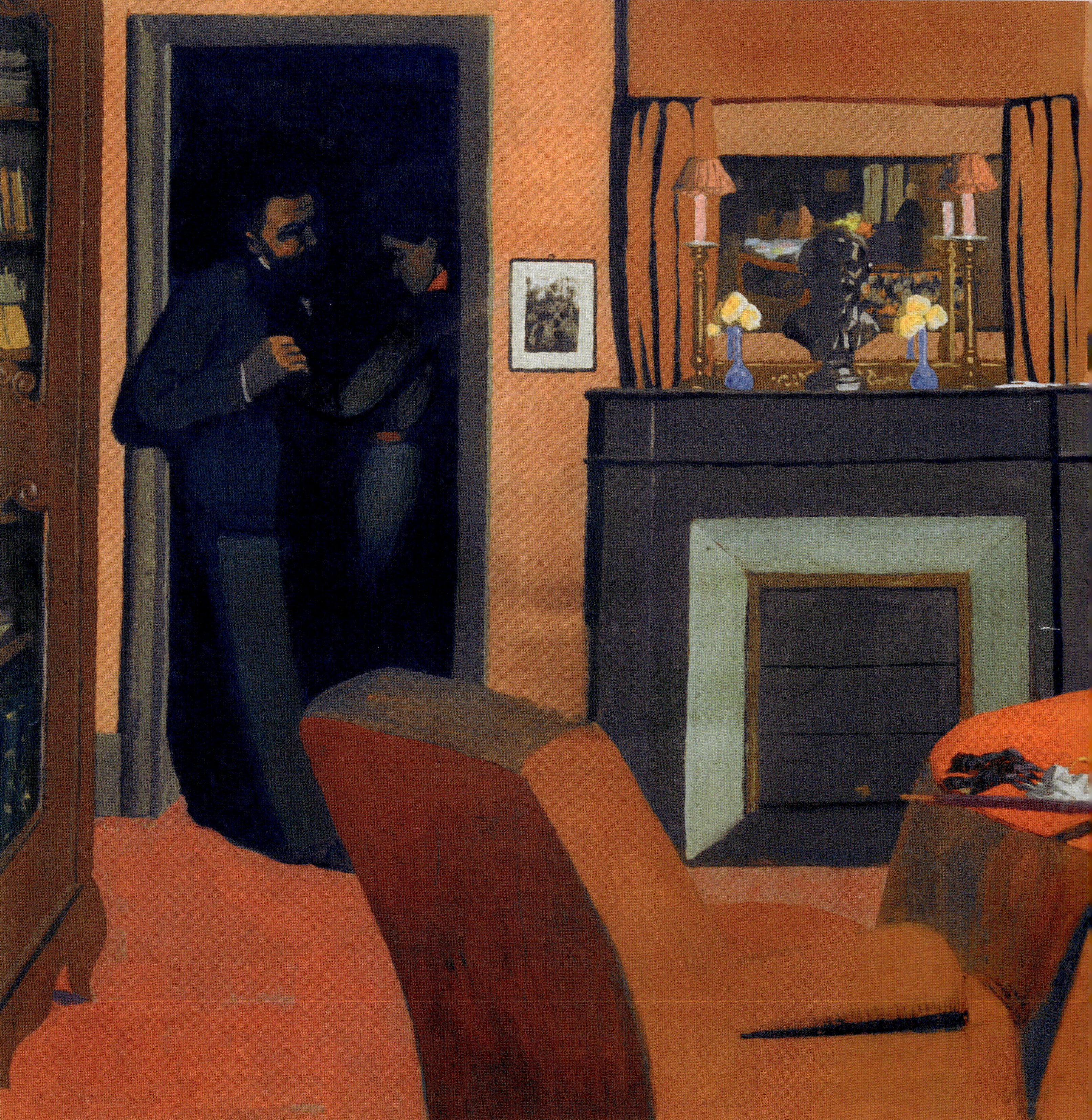

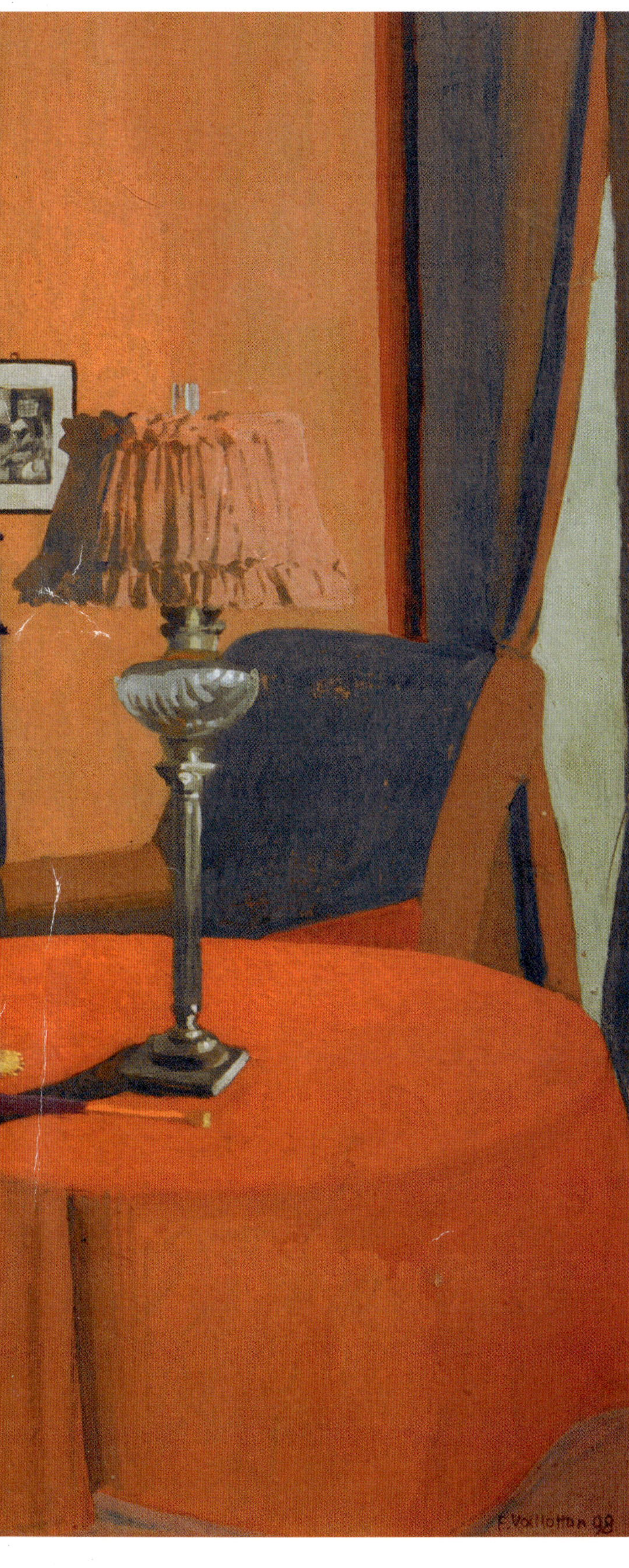

prostitution—which it was for a long time—it remains the color of eroticism and femininity.

Red, the color of pleasure, is also the color of joy and holidays. Christmas, for example, which takes place not long after winter solstice in the calendar year, brings together the green of the fir tree, the white of snow, and the red of Father Christmas. That figure, it must be said, does not in the least owe his red suit to 1930s advertisements for Coca-Cola, as some would claim, but to Saint Nicholas, protector and benefactor of children, depicted wearing a miter and a red cloak in images as far back as the late Middle Ages. The saint's day falls on December 6, and that was the day that children received their gifts (which is still the case in much of Europe). Father Christmas, heir to Saint Nicholas, appeared only much later, and the pagan excesses and commercialism of December 25 even later still.[53]

But there are many other festivities in which red has the place of honor. One example is the truly epiphanic ritual of raising or opening a red curtain to reveal the stage for a musical or theatrical event. In the movie theater, this ritual has become debased, but for live theater and opera it still retains something of its solemnity. Moreover, that curtain has not always been red. In the eighteenth century it was usually blue, but it gradually evolved toward red, not only because tastes changed but also and more important because new lighting showed actors to best advantage in an ambience of red. Actresses and singers especially complained of appearing pale and lifeless when they were surrounded by blue or green. The curtain and the stage then switched to red, after which the entire hall did the same. Little

The Mystery of the Red Chamber

The empty space in conjunction with the ubiquitous reds makes this one of the strangest and most disturbing pictures in the whole history of painting. The mysterious visitor has left his cane and gloves on the table; he lurks in the shadows, hands bare. What is about to happen? A simple romance? Prostitution? Incest? A blood crime? In contrast, the painting by Édouard Vuillard reflected in the mirror above the mantle seems very peaceful.

Félix Vallatton, *The Red Room*, 1898. Lausanne, Switzerland, Musée Cantonal des Beaux-Arts.

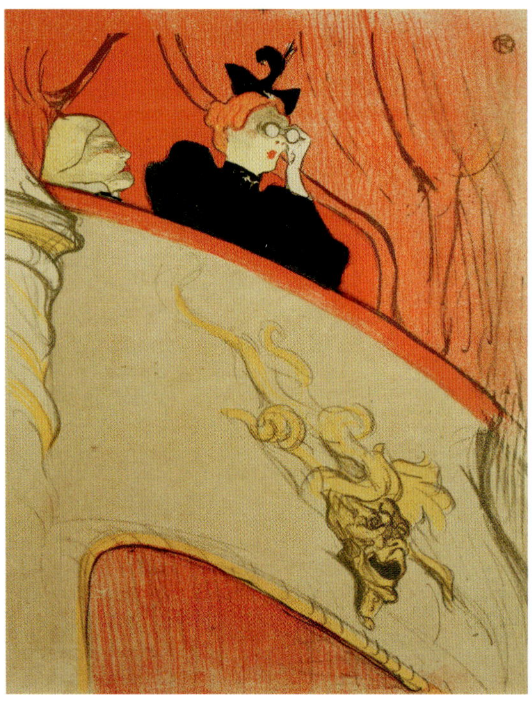

Red's Theatricality

Ever since Roman antiquity red has been—even more than the color of the theater—the color of theatricality.

Henri de Toulouse-Lautrec, *The Box with the Golden Mask*, oil on paperboard, 1894. Vienna, Albertina, Graphic Arts Collection.

by little, whether paired with gold or not, red became the emblematic color of the theater and the opera. It remains so to this day.

A few striking events sealed this now mythical bond between red and the theater, among them the famous "battle of *Hernani*," in Paris, on February 25, 1830. For *Hernani*'s premier performance that evening, the "Romantic army," that is the friends of Victor Hugo—Alexandre Dumas, Théophile Gautier, Gérard de Nerval, Hector Berlioz, and many others—had come to defend their leader's play, controversial even before being staged, a play brimming with youth and passion growing out of the new concept of theater advocated by Hugo and his followers. Théophile Gautier wore a red silk waistcoat that became the evening's emblem. He and his friends had arrived at the Théâtre-Français early to occupy their seats ahead of the supporters of classical

The Battle of *Hernani*

On February 25, 1830, the whole "Romantic army" came to defend Victor Hugo's play on its opening night and with it a new concept of theater. Théophile Gautier wore a red-satin waistcoat, which became the evening's banner, handed down to posterity.

Albert Besnard, *Performance of "Hernani" by Victor Hugo*, 1903. Paris, Maison de Victor Hugo.

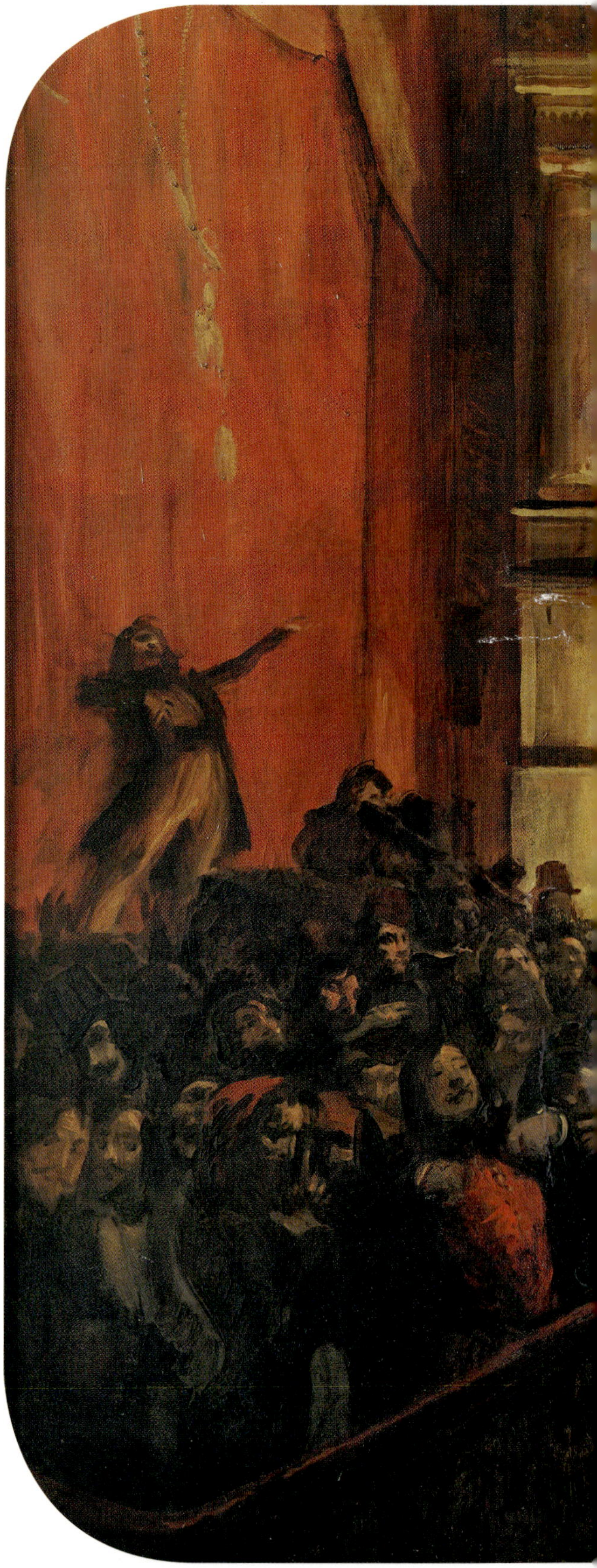

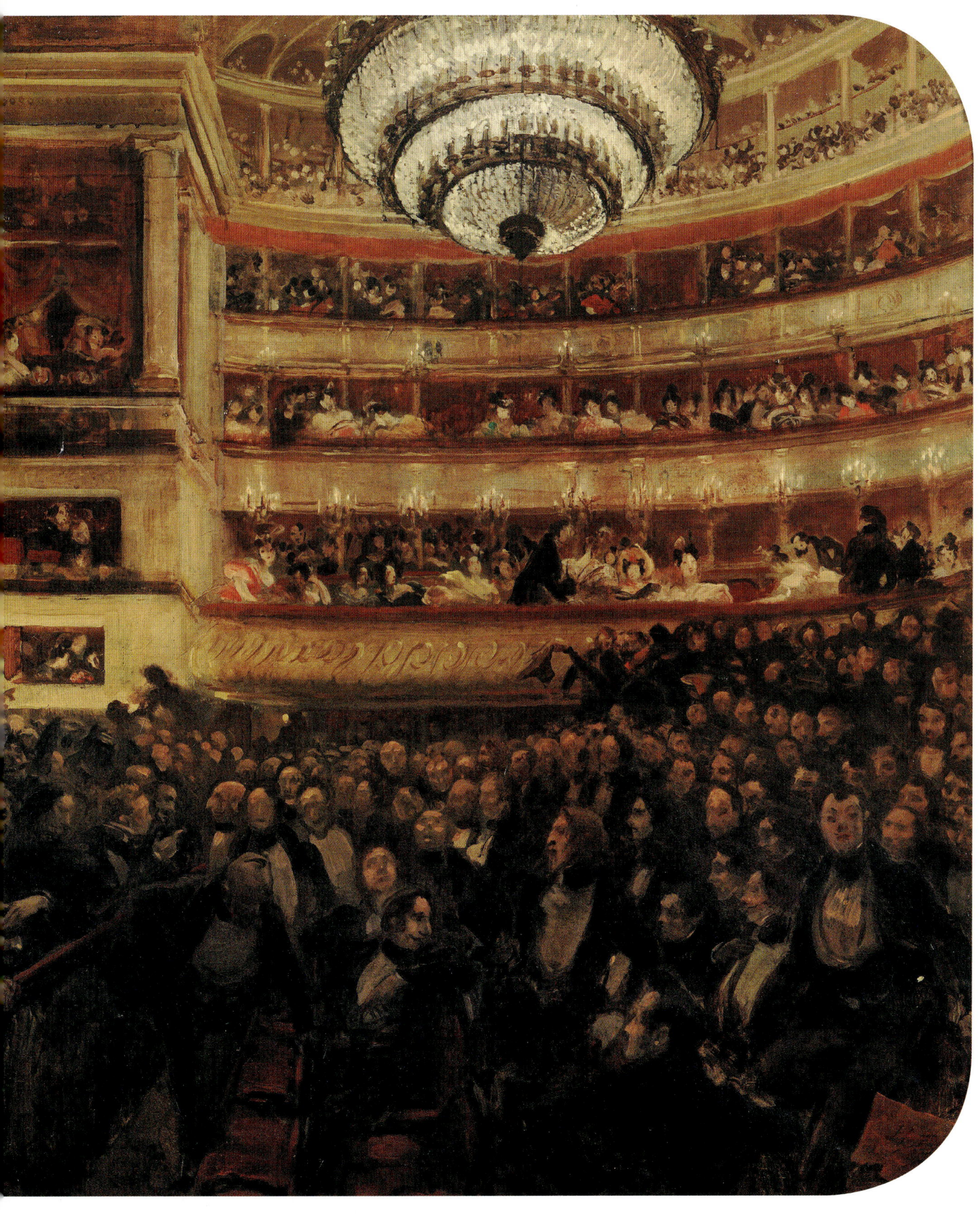

The Music of Color

Certain abstract painters are tremendous colorists: Paul Klee, Nicolas de Staël, Serge Poliakoff. Joining that number, Mark Rothko often plays with the rhythms of color to create sonorous effects. This can be seen and heard especially when several of his canvases are placed side by side; they form a veritable chromatic symphony. Few artists have achieved such a fusion of color and music, though it occurs continually in our vocabulary: scale, tone, value, nuance, intensity, chromaticism.

Mark Rothko, *No. 16 (Red, White, and Brown)*, 1957. Basil, Switzerland, Kunstmuseum.

theater. Dispersed throughout the hall, waving large red cardboard cards that served as their rallying sign, applauding and cheering at every occasion, the Romantics formed an unusual claque. They triumphed over the classicists and ensured the success of both the play and the new dramatic concept.[54]

Cousin to theatrical red is the red of official ceremonies. It is very much older, already present in the ancient Roman Senate and the papal Curia—its heir—in the late Middle Ages. Here the color has less to do with performance than with solemnity. Such red spans the centuries, but it was in the nineteenth century that it became associated definitively with the display of state power. Napoleon and other rulers often turned to it, but so did many republics, seeking in red a kind of majesty sometimes reminiscent of the Ancien Régime. That red has not disappeared, notably in appointment or inauguration ceremonies (during which a "red ribbon" is cut), or when welcoming foreign heads of states (for whom the "red carpet" is rolled out).

It is a short step from decor to decoration. Red "honors" can be found in chivalric orders and rewards for national service, which are the present-day extensions of medieval practices. The Order of the Golden Fleece, for example, established by the Duke of Burgundy, Philip the Good, in 1430, was particularly devoted to this color; the great mantle of the knights was red, and during formal chapter meetings the walls were hung with red, black, and gold. Many modern orders sought to imitate the Golden Fleece, and the ribbons and insignia of contemporary orders give red primacy over the other colors. In France, the Legion of Honor, the highest reward for national service, established by Bonaparte in 1802, is no exception. Almost everything is red: bar, rosette, ribbon, tie. That is why to bear the Legion of Honor is "to have the measles" in French slang, and to wait impatiently to receive it is "to have the red fever."

This does not in the least keep red from remaining a color full of majesty and distinction. But it is also, now as ever, a vibrant, stimulating, even aggressive color. Red wine is thought to be more invigorating than white, red meat more fortifying than white, red cars—think of Ferraris or Maseratis—faster than others. And in the sports world, if we are to believe a persistent legend, teams that play in red jerseys intimidate their opponents and rarely lose.

That is the paradox of red today. No longer our favorite, it has increasingly withdrawn from our everyday environment, and in many areas it has been outstripped by blue or else by green, but it remains the strongest color symbolically. It is a strange fate for a color with so long a past and so laden with meaning, legends, and dreams. But its long history has no doubt become too heavy a burden for our contemporary societies, tired of no longer believing in their own values and each day turning their backs further on their past, their myths, their symbols, and their colors.

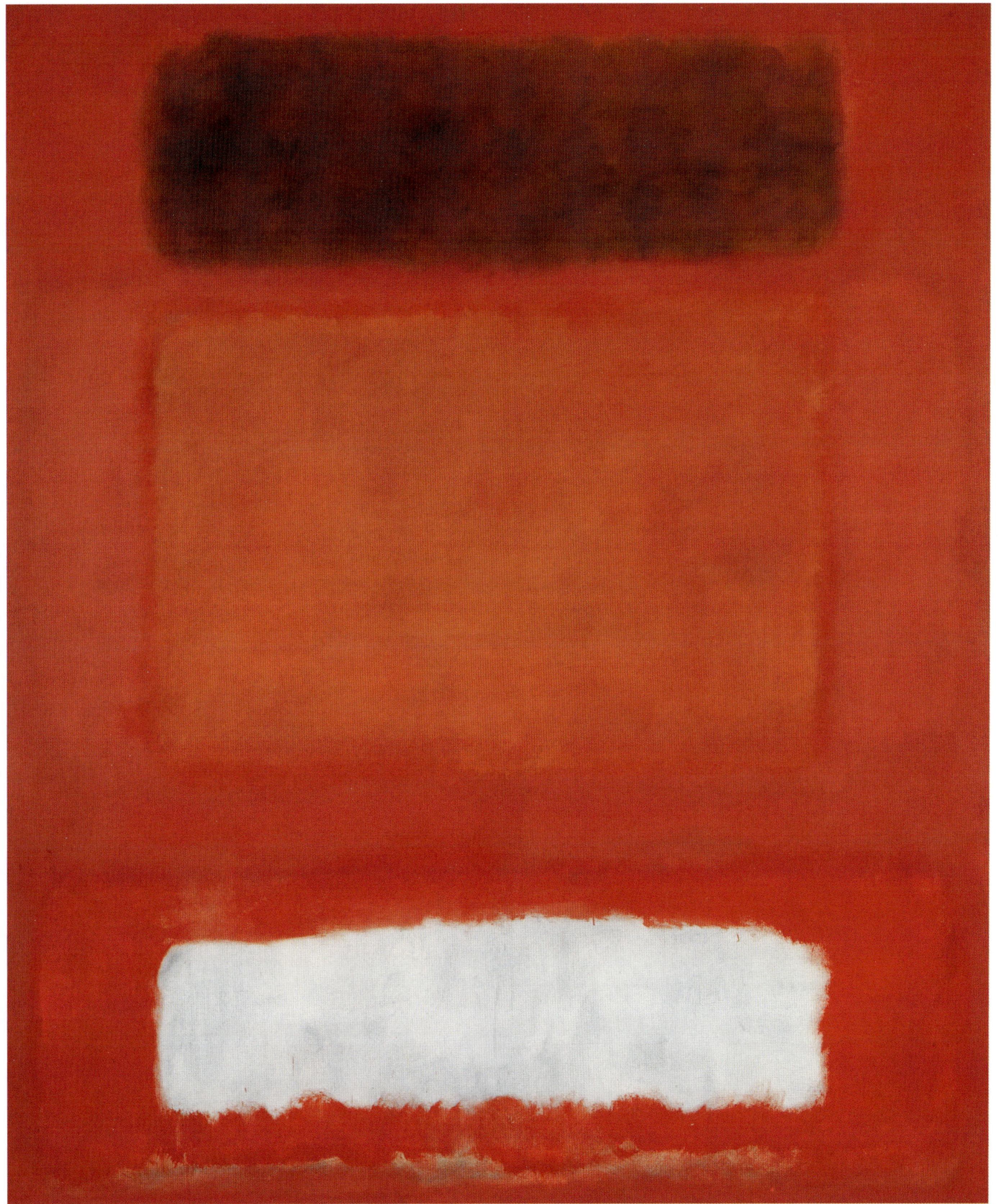

Notes

THE FIRST COLOR

1. When it means red, *coloratus* applies above all to the redness of the body or face, especially the tanned or sunburned face. See J. André, *Étude sur les termes de couleur dans la langue latine* (Paris, 1949), 125–26.

2. Moscow's Red Square (*Krasnaïa Plochad*), a wide rectangular esplanade marking the center of the city, was already called that in the time of the czars, well before the Communist regime was established. It is called "red" not because of the color of the brick buildings that surround it but because it was considered the city's most beautiful square.

3. B. Berlin and P. Kay, *Basic Color Terms: Their Universality and Evolution* (Berkeley, 1969).

4. The presence of realgar in Egyptian painting has sometimes been questioned, but recently analyses have absolutely confirmed it. See *Ancient Egyptian Materials and Technology*, ed. P.T. Nicholson and I. Shaw (Cambridge, 2000), 113–14.

5. The silicate double of copper and calcium. On this famous Egyptian blue, see J. Riederer, "Egyptian Blue," in E.W. Fitzhugh, ed., *Artists' Pigments*, vol. 3 (Oxford, 1997), 23–45.

6. Yellow ocher is clay soil colored with hydrated iron oxide. Through cooking it, the water evaporates completely and the color changes, turning from yellow to red and then to brown.

7. H. Magnus, *Die geschichtliche Entwicklung des Farbensinnes* (Leipzig, 1877); F. Marty, *Die Frage nach der geschichtlichen Entwicklung des Farbensinnes* (Vienna, 1879); G. Allen, *The Colour Sense: Its Origin and Development* (London, 1879). On these questions, see the historiographical summary by Adeline Grand-Clément, "Couleur et esthétique classique au XIXe siècle: L'art grec antique pouvait-il être polychrome?" *Ithaca: Quaderns Catalans de cultura clàssica*, 2 (1): 139–60; also see M. Pastoureau, *Vert: Histoire d'une couleur* (Paris, 2013), 14–20.

8. The long accepted idea that infants see red before other colors has also now been abandoned. P. Lanthony, *Histoire naturelle de la vision colorée* (Paris, 2012).

9. In the West, for example, green was long associated with water and white with air before blue replaced them in these two roles; similarly, black was first associated with night, darkness, and the subterranean world before being associated with fertility, creativity, and authority.

10. C. Perlès, *Préhistoire du feu* (Paris, 1977); J. Collina-Girard, *Le Feu avant les allumettes* (Paris, 1998); B. Roussel, *La Grande Aventure du feu* (Paris, 2006); R. W. Wrangham, *Catching Fire* (New York, 2009).

11. Prometheus was a Titan in constant struggle with Zeus and the gods of Olympus. After having created humans from water and earth, he stole fire from the gods to entrust it to humans and to teach them the arts and metallurgy. Zeus took it back from them and, to punish Prometheus, had him chained naked to a rock in the Caucasus Mountains, where each day an eagle came to eat his liver, which grew back during the night, thus prolonging the Titan's torture indefinitely.

12. On Hephaestus and his physical appearance in the iconography and Greek legends, see M. Delcourt, *Héphaïstos ou la Légende du magicien* (Paris, 1957).

13. On the history and mythology of blood: J.-P. Roux, *Le Sang: Mythes, symboles et réalités* (Paris, 1988); J. Bernard, *La Légende du sang* (Paris, 1992); G. Tobelem, *Histoire du sang* (Paris, 2013).

14. There are numerous occurences in the books of Exodus (12:13; 24:4–8; 30:10) and Leviticus (4:1; 12:6; 14:10; 16:15–16; 19:20). Also see what Saint Paul said in his letter to the Hebrews (9:19–22).

15. Prudentius, *Prudentius Volume II: Against Symmachus 2. Crown of Martyrdom. Scenes from History. Epilogue*, trans. H. J. Thomson (Cambridge, MA, 1953), 295–97.

16. E. Wunderlich, *Die Bedeutung der roten Farbe im Kultus der Griechen und Römer* (Giessen, 1925).

17. Virgil, *The Aeneid*, trans. Robert Fagles (New York and London, 2006), bk. 5, lines 91–99, 156.

18. Quoted by J.-C. Belfiore, *Dictionnaire des croyances et symboles de l'Antiquité* (Paris, 2010), 857.

19. On ancient Greek painting: M. Robertson, *La Peinture grecque* (Geneva, 1959); A. Rouveret, *Histoire et imaginaire de la peinture ancienne (Ve siècle av. J.-C. -1er siècle ap. J.-C.)*, 2nd ed. (Rome, 2014).

20. P. Jockey, *Le Mythe de la Grèce blanche: Histoire d'un rêve occidental* (Paris, 2013).

21. In the Romantic period, the architects sent these accounts to renowned scholars in the academies of London, Paris, and Berlin, but the scholars did not believe them, and it would be a very long time before the existence of a polychromatic antiquity was generally acknowledged by archaeologists.

22. See the spectacular attempts at recreating this polychromy in the catalog for the traveling exhibition *Die bunten Götter: Die Farbigkeit antiker Skulptur* (Munich, 2004).

23. P. Jockey, *Le Mythe de la Grèce blanche*, cited in note 20; A. Grand-Clément, *La Fabrique des couleur: Histoire du paysage sensible des Grecs anciens (VIIIe–début du Ve siècle av. notre ère)* (Paris, 2011).

24. On the painting of Greek vases: J. Montagu, *Les Secrets de fabrication des céramiques antiques* (Saint-Vallier, 1978); C. Bérard, et al., *La Cité des images: Religion et société en Grèce antique* (Paris, 1984); J. Boardman, *La Céramique antique* (Paris, 1985); R. Cook, *Greek Painted Pottery*, 3rd ed. (London, 1997).

25. On ancient Roman painting, for French readers: A. Barbet, *La Peinture murale romaine: Les Style décoratifs pompéiens* (Paris, 1985); I. Baldassare, A. Pontrandolfo, A. Rouveret, and M. Salvadori, *La Peinture romaine, de l'époque hellénistique à l'Antiquité tardive* (Arles, 2006); *L'Empire de la couleur, de Pompéi au sud des Gaules*, ed. A. Dardenay and P. Capus, exhibition (Toulouse, 2014).

26. On this important issue, see J. André, *Étude sur les termes de couleur dans la langue latine* (Paris, 1949), 239–40.

27. Pliny often assumes that his reader has a knowledge of painters and their works that we no longer possess. Sometimes, with regard to a pigment, he stresses how limited the Latin lexicon is and what difficulties he himself has encountered in trying to name pigments precisely.

28. For example, that is the case with Julius von Schlosser (*La Littérature artistique . . .* , new ed. [Paris, 1984], 45–60) and all the art historians—and they are many—who followed him. Schlosser goes as far as characterizing Pliny's discourse on Greek and Roman art as a "veritable tomb of knowledge on ancient art." That is absurd. Other scholars reproach Pliny for getting tangled up in his notes and files, confusing different artists, contradicting himself, and even not understanding what he had recopied from some previous author. These criticisms are excessive and anachronistic; moreover, Pliny has often been badly translated. See clarifications by J.-M. Croisille, "Pline et la peinture d'époque romaine," in *Pline l'Ancien témoin de son temps* (Salamanque and Nantes, 1987), 321–37; and by J. Pigeaud, *L'Art et le Vivant* (Paris, 1995), 199–210.

29. *Historia naturalis*, bk. 35, chap. 12 (sec. 6).

30. Ibid., bk. 33, chap. 38, and bk. 35, chap. 27. See the fine study by J. Trinquier, "*Cinaberis* et sang-dragon: Le Cinabre des Anciens, entre minéral, végétal et animal," in *Revue archéologique* 56 (2013): fasc. 2, 305–46.

31. On Pliny as conservative or "reactionary," see various contributions to the proceedings from the major conference *Pline l'Ancien témoin de son temps*, cited in note 28. See also H. Naas, *Le Projet encyclopédique de Pline l'Ancien* (Rome, 2002), passim.

32. Vitruvius, *De architectura*, bk. 7, chaps. 7–14.

33. For mural painting, see the texts from a very comprehensive conference that examined the state of our knowledge at the end of the twentieth century: *Roman Wall Painting: Materials, Techniques, Analysis and Conservation. Proceedings of the International Workshop (Fribourg, 7-9 March 1996)*, ed. H. Bearat, M. Fuchs, M. Maggetti, and D. Paunier (Fribourg, 1997). See in particular the contribution by H. Bearat, "Quelle est la gamme exacte des pigments romains?" 11–34.

34. In addition to the study by H. Bearat cited in the preceding note, see the major article by J. Trinquier cited in note 30.

35. In Pompeii, some ocher-based reds may have originally been yellow ochers that the heat from the eruption of Vesuvius transformed into red ochers. Thus, the omnipresence of red tones on the walls of houses today may be greater than before the explosion, when yellow and red shared wall surfaces equally. At least that is one recently advanced hypothesis.

36. The Latin word was retained in French and English. In mural painting, especially with frescoes, a *sinopia* is a preliminary drawing done in red on the first coat.

37. The principal mines were near Pozzuoli in Campania, Italy.

38. By a more simple procedure, strips of lead can be oxidized with lime, fermented urine, or vinegar.

39. Pliny gives this mixture the name *sandyx* (*Historia naturalis*, bk. 35, chap. 40).

40. On pigments used in ancient Rome, beyond the work cited above in note 33, see the useful compendium by N. Eastaugh, V. Walsh, T. Chaplin, and R. Siddall, *The Pigment Compendium: A Dictionary of Historical Pigments* (Leyde, 2004).

41. Vitruvius, *De architectura*, bk. 7, chap. 14.

42. F. Brunello, *The Art of Dyeing in the History of Mankind* (Vicenza, 1973), 38–46.

43. Ibid., 14–15.

44. Pliny, *Historia naturalis*, bk. 24, chaps. 56–57.

45. Legend holds that the guild was established as early as the seventh century BCE by King Numa Pompilius (who, according to tradition, ruled from 715 to 673). This is obviously only a legend, but it is valuable for emphasizing how very ancient the dyers' guild was; dyers were among the earliest artisans in ancient Rome.

46. Brunello, *The Art of Dyeing*, 104–5.

47. In antiquity, as in most of the Middle Ages for that matter, dyeing in true white was a nearly impossible endeavor.

48. Rome long maintained the custom of dressing the Capitoline statue of Jupiter in a purple cloak (sometimes the stone itself was covered with red lead or cinnabar). See E. Wunderlich, *Die Bedeutung der roten Farbe*, cited in note 16.

49. On antique purple, the bibliography is very abundant but uneven; let us cite: W. Born, "Purple in Classical Antiquity," in *Ciba Review* 1–2, 1937–39: 110–19; M. Reinhold, *History of Purple as a Status Symbol in Antiquity* (Brussels, 1970) (*Latomus*, vol. 116); J. Daumet, *Étude sur la couleur de la pourpre ancienne* (Beirut, 1980); H. Stulz, *Die Farbe Purpur im frühen Griechentum* (Stuttgart, 1990).

50. Eighteenth- and nineteenth-century zoologists engaged in endless debates assigning this or that vocable to this or that mollusk, an exercise totally in vain because the same word designates many shellfish and the same shellfish is designated by many terms. Added to these difficulties is the question of simple varieties often taken to be distinctive species. See the texts cited by A. Dedekind, *Ein Beitrag zur Purpurkunde* (Berlin, 1898).

51. Pliny, *Historia naturalis*, bk. 9, chaps. 61–65.

52. Under the empire, it was not uncommon to mix, in variable proportions, murex (*buccinum*) and purpura (*pelagium*) juices to obtain new or unusual shades of color.

53. On the extreme diversity in the shades of Roman purple and its accompanying lexicon, see J. André, *Étude sur les termes de couleur*, cited in note 26, 90–105.

54. The ancients used purple dyes for textiles of animal origin, wool and silk, but rarely for cotton and never for linen. Wool was dyed in the untreated state. After being soaked in an alum decoction, it was immersed in a hot vat of purple and remained there for a relatively long time, until it was completely permeated with the purple juice. To obtain the desired shade, various products, some of which were colorants, some not, were added to this bath: orcein, madder, honey, bean powder, wine, and water.

55. M. Besnier, "Purpura," in *Dictionnaire des antiquités grecques et romaines*, vol. 4: 1, ed. C. Daremberg and E. Saglio (Paris, 1905), 769–78; K. Schneider, "Purpura," in *Realencyclopädie der klassichen Altertumswissenchaft (Pauly-Wissowa)* (Stuttgart, 1959), vol. 23: 2, cols. 2000–2020.

56. Suetonius, *Caligula* (*The Twelve Caesars*), chap. 35.

57. Horace, *Satyrae*, bk. 2, sat. 8: 10–11.

58. Jockey, *Le Mythe de la Grèce blanche*, cited in note 20.

59. Juvenal, *Satires*, bk. 3, line 196, in *Juvenal and Persius*, ed. and trans. Susanna Morton Braund (Cambridge, MA, 2004), 183. Also see the testimony of Ulpian, jurisconsult and prefect of the praetorium in the early third century, who complained of the multiple fires that broke out in the city each day: *plurimis uno die incendiis exortis* (*Dig.*, I, 15, 2).

60. J. Marquardt, *Le Vie privée des Romains*, vol. 2 (Paris, 1892), 123.

61. Juvenal, *Satyrae*, bk. 10, lines 37–39; Martial, *Epigrammata*, bk. 2, lines 29–37.

62. *Rubrica* was a red makeup with an ocher or iron-oxide-rich clay base; *fucus* was a red makeup with an orcein base.

63. Ovid, *Ovid's Erotic poems: "Amores" and "Ars amatoria,"* trans. Len Krisak (Philadelphia, 2014), bk. 3, line 210.

64. Martial, *Epigrams* (Cambridge, MA, 1919), bk. 9, lines 37–41, vol. 2, p. 259.

65. André, *Étude sur les termes de couleur*, 323–71.

66. Pliny, *Natural History: Preface and Books 1–2*, trans. Harris Rackham (Cambridge, MA, 2006), vol. 3, bk. 10, p. 323.

67. Titus Livius, *Ab urbe condita libri* (*History of Rome*), bk. 21, chap. 62.

68. André, *Étude sur les termes de couleur*, 81–83.

69. F. Jacquesson, *Les Mots de couleurs dans les textes bibliques* (Paris, 2008), online version at the LACITO-CNRS research site, in conjunction with the study by the same author, "Les mots de la couleur en hébreu ancien," *Histoire et géographie de la couleur*, ed. P. Dollus, F. Jacquesson, and M. Pastoureau (Paris, 2013), 67–130 (*Cahiers du Léopard d'Or*, vol. 13).

70. Ibid., 70.

71. B. Berlin and P. Kay, *Basic Color Terms: Their Universality and Evolution* (Berkeley, 1969).

72. H. C. Conklin, "Color Categorization," *American Anthropologist* 24, no. 4 (1973): 931–42; B. Saunders, "Revisiting *Basic Color Terms*," *Journal of the Royal Anthropological Institute* 6 (2000): 81–99.

73. In classical Latin, *roseus*, when used as a color adjective, never means "pink," but rather "red," most often a beautiful, vivid, luminous red. The best translation in modern French is "*vermeil*," or "vermilion" in English.

74. On the lexicon of reds in classical Latin, see André, *Étude sur les termes de couleur*, 75–127.

75. At least if we are to believe Plutarch and Suetonius. Amid the abundant literature, see M. Dubuisson, "*Verba uolant:* Réexamen de quelques mots historiques romains," *Revue belge de philologie et d'histoire* 78 (2000): 147–69.

76. Exodus 14:1–31.

THE FAVORITE COLOR

1. On these complex questions that run through my studies on the history of colors, I hope soon to have the opportunity to give my position: M. Pastoureau, *Qu'est-ce que la couleur? Trois essais en quête d'une définition* (Paris: Éditions du Seuil, forthcoming).

2. It is absurd to rely on a modern translation of the Bible to study historical questions connected to biblical passages. The biblical text is a fluid text. We must always make the effort to discover the state of the text used in a given period, consulted by a given author, or commented upon by yet another author; otherwise, all our analyses are in vain.

3. On the symbolism of colors among the Church Fathers, see C. Meier and R. Suntrup, *Zum Lexicon der Farbenbedeutungen im Mittelalter* (Cologne and Vienna, 2011, CD-ROM [print version not yet available]).

4. C. Meier and R. Suntrup, "Zum Lexicon der Farbenbedeutungen im Mittelalter: Einführung zu Gegenstand und Methoden sowie Probeartikel aus dem Farbenbereich Rot" *Frühmittelalterliche Studien* 21 (1987): 390–478;

M. Pastoureau, "Ceci est mon sang: Le christianisme médiéval et la couleur rouge" *Le Pressoir mystique: Actes du colloque de Recloses*, ed. D. Alexandre-Bidon (Paris, 1990), 43–56.

5. The Church Fathers sometimes associated the "dragon red as fire" with the coat of the horse ridden by the second horseman of the Apocalypse, which is also "red as fire" (Rev. 6:4). It symbolized war.

6. Luke 12:49.

7. Pliny, *Natural History: Preface and Books 1–2*, trans. Harris Rackham (Cambridge, MA, 2006), vol. 3, bk. 10, 323.

8. On the misogyny of medieval monks and preachers: M.-T. d'Alverny, "Comment les théologiens et les philosophes voient la femme," *Cahiers de civilization médiévale* 20 (1977): 105–29; R. H. Bloch, "La misogynie médiévale et l'invention de l'amour en Occident," *Cahiers du GRIF* 43 (1993): 9–23. Many references to the misogyny of preachers can also be found in the work by J. Horowitz and S. Ménache, *L'Humour en chaire: Le rire dans la prédication médiévale* (Geneva, 1994), especially 190–93.

9. Cyprian of Carthage, *The Letters of St. Cyprian of Carthage*, trans. G. W. Clarke (New York and New Jersey, 1984), letter 10, sec. 5.2, 75.

10. On the worship of the Precious Blood: G. Schury, *Lebensflut: Eine Kulturgeschichte des Blutes* (Leipzig, 2001); C. Walker Bynum, *The Blood of Christ in the Later Middle Ages* (Cambridge, 2002); *1200 Jahre Heilig-Blut-Tradition: Katalog zur Jubiläumsausstellung der Stadt Weingarten, 20 Mai–11 Juli, 2004*, ed. N. Kruse (Weingarten, 2004).

11. On the theme of the mystic wine-press, see *Le Pressoir mystique: Actes du colloque de Recloses*, ed. D. Alexandre-Bidon, cited in note 4.

12. C. H. Hefele, *Histoire des conciles d'après les documents généraux*, vol. 5 (1863), 398–424; *Le Concile de Clermont de 1095 et l'Appel à la croisade: Actes du colloque universitaire international de Clermont-Ferrand, 23–25 juin 1995*, École française de Rome, ed. (Rome, 1997); J. Heers, *La Première Croisade* (Paris, 2002).

13. M. Pastoureau, "La coquille et la croix: les emblèmes des croisés," *L'Histoire* 47 (July 1982): 68–72; A. Demurger, *Croisades et croisés au Moyen Âge* (Paris, 2006), 46.

14. A. Paravicini Bagliani, *Le Chiavi e la Tiara: Immagini e simboli del papato medievale* (Rome, 2005); and A. Paravicini Bagliani, *Il potere del papa: Corporeità, autorappresentazione, simboli* (Florence, 2009).

15. Éginhard, *Vita Karoli Magni Imperatoris*, L. Halphen, ed. (Paris, 1923), 46. See also R. Folz, *Le Souvenir et la Légende de Charlemagne dans l'Empire germanique médiéval* (1950); and R. Folz, *Le Couronnement impérial de Charlemagne (25 decembre 800)* (Paris, 1964).

16. P. E. Schramm, *Die zeitgenössischen Bildnisse Karls des Grossen* (Leipzig, 1928); and P. E. Schramm, *Herrschaftszeichen und Staatssymbolik: Beiträge zu ihrer Geschichte vom dritten bis zum sechzehnten Jarhundert*, 3 vols. (Stuttgart, 1954–56).

17. This mantle is now held in the Kunsthistorisches Museum in Vienna; it weighs almost fifty kilos. See the note by R. Bauer, "Il manto di Ruggero II," in the catalog from the exhibition *I Normanni, popolo d'Europa (1030–1200)* (Rome, 1994), 279–87; as well as W. Tronzo, "The Mantle of Roger II of Sicily," in *Investiture* (Cambridge, 2001), 241–53.

18. On the coronation mantle of the kings of France, see H. Pinoteau, "La tenue de sacre de saint Louis," *Itinéraires* 62 (1972): 120–62; see also, by the same author, *La Symbolique royale française (V^e–XVIIIe siècle)* (La Roche-Rigault, 2004), passim.

19. *La Chanson de Roland*, ed. G. Moignet (Paris, 1970), verse 2653. See A. Lombard-Jourdan, *Fleur de lis et oriflamme: Signes célestes du royaume de France* (Paris, 1991), 220–30.

20. On the oriflamme, see P. Contamine, *L'Oriflamme de Saint-Denis aux XIVe and XVe siècles: Étude de symbolique religieuse et royale* (Nancy, 1975).

21. I thank my friend Marguerite Wilska for having drawn my attention to these curious Polish practices. On the cochineal insect as feudal payment, see M. Wilska, "Du symbole au vêtement: Fonction et signification de al couleur dans la culture courtoise de la Pologne médiévale," in *Le Vêtement: Histoire, archéologie et symbolique vestimentaires au Moyen Âge, Cahiers du Léopard d'Or*, vol. 1 (Paris, 1986), 307–24.

22. R. Jacob, *Images de la Justice: Essai sur l'iconographie judiciaire du Moyen Âge à l'âge classique* (Paris, 1994), 67–68.

23. The appearance of coats of arms in the West about the mid-twelfth century was first linked to a practical cause: the development of military equipment. Changes in helmets and hauberks made knights unrecognizable in battles and tournaments, so they gradually adopted the custom of having the large surfaces of their shields painted with figures (animals, plants, geometric shapes), making them recognizable in the fray. We can speak of coats of arms beginning from when a single knight painted his shield the same way consistently over a long period of his life, using the same figures and colors, and when a few principles of composition, simple but strict, played a part in the design. Nevertheless this practical cause does not explain everything. The appearance of coats of arms is more deeply rooted in the new social order that affected Western society in the seignorial period. Henceforth that society sought out signs of identity (patronymics, coats of arms, vestmental insignia).

24. After a fairly long, slow development, true coats of arms made their appearance on battle and tournament fields in the mid-twelfth century. First intended only as signs for recognizing the combatants, their use spread to all nobility—including women—and then beginning in the thirteenth century to other social classes and categories, for which they played the role of signs of identity, marks of possession, and sometimes decorative ornaments. For the whole medieval period and all of Western Europe, we can recognize about a million different coats of arms. Three-quarters of them we know through seals, that is to say, without their colors.

25. See the numbers presented by M. Pastoureau, *Traité d'héraldique*, 2nd ed. (Paris, 1993), 113–21.

26. On the etymology and appearance of these terms in the language of heraldry, see ibid., 103. Heraldry does not employ its six colors randomly. They are divided into two groups: in the first are white and yellow; in the second are red, black, blue, and green. The fundamental rule for using colors forbids juxtaposing or superimposing two colors that belong to the same group (except with regard to small details, such as the tongues or claws of animals).

27.   Later, in the fourteenth century, the king of Sweden also adopted coats of arms with a blue field: *d'azur à trois couronnes d'or.*

28.   See the summary of this issue offered by K. Nirop, "*Gueules*: Histoire d'un mot," *Romania* 68 (1922): 559-70. Since then our knowledge has hardly advanced. The low Latin term *tegulatus*, which sometimes has a chromatic meaning ("the color of tile") seems to provide a more solid lead than Gallic, Persian, or Frankish, but no scholar seems to have considered it.

29.   The terms *or*, *argent*, and *azur* pose no problem. The first two come from Latin, the third from Arabic. *Sable* comes from the German *sabeln*, which itself comes from the old Slavic *sobol*, designating the black fur of the sable marten. As for *sinople*, it comes from the Latin *sinopia*, which designates the red clay found in abundance in the region of Sinop, now a city in Turkey, on the shores of the Black Sea. This term long signified "red," before taking on the meaning of "green" in the language of heraldry in the second half of the fourteenth century. The reasons for this change in meaning are still unknown.

30.   M. Pastoureau, "*De gueules plain*: Perceval et les origines héraldique de la maison d'Albret," *Revue française d'héraldique et de sigillographie* 61 (1991): 63-81.

31.   I offer here a translation into modern French (translated to English for this edition) from the extract of the treatise attributed to Banyster, edited by C. Boudreau, *L'Héritage symbolique des hérauts d'armes: Dictionnaire encyclopédique de l'enseignement du blason ancien (XIVᵉ-XVIᵉ s.)*, vol. 2 (Paris, 2006), 781.

32.   For this adaptation into modern French (here translated to English), I have not followed the mediocre edition by H. Cocheris (cited in the following note), which relies on later printings, but on the manuscript from the Vatican Library Ottob. Lat. 2257, as well as the Lyonnaise printing issued from the offices of Rouillé and Arnouillet in 1515.

33.   A new edition of the *Blason des couleurs* would be welcome. The old edition by H. Coheris (Paris, 1860), often cited, is faulty and was based on copies printed at the end of the sixteenth century and not on manuscripts from the late fifteenth century or printed copies from the 1500s. Now there are many variants between these versions, especially because of the evolution in the clothing colors actually worn between the beginning and end of the sixteenth century. The text has been altered and adapted many times. See my study cited in the following note, as well as that of C. Boudreau, "Historiographie d'une méprise: À propos de l'incunable du *Blason des couleurs du héraut Sicile*," *Études médiévales*, 69ᵉ congrès de l'AFCAS (University of Montreal, May 1994) (Montreal, 1994), 123-29.

34.   M. Pastoureau, "Le blanc, le bleu et le tanné: Beauté, harmonie et symbolique des couleurs à l'aube des temps modernes," in *Désir n'a repos: Hommage à Danielle Bohler*, ed. F. Bouchet and D. James-Raoul (Bordeaux, 2016), 115-32.

35.   B. Milland-Bove, *La Demoiselle arthurienne: Écriture du personnage et art du récit dans les romans en prose du XIIIᵉ siècle* (Paris, 2006).

36.   That is, in this order: light blue, blue-gray, blue-green, deep blue, very deep blue.

37.   C.-V. Langlois, *La Vie en France au Moyen Âge, de la fin du XIIᵉ siècle au milieu du XIVᵉ, d'après les romans mondains du temps* (Paris, 1926), passim; *Les Soins de beauté au Moyen Âge*, ed. D. Menjot (Nice, 1987); *Le Bain et le Miroir: Soins du corps et cosmétiques de l'Antiquité à la Renaissance*, exhibition (Paris, Musée de Cluny, 2009). For the end of the Middle Ages and the modern era, see also: C. Lanoë, *La Poudre et le Fard: Une histoire des cosmétiques de la Renaissance aux Lumières* (Seyssel, 2008).

38.   Wolfram von Eschenbach (c. 1170-c. 1230), the Bavarian poet and knight, was the greatest epic poet of the German Middle Ages. His *Parzival*, inspired by Chrétien de Troyes's *Le Conte du Graal*, served as Richard Wagner's source for his two operas *Parsifal* and *Lohengrin*.

39.   On the Grail, for which there is abundant and often uneven literature, see especially: J. Marx, *La Légende arthurienne et le Graal* (Paris, 1952); R. S. Loomis, *The Grail: From Celtic Myth to Christian Symbol* (Cardiff, 1963); D.D.R. Owen, *The Evolution of the Grail Legend* (Edinburgh, 1968); J. Frappier, *Autour de Graal* (Geneva, 1977); J. Frappier,

Chrétien de Troyes et le mythe du Graal, 2nd ed. (Paris, 1979); P. Walter, ed., *Le Livere du Graal*, 3 vols. (Paris, 2001–9).

40. J. Rossiaud, *La Prostitution médiévale* (Paris, 1988), passim.

41. Rev. 17:3–4.

42. Heidelberg, Universitätsbibliothek, Cpg 848.

43. The image of a lady offering her sleeve to a knight was not a creation of the Romantic era. It is well attested in the courtly romances of the twelfth and thirteenth centuries, notably those by Chrétien de Troyes (*Le Chevalier au lion, Le Conte du Graal*), and a century later, in *Sone de Nansay*, composed by an anonymous author from Lorraine or Champagne.

44. The fig and pear have retained sexual meanings even in contemporary slang. See J. Cellard and A. Rey, *Dictionnaire du français non conventionnel* (Paris, 1991).

45. Chrétien de Troyes, *Le Conte du Graal*, vol. 2, ed. F. Lecoy (Paris, 1970), lines 4109 and following. This passage has been commented upon many, many times. See especially, H. Rey-Flaud, "Le sang sur la neige: Anaylse d'une image-écran de Chrétien de Troyes," *Littérature* 37 (1980): 15–24; D. Poiron, "Du sang sur la neige: Nature et fonction de l'image dans *Le Conte du Graal*," in D. Hüe, ed., *Polyphonie du Graal* (Orléans, 1998), 99–112.

46. The practice of wearing dark clothes for mourning was already present in early Christian art. In Rome of the late empire, black or dark clothes were worn by new magistrates in mourning for their predecessors, and this practice found its extension in Carolingian and Ottonian art.

47. On the Saint-Denis blue that became the Chartres blue: J. Gage, *Colour and Culture: Practice and Meaning from Antiquity to Abstraction* (London, 1993), 69–78; M. Pastoureau, *Bleu: Histoire d'une couleur*, 2nd ed. (Paris, 2006), 37–42.

48. Among the major studies that I devoted to this color before the publication of the book cited in the preceding note, see especially: "Et puis vint le bleu," in D. Regnier-Bohler, ed., *Le Moyen Âge aujourd'hui, Europe*, no. 654 (Oct., 1983): 43–50; "Vers une histoire de la couleur bleu," in *Sublime indigo*, exhibit (Marseilles, 1987, Fribourg, 1987), 19–27; "La promotion de la couleur bleue au XIIIe siècle: Le témoignage de l'héraldique et de l'emblématique," in *Il colore nel Medioevo: Arte, simbolo, tecnica; Atti delle giornate di studi (Lucca, 5–6 maggio 1995)* (Lucca, 1996), 7–16; "Voir les couleurs au XIIIe siècle," in A. Paravicini Bagliani, ed., *La visione e lo sguardo nel Medioevo* (1998), 147–165 (*Micrologus: Natura, scienze e società medievali*, vol. 6/2).

49. M. Pastoureau, *Bleu: Histoire d'une couleur*, cited in note 47, 53–56.

50. J. Le Goff, *La Civilisation de l'Occident médiéval*, 2nd ed. (Paris, 1982), p. 330.

51. It was in fact animal matter, extracted from the dried bodies of various insects collected from the leaves of many varieties of oaks growing in areas of the Mediterranean and eastern Europe. For the dye, only the females were used and had to be caught at the time when they were preparing to lay their eggs. Sprayed with vinegar, then dried in the sun, the insect bodies were transformed into a sort of brownish seed that, when crushed, secreted a bit of intense red juice. The dye was solid, saturated, and luminous in color, but it took considerable quantities of insects to obtain a small amount of dyestuff, hence the high price of medieval kermes, reserved for very expensive fabrics.

52. A. Ott, *Études sur les termes de couleur en vieux français* (Paris, 1900), 129–31.

53. J. B. Weckerlin, *Le Drap "escarlate" au Moyen Âge: Essai sur l'étymologie et la signification du mot écarlate et notes techniques sur la fabrication de ce drap de laine au Moyen Âge* (Lyon, 1905); W. Jervis Jones, *German Colour Terms: A Study in Their Historical Evolution from Earliest Times to the Present* (Amsterdam, 2013), 338–40.

54. Florence, Archivo di Stato, Giudice degli appelli di nullita, ms. 117. The volume includes 308 pages and measures 30 × 24 cm. The title *Prammatica* (meaning "regulatory practices") seems to have been given to it in the sixteenth century.

55. L. Gérard-Marchant, "Compter et nommer l'étoffe à Florence au Trecento (1343)," *Médiévales* 29 (1995): 87–104. The manuscript, copied on paper, was badly damaged and remains difficult to read. Despite skillful restoration, about 10 percent of the text was permanently lost.

56. L. Eisenbart, *Kleiderordnungen der deutschen Städte* (Göttingen, 1962); A. Hunt, *A History of Sumptuary Laws* (New York, 1996); M. A. Ceppari Ridolfi and P. Turrini, *Il mulino delle vanità* (Sienna, 1996); M. G. Muzzarelli, *Guardaroba medievale: Vesti e società dal XIII al XVI secolo* (Bologna, 1999).

57. L. Gérard-Marchant, C. Klapisch-Zuber, et al., *Draghi rossi e querce azzurre: Elenchi descrittivi di abiti di lusso, Firenze, 1343–1345* (Florence, 2013) (SISMEL, *Memoria scripturarum 6, testi latini 4*).

A CONTROVERSIAL COLOR

1. M. Pastoureau, "Le blanc, le bleu et le tanné: Beauté, harmonie et symbolique des couleurs à l'aube des temps modernes," in *Désir n'a repos: Hommage à Danielle Bohler*, ed. F. Bouchet and D. James-Raoul (Bordeaux, 2016), 115–32.

2. C. Casagrande and S. Vecchio, *I sette vizi capitali: Storia dei paccati nel Medioevo* (Turin, 2000).

3. There is a similar system for the seven virtues. These two systems, the colors of the seven sins and seven virtues, are known to us through books of emblems, treatises on heraldry, and related literature. Their influence made itself felt on poetic and artistic creation until the mid-seventeenth century. Rabelais mocks them with much irony in connection with the colors of Gargantua's livery.

4. On the medieval iconography of hell, see J. Baschet, *Les Justices de l'au-delà: Les représentations de l'enfer en France et en Italie (XIIᵉ–XVᵉ siècle)* (Rome, 1993).

5. On the colors of the Devil, see M. Pastoureau, *Noir: Histoire d'une couleur* (Paris, 2008), 47–56. English edition: *Black: History of a Color*, trans. J. Gladding (Princeton, 2009), 47–56.

6. This combination of black and red was practically absent from the wardrobes of the Florentine ladies discussed in the last chapter; see "The Wardrobes of Beautiful Florentine Ladies." See also the last part of a curious treatise on heraldry and clothing, compiled about 1480–85 and wrongly attributed to the Sicily Herald (who died in 1437), *Le Blason des couleurs*, ed. H. Coheris (Paris, 1860), 80–81. The author sees in this combination of colors a sign of despair, evoking the final end.

7. On this rule, see M. Pastoureau, *L'Art héraldique au Moyen Âge* (Paris, 2009), 26–32.

8. At the end of the Middle Ages the idea gradually took hold that the black-white pairing was richer in significance than the white-red pairing. Beginning in the 1360s–80s, the color black had indeed experienced a remarkable ascent. From the color of the Devil, death, and sin, it had become the color of humility and temperance, two virtues then on the rise. Moreover, Aristotle's theories on the classification of colors had circulated widely, and made black and white the two opposite poles of all chromatic axes. From then on in many domains the opposition of white and black began to be considered stronger and richer than that of white and red, notably on the chessboard. See M. Pastoureau, *Le Jeu d'échecs médiéval* (Paris, 2012), 30–34.

9. The red of justice is still present today in the robes of certain magistrates—at least for formal occasions—and within the university, in the gowns of law professors. Indeed throughout Europe, law schools use red for their emblematic color, while green is the color of the sciences and medicine, and yellow the color of the arts and humanities.

10. The works on the iconography of Judas are quite limited in number and generally old. The best summary, constructed around the question of Judas's red hair, is by Ruth Mellinkoff, "Judas's Red Hair and the Jews," *Journal of Jewish Art* 9 (1982): 31–46. It can be supplemented with the large work by the same author, *Outcasts: Signs of Otherness in Northern European Art of the Late Middle Ages*, 2 vols. (Berkeley, 1993). See especially vol. 1, 145–59. Contrary to R. Mellinkoff's opinion, the thesis by Wilhelm Porte, *Judas Ischariot in der bildenden Kunst* (Berlin, 1883), is still worth consulting.

11. The list and critical studies of these attributes can be found in the usual iconographic repertoires, notably: L. Réau, *Iconographie de l'art chrétien*, vol. 2/2 (Paris, 1957), 406–10; G. Schiller, *Iconography of Christian Art*, vol. 2 (London, 1972), 29–30, 164–80, 494–501, and passim; E. Kichbaum, ed., *Lexikon der christlichen Ikonographie*, vol. 2 (Freiburg, 1970), col. 444–48.

12. R. Mellinkoff, *The Mark of Cain* (Berkeley, 1981).

13. C. Raynaud, "Images médiévales de Ganelon," in *Félonie, trahison and reniements au Moyen Âge* (Montpellier, 1996), 75–92.

14. See the impressive body of images collected in R. Mellinkoff, *Outcasts* (cited in note 10), especially vol. 2, 1–38, and plate VII.

15. The name "Fauvel" is an acrostic. Each of the letters composing it is the initial of a vice: Flattery, Avarice, Villany, Variety (inconstancy), Envy,

Laches (cowardice). On the *Roman de Fauvel*, a political and social satire composed at the royal chancery between 1310 and 1314, see especially J.-C. Mühlethaler, *Fauvel au pouvoir: Lire la satire médiévale* (Geneva, 1994).

16. This issue of ignominious or distinguishing marks imposed upon certain social classes in the medieval West has yet to be the subject of truly satisfactory comprehensive works. Thus we must still return to the old and cursory study by Ulysse Robert, *Les Signes d'infamie au Moyen Âge* (Paris, 1891). On the other hand, there are many quality works available to us on the marks and insignia imposed upon Jews: G. Kisch, "The Yellow Badge in History," *Historia Judaica* 19 (1957): 89–146; B. Ravid, "From Yellow to Red: On the Distinguishing Head Coverings of the Jews of Venice," *Jewish History*, vol. 6 (1992), fasc. 1–2, 179–210; D. Sansy, "Chapeau juif ou chapeau pointu? Esquisse d'un sign d'infamie," *Symbole des Alltags, Alltag der Symbole: Festschrift für Harry Kühnel* (Graz, 1992), 349–75; D. Sansy, "Marquer la différence: L'imposition de la rouelle aux XIIIᵉ et XIVᵉ siècles," *Médiévales* 41 (2001): 15–36.

17. We must note that neither Jacob nor Rebecca is portrayed negatively in medieval imagery. Their tricks and unjust behavior toward Esau do not seem to have been judged pejoratively by either theologians or artists.

18. On the iconography of Saul, see the *Lexikon der christlichen Ikonographie* (cited in note 11), vol. 4 (Freiburg, 1972), col. 50–54.

19. On the iconography of Caiaphas, who is often depicted with dark skin and with hair that is both red and curly, triple attributes that make him more negative than Pilate or Herod, see ibid., vol. 4, col. 233–34.

20. Unlike the Vulgate, which uses the word *rufus* to describe David, some modern French translations, especially in Protestant bibles, replace "red" with "blond." Must this be seen as a relic of the rejection of red hair, incompatible with the idea of beauty? There are many works on the iconography of David; a summary and a bibliography of them can be found in C. Hourihane, *King David in the Index of Christian Art* (Princeton, 2002).

21. On the relationship between Seth and Typhon, see F. Vian, "Le mythe de Typhée . . ." *Élements orientaux dans la mythologie grecque* (Paris, 1960), 19–37; J. B. Russell, *The Devil* (Ithaca and London, 1977), 78–79 and 253–55.

22. See the catalog by W. D. Hand, *A Dictionary of Words and Idioms Associated with Judas Iscariot* (Berkeley, 1942).

23. Martial, *Epigrams*, ed. and trans. D. R. Shackleton Bailey (Cambridge, MA, and London, 1993), bk. 12, verse 54, p. 135; and bk. 14, verse 176, p. 295.

24. Adage quoted by E. C. Evans, "Physiognomics in the Ancient World," *Transactions of the American Philosophical Society* 59 (1969): 5–101 (here, p. 64).

25. H. Bächtold-Stäubli, ed., *Handwörterbuch des deutschen Aberglaubens*, vol. 3 (Berlin and Leipzig, 1931), col. 1249–54.

26. See the usual collections by: H. Walter, *Proverbia sententiaeque latinitatis Medii ac Recentioris Aevi*, 6 vols. (Göttingen, 1963–69); J. W. Hassell, *Middle French Proverbs, Sentences and Proverbial Phrases* (Toronto, 1982); G. DiStefano, *Dictionnaire des locutions en moyen français* (Montreal, 1991).

27. On the continuation of these beliefs into the modern era, see the little book by X. Fauche, *Roux et rousses: Un éclat très particulier* (Paris, 1997).

28. M. Trotter, "Classifications of Hair Color," *American Journal of Physical Anthropology* 24 (1938): 237–59; to be qualified by J. V. Neel, "Red Hair Colour as a Genetical Character," *Annals of Eugenics* 17 (1952–53): 115–39.

29. Contrary to a widely held but false idea, redheads are not more numerous than blonds in Scandinavia, Ireland, or Scotland. Very much the opposite, they represent a minority there, as in Mediterranean societies, even though quantitatively and proportionally, that minority is larger than elsewhere.

30. In the Middle Ages, to be redheaded was not only to combine in one's person the negative aspects of red and yellow. Being redheaded also meant having skin freckled with reddish spots; it was to be spotted and thus impure, partaking of a certain bestial state. The medieval sensibility had a horror of what was spotted; the beautiful was the pure, and the pure was uniform. Stripes were always demeaning and spots were particularly worrisome, not surprising in a world where skin disease was frequent and formidable, and where the most extreme form of it, leprosy, banished from society those who contracted it.

31. Listed here in order of decreasing preference. See E. Heller, *Psychologie de la couleur: Effets et symboliques* (Paris, 2009), 4 and pl. 1.

32. See "The Wardrobes of Beautiful Florentine Ladies" in the preceding chapter.

33. J. Rossiaud, *L'Amour vénal: La prostitution en Occident (XIIᵉ–XVIᵉ)* (Paris, 2010), 87.

34. U. Robert, *Les Signes d'infamie,* cited in note 16.

35. M. Pastoureau, *Noir: Histoire d'une couleur,* cited in note 5, 124–33.

36. Also see the statement of the sins of Jerusalem, especially the excessive luxury of decor, finery, and colors in Ezek. 8:10–13.

37. On Protestant iconoclasm, many works exist: J. Philips, *The Reformation of Images: Destruction of Art in England (1553–1660)* (Berkeley, 1973); M. Warnke, *Bildersturm: Die Zerstörung des Kunstwerks* (Munich, 1973); M. Stirm, *Die Bilderfrage in der Reformation* (Gütersloh, 1977) (*Forschungen zur Reformationsgeschichte,* 45); C. Christensen, *Art and the Reformation in Germany* (Athens, GA, 1979); S. Deyon and P. Lottin, *Les Casseurs de l'été 1566: L'iconoclasme dan le Nord* (Paris, 1981); G. Scavizzi, *Arte e architettura sacra: Cronache e documenti sulla controversia tra riformati e cattolici (1500–1550)* (Rome, 1981); H. D. Altendorf and P. Jezler, eds., *Bilderstreit: Kulturwandel in Zwinglis Reformation* (Zurich, 1984); D. Freedberg, *Iconoclasts and Their Motives* (Maarsen, Holland, 1985); C. M. Eire, *War against the Idols: The Reformation of Worship from Erasmus to Calvin* (Cambridge, MA, 1986); D. Crouzet, *Les Guerriers de Dieu: La violence au temps des guerres de Religion,* 2 vols. (Paris, 1990); O. Christin, *Une révolution symbolique: L'Iconoclasme huguenot et la reconstruction catholique* (Paris, 1991). To these individual or collective works must be added the scholarly and voluminous catalog of the *Iconoclasme* exhibition (Berne and Strasbourg, 2001).

38. M. Pastoureau, "Naissance d'un monde en noir et blanc: L'Église et la couleur des origines à la Réforme," *Une histoire symbolique du Moyen Âge occidental* (Paris, 2004), 135–71.

39. *Oratio contra affectationem novitatis in vestitu* (1527), a violent sermon in which Melanchthon recommended that all honest Christians wear sober, somber clothing and not *distinctum a variis coloribus velut pavo* (be adorned with varied colors like a peacock). *Corpus reformatorum*, vol. 11, 139–49. See also vol. 2, 331–38. Let us note that the family name of Philipp Melanchthon, both in its German form (Schwarzert) and in the Greek form that he himself adopted, strongly evokes the color black.

40. P. Charpenne, *L'Histoire de la Réforme et des réformateurs de Genève* (Geneva, 1861); R. Guerden, *La Vie quotidienne à Genève au temps de Calvin* (Paris, 1973); W. Monter, "Women in Geneva," in *Enforcing Morality in Early Modern Europe* (London, 1987), 205–32.

41. J. Calvin, *Institution de la vie chrétienne* (1560 text) III, X, 2.

42. Pliny the Elder, *Historia naturalis,* bk. 35, chaps. 12–31.

43. B. Guinneau, *Glossaire des matériaux de la couleur et des termes techniques employés dans les recettes de couleurs anciennes* (Turnhout, 2005), passim.

44. I owe this example to the late-lamented Enrico Castelnuovo, a great medieval art historian, who sadly did not give me the shelf designation of the manuscript where he found this astonishing recipe. It involves transforming fabric permeated with ox blood into red pigment through a process like the one used for a kermes lacquer.

45. While we color historians await more numerous collections, editions, and studies of these recipe books, they all raise the same questions for us: What use could medieval painters have made of these texts that are always more speculative than practical? Were their authors actually practitioners? For whom were these recipes really meant? What was the exact role of the copier in their production? These are difficult questions to answer, given the current extent of our knowledge. On the history of recipe collections and the issues they raise, see relevant remarks in R. Halleux, "Pigments et colorants dans *Mappae Clavicula,*" in *Pigments et colorants de l'Antiquité et du Moyen Âge, Colloque international du CNRS,* ed. B. Guineau (Paris, 1990), 173–80.

46. It was primarily from the fruit of this palm—*Calamus draco*—that sandarac was obtained. Its fronds also provided rattan, gradually imported into Europe.

47. C. Gaignebet, "Le sang-dragon au *Jardin des délices,*" *Enthnologie française* 20, no. 4 (Oct.–Dec. 1990): 378–90.

48. M. Pastoureau, *Bestiaires du Moyen Âge* (Paris, 2011), 205–8.

49. Detailed commentary on this diagram can be found in M. Pastoureau, *Noir: Histoire d'une couleur,* cited in note 5, 140–43.

50. L. Savot, *Nova seu verius nova-antiqua de causis colorum sententia* (Paris, 1609).

51. A. De Boodt, *Gemmarum et lapidum historia* (Hanau, 1609).

52. F. d'Aguilon, *Opticorum libri sex* (Anvers, 1613).

53. An expression like "pure color," for example, is equivocal and can designate a natural pigment or a basic color or even a color to which neither white nor black is added.

54. Pliny, *Historia naturalis*, bk. 33, chap. 56 (sec. 158). Understanding this term, extremely rare in classical Latin, is all the more difficult because Pliny speaks more of pigments and dyestuffs than of coloration. See J. Gage, *Couleur et culture* (Paris, 2010), 35.

55. On this invention, see the scholarly catalog from the exhibition, *Anatomie de la couleur* (Paris, Bibliothèque Nationale de France, 1995) ed. F. Rodari and M. Préaud. See also the treatise by J. C. Le Blon, *Coloritto, or the Harmony of Colouring in Painting Reduced to Mechanical Practice* (London, 1725), which acknowledges its debt to Newton and affirms the primacy of three basic colors: red, blue and yellow. On the history of color engraving, considered from a long-term perspective, see the study by J. M. Friedman, *Color Printing in England, 1486–1870* (New Haven, CT, 1978).

56. R. Boyle, *Experiments and Considerations Touching Colours* (London, 1664), 219–20.

57. On Newton's discoveries and the importance of the spectrum, see M. Blay, *La Conception newtonienne des phénomènes de la couleur* (Paris, 1983).

58. I. Newton, *Opticks: or, A Treatise of the Reflexions, Refractions, Inflexions and Colours of Light . . .* (London, 1704); *Optice sive de relectionibus, refractionibus et inflectionibus et coloribus lucis . . .*, Latin trans. S. Clarke (London, 1707, reprinted Geneva, 1740).

58. N. J. Thiéry de Ménouville, *Traité de la culture du nopal et de l'éducation de la cochenille dans les colonies françaises de l'Amerique*, 2 vols. (Cap-Français, 1787).

60. On this commercial war and the history of Mexican cochineal, see A. B. Greenfield, *A Perfect Red: Empire, Espionage, and the Quest for the Color of Desire* (New York, 2005). French translation: *L'Extraordinaire Saga du rouge: Le pigment le plus convoité* (Paris, 2009).

61. M. Proust, *Le Côté de Guermantes*, vol. 1 (Paris, 1920), 14–15. English translation: *The Guermantes Way*, trans. C.K.S. Moncrieff and T. Kilmartin (New York, 1981), 9.

62. The French shoe designer Christian Louboutin, perhaps inspired by pop art, recently based the uniqueness of his brand on a red leather sole aimed at becoming a kind of signature or logo. Considering the sale price of such shoes, it is tempting to make the comparison with the earlier *talons rouges* of the aristocracy.

63. O. de Serres, *Theatre d'agriculture et mesnage des champs* (Paris, 1600), 562.

64. P. Eisenberg, *Grundiss der deutschen Grammatik*, 2nd ed. (Stuttgard, 1989), 219–22. W. Jervis Jones, *German Colour Terms: A Study in Their Historical Evolution from Earliest Times to the Present* (Amsterdam, 2013), 419–20 and 474–76.

65. Egbert de Liège, *Fecunda ratis*, ed. E. Voigt (Halle, 1889), 232–33 (the poem's title is *De puella a lupellis servata*, The little girl saved from wolf cubs). On this very old version see: G. Lontzen, "Das Gedicht *De puella a lupellis servata* von Egbert von Lüttich," in *Merveilles et contes*, vol. 6 (1992), 20–44; C. Brémont, C. Velay-Valentin, and J. Berlioz, *Formes médiévales du conte merveilleux* (Paris, 1989), 63–74.

66. Because I have written extensively on red in "Little Red Riding Hood," I am summarizing here the many studies and articles I have published in various places since 1990.

67. V. Hugo, "The Ballad of the Nun," in *The Works of Victor Hugo: Poems* (Boston, 1909), 88.

68. See the study by G. Lontzen cited in note 65.

69. E. Heller, *Psychologie de la couleur*, cited in note 31, here 47–48.

70. R. Schneider, *Die Tarnkappe* (Wiesbaden, 1951).

71. B. Bettelheim, *The Uses of Enchantment* (New York, 1976), 47–86.

72. M. Pastoureau, *Vert: Histoire d'une couleur* (Paris, 2013), 71–78. English edition: *Green: History of a Color*, trans. J. Gladding (Princeton, 2014), 71–78.

73. Thanks to François Poplin for drawing my attention to the distributional role of these three colors in tales and fables.

A DANGEROUS COLOR?

1. See the figures resulting from recent surveys conducted in this area in E. Heller, *Psychologie de la couleur: Effets et symboliques* (Paris, 2009), 4–9 and pl. 1 and 2.

2. J. Gage, *Colour and Culture* (London, 1993), 153–76 and 227–36.

3. J. André, *Étude sur les termes de couleur dans la langue latine* (Paris, 1949).

4. Ibid., 111–12 and 116–17.

5. "When the child of morning, rosy-fingered Dawn, appeared." In many books of the *Odyssey*, Homer uses this line as an expression to begin the storytelling again or to introduce new developments.

6. C. Joret, *La Rose dans l'Antiquité et au Moyen Âge: Histoires, légendes et symbolisme* (Paris, 1892).

7. Other adjectives could also work to name pink: *pallescens, rubellus, subrubeus*. J. André, *Étude sur les termes de couleur* (cited in note 3), 139–47 and passim.

8. A. Ott, *Étude sur les couleurs en vieux français* (Paris, 1899); B. Schäfer, *Die Semantik der Farbedjektive im Altfranzösischen* (Tübingen, 1987).

9. To transform dyestuff into pigment, a certain quantity of the dyestuff, still very concentrated, had to be collected on fabric and then chemically precipitated onto a metallic salt (for example, aluminum salts). A lacquer was thus obtained.

10. A. M. Kristol, *Color: Les langues romanes devant le phénomène de la couleur* (Berne, 1978).

11. Jean Robertet, *Oeuvres*, ed. M. Zsuppàn (Geneva, 1970), epistle 16, 139.

12. That is why in sixteenth- and seventeenth-century French, the word *jaune* itself can sometimes be translated into modern French as *rose* and not as *jaune* (yellow).

13. P. Ball, *Histoire vivante des couleurs: 5,000 ans de peinture racontée par les pigments* (Paris, 2010), 207–8.

14. Let us cite: George Romney, Franz Xaver Winterhalter, James Tissot, Mary Cassatt, Henry Caro-Delvaille.

15. M. Pastoureau, "Rose Barbie," in A. Monier, ed., *Barbie*, exhibition (Musée des Arts Décoratifs, Paris, 2016), 92–98.

16. Until the first half of the nineteenth century, throughout Europe, individuals belonging to the aristocracy or the upper middle classes had to have the lightest possible skin to distinguish themselves from the peasants. But those values changed in the second half of the century, when "good society" began to frequent seashores and later mountains. It then became more fashionable to flaunt a tan or skin darkened by the sun, because now it was no longer a matter of distinguishing oneself from peasants but from workers, who were increasing in number. They lived in cities, worked indoors, and thus had white skin, pallid coloring, and pale or grayish faces. It was especially important not to resemble a worker, a creature much worse off than a simple peasant. These new values and the quest for sun that accompanied them would become more pronounced over the decades. They seemed to reach their height in the 1930s–60s: suntans were then all the rage; one had to be tanned. That would not last, however. Beginning in the mid-1960s, when seaside vacations and outdoor winter sports expanded to the middle and even to the lower classes, "good society" gradually rejected tanning, because it had come within everyone's or almost everyone's reach. Those on "paid vacations" especially tried to get tans: how disagreeable, if not grotesque! Henceforth, the great fashion was to be not tan, especially if one was returning from the ocean or the mountains. Subsequently that attitude, which began as disdainful snobbery, gradually gained ground. But this time it was for health reasons. The marked increase in skin cancers and diseases from prolonged exposure to the sun led to the decline of tanning, especially among the middle classes. Being tan was no longer prestigious, very much to the contrary. As is often the case in the history of value systems, the pendulum had swung in the other direction. But for how long?

17. Quoted in the scholarly study by C. Lanoë, *La Poudre et le Fard: Une histoire des cosmétiques de la Renaissance aux Lumières* (Seyssel, 2008), 142.

18. In August 1914, French soldiers left for combat wearing pants of a particularly loud madder red. It is likely that this excessively vivid color cost many tens of thousands of men their lives. By December, the decision was made to replace this red with blue, a dull, grayish, subdued blue. But finding the quantities of synthetic indigo necessary to dye fabric for pants for all the soldiers was a long and complex operation. It was not until spring 1915 that all French troups were finally dressed in this new blue, called "horizon blue," in reference to "the indefinable color of the line at the horizon that seems to separate sky from earth." M. Pastoureau, *Bleu: Histoire d'une couleur* (Paris, 2000), 187–88, 202. English edition: *Blue: History of a Color*, trans. M. Cruse (Princeton, 2001), 162–63.

19. M. Proust, *La Prisonnière*, vol. 1 (Paris, 1919), 47. English translation: *The Captive*, trans. C.K.S. Moncrieff, T. Kilmartin, and A. Mayor (New York, 1981), 30.

20. Let us add that some redheaded women, even today, avoid wearing red, a color that is supposed to clash with their hair. But others, to express their freedom or contrariness, make a point of wearing it.

21. On the stormy history of the red flag, the best study remains the one by M. Dommanget, *Histoire du drapeau rouge: Des origines à la guerre de 1939* (Paris, 1967). On the history of *bonnet rouge*, see: M. Agulhon, *Marianne au combat: L'imagerie et la symbolique républicaines de 1789 à 1880* (Paris, 1979), 21–53; E. Liris, "Autour des vignettes révolutionnaires: La symbolique du bonnet phrygien," in M. Vovelle, ed. *Les Images de la Révolution française* (Paris, 1988), 312–23; J.-C. Benzaken, "L'allégorie de la Liberté et son bonnet dans l'iconologie des monnaies et médailles de la Révolution française (1789–1799)," in *La Gazette des Archives* 146–47 (1989): 338–77; M. Pastoureau, *Les Emblèmes de la France* (Paris, 1997), 43–49.

22. Let us note that the adjective *martial* refers to Mars, the Roman god of war, whose emblematic color was red.

23. Cited by M. Dommanget, *Histoire du drapeau rouge* (see note 21), 26.

24. M. Agulhon, *Marianne au combat* (cited note 21), 16.

25. C. Ripa, *Iconologia*, new edition in collaboration with L. Faci (Rome, 1603).

26. See the fine book by Jean Starobinski, *L'Invention de la liberté (1700–1789)* (Geneva, 1964).

27. V. Hugo, *Les Misérables*, trans. Julie Rose (New York, 2008), pt. 4, bk. 14, chap. 1 and 2, 929–30.

28. A. de Lamartine, *Histoire de la révolution de 1848*, vol. 1 (Paris, 1849), 393–406.

29. After the events of February 25, 1848, the insurgents demanded that the provisional government include the red cap in the white part of the tricolor flag. But that did not last long. This same cap disappeared from the seal of the Second Republic and never reappeared. On the other hand, under the Third Republic, it returned to the foreground adorning the busts and statues of "Marianne," the allegorized feminine image of Liberty, and then of the Republic.

30. Sometimes a five-pointed star symbolizing the unity of the workers across five continents appears above the hammer and sickle.

31. On the history of the flags of China and the USSR, see W. Smith and O. Neubecker, *Die Zeichen der Menschen und Völker* (Lucerne, 1975), 108–13 and 114–78.

32. In 1971, the French Socialist Party, reshaped by F. Mitterrand, adopted a new symbol: a fist holding a rose, an alliance of force and gentleness. That rose evoked the color pink that sometimes symbolized socialist parties in countries where a communist party existed. That was the case sporadically in France beginning in 1920. See M. Agulhon, "Les couleurs dans la politique française," in *Ethnologie française* 20 (1990): fasc. 4, 391–98.

33. This meaning was already attested during the French Revolution in 1789–99. See A. Geffroy, "Étude en rouge, 1789–1798," in *Cahiers de lexicologie* 51 (1988): 119–48.

34. M. Agulhon, "Les couleurs dans la politique française" (cited in note 32).

35. M. Pastoureau, *Vert: Histoire d'une couleur* (Paris, 2013), 217–22.

36. The German language possesses two words to distinguish the flag as physical object from the emblematic image appearing on any medium: *Flagge* and *Fahne*. Almost all other Western languages have only one. See the relevant distinctions proposed by O. Neubecker, *Fahnen und Flaggen* (Leipzig, 1939), passim.

37. Allow me to cite my programmatic article here, "Du vague des drapeaux," which appeared in *Le Genre humain* 20 (1989): 119–34.

38. As a general rule, the colors of flags are abstract colors, their shades do not matter. For most countries, no part of the constitution specifies that the red, green, or blue of the flag must be a particular shade, defined in relationship to a reference shade. But there are exceptions, especially in the case of young countries, when the flag is less than half a century old. In older countries, the exceptions most often involve blue, sometimes specified as "light" and not left indefinite (Argentina, Uruguay, more recently Israel).

39. To do this—necessarily brief—breakdown, I consulted two recent indexes. I did not include small insignia, badges, or even coats of arms that sometimes appear on certain flags and whose use seems optional (sometimes present, sometimes absent). The flags are not all bi- or tri-chromatic, but among the tricolors, the blue-white-red triad dominates.

40. Let us note nevertheless that in the countries of the former Eastern Europe, many flags borrowed their colors not from communist ideology but from earlier royal or princely coats of arms (Poland, Czechoslovakia, Romania).

41. On the history of the Japanese flag, there are many studies published in Japanese. A few that have appeared in European languages can be found in W. Smith and O. Neubecker, *Die Zeichen der Menschen und Volker* (note 31), 164–73.

42. Heraldry uses only six colors, which it divides into two groups. In the first group are white and yellow (I am using the terms of ordinary language here); in the second are red, blue, green, and black. Very strict rules of use for these colors forbid juxtaposing or superimposing two colors that belong to the same group. This rule was in existence by the twelfth century, when coats of arms first appeared, and until the eighteenth century infractions represented less than 1 percent of cases. Vexillology adopted this rule for its own, but sees a higher percentage of infractions (10 or 12 percent). Today, among the twenty-eight countries of the European Union, only Portugal (green and red touch) and Germany (black and red touch) display flags that break the rule. See M. Pastoureau, *Figures de l'héraldique* (Paris, 1996), 44–49.

43. Maritime and railway signs have prompted very little research. A brief survey on the emergence of an international code of maritime signs can be found in US Navy, *The International Code of Signals: For the Use of All Nations* (New York, 1890); and a bit more information for sea, rail, and road in M. Vanns, *An Illustrated History of Signalling* (Shepperton, UK, 1997). For the French railway, there is the excellent summary by A. Gernigon, *Histoire de la signalisation ferroviaire française* (Paris, 1998).

44. On the history of road signs in France: M. Duhamel, *Un demi-siècle de signalisation routière en France 1894–1946* (Paris, 1994); M. Duhamel-Herz and J. Nouvier, *La Signalisation routière en France, de 1946 à nos jours* (Paris, 1998).

45. I know of no serious study on the history of traffic lights; it has yet to be written.

46. Consider the crossing of the Red Sea, ordinarily an impassible barrier, which opened at a sign from heaven and let the Hebrews flee Egypt (Ex. 14:15–31).

47. M. Pastoureau, *Vert: Histoire d'une couleur* (Paris, 2013). English edition: *Green: History of a Color* (Princeton, 2014).

48. Today in some countries, it is not green but rather blue that authorizes passage. In others, Japan for example, the traffic light's "go" signal is called blue but is actually green.

49. Since 2005, the red crystal, a humanitarian emblem chosen by countries that consider the red cross too Christian and the red crescent too Muslim, is equally protected by the International Geneva Convention.

50. On these expressions and idioms in French, see A. Mollard-Desfour, *Le Rouge: Dictionnaire des mots et expressions de couleur*, 2nd ed. (Paris, 2009).

51. E. Heller, *Psychologie de la couleur: Effets et symboliques* (cited in note 1), 4–9 and pl. 1 and 2.

52. In contrast to white, a virtuous and hygienic color, black was long considered indecent, immoral, and reserved for professions that involved debauchery. Today that is no longer the case. If it remains off-limits to young girls, black no longer connotes prostitution as it formerly did, or even provocation. Some women prefer wearing black underwear rather than white when they have on a black skirt or blouse. Others think that black best suits the color of their complexion. Many note as well that with today's synthetic fabrics, black holds up longest to frequent washing. Thus it may be that in our time, red rather than black is considered the most seductive color, at least if we are to believe women's magazines and opinion polls.

53. On the history of Father Christmas, see V. Timtcheva, *Le Mythe du Père Noël: Origines et évolution* (Paris, 2006); N. Cretin, *Histoire du Père Noël* (Toulouse, 2010).

54. On the battle of *Hernani*: A. Dumas, *Mes Mémoires*, vol. 5 (Paris, 1852); T. Gautier, *Histoire du romantisme* (Paris, 1877); E. Blewer, *La Campagne d'*Hernani (Paris, 2002).

Bibliography

— 1 —
GENERAL WORKS

Berlin, Brent, and Paul Kay. *Basic Color Terms: Their Universality and Evolution.* Berkeley, CA, 1969.

Birren, Faber. *Color: A Survey in Words and Pictures.* New York, 1961.

Brusatin, Manlio. *Storia dei colori.* 2nd ed. Turin, 1983. Translated as *Histoire des couleurs,* Paris, 1986.

Conklin, Harold C. "Color Categorization." *American Anthropologist* 75, no. 4 (1973): 931–42.

Eco, Renate, ed. "Colore: Divietti, decreti, discute." Special number of *Rassegna* (Milan) 23 (September 1985).

Gage, John. *Colour and Culture: Practice and Meaning from Antiquity to Abstraction.* London, 1993.

Heller, Eva. *Wie Farben wirken: Farbpsychologie, Farbsymbolik, Kreative Farbgestaltung.* 2nd ed. Hamburg, 2004.

Indergand, Michel and Philippe Fagot. *Bibliographie de la couleur.* 2 vols. Paris, 1984–88.

Meyerson, Ignace, ed. *Problèmes de la couleur.* Paris, 1957.

Pastoureau, Michel. *Bleu: Histoire d'une couleur.* Paris, 2000.

———. *Dictionnaire des couleurs de notre temps: Symbolique et société.* 4th ed. Paris, 2007.

———. *Noir: Histoire d'une couleur.* Paris, 2007.

———. *Vert: Histoire d'une couleur.* Paris, 2013.

Portmann, Adolf, and Rudolf Ritsema, eds. *The Realms of Colour. Die Welt der Farben.* Leiden, 1974. (*Eranos Yearbook,* 1972).

Pouchelle, Marie-Christine, ed. "Paradoxes de la couleur." Special number of *Ethnologie française* (Paris) 20, no. 4 (October–December, 1990).

Rzepinska, Maria. *Historia coloru u dziejach malatstwa europejskiego,* 3rd ed. Warsaw, 1989.

Tornay, Serge, ed. *Voir et nommer les couleurs.* Nanterre, 1978.

Valeur, Bernard. *La Couleur dans tous ses états.* Paris, 2011.

Vogt, Hans Heinrich. *Farben und ihre Geschichte.* Stuttgart, 1973.

Zahan, Dominique. "L'homme et la couleur." In *Histoire des mœurs,* ed. Jean Poirier, vol. 1, *Les Coordonnées de l'homme et la culture matérielle,* 115–80. Paris, 1990.

Zuppiroli, Libero, ed. *Traité des couleurs.* Lausanne, 2001.

— 2 —
ANTIQUITY AND THE MIDDLE AGES

Beta, Simone, and Maria Michela Sassi, eds. *I colori nel mondo antiquo: Esperienze linguistiche e quadri simbolici.* Siena, 2003.

Bradley, Mark. *Colour and Meaning in Ancient Rome.* Cambridge, 2009.

Brinkmann, Vinzenz, and Raimund Wünsche, eds. *Bunte Götter: Die Farbigkeit antiker Skulptur.* Munich, 2003.

Brüggen, Elke. *Kleidung und Mode in der höfischen Epik.* Heidelberg, 1989.

Carastro, Marcello, ed. *L'Antiquité en couleurs: Catégories, pratiques, représentations,* 187–205. Grenoble, 2008.

Cechetti, Bartolomeo. *La vita dei Veneziani nel 1300: Le veste.* Venice, 1886.

Centre Universitaire d'Études et de Recherches Médiévales d'Aix-en-Provence. *Les Couleurs au Moyen Âge. Senefiance,* vol. 24. Aix-en-Provence, France, 1988.

Ceppari Ridolfi, Maria A., and Patrizia Turrini. *Il mulino delle vanità: Lusso e cerimonie nella Siena medievale.* Siena, 1996.

Descamps-Lequime, Sophie, ed. *Couleur et peinture dans le monde grec antique.* Paris, 2004.

Dumézil, Georges. "*Albati, russati, virides.*" In *Rituels indoeuropéens à Rome,* 45–61. Paris, 1954.

Frodl-Kraft, Eva. "Die Farbsprache der gotischen Malerei: Ein Entwurf." *Wiener Jahrbuch für Kunstgeschichte* 30–31 (1977–78): 89–178.

Grand-Clément, Adeline. *La Fabrique des couleurs: Histoire du paysage sensible des Grecs anciens.* Paris, 2011.

Haupt, Gottfried. *Die Farbensymbolik in der sakralen Kunst des abendländischen Mittelalters.* Leipzig, 1941.

Istituto Storico Lucchese. *Il colore nel Medioevo: Arte, simbolo, tecnica: Atti delle Giornate di studi.* 2 vols. Lucca, 1996–98.

Luzzatto, Lia, and Renata Pompas. *Il significato dei colori nelle civiltà antiche.* Milan, 1988.

Pastoureau, Michel. *Figures et couleurs: Études sur la symbolique et la sensibilité médiévales*. Paris, 1986.

———. "L'Église et la couleur des origines à la Réforme." *Bibliothèque de l'École des chartes* 147 (1989): 203-30.

———. "Voir les couleurs au XIIIᵉ siècle." In *View and Vision in the Middle Ages*, 2: 147-65. *Micrologus: Nature, Science and Medieval Societies*, vol. 6. Florence, 1998.

Rouveret, Agnès. *Histoire et imaginaire de la peinture ancienne*. Paris, 1989.

Rouveret, Agnès, Sandrine Dubel, and Valérie Naas, eds. *Couleurs et matières dans l'Antiquité: Textes, techniques et pratiques*. Paris, 2006.

Sicile, héraut d'armes du XVᵉ siècle. *Le Blason des couleurs en armes, livrées et devises*. Ed. H. Cocheris. Paris, 1857.

Tiverios, Michales A., and Despoina Tsiafakis, eds. *The Role of Color in Ancient Greek Art and Architecture (700-31 B.C.)*. Thessaloniki, 2002.

Villard, Laurence, ed. *Couleur et vision dans l'Antiquité classique*. Rouen, 2002.

— 3 —

MODERN AND CONTEMPORARY TIMES

Batchelor, David. *La Peur de la couleur*. Paris, 2001.

Birren, Faber. *Selling Color to People*. New York, 1956.

Brino, Giovanni, and Franco Rosso. *Colore e città: Il piano del colore di Torino, 1800-1850*. Milan, 1980.

Laufer, Otto. *Farbensymbolik im deutschen Volsbrauch*. Hamburg, 1948.

Lenclos, Jean-Philippe, and Dominique Lenclos. *Les Couleurs de la France: Maisons et paysage*. Paris, 1982.

———. *Les Couleurs de l'Europe: Géographie de la couleur*. Paris, 1995.

Noël, Benoît. *L'Histoire du cinéma couleur*. Croissy-sur-Seine, 1995.

Pastoureau, Michel. "La Réforme et la couleur." *Bulletin de la Société d'histoire du Protestantisme français* 138 (July-September 1992): 323-42.

———. "La couleur en noir et blanc (XVᵉ-XVIIIᵉ siècle)." In *Le Livre et l'Historien: Études offertes en l'honneur du Professeur Henri-Jean Martin*, 197-213. Geneva, 1997.

———. *Les Couleurs de nos souvenirs*. Paris, 2010.

— 4 —

PROBLEMS OF PHILOLOGY AND TERMINOLOGY

André, Jacques. *Étude sur les termes de couleur dans la langue latine*. Paris, 1949.

Brault, Gerard J. *Early Blazon. Heraldic Terminology in the XIIth and XIIIth Centuries, with Special Reference to Arthurian Literature*. Oxford, 1972.

Crosland, Maurice P. *Historical Studies in the Language of Chemistry*. London, 1962.

Giacolone Ramat, Anna. "Colori germanici nel mondo romanzo." *Atti e memorie dell'Academia toscana di scienze e lettere La Colombaria* (Florence) 32 (1967): 105-211.

Gloth, Walther. *Das Spiel von den sieben Farben*. Königsberg, 1902.

Grossmann, Maria. *Colori e lessico: Studi sulla struttura semantica degli aggetivi di colore in catalano, castigliano, italiano, romano, latino ed ungherese*. Tübingen, 1988.

Irwin, Eleanor. *Colour Terms in Greek Poetry*. Toronto, 1974.

Jacobson-Widding, Anita. *Red-White-Black, as a Mode of Thought*. Stockholm, 1979.

Kristol, Andres M. *Color: Les Langues romanes devant le phénomène de la couleur*. Berne, 1978.

Maxwell-Stuart, P. G. *Studies in Greek Colour Terminology*, vol. 2: XΛΩΡΟΣ. Leiden, 1998.

Meunier, Annie. "Quelques remarques sur les adjectifs de couleur." *Annales de l'Université de Toulouse* 11, no. 5 (1975): 37-62.

Mollard-Desfour, Annie. *Le Dictionnaire des mots et expressions de couleur*. 7 vols. Paris, 2000-2016.

Ott, André. *Études sur les couleurs en vieux français*. Paris, 1899.

Schäfer, Barbara. *Die Semantik der Farbadjektive im Altfranzösischen*. Tübingen, 1987.

Sève, Robert, Michel Indergand, and Philippe Lanthony. *Dictionnaire des termes de la couleur*. Paris, 2007.

Wackernagel, Wilhelm. "Die Farben- und Blumensprache des Mittelalter." In *Abhandlungen zur deutschen Altertumskunde und Kunstgeschichte*, 143-240. Leipzig, 1872.

Wierzbicka, Anna. "The Meaning of Color Terms: Cromatology and Culture." *Cognitive Linguistics* 1, no. 1 (1990): 99-150.

— 5 —

THE HISTORY OF DYES AND DYERS

Brunello, Franco. *L'arte della tintura nella storia dell'umanita*. Vicenza, 1968.

———. *Arti e mestieri a Venezia nel medioevo e nel Rinascimento*. Vicenza, 1980.

Cardon, Dominique, and Gaëtan Du Châtenet. *Guide des teintures naturelles.* Paris, 1990.

Chevreul, Michel Eugène. *Leçons de chimie appliquées à la teinture.* Paris, 1829.

Edelstein, Sidney M., and Hector C. Borghetty. *The "Plictho" of Giovan Ventura Rosetti.* London and Cambridge, MA, 1969.

Gerschel, Lucien. "Couleurs et teintures chez divers peuples indo-européens." *Annales ESC* 21 (1966): 608-63.

Hellot, Jean. *L'Art de la teinture des laines et des étoffes de laine en grand et petit teint.* Paris, 1750.

Jaoul, Martine, ed. *Des teintes et des couleurs.* Exhibition catalog. Paris, 1988.

Lauterbach, Fritz. *Geschichte der in Deutschland bei der Färberei angewandten Farbstoffe, mit besonderer Berücksichtigung des mittelalterlichen Waidblaues.* Leipzig, 1905.

Legget, William F. *Ancient and Medieval Dyes.* New York, 1944.

Lespinasse, René de. *Histoire générale de Paris: Les métiers et corporations de la ville de Paris.* Vol. 3, *Tissus, étoffes. . . .* Paris, 1897.

Pastoureau, Michel. *Jésus chez le teinturier: Couleurs et teintures dans l'Occident médiéval.* Paris, 1998.

Ploss, Emil Ernst. *Ein Buch von alten Farben: Technologie der Textilfarben im Mittelalter.* 6th ed. Munich, 1989.

Rebora, Giovanni. *Un manuale di tintoria del Quattrocento.* Milan, 1970.

Varichon, Anne. *Couleurs: Pigments et teintures dans les mains des peuples.* 2nd ed. Paris, 2005.

— 6 —
THE HISTORY OF PIGMENTS

Ball, Philip. *Histoire vivante des couleurs: 5000 ans de peinture racontée par les pigments.* Paris, 2005.

Bomford, David, et al. *Art in the Making: Italian Painting before 1400.* London, 1989.

———. *Art in the Making: Impressionism.* London, 1990.

Brunello, Franco. *"De arte illuminandi" e altri trattati sulla tecnica della miniatura medievale.* 2nd ed. Vicenza, 1992.

Feller, Robert L., and Ashok Roy. *Artists' Pigments: A Handbook of Their History and Characteristics.* 2 vols. Washington, D.C., 1985-86.

Guineau, Bernard, ed. *Pigments et colorants de l'Antiquité et du Moyen Âge.* Paris, 1990.

Harley, Rosamond D. *Artists' Pigments (c. 1600-1835).* 2nd ed. London, 1982.

Hills, Paul. *The Venetian Colour.* New Haven, 1999.

Kittel, Hans, ed. *Pigmente.* Stuttgart, 1960.

Laurie, Arthur P. *The Pigments and Mediums of Old Masters.* London, 1914.

Loumyer, Georges. *Les Traditions techniques de la peinture médiévale.* Brussels, 1920.

Merrifield, Mary P. *Original Treatises Dating from the XIIth to the XVIIIth Centuries on the Art of Painting.* 2 vols. London, 1849.

Montagna, Giovanni. *I pigmenti: Prontuario per l'arte e il restauro.* Florence, 1993.

Reclams Handbuch der künstlerischen Techniken. Vol. I, *Farbmittel, Buchmalerei, Tafel- und Leinwandmalerei.* Stuttgart, 1988.

Roosen-Runge, Heinz. *Farbgebung und Technik frühmittelalterlicher Buchmalerei.* 2 vols. Munich, 1967.

Smith, Cyril S., and John G. Hawthorne. *Mappae clavicula: A Little Key to the World of Medieval Techniques.* Philadelphia, 1974. (*Transactions of the American Philosophical Society* 64/4).

Technè: La science au service de l'art et des civilisations. Vol. 4, *La couleur et ses pigments.* 1996.

Thompson, Daniel V. *The Material of Medieval Painting.* London, 1936.

— 7 —
THE HISTORY OF CLOTHING

Baldwin, Frances E. *Sumptuary Legislation and Personal Relation in England.* Baltimore, 1926.

Baur, Veronika. *Kleiderordnungen in Bayern von 14. bis 19. Jahrhundert.* Munich, 1975.

Boehn, Max von. *Die Mode: Menschen und Moden vom Untergang der alten Welt bis zum Beginn des zwanzigsten Jahrhunderts.* 8 vols. Munich, 1907-25.

Boucher, François. *Histoire du costume en Occident de l'Antiquité à nos jours.* Paris, 1965.

Bridbury, Anthony R. *Medieval English Clothmaking: An Economic Survey.* London, 1982.

Eisenbart, Liselotte C. *Kleiderordnungen der deutschen Städte zwischen 1350-1700.* Göttingen, 1962.

Harte, N. B., and Kenneth G. Ponting, eds. *Cloth and Clothing in Medieval Europe: Essays in Memory of E. M. Carus-Wilson.* London, 1982.

Harvey, John. *Men in Black.* London, 1995. Translated as *Des hommes en noir.*

Du costume masculin à travers les âges. Abbeville, 1998.

Hunt, Alan. *Governance of the Consuming Passions: A History of Sumptuary Laws.* London and New York, 1996.

Lurie, Alison. *The Language of Clothes.* London, 1982.

Madou, Mireille. *Le Costume civil: Typologie des sources du Moyen Âge occidental,* vol. 47. Turnhout, 1986.

Mayo, Janet. *A History of Ecclesiastical Dress.* London, 1984.

Nixdorff, Heide, and Heidi Müller, eds. *Weisse Vesten, roten Roben: Von den Farbordnungen des Mittelalters zum individuellen Farbgeschmak.* Exhibition catalog. Berlin, 1983.

Page, Agnès. *Vêtir le prince: Tissus et couleurs à la cour de Savoie (1427–1447).* Lausanne, 1993.

Pellegrin, Nicole. *Les Vêtements de la liberté: Abécédaires des pratiques vestimentaires françaises de 1780 à 1800.* Paris, 1989.

Piponnier, Françoise. *Costume et vie sociale: La cour d'Anjou, XIVᵉ–XVᵉ siècles.* Paris, 1970.

Piponnier, Françoise, and Perrine Mane. *Se vêtir au Moyen Âge.* Paris, 1995.

Quicherat, Jules. *Histoire du costume en France depuis les temps les plus reculés jusqu'à la fin du XVIIIᵉ siècle.* Paris, 1875.

Roche, Daniel. *La Culture des apparences: Une histoire du vêtement (XVIIᵉ–XVIIIᵉ siècles).* Paris, 1989.

Roche-Bernard, Geneviève, and Alain Ferdière. *Costumes et textiles en Gaule romaine.* Paris, 1993.

Vincent, John M. *Costume and Conduct in the Laws of Basel, Bern, and Zurich.* Baltimore, 1935.

— 8 —

THE PHILOSOPHY AND HISTORY OF SCIENCE

Albert, Jean-Pierre, et al., eds. *Coloris Corpus.* Paris, 2008.

Blay, Michel. *La Conceptualisation newtonienne des phénomènes de la couleur.* Paris, 1983.

———. *Les Figures de l'arc-en-ciel.* Paris, 1995.

Boyer, Carl B. *The Rainbow from Myth to Mathematics.* New York, 1959.

Goethe, Johann Wolfgang von. *Zur Farbenlehre.* 2 vols. Tübingen, 1810.

———. *Materialen zur Geschichte der Farbenlehre.* 2 vols. Munich, 1971.

Halbertsma, Klaas Tjalling Agnus. *A History of the Theory of Colour.* Amsterdam, 1949.

Hardin, Clyde L. *Color for Philosophers: Unweaving the Rainbow.* Cambridge, MA, 1988.

Lindberg, David C. *Theories of Vision from Al-Kindi to Kepler.* Chicago, 1976.

Magnus, Hugo. *Histoire de l'évolution du sens des couleurs.* Paris, 1878.

Newton, Isaac. *Opticks or a Treatise of the Reflexions, Refractions, Inflexions and Colours of Light.* London, 1704.

Pastore, Nicholas. *Selective History of Theories of Visual Perception, 1650–1950.* Oxford, 1971.

Sepper, Dennis L. *Goethe contra Newton: Polemics and the Project of a New Science of Color.* Cambridge, 1988.

Sherman, Paul D. *Colour Vision in the Nineteenth Century: The Young-Helmholtz-Maxwell Theory.* Cambridge, 1981.

Westphal, John. *Colour: A Philosophical Introduction.* 2nd ed. London, 1991.

Wittgenstein, Ludwig. *Bemerkungen über die Farben.* Frankfurt am Main, 1979.

— 9 —

THE HISTORY AND THEORIES OF ART

Aumont, Jacques. *Introduction à la couleur: Des discours aux images.* Paris, 1994.

Ballas, Guila. *La Couleur dans la peinture moderne: Théorie et pratique.* Paris, 1997.

Barasch, Moshe. *Light and Color in the Italian Renaissance Theory of Art.* New York, 1978.

Dittmann, Lorenz. *Farbgestaltung und Fartheorie in der abendländischen Malerei.* Stuttgart, 1987.

Gavel, Jonas. *Colour: A Study of Its Position in the Art Theory of the Quattro- and Cinquecento.* Stockholm, 1979.

Hall, Marcia B. *Color and Meaning: Practice and Theory in Renaissance Painting.* Cambridge, MA, 1992.

Imdahl, Max. *Farbe: Kunsttheoretische Reflexionen in Frankreich.* Munich, 1987.

Kandinsky, Vassily. *Über das Geistige in der Kunst.* Munich, 1912.

Le Rider, Jacques. *Les Couleurs et les mots.* Paris, 1997.

Lichtenstein, Jacqueline. *La Couleur éloquent: Rhétorique et peinture à l'âge classique.* Paris, 1989.

Roque, Georges. *Art et science de la couleur: Chevreul et les peintres de Delacroix à l'abstraction.* Nîmes, 1997.

Shapiro, Alan E. "Artists' Colors and Newton's Colors." *Isis* 85 (1994): 600–630.

Teyssèdre, Bernard. *Roger de Piles et les débats sur le coloris au siècle de Louis XIV.* Paris, 1957.

— 10 —
THE HISTORY OF THE COLOR RED

Antiquity

Besnier, Maurice. "Purpura." In *Dictionnaire des antiquités grecques et romaines*, vol. 4/1, ed. C. Daremberg and E. Saglio, 769–78. Paris, 1905.

Dedekind, Alexander. *Ein Beitrag zur Purpurkunde*. Berlin, 1898.

Doumet, Joseph. *Étude sur la couleur de la pourpre ancienne*. Beirut, 1980.

Reinhold, Meyer. *History of Purple as a Status Symbol in Antiquity*. Brussels, 1970. (*Latomus*, vol. 116).

Schneider, Kurt. "Purpura." In *Realencyclopädie der klassischen Altertumwissenschaft (Pauly-Wissowa)*, vol. 33/2, col. 2000–2020. Stuttgart, 1959.

Stulz, Heinke. *Die Farbe Purpur im frühen Griechentum*. Stuttgart, 1990.

Trinquier, Jean. "*Cinaberis* et sang-dragon: Le cinabre des Anciens, entre minéral, végétal et animal." In *Revue archéologique* 56, fasc. 2 (2013): 305–46.

Wunderlich, Eva. *Die Bedeutung der roten Farbe im Kultus der Griechen und Römer*. Giessen, 1925.

The Middle Ages

Contamine, Philippe. *L'Oriflamme de Saint-Denis aux XIVᵉ et XVᵉ siècles: Étude de symbolique religieuse et royale*. Nancy, 1975.

Gaignebet, Claude. "Le sang-dragon au *Jardin des délices*." In *Ethnologie française* 20, no. 4 (October–December 1990): 378–90.

Lontzen, Günter. "Das Gedicht *De puella a lupellis servata* von Egbert von Lüttich." In *Merveilles et contes* 6 (1992): 20–44.

Meier, Christel, and Rudolf Suntrup. "Zum Lexikon der Farbenbedeutungen im Mittelalter: Einführung zu Gegenstand und Methoden sowie Probeartikel aus dem Farbenbereich Rot." In *Frühmittelalterliche Studien* 21 (1987): 390–478.

Mellinkoff, Ruth. "Judas's Red Hair and the Jews." In *Journal of Jewish Art* 9 (1982): 31–46.

Nyrop, Kristoffer. "*Gueules*: Histoire d'un mot." In *Romania* 68 (1922): 559–70.

Pastoureau, Michel. "Ceci est mon sang: Le christianisme médiéval et la couleur rouge." In *Le Pressoir mystique: Actes du colloque de Recloses*, ed. D. Alexandre-Bidon, 43–56. Paris, 1990.

———. "*De gueules plain*: Perceval et les origines héraldique de la maison d'Albret." In *Revue française d'héraldique et de sigillographie* 61 (1991): 63–81.

Poiron, Daniel. "Du sang sur la neige: Nature et fonction de l'image dans *Le Conte du Graal*." In *Polyphonie du Graal*, ed. D. Hüe, 99–112. Orléans, 1998.

Ravid, Benjamin. "From Yellow to Red: On the Distinguishing Head Covering of the Jews of Venice." In *Jewish History* 6, fasc. 1–2 (1992): 179–210.

Rey-Flaud, Henri. "Le sang sur la neige: Analyse d'une image-écran de Chrétien de Troyes." In *Littérature* 37 (1980): 15–24.

Walker Bynum, Caroline. *The Blood of Christ in the Later Middle Ages*. Cambridge, 2002.

Weckerlin, Jean Baptiste. *Le Drap escarlate au Moyen Âge: Essai sur l'étymologie de la signification du mot écarlate et notes techniques sur la fabrication de ce drap de laine au Moyen Âge*. Lyon, 1905.

Modern and Contemporary Times

Agulhon, Maurice. "Les couleurs dans la politique française." In *Ethnologie française* 20, fasc. 4 (1990): 391–98.

Cretin, N. *Histoire du Père Noël*. Toulouse, 2010.

Dommanget, Maurice. *Histoire du drapeau rouge, des origines à la guerre de 1939*. Paris, 1967.

Fauche, Xavier. *Roux et rousses: Un éclat très particulier*. Paris, 1997.

Geffroy, Anne. "Étude en rouge, 1789–1798." In *Cahiers de lexicologie* 51 (1988): 119–148.

Greenfield, Amy Butler. *A Perfect Red: Empire, Espionage, and the Quest for the Color of Desire*. New York, 2005. Translated as *L'Extraordinaire Saga du Rouge: Le pigment le plus convoité*. Paris, 2009.

Lanoë, Catherine. *La Poudre et le Fard: Une histoire des cosmétiques de la Renaissance aux Lumières*. Seyssel, 2008.

Mollard-Desfour, Annie. *Le Rouge: Dictionnaire des mots et expressions de couleur*. 2nd ed. Paris, 2009.

Thiéry de Ménonville, N. J. *Traité de la culture du nopal et de l'éducation de la cochenille dans les colonies françaises de l'Amérique*. 2 vols. Cap-Français, 1787.

Timtcheva, Viara. *Le Mythe du Père Noël: Origines et évolution*. Paris, 2006.

Photography Credits

Josef Albers's Stained Glass

A student of Klee and Itten, Albers enlivened and then directed the Bauhaus stained glass studio from 1920 to 1933. As a color theorist and great admirer of Matisse, he sought to give red a much greater place in abstract stained glass, long limited to blue and green.

Josef Albers, *Stained Glass for the Waiting room of Walter Gropius's Office at the Bauhaus School of Weimar*, 1923. Destroyed, then reconstructed by Luc-Benoît Brouard, 2008, 216.5 x 128 cm. Le Cateau-Cambrésis, Musée Départemental Matisse.

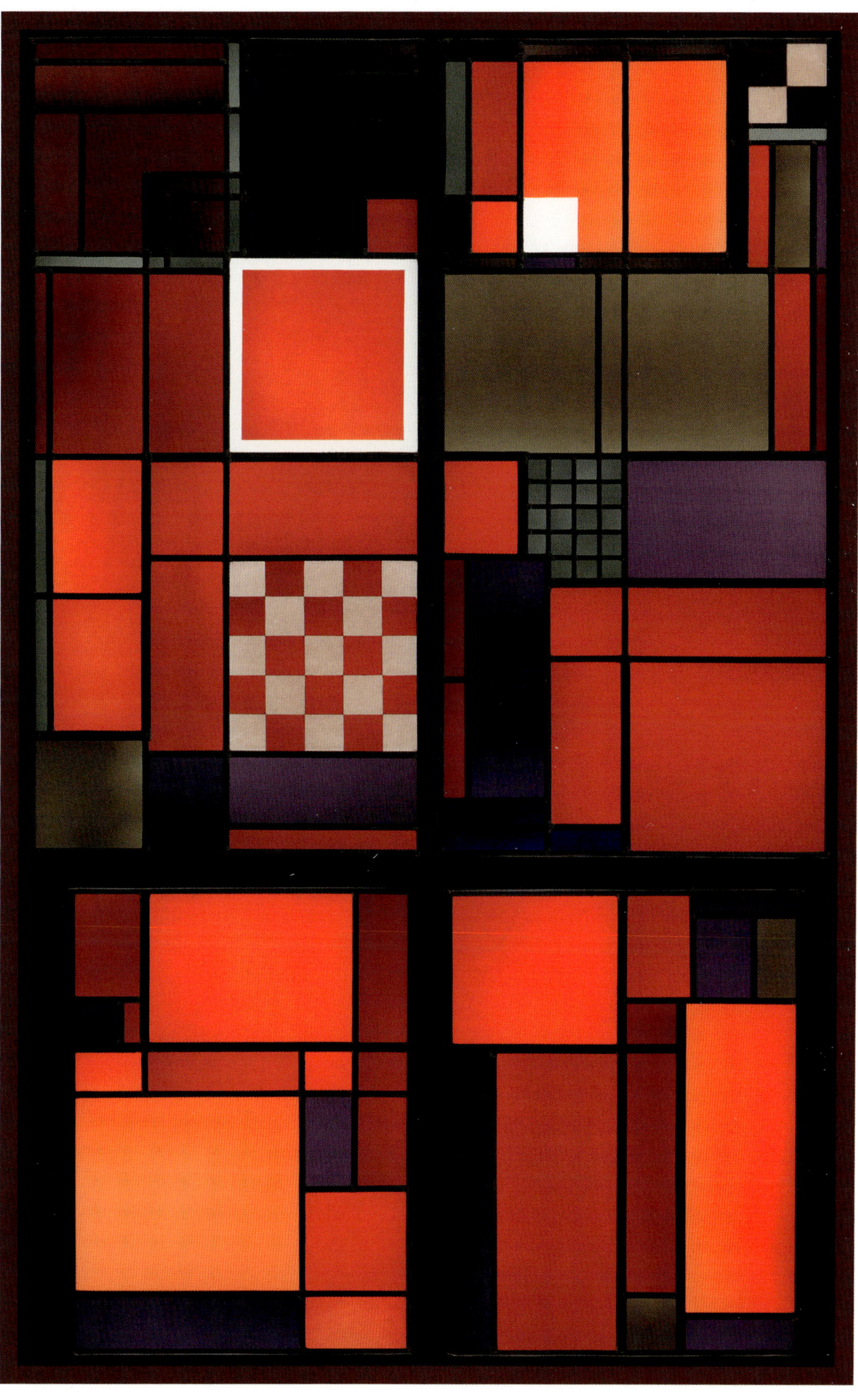

Acknowledgments

Before taking the form of a book, this social and cultural history of the color red in Europe was the subject of my seminars for many years at both the École Practique des Hautes Études and the École des Hautes Études en Sciences Sociales. I thank all my students and auditors for the fruitful exchanges we had for over thirty years on the subject of colors.

I would also like to thank all those close to me—friends, relatives, colleagues, students—whose advice, comments, and suggestions I have profited from, in particular: Thalia Brero, Brigitte Buettner, Pierre Bureau, Yvonne Cazal, Marie Clauteaux, Claude Coupry, Lydia Flem, Adeline Grand-Clément, Éliane Hartmann, François Jacquesson, Christine Lapostolle, Maurice Olender, Dominque Poirel, François Poplin, Anne Ritz-Guilbert, Olga Vassilieva-Codognet.

Thanks as well to Éditions du Seuil, especially to the whole Beaux Livres team, Nathalie Beaux, Caroline Fuchs, Karine Benzaquin-Laidain, Claude Hénard, and graphic designer François-Xavier Delarue, and to my publishing assistants, Maud Boulard and Marie-Claire Chalvet. Everyone has worked to make the present volume a very beautiful one that, like its predecessors, will be available to a wide readership.

Finally, I offer an affectionate, warm, and immense thanks to Claudia Rabel, who once again has made me the beneficiary of her constructive criticism and efficacious rereadings.

Photogravure : Quadrilaser, Ormes, France

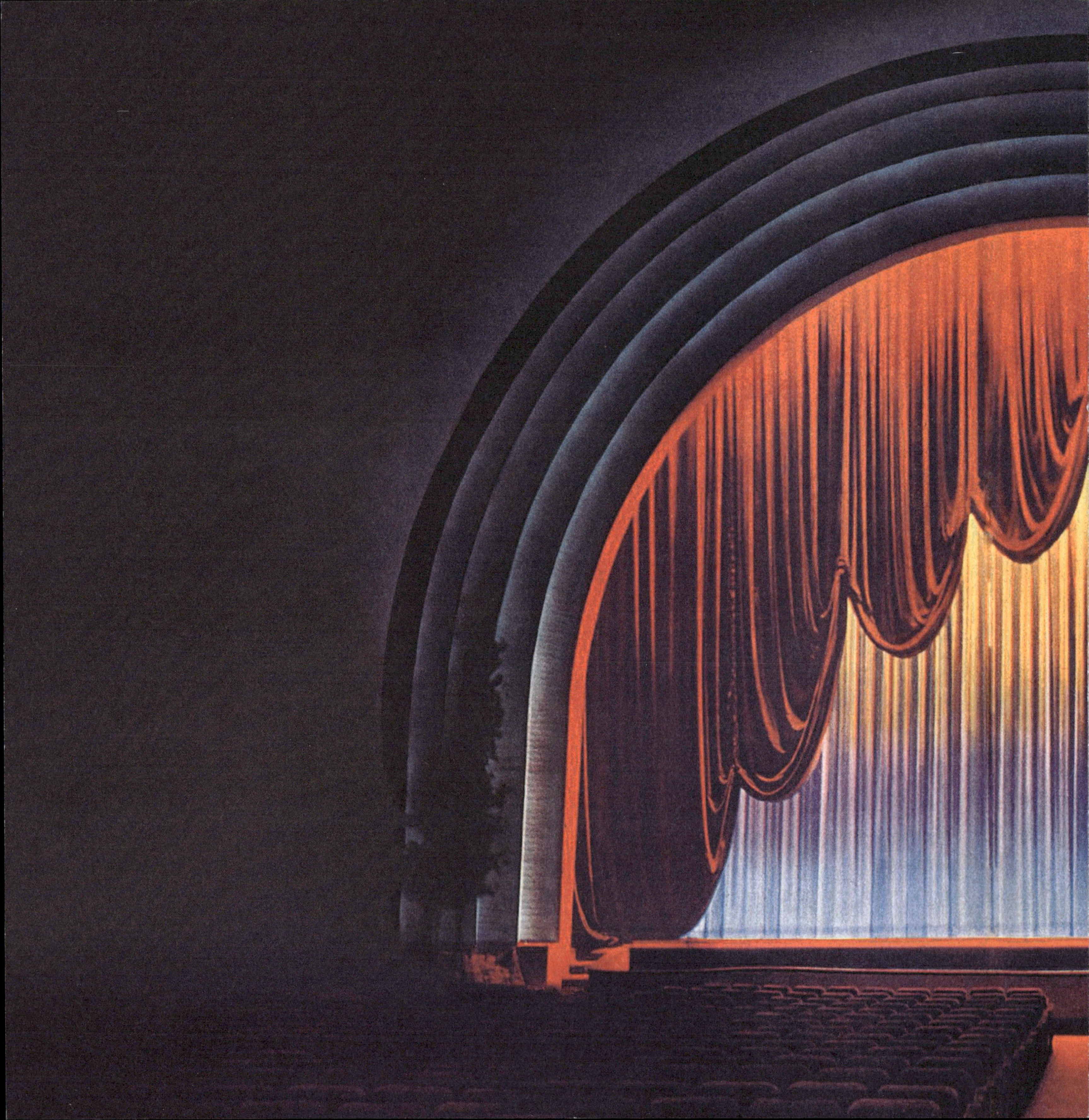